Natsume's
BOOK of FRIENDS

Shojo Beat

Natsume's BOOK of FRIENDS

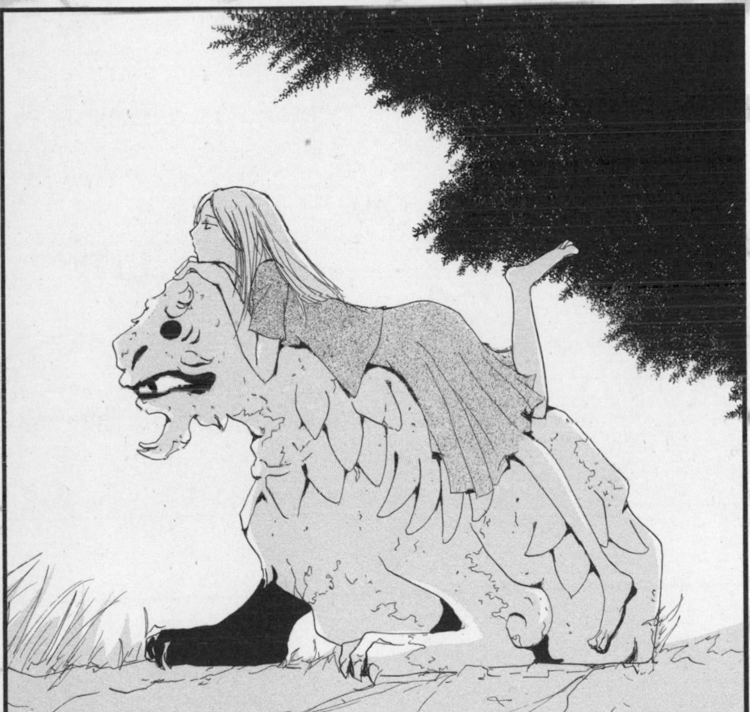

STORY and ART by
Yuki Midorikawa

VOLUME 13

Natsume's
BOOK of FRIENDS
VOLUME 13 CONTENTS

chapter 52 —— 5

chapter 53 —— 37

chapter 54 —— 68

Special Episode 10
Nishimura and Natsume
—————— 109

Special Episode 11
Kitamoto and Natsume
—————— 141

Afterword —— 181

End Notes —— 185

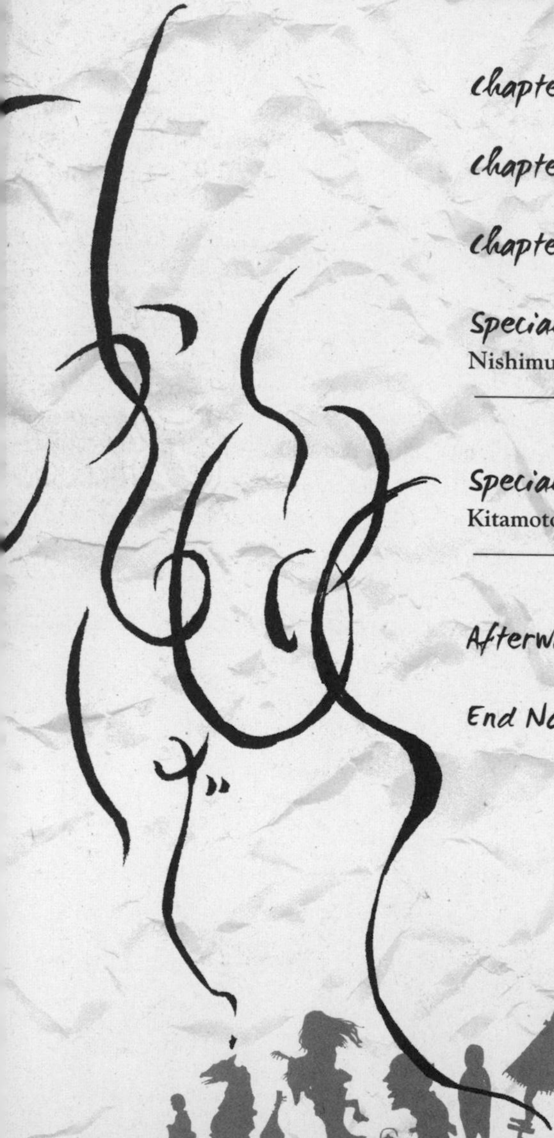

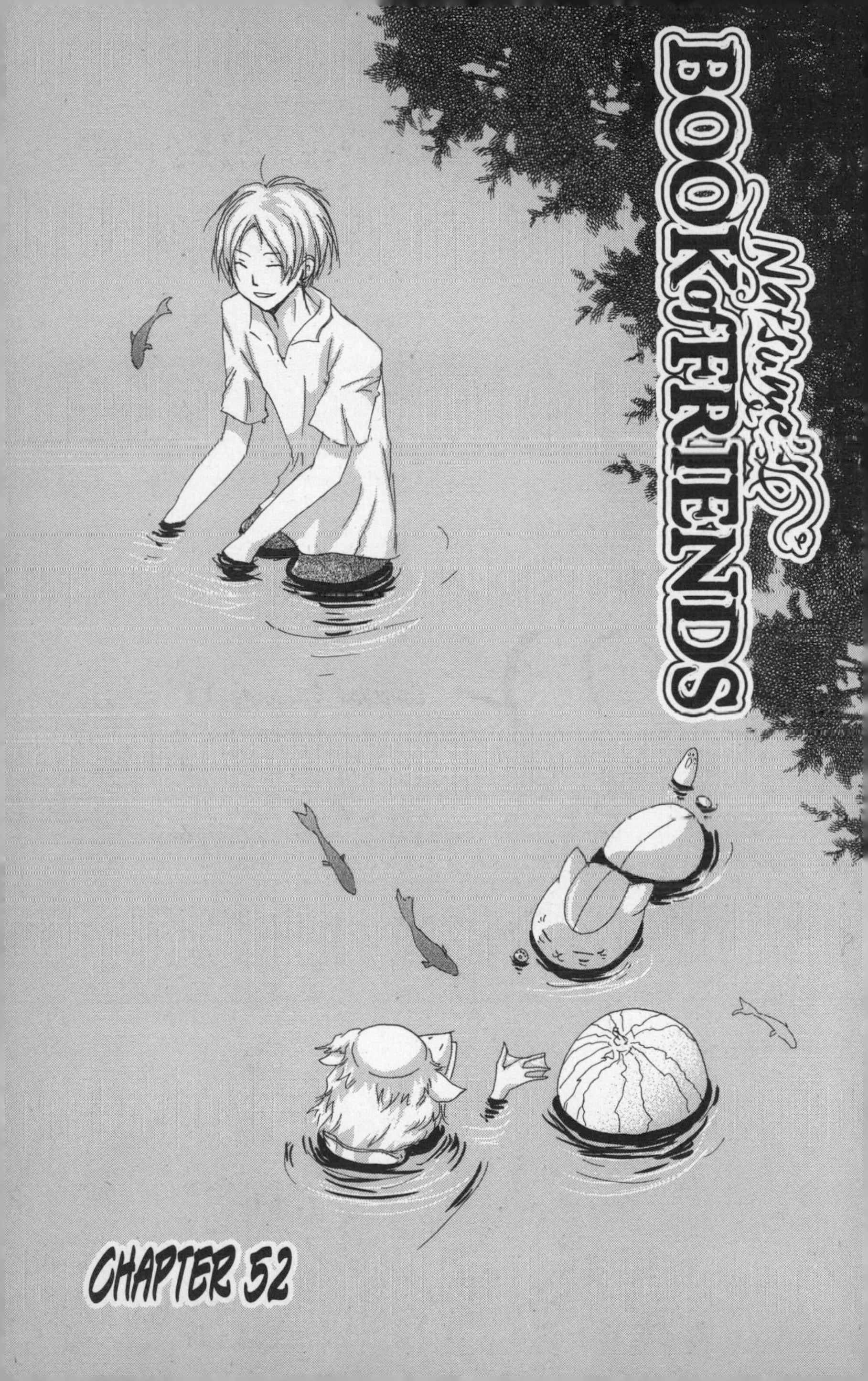
Natsume's
BOOK of FRIENDS
CHAPTER 52

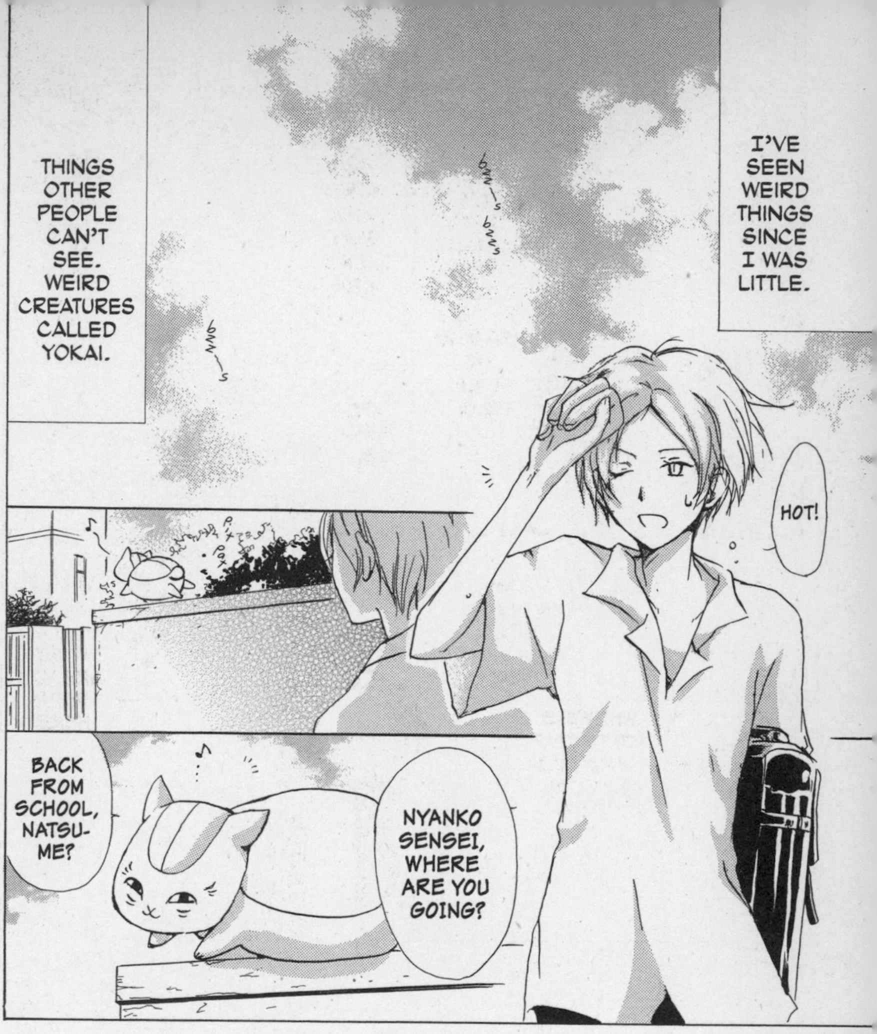
I'VE SEEN WEIRD THINGS SINCE I WAS LITTLE.
THINGS OTHER PEOPLE CAN'T SEE. WEIRD CREATURES CALLED YOKAI.
HOT!
NYANKO SENSEI, WHERE ARE YOU GOING?
BACK FROM SCHOOL, NATSUME?

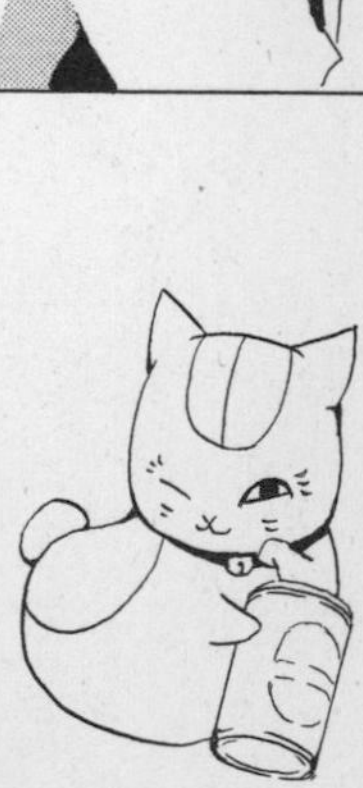

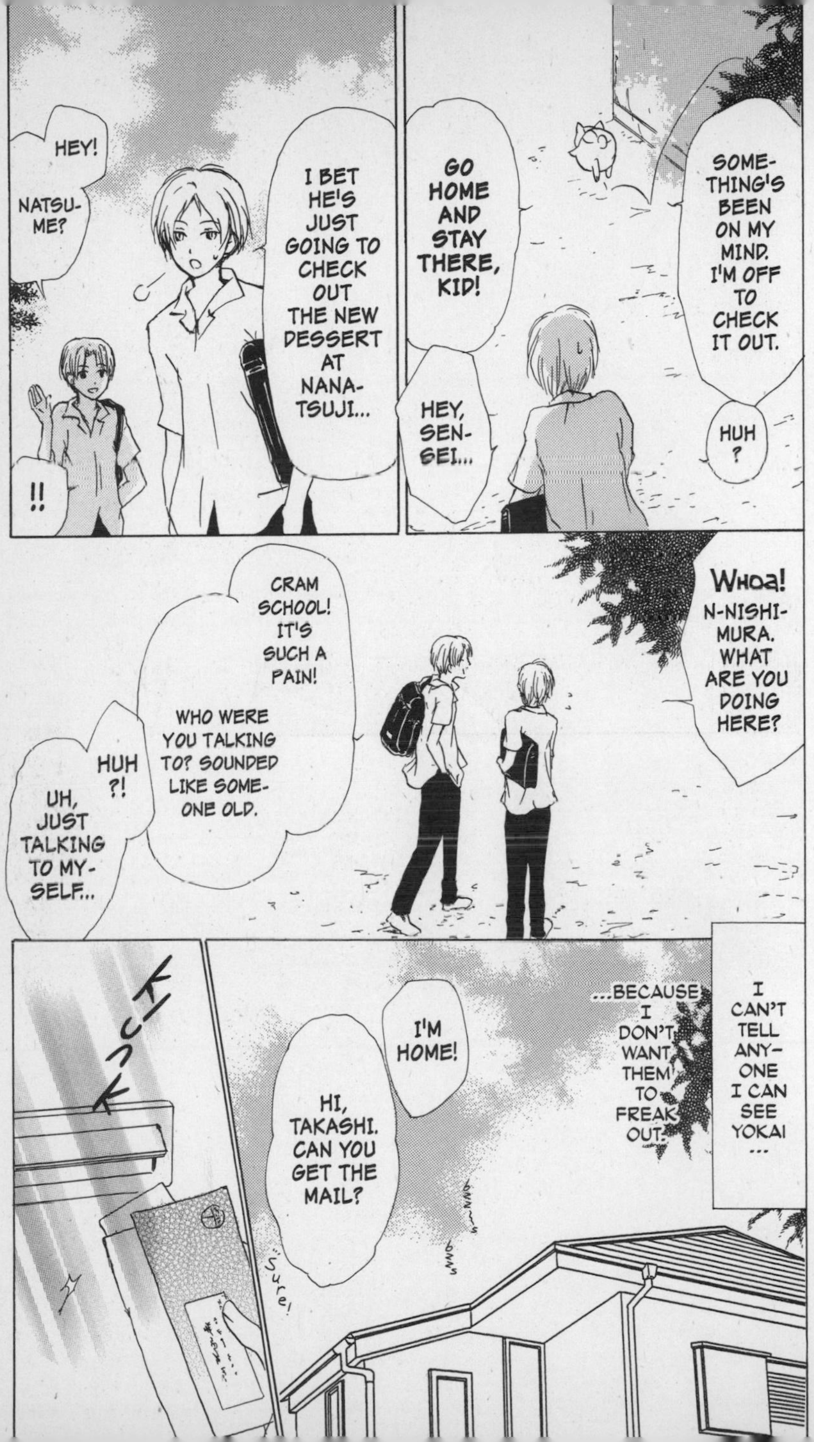
SOME-THING'S BEEN ON MY MIND. I'M OFF TO CHECK IT OUT.
HUH?
GO HOME AND STAY THERE, KID!
HEY, SEN-SEI...
I BET HE'S JUST GOING TO CHECK OUT THE NEW DESSERT AT NANA-TSUJI...
HEY!
NATSU-ME?
!!
Whoa!
N-NISHI-MURA. WHAT ARE YOU DOING HERE?
CRAM SCHOOL! IT'S SUCH A PAIN!
WHO WERE YOU TALKING TO? SOUNDED LIKE SOME-ONE OLD.
HUH?!
UH, JUST TALKING TO MY-SELF...
I CAN'T TELL ANY-ONE I CAN SEE YOKAI...
...BECAUSE I DON'T WANT THEM TO FREAK OUT.
I'M HOME!
HI, TAKASHI. CAN YOU GET THE MAIL?
Sure!
KLUNK

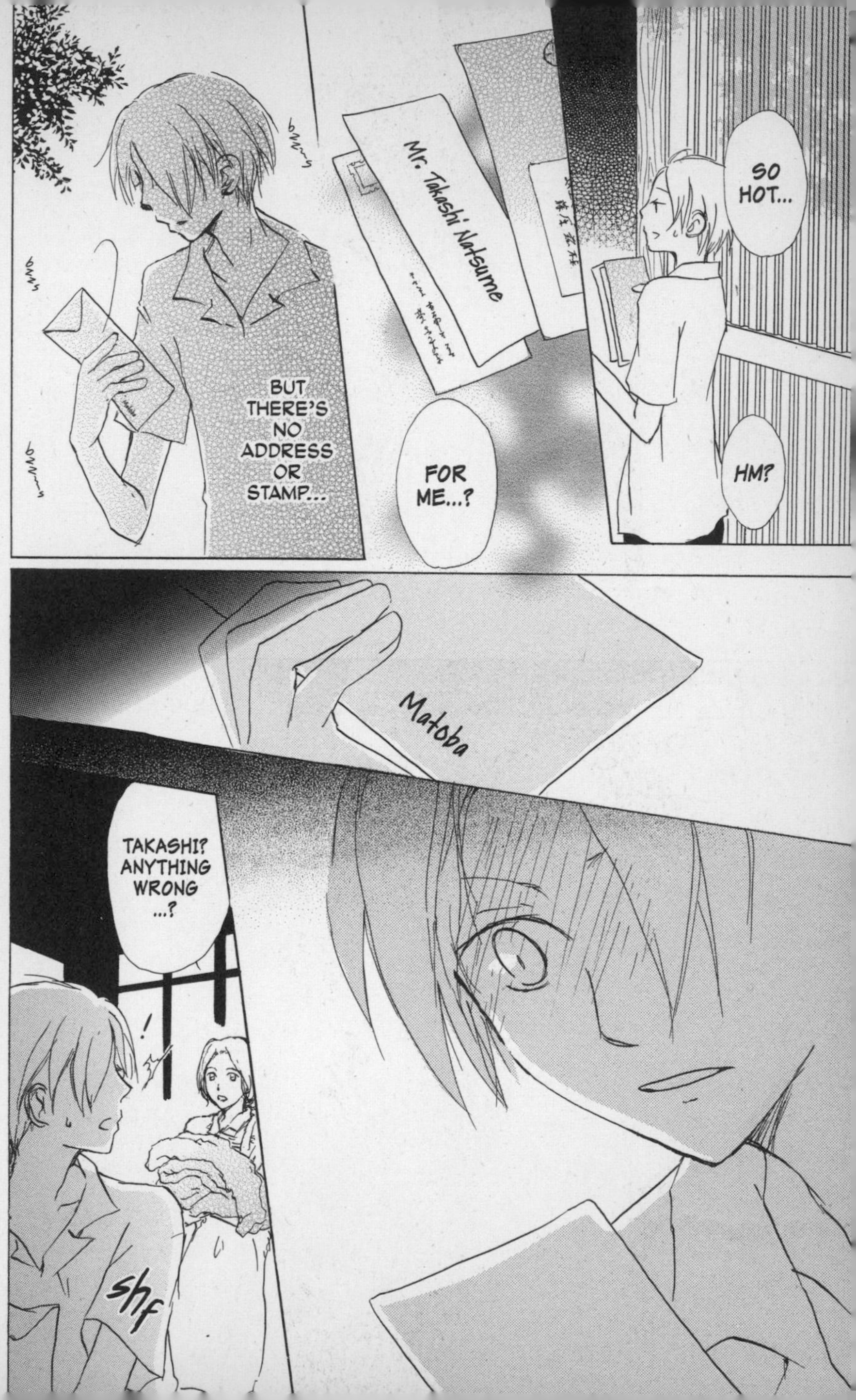
SO HOT...
HM?
Mr. Takashi Natsume
FOR ME...?
BUT THERE'S NO ADDRESS OR STAMP...
Matoba
TAKASHI? ANYTHING WRONG ...?
!
shf

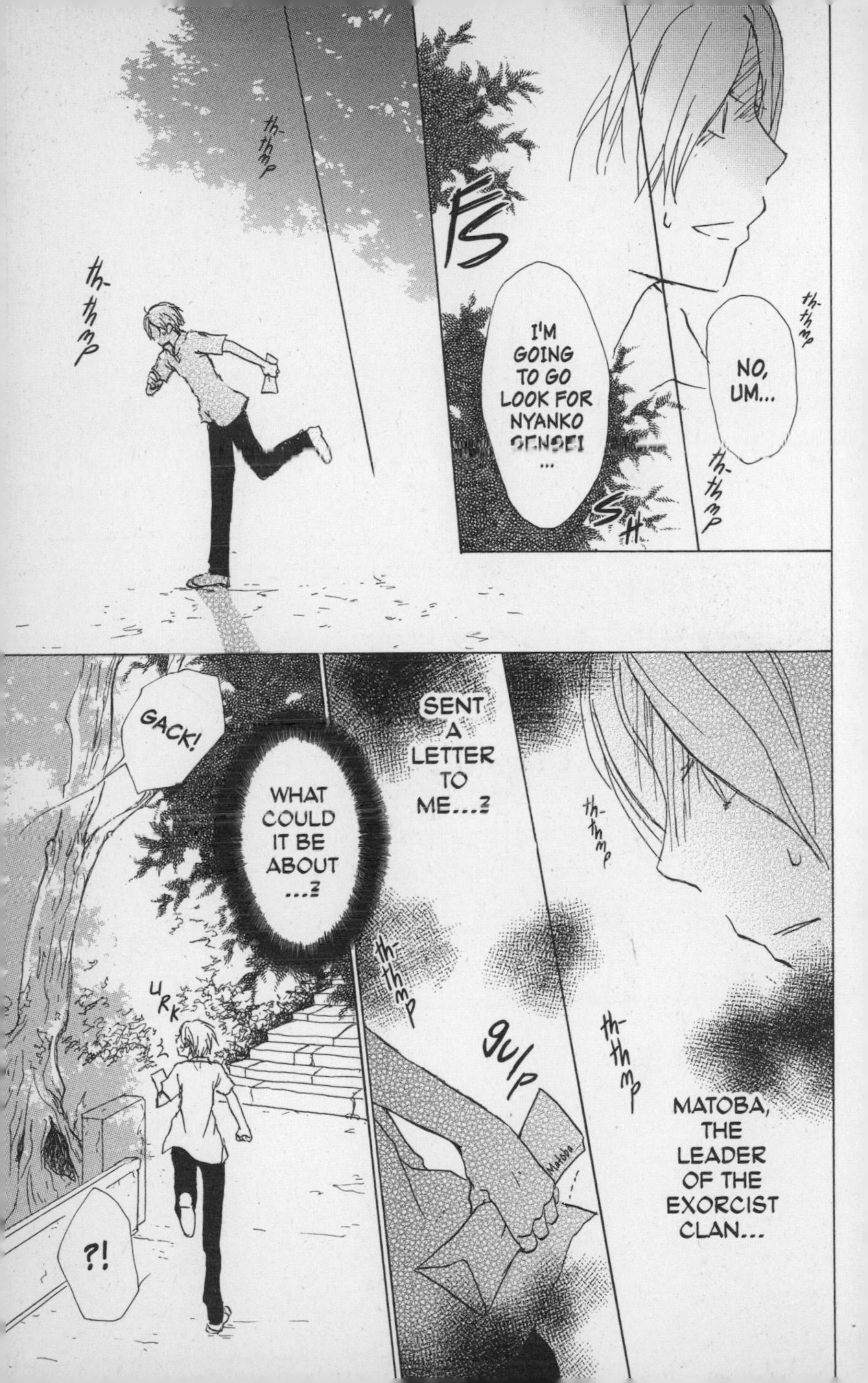
th-thmp
NO, UM...
th-thmp
FS
I'M GOING TO GO LOOK FOR NYANKO SENSEI...
SH
th-thmp
th-thmp
th-thmp
th-thmp
MATOBA, THE LEADER OF THE EXORCIST CLAN...
SENT A LETTER TO ME...?
gulp
Matoba
th-thmp
GACK!
WHAT COULD IT BE ABOUT...?
URK
?!

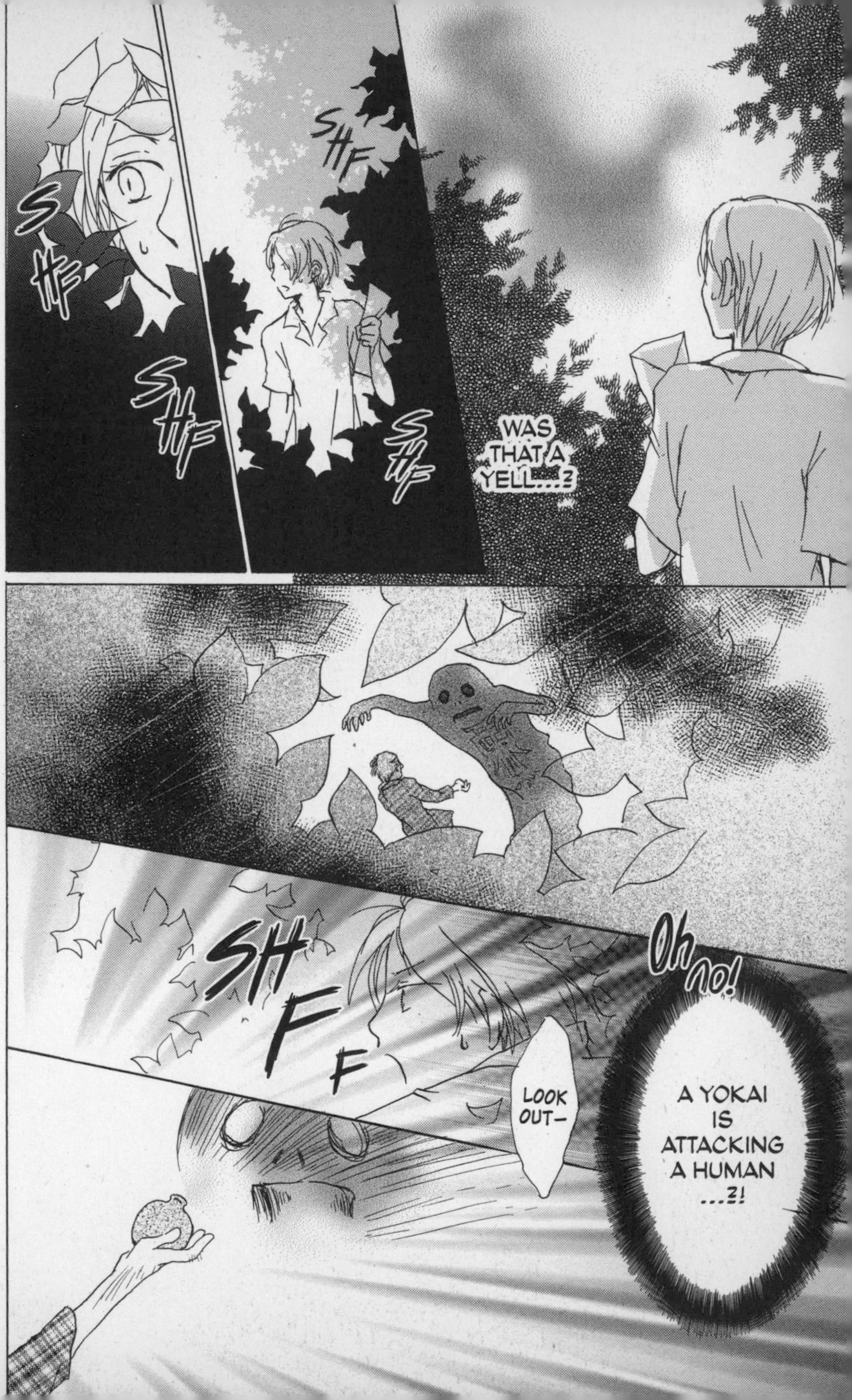
WAS THAT A YELL...?
SHF
SHF
SHF
SHF
SHFF
Oh no!
A YOKAI IS ATTACKING A HUMAN ...?!
LOOK OUT—

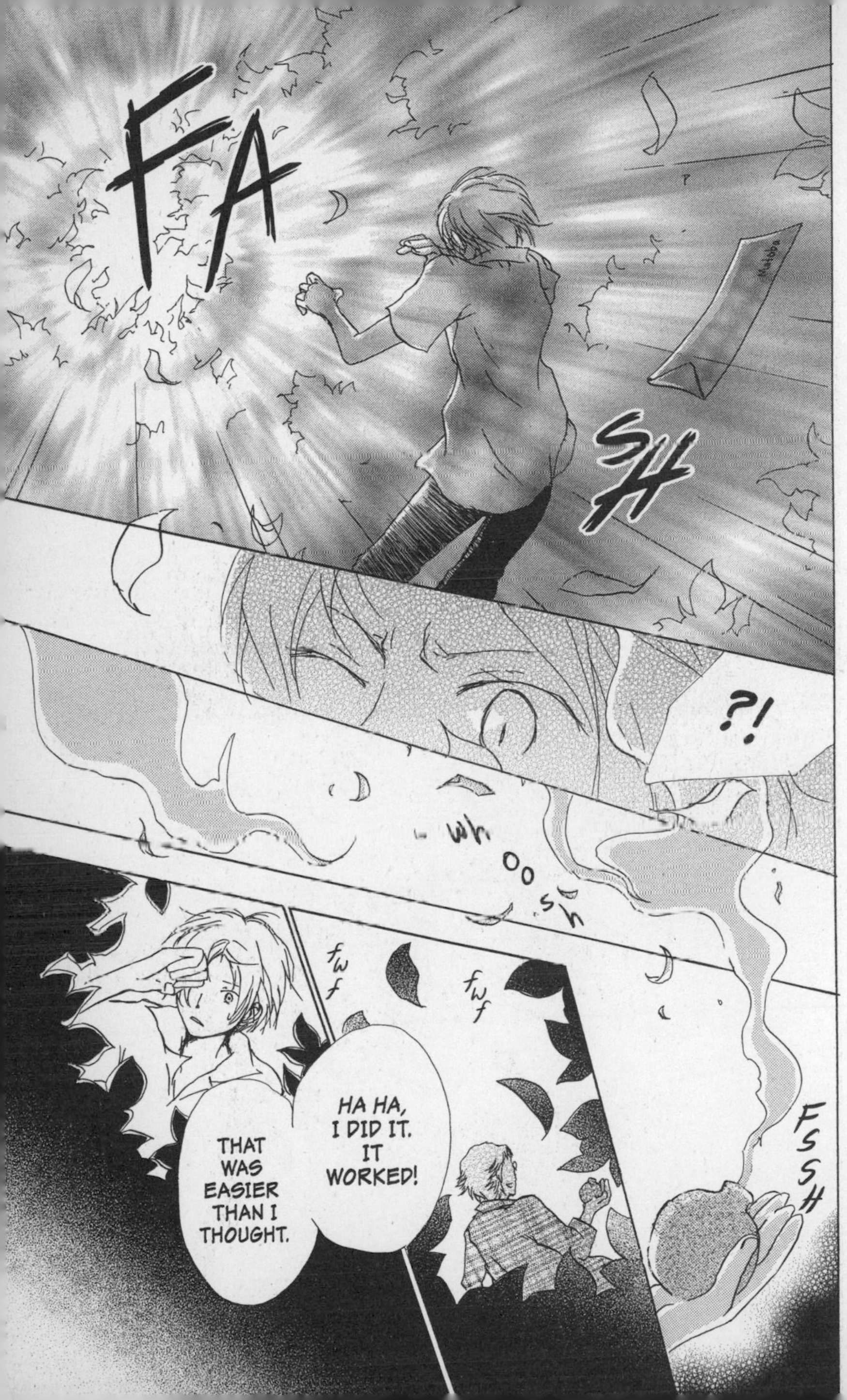
FA
SH
?!
whoosh
FSSH
fwf
fwf
HA HA, I DID IT. IT WORKED!
THAT WAS EASIER THAN I THOUGHT.

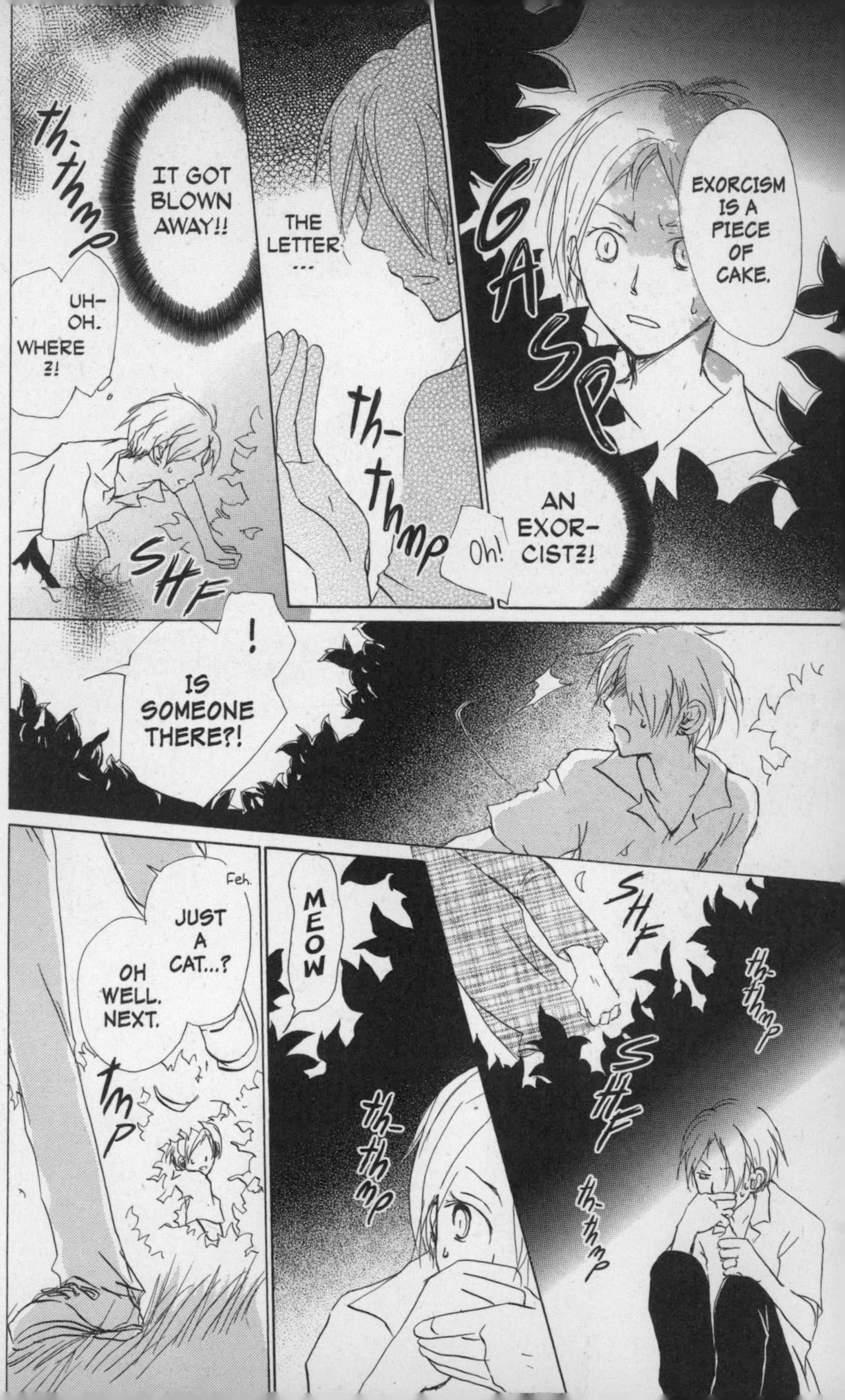
EXORCISM IS A PIECE OF CAKE.
GASP
AN EXOR-CIST?!
Oh!
THE LETTER...
th-thmp
IT GOT BLOWN AWAY!!
th-thmp
UH-OH. WHERE?!
SHF
!
IS SOMEONE THERE?!
SHF
th-thmp
SHF
th-thmp
th-thmp
MEOW
Feh.
JUST A CAT...?
OH WELL. NEXT.
tmp

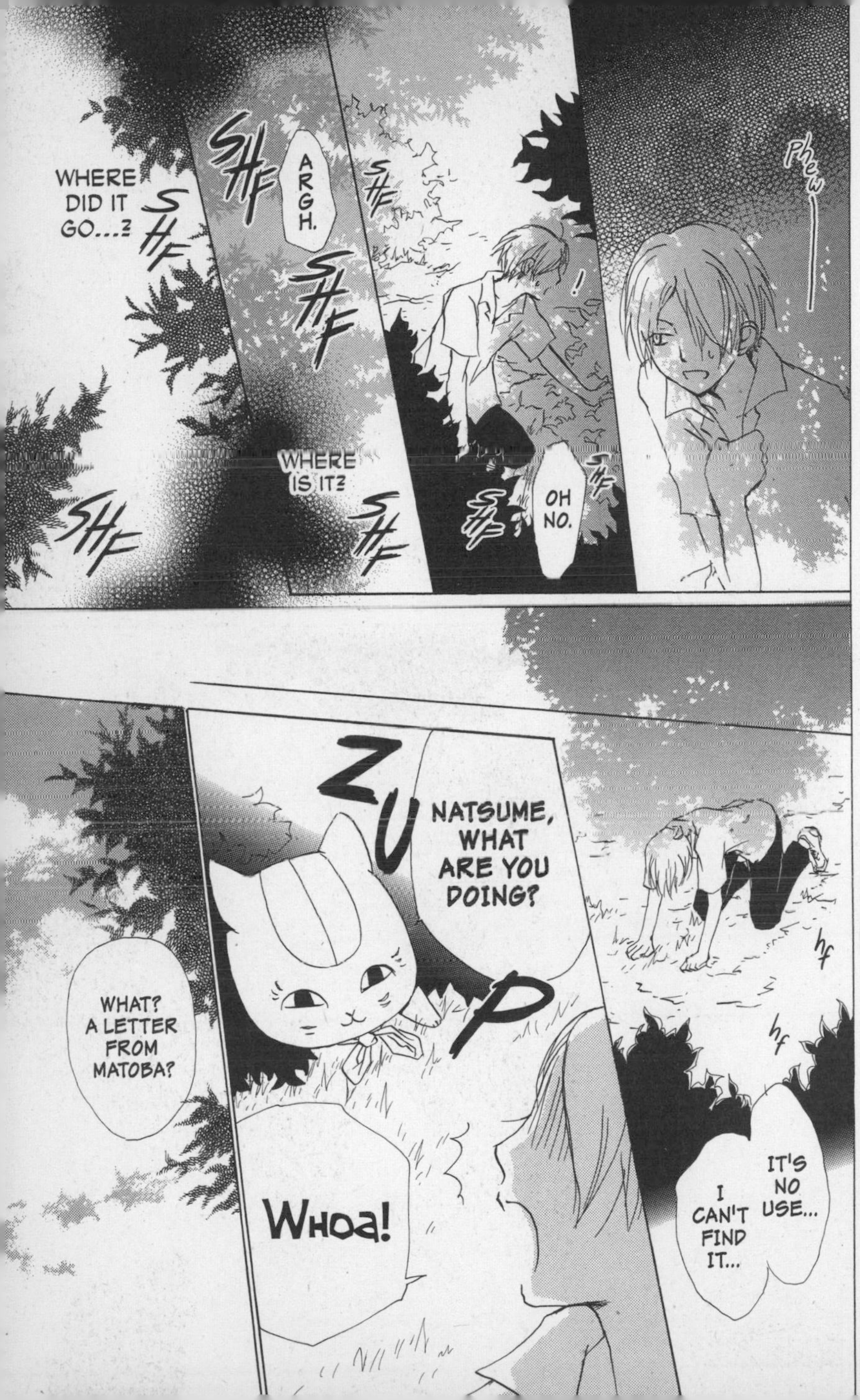
Phew—
!
SHF
SHF
OH NO.
SHF
ARGH.
SHF
SHF
WHERE IS IT?
SHF
WHERE DID IT GO...?
SHF
SHF
hf
hf
IT'S NO USE...
I CAN'T FIND IT...
ZUP
NATSUME, WHAT ARE YOU DOING?
WHAT? A LETTER FROM MATOBA?
Whoa!

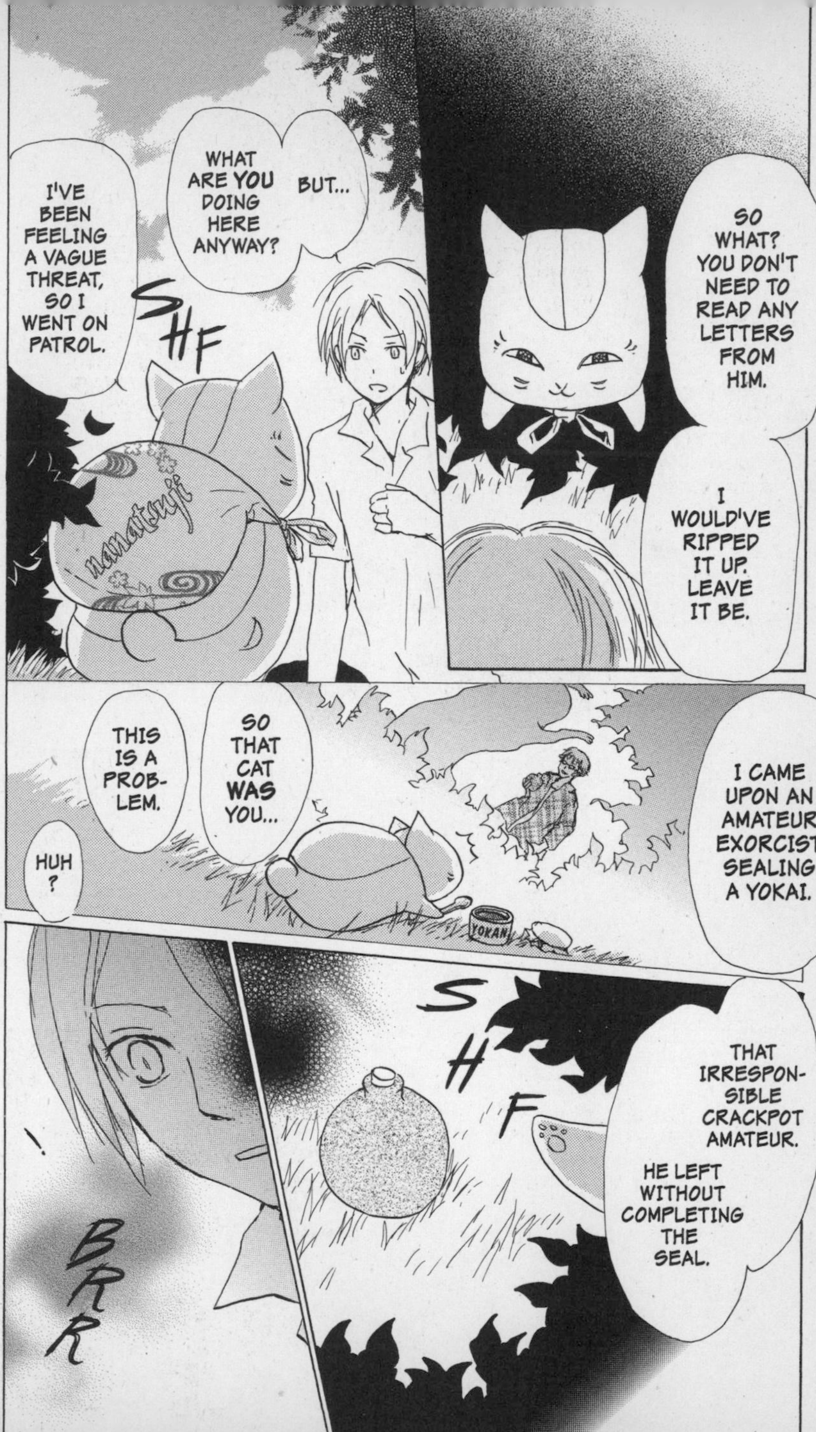
SO WHAT? YOU DON'T NEED TO READ ANY LETTERS FROM HIM.
I WOULD'VE RIPPED IT UP. LEAVE IT BE.
BUT...
WHAT ARE YOU DOING HERE ANYWAY?
I'VE BEEN FEELING A VAGUE THREAT, SO I WENT ON PATROL.
SHF
nanatsuji
I CAME UPON AN AMATEUR EXORCIST SEALING A YOKAI.
YOKAN
SO THAT CAT WAS YOU...
THIS IS A PROB-LEM.
HUH?
SHF
THAT IRRESPON-SIBLE CRACKPOT AMATEUR.
HE LEFT WITHOUT COMPLETING THE SEAL.
!
BRR

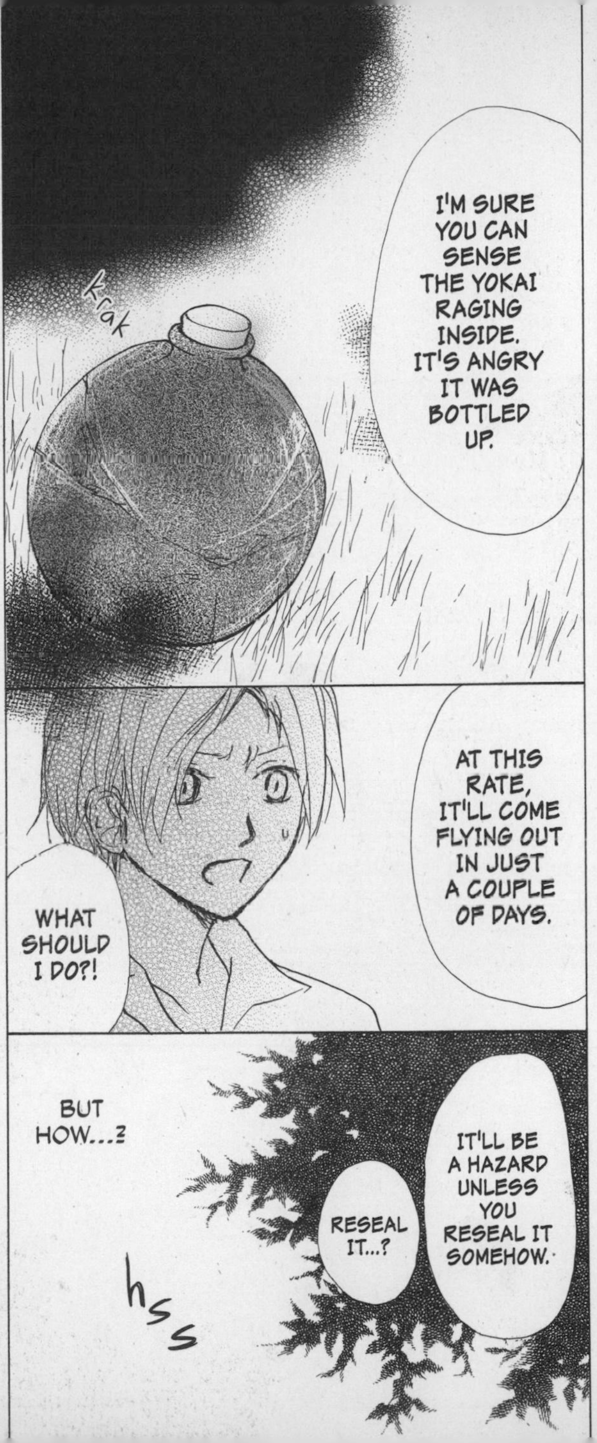
krak
I'M SURE YOU CAN SENSE THE YOKAI RAGING INSIDE. IT'S ANGRY IT WAS BOTTLED UP.
AT THIS RATE, IT'LL COME FLYING OUT IN JUST A COUPLE OF DAYS.
WHAT SHOULD I DO?!
IT'LL BE A HAZARD UNLESS YOU RESEAL IT SOMEHOW.
RESEAL IT...?
BUT HOW...?
hss

01

Hello, I'm Midorikawa. This is my 21st total graphic novel.

I'm so happy and grateful. I'd like to keep working hard to make many manga for people to enjoy.

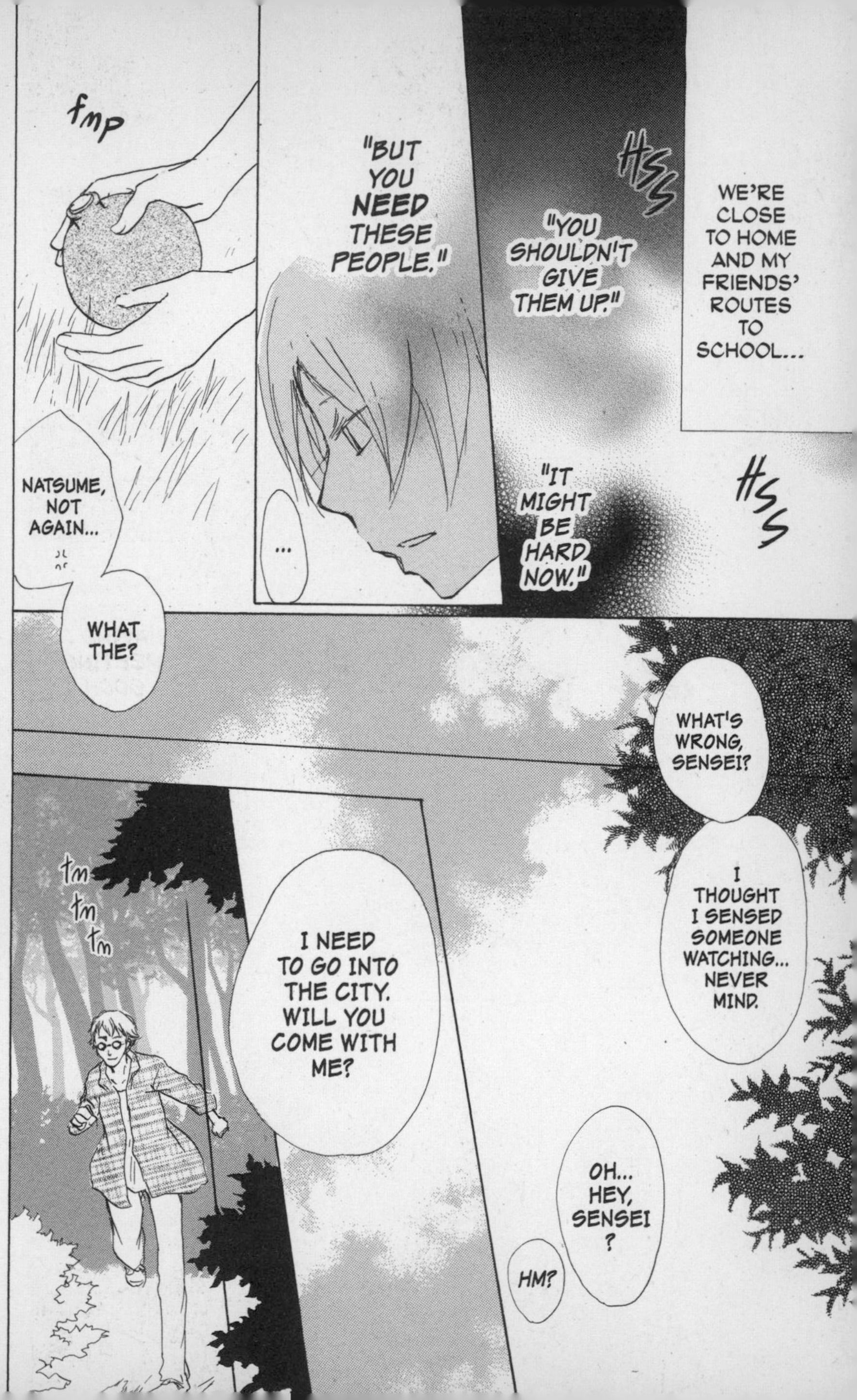
WE'RE CLOSE TO HOME AND MY FRIENDS' ROUTES TO SCHOOL...
HSS
HSS
"YOU SHOULDN'T GIVE THEM UP."
"IT MIGHT BE HARD NOW."
"BUT YOU NEED THESE PEOPLE."
...
fmp
NATSUME, NOT AGAIN...
WHAT THE?
WHAT'S WRONG, SENSEI?
I THOUGHT I SENSED SOMEONE WATCHING... NEVER MIND.
OH... HEY, SENSEI?
HM?
tm tm tm
I NEED TO GO INTO THE CITY. WILL YOU COME WITH ME?

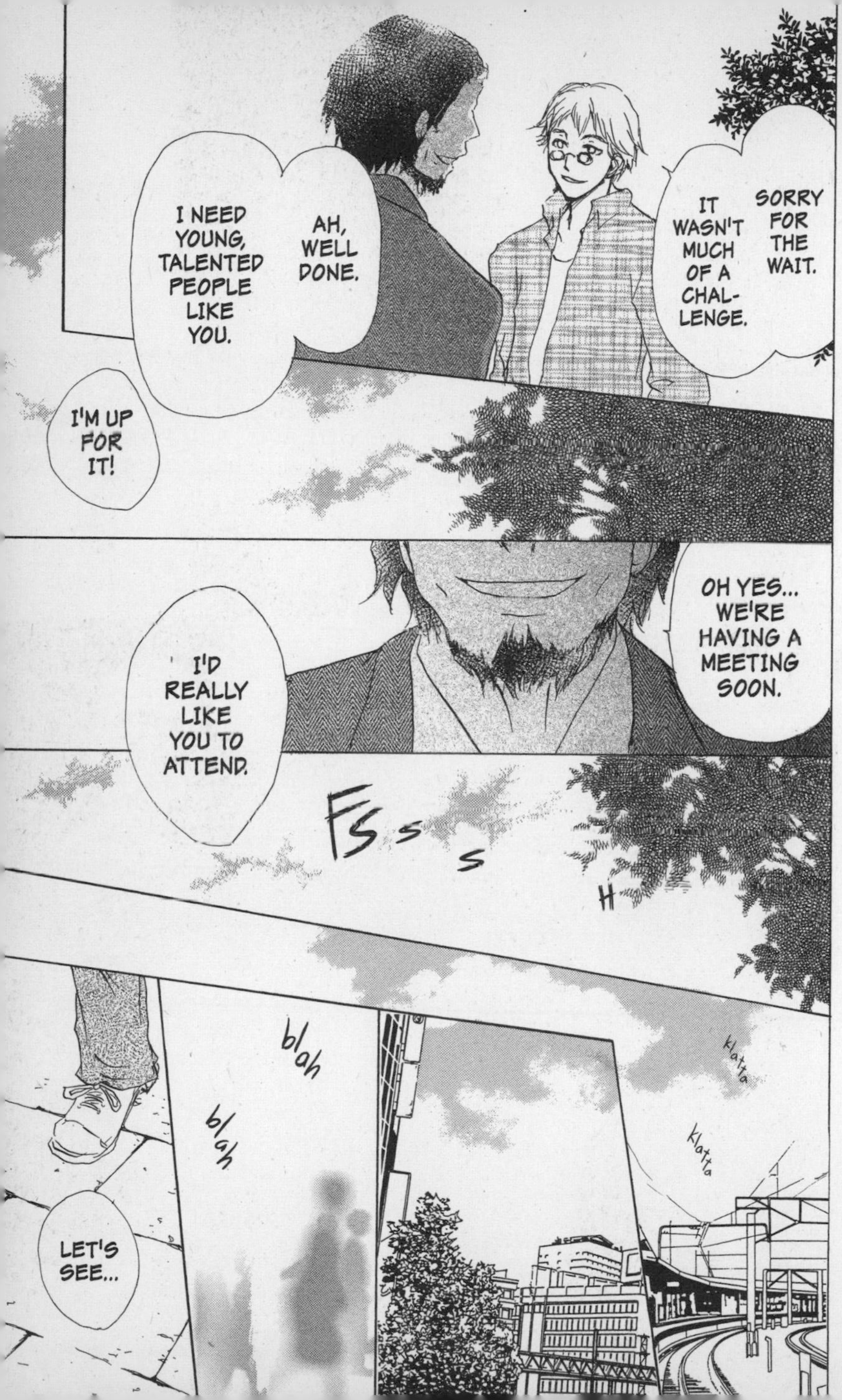
SORRY FOR THE WAIT.
IT WASN'T MUCH OF A CHAL-LENGE.
AH, WELL DONE.
I NEED YOUNG, TALENTED PEOPLE LIKE YOU.
I'M UP FOR IT!
OH YES... WE'RE HAVING A MEETING SOON.
I'D REALLY LIKE YOU TO ATTEND.
FSSSH
klatta
klatta
blah
blah
LET'S SEE...

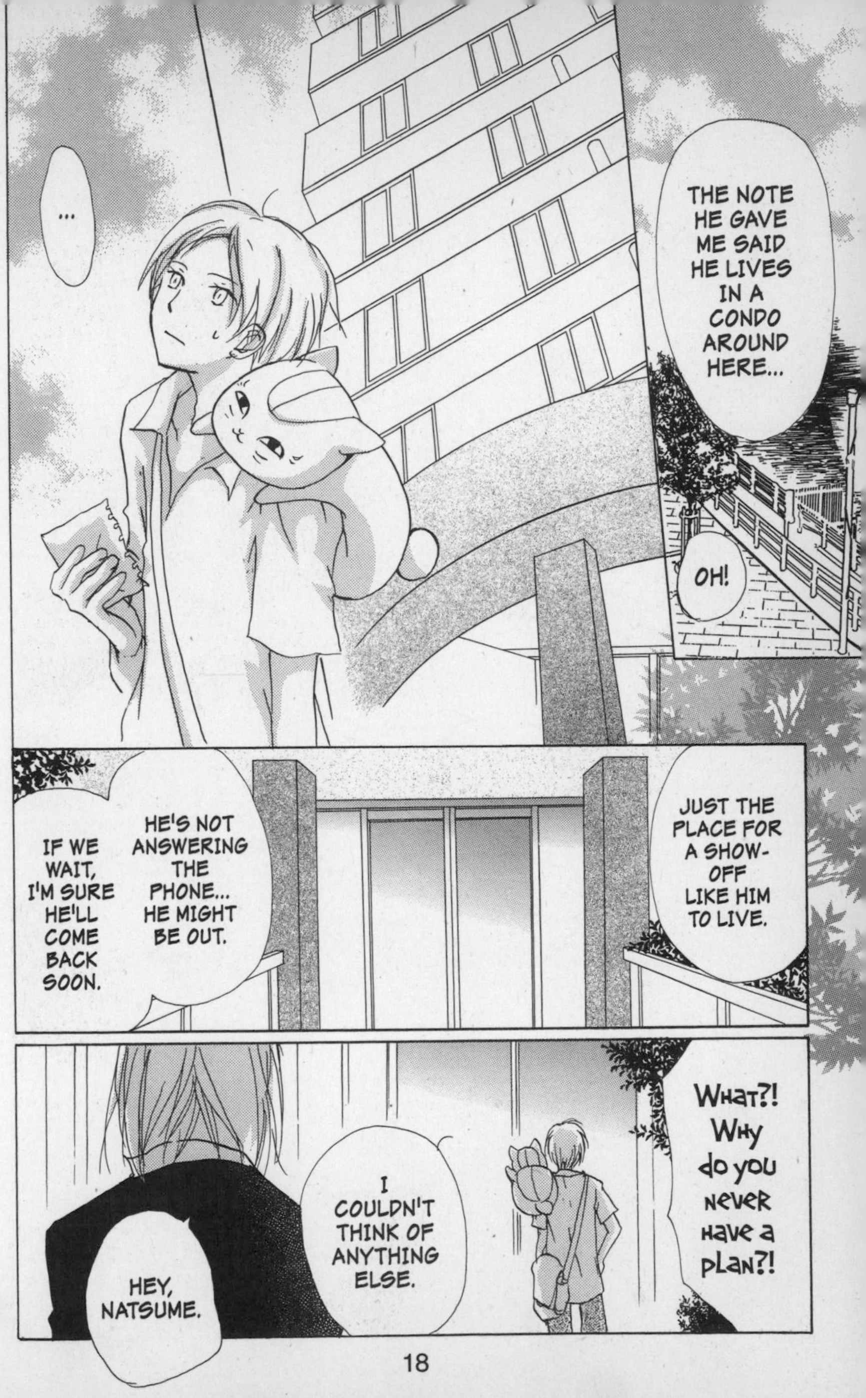
THE NOTE HE GAVE ME SAID HE LIVES IN A CONDO AROUND HERE...
OH!
...
JUST THE PLACE FOR A SHOW-OFF LIKE HIM TO LIVE.
HE'S NOT ANSWERING THE PHONE... HE MIGHT BE OUT.
IF WE WAIT, I'M SURE HE'LL COME BACK SOON.
WHAT?! WHY DO YOU NEVER HAVE A PLAN?!
I COULDN'T THINK OF ANYTHING ELSE.
HEY, NATSUME.

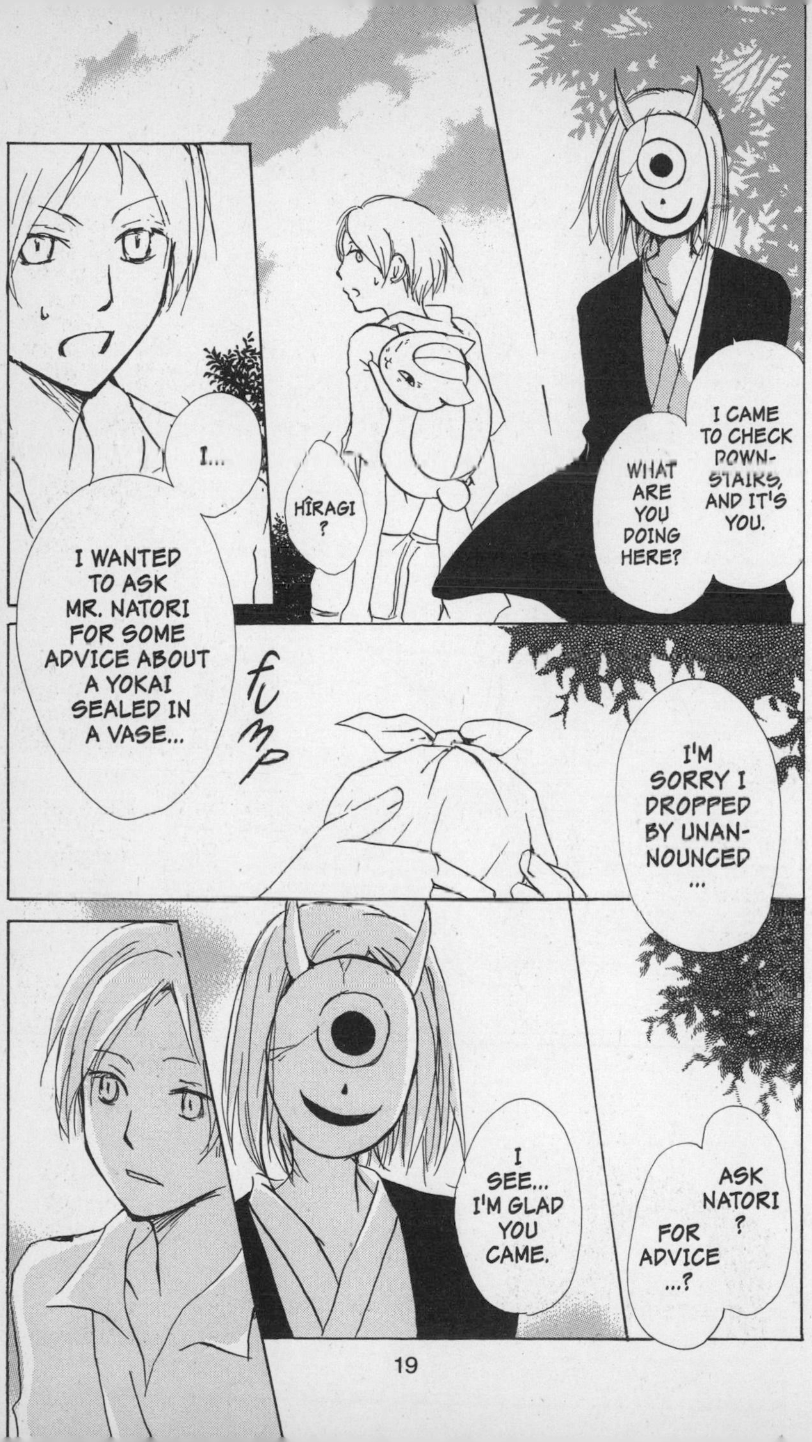
I CAME TO CHECK DOWN-STAIRS, AND IT'S YOU.
WHAT ARE YOU DOING HERE?
HÎRAGI?
I...
I WANTED TO ASK MR. NATORI FOR SOME ADVICE ABOUT A YOKAI SEALED IN A VASE...
I'M SORRY I DROPPED BY UNAN-NOUNCED...
FLUMP
ASK NATORI?
FOR ADVICE...?
I SEE... I'M GLAD YOU CAME.

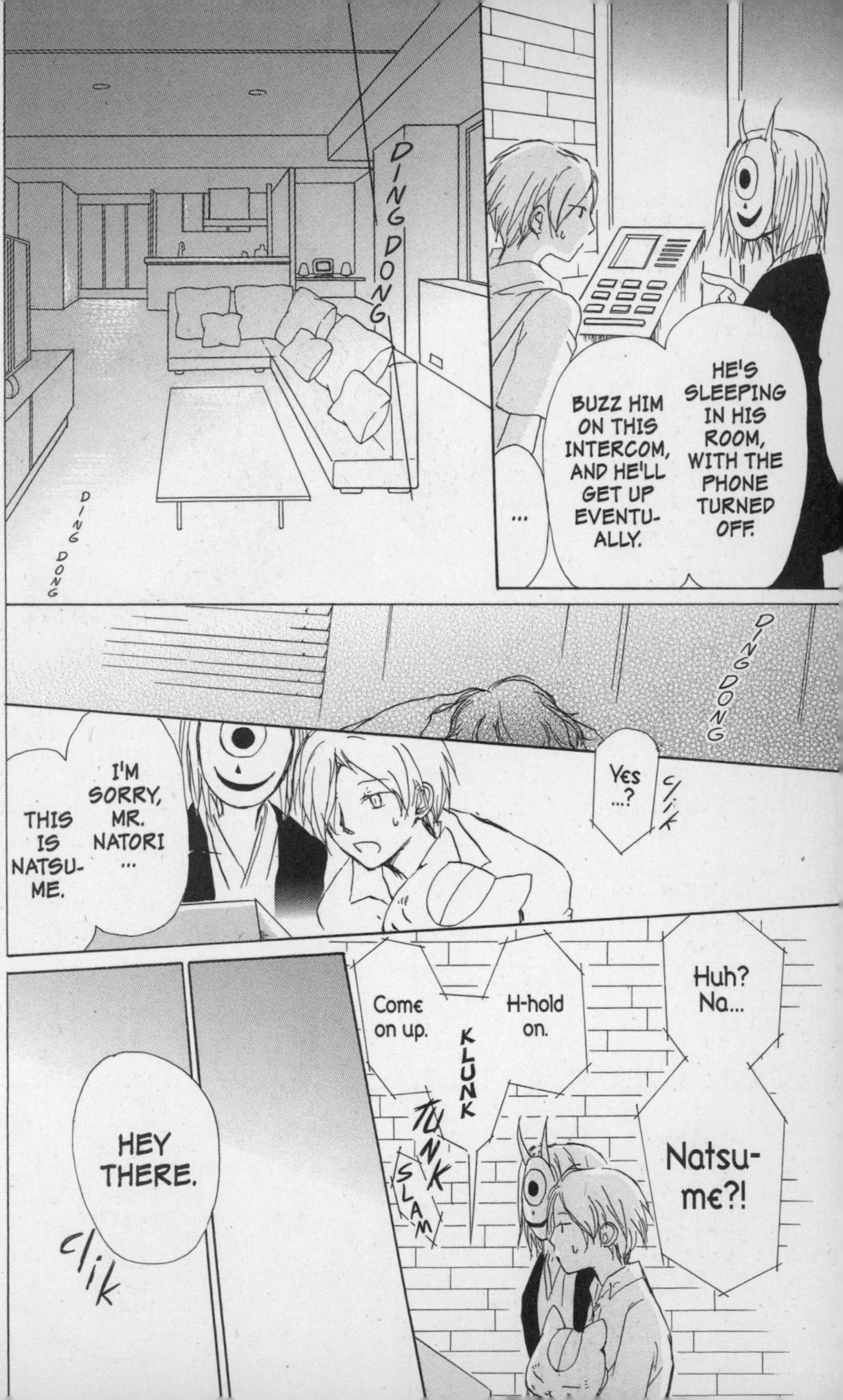
HE'S SLEEPING IN HIS ROOM, WITH THE PHONE TURNED OFF.
BUZZ HIM ON THIS INTERCOM, AND HE'LL GET UP EVENTU-ALLY.
...
DING DONG
DING DONG
DING DONG
Yes ...?
clik
I'M SORRY, MR. NATORI ...
THIS IS NATSU-ME.
Huh? Na...
Natsu-me?!
H-hold on.
Come on up.
KLUNK
TUNK
SLAM
HEY THERE.
clik

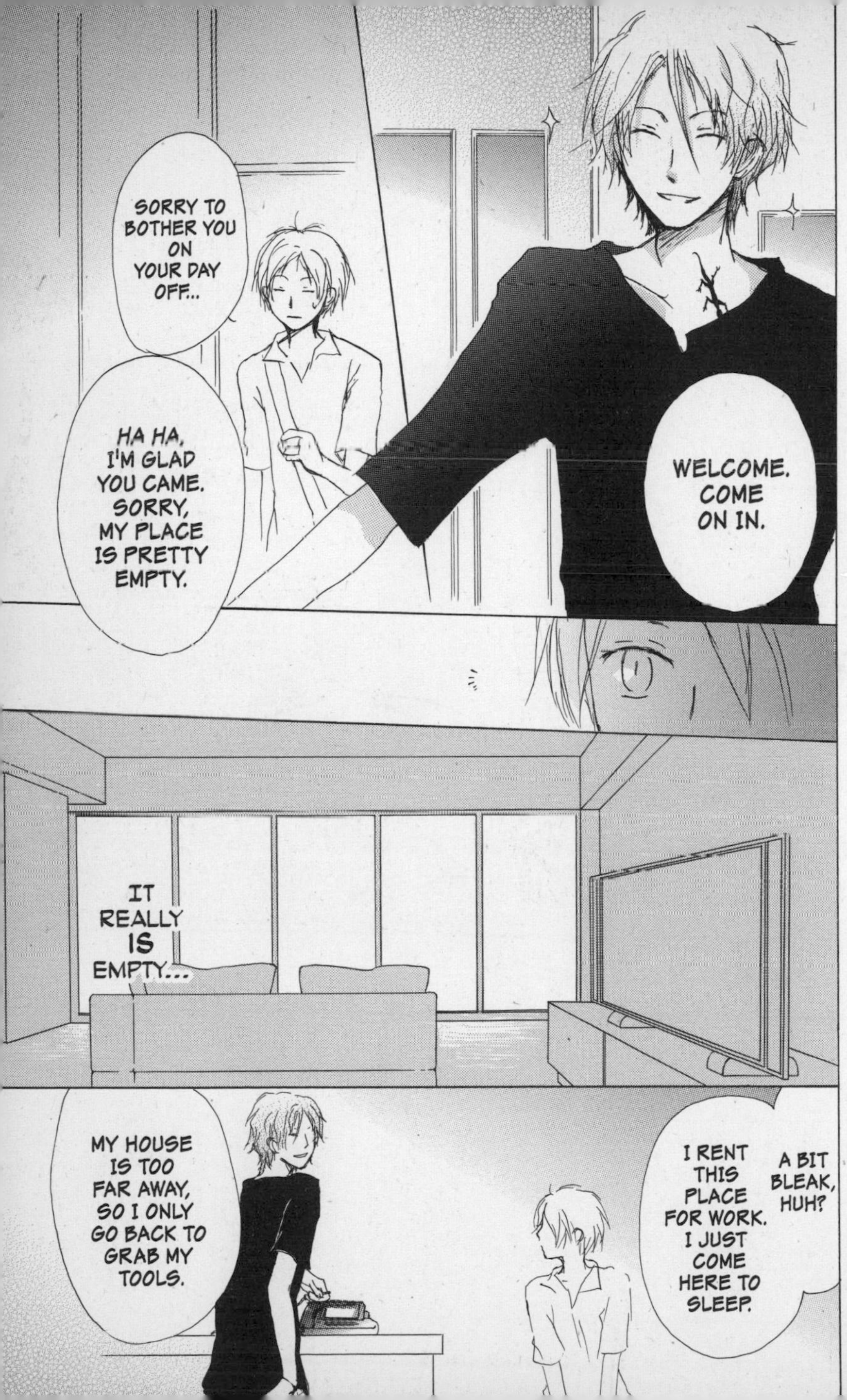
WELCOME. COME ON IN.
SORRY TO BOTHER YOU ON YOUR DAY OFF...
HA HA, I'M GLAD YOU CAME. SORRY, MY PLACE IS PRETTY EMPTY.
IT REALLY IS EMPTY...
A BIT BLEAK, HUH?
I RENT THIS PLACE FOR WORK. I JUST COME HERE TO SLEEP.
MY HOUSE IS TOO FAR AWAY, SO I ONLY GO BACK TO GRAB MY TOOLS.

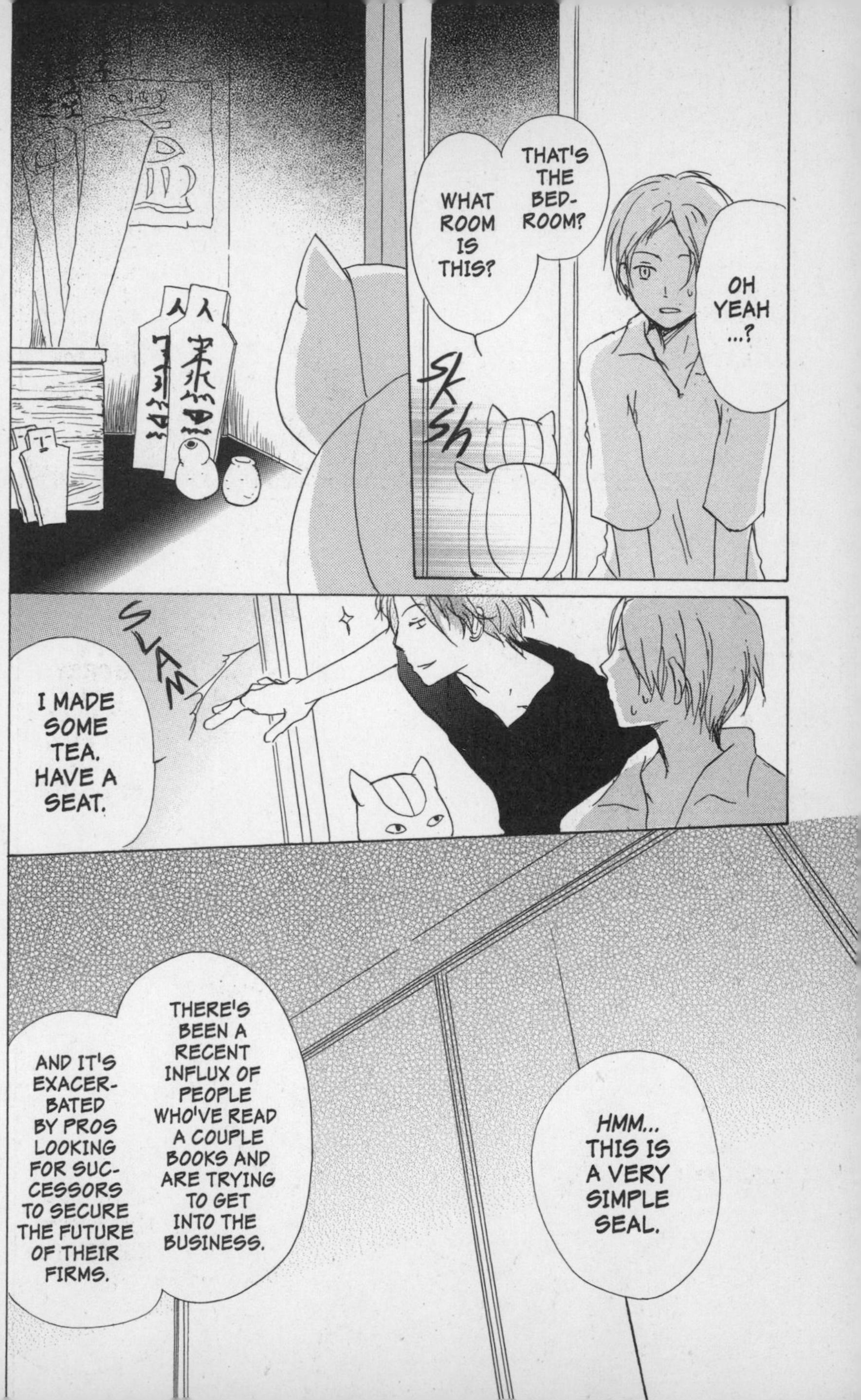
WHAT ROOM IS THIS?
THAT'S THE BED-ROOM?
OH YEAH ...?
SKSH
SLAM
I MADE SOME TEA. HAVE A SEAT.
HMM... THIS IS A VERY SIMPLE SEAL.
THERE'S BEEN A RECENT INFLUX OF PEOPLE WHO'VE READ A COUPLE BOOKS AND ARE TRYING TO GET INTO THE BUSINESS.
AND IT'S EXACER-BATED BY PROS LOOKING FOR SUC-CESSORS TO SECURE THE FUTURE OF THEIR FIRMS.

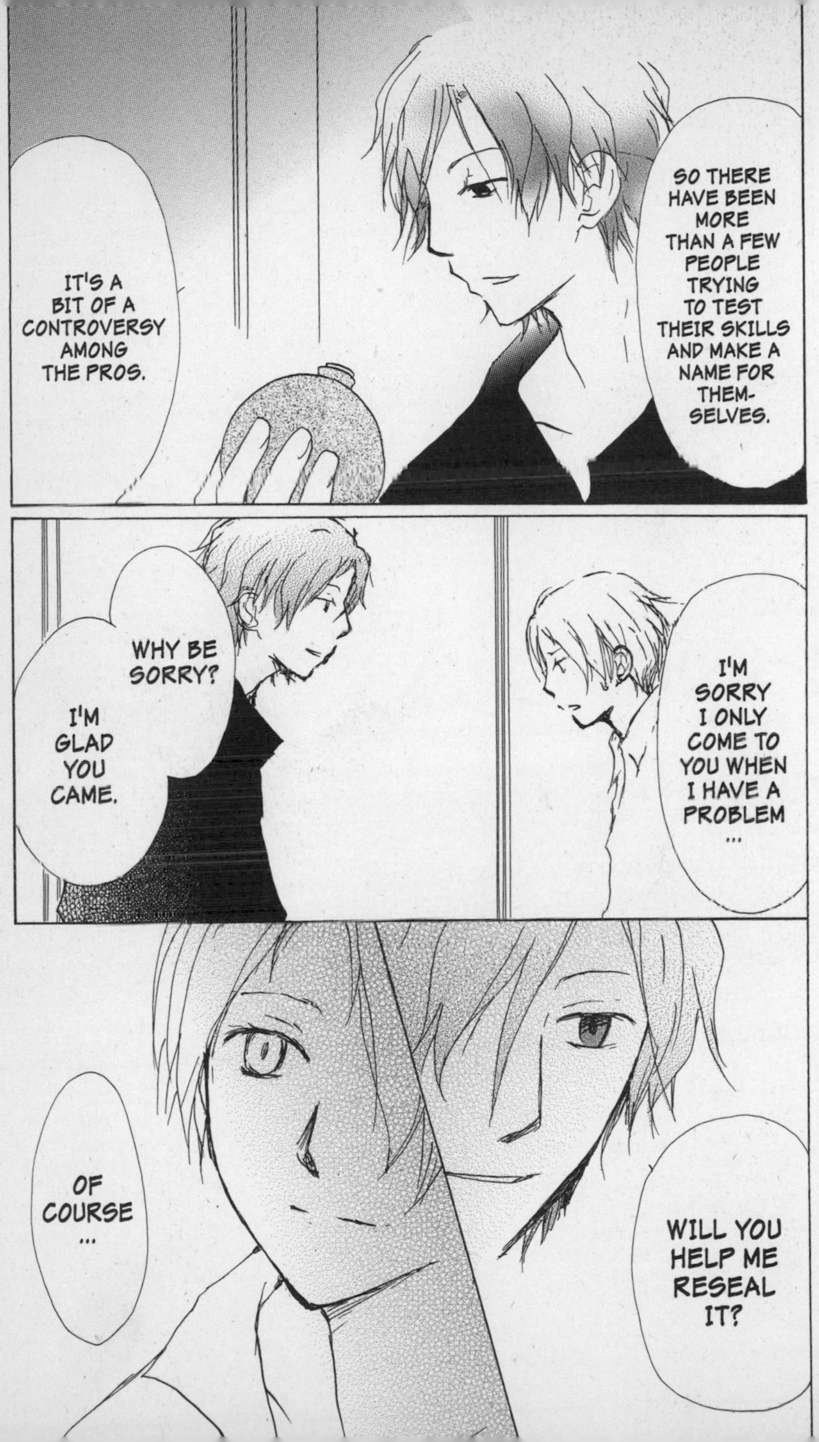
SO THERE HAVE BEEN MORE THAN A FEW PEOPLE TRYING TO TEST THEIR SKILLS AND MAKE A NAME FOR THEM-SELVES.
IT'S A BIT OF A CONTROVERSY AMONG THE PROS.
I'M SORRY I ONLY COME TO YOU WHEN I HAVE A PROBLEM ...
WHY BE SORRY?
I'M GLAD YOU CAME.
WILL YOU HELP ME RESEAL IT?
OF COURSE ...

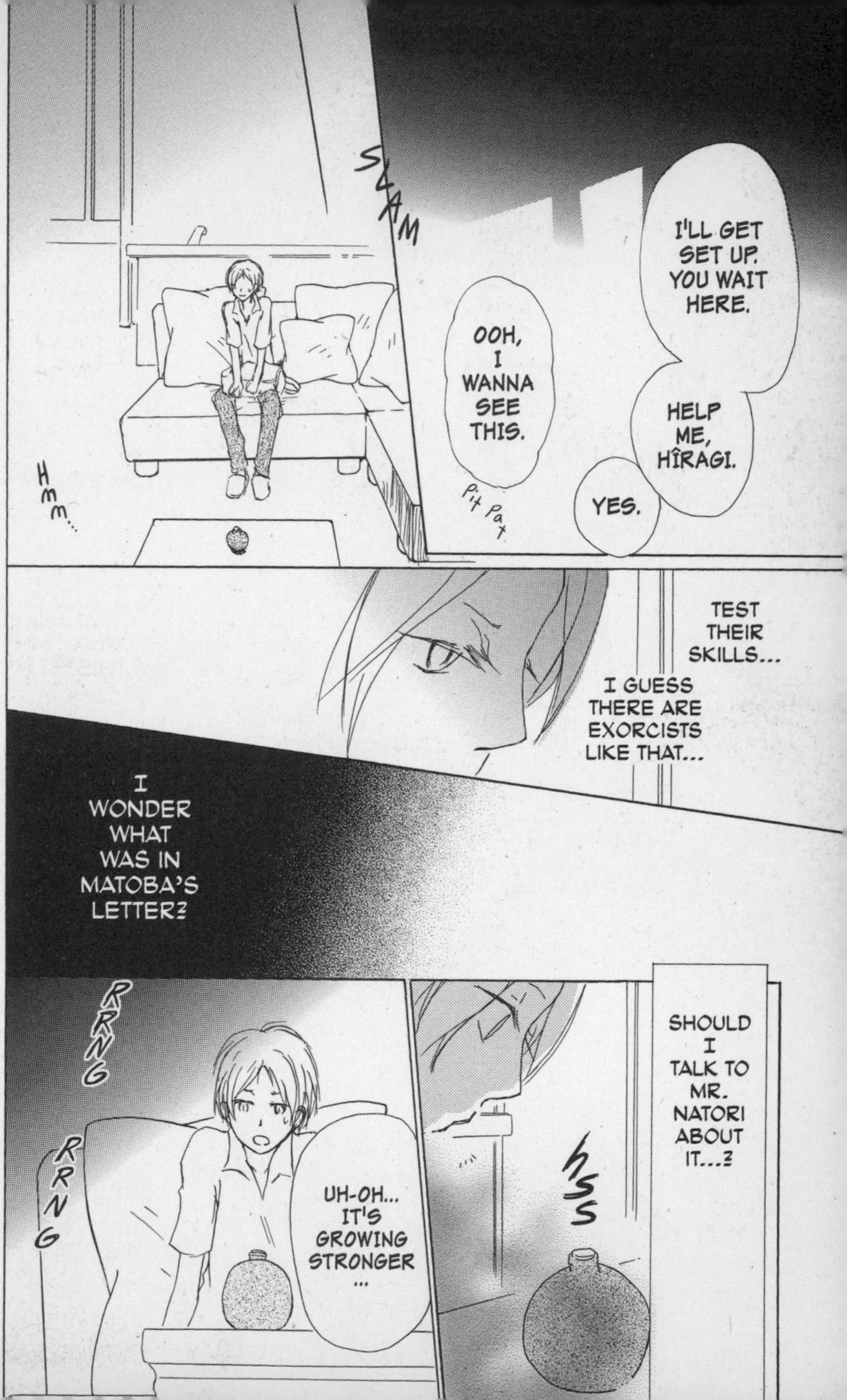

I'LL GET SET UP. YOU WAIT HERE.
HELP ME, HÎRAGI.
YES.
OOH, I WANNA SEE THIS.
Pit Pat
SLAM
Hmm...
TEST THEIR SKILLS...
I GUESS THERE ARE EXORCISTS LIKE THAT...
I WONDER WHAT WAS IN MATOBA'S LETTER?
SHOULD I TALK TO MR. NATORI ABOUT IT...?
HSS
RRNG
RRNG
UH-OH... IT'S GROWING STRONGER...

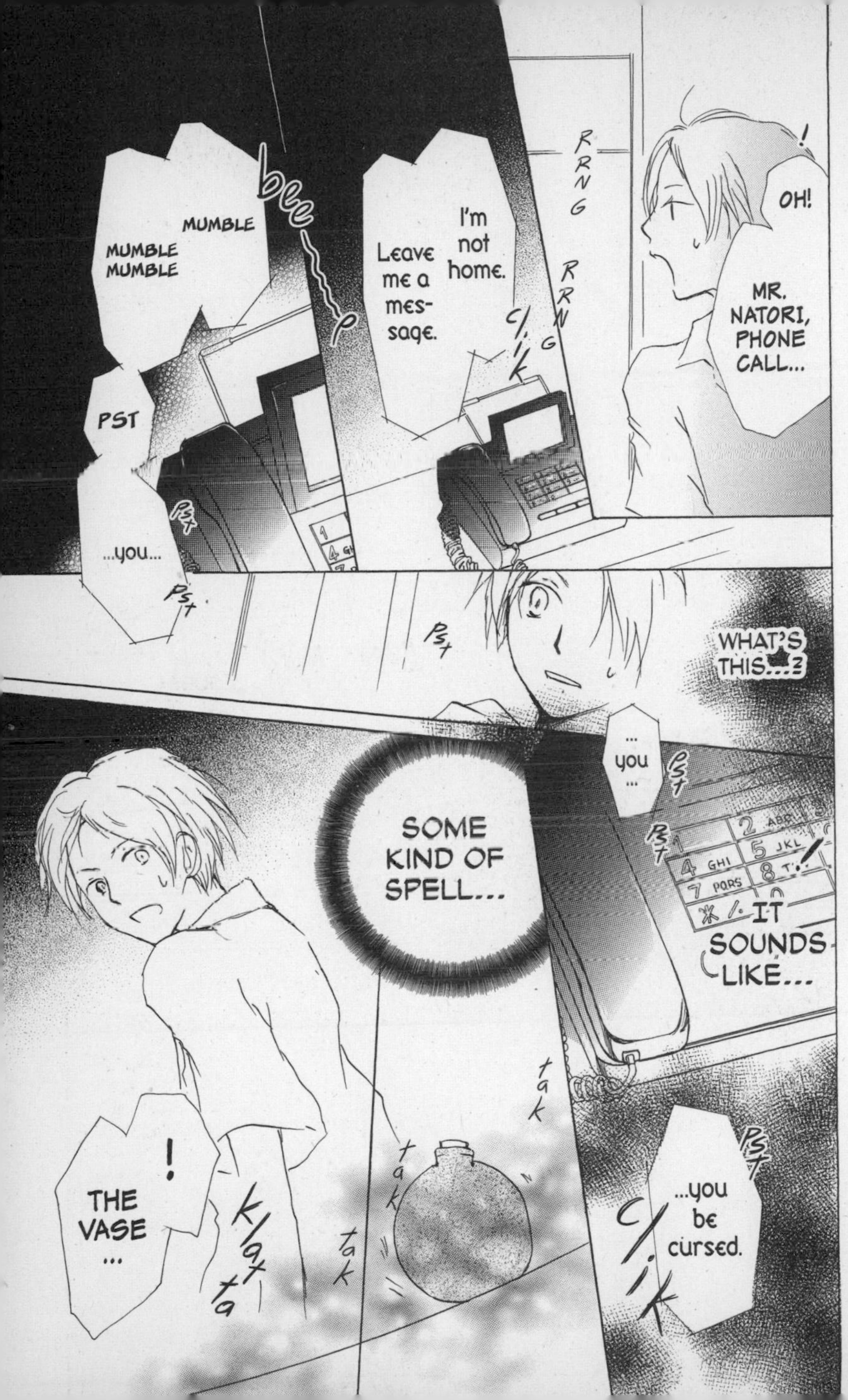
!
OH!
MR. NATORI, PHONE CALL...
RRNG RRNG
I'm not home.
Leave me a mes-sage.
CLIK
bleeep
MUMBLE
MUMBLE MUMBLE
PST
PST
...you...
PST
PST
WHAT'S THIS...?
... you ...
PST
PST
IT SOUNDS LIKE...
SOME KIND OF SPELL...
PST
...you be cursed.
CLIK
tak
tak
tak
!
THE VASE ...
klatta

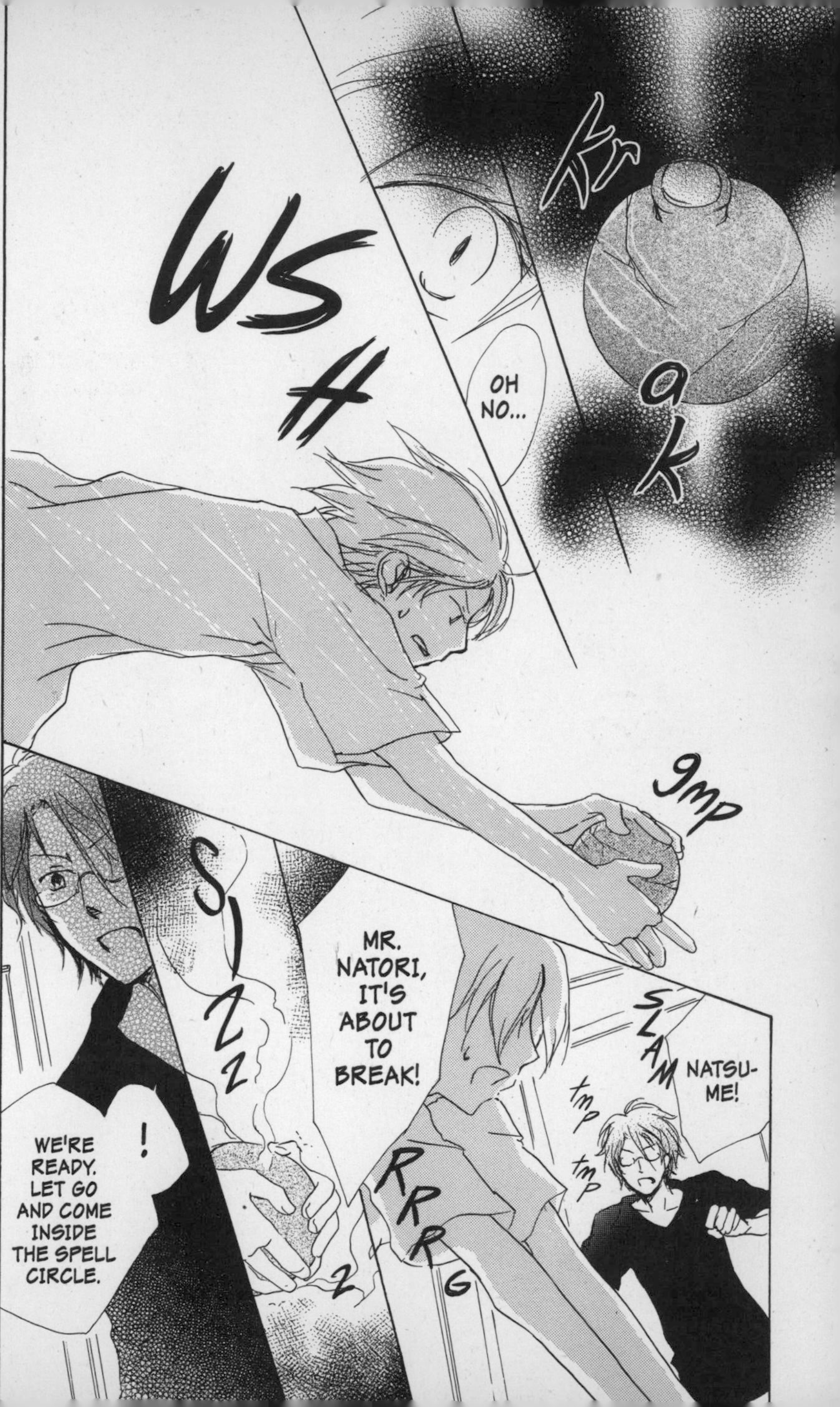
krak
OH NO...
WSH
gmp
SLAM
NATSU-ME!
tmp tmp
MR. NATORI, IT'S ABOUT TO BREAK!
RRRG
SIZZZ
!
WE'RE READY. LET GO AND COME INSIDE THE SPELL CIRCLE.

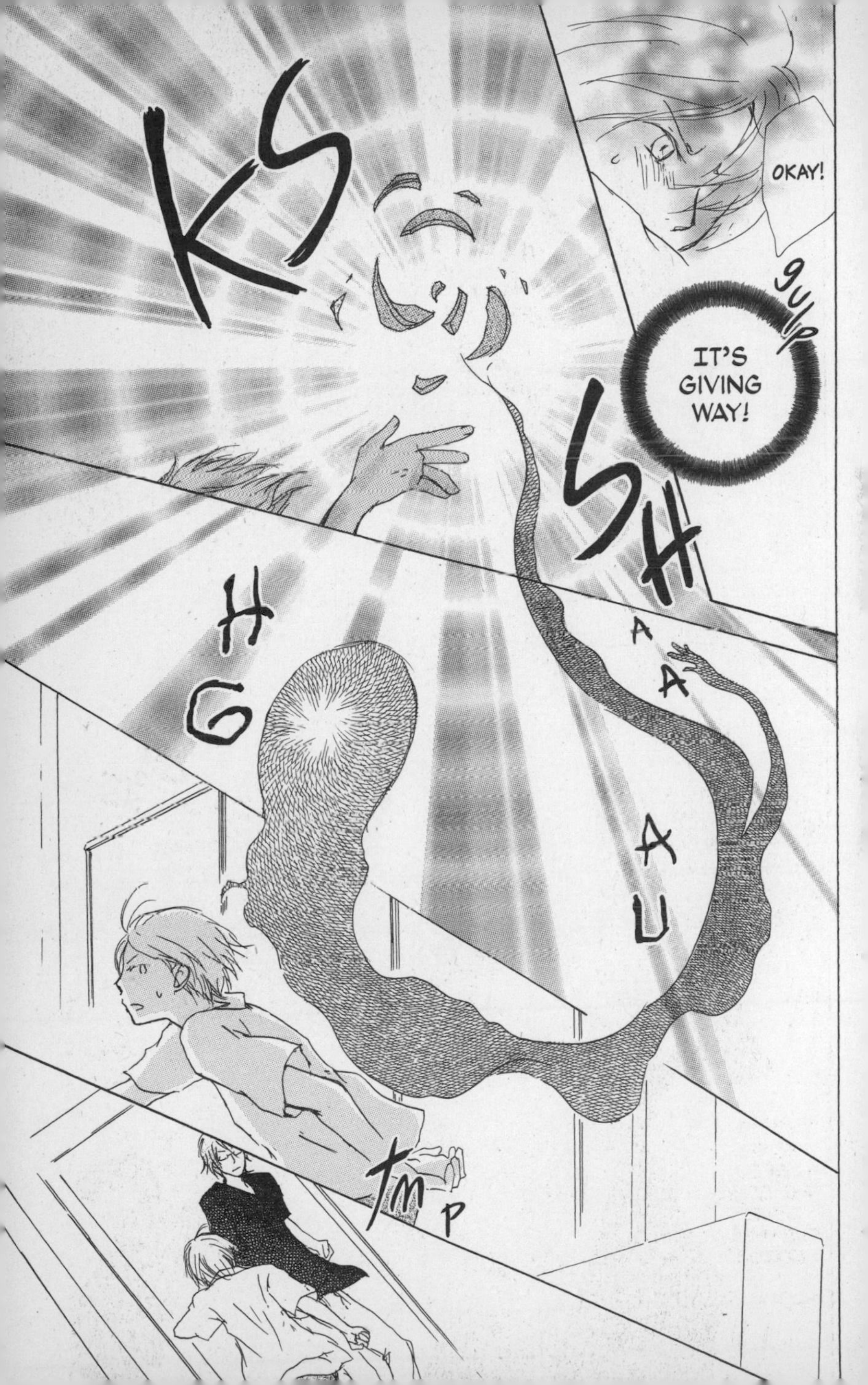
OKAY!
gulp
IT'S GIVING WAY!
KS
SH
HAAAU
GH
tmp

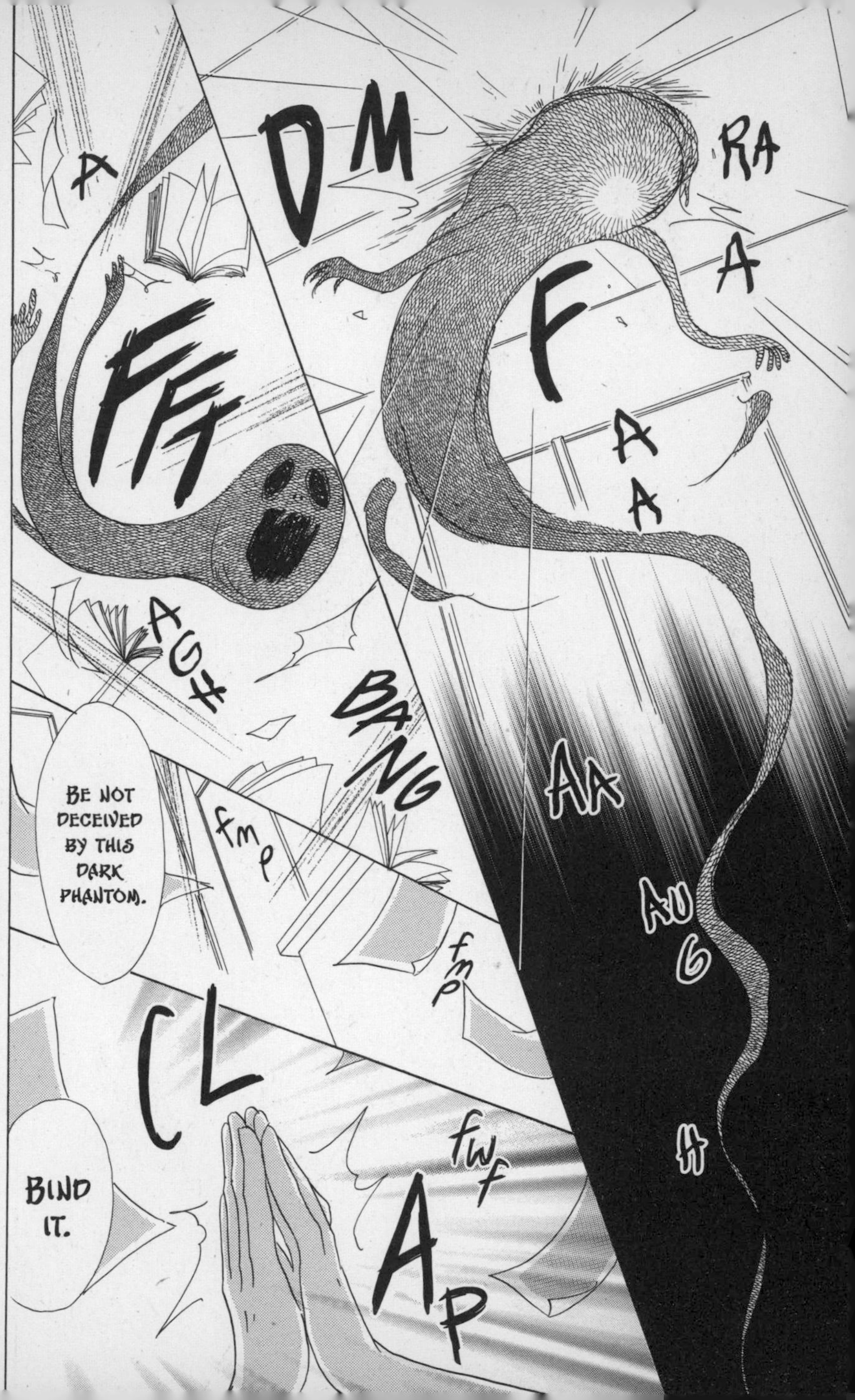

RA
A
F
A
A
DM
A
FF
AGH
BANG
fmp
AA
AUG
H
BE NOT DECEIVED BY THIS DARK PHANTOM.
fmp
CL
AP
fwf
BIND IT.

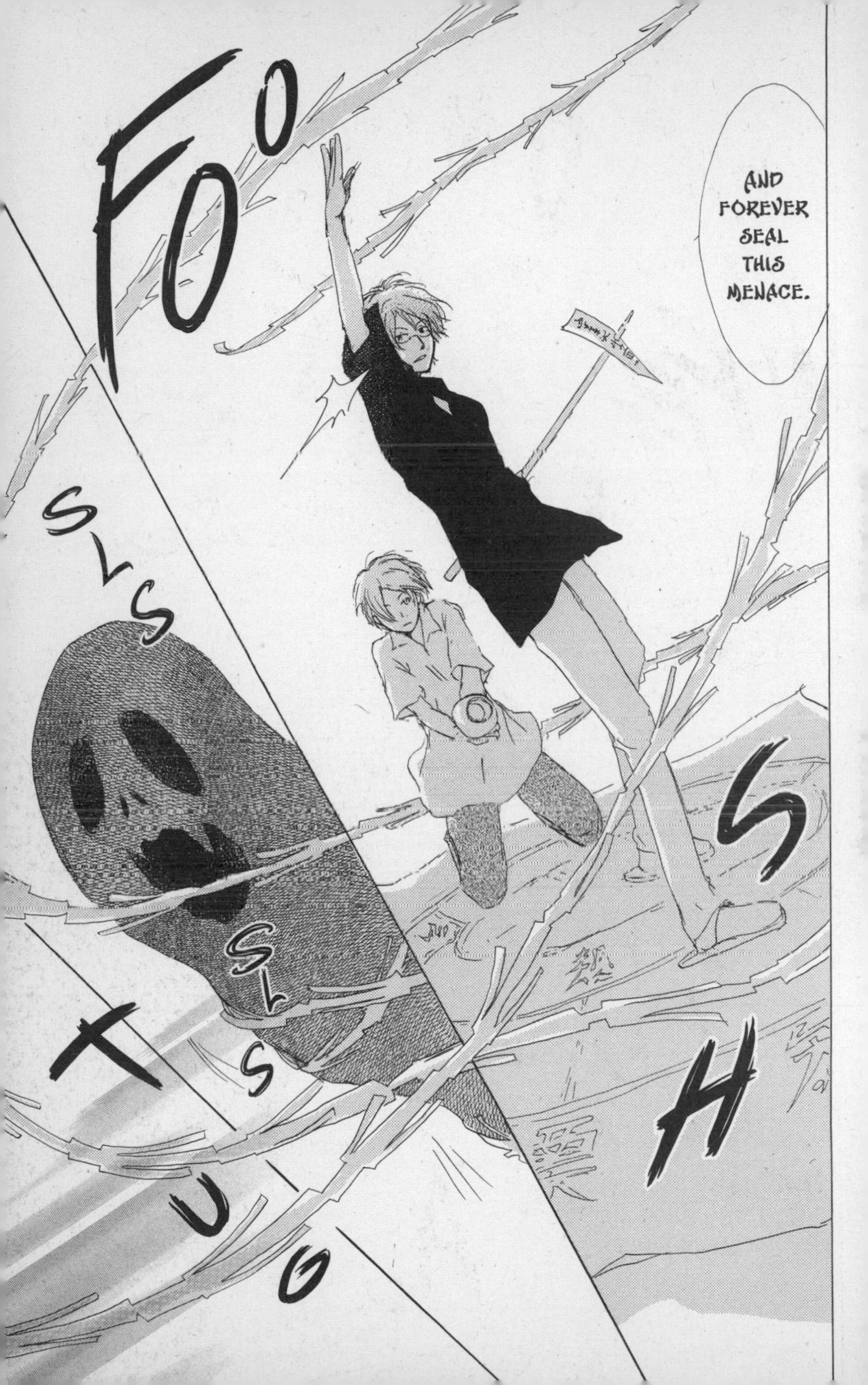
AND FOREVER SEAL THIS MENACE.
FOO
SLSS
SLSLS
SH
FUSH

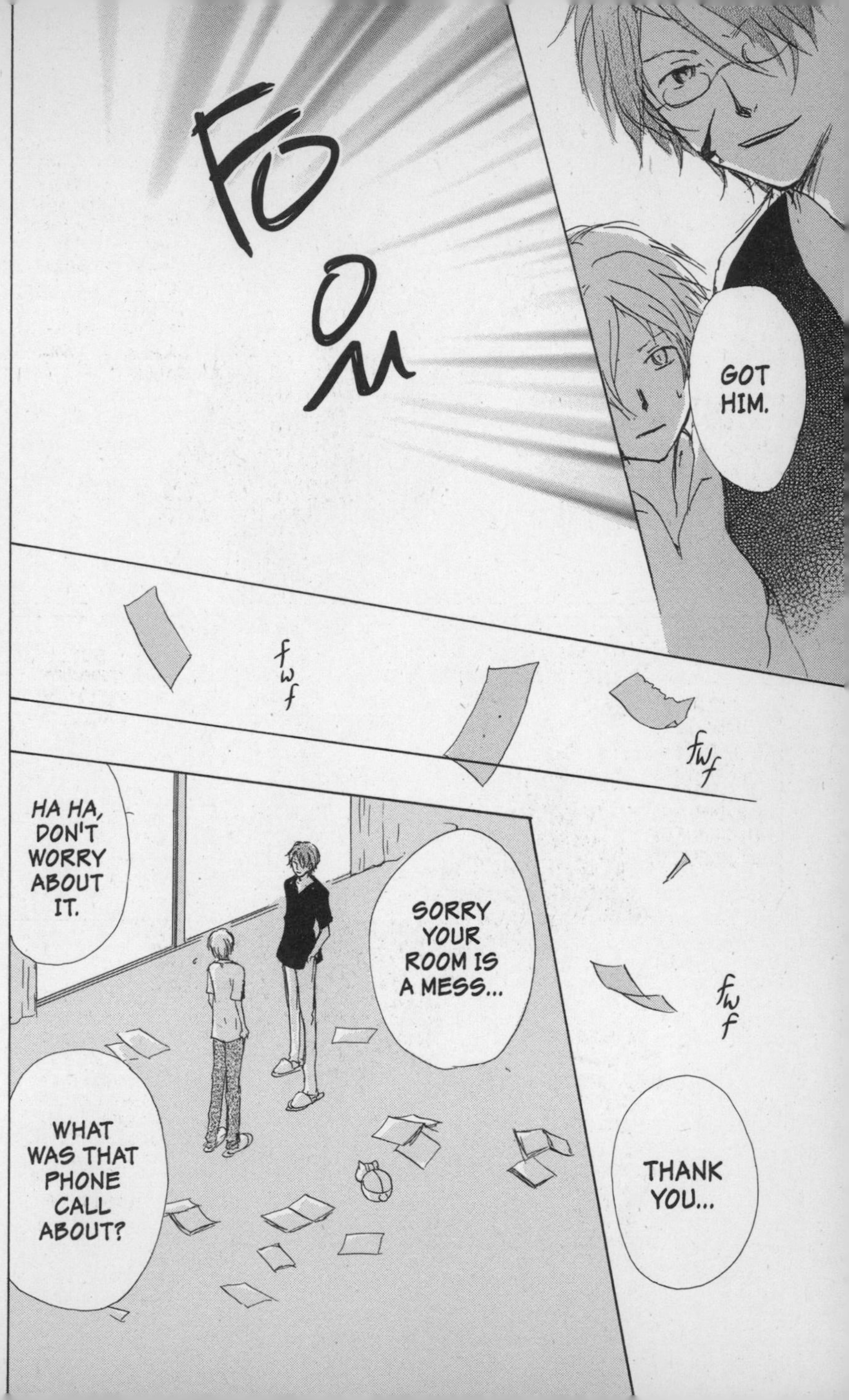
GOT HIM.
FOOM
fwf
fwf
fwf
SORRY YOUR ROOM IS A MESS...
HA HA, DON'T WORRY ABOUT IT.
THANK YOU...
WHAT WAS THAT PHONE CALL ABOUT?

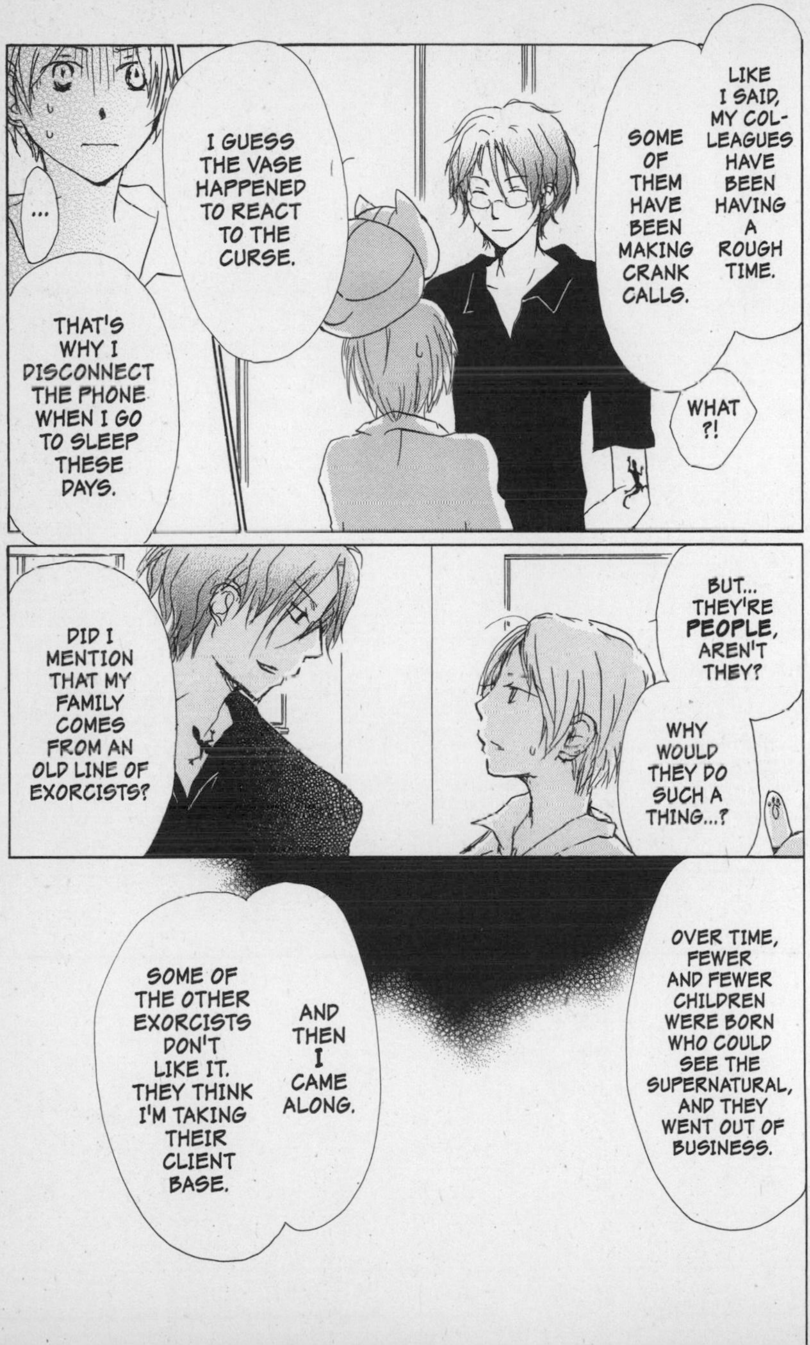
LIKE I SAID, MY COLLEAGUES HAVE BEEN HAVING A ROUGH TIME.
SOME OF THEM HAVE BEEN MAKING CRANK CALLS.
WHAT?!
I GUESS THE VASE HAPPENED TO REACT TO THE CURSE.
...
THAT'S WHY I DISCONNECT THE PHONE WHEN I GO TO SLEEP THESE DAYS.
BUT... THEY'RE **PEOPLE**, AREN'T THEY?
WHY WOULD THEY DO SUCH A THING...?
DID I MENTION THAT MY FAMILY COMES FROM AN OLD LINE OF EXORCISTS?
OVER TIME, FEWER AND FEWER CHILDREN WERE BORN WHO COULD SEE THE SUPERNATURAL, AND THEY WENT OUT OF BUSINESS.
AND THEN **I** CAME ALONG.
SOME OF THE OTHER EXORCISTS DON'T LIKE IT. THEY THINK I'M TAKING THEIR CLIENT BASE.

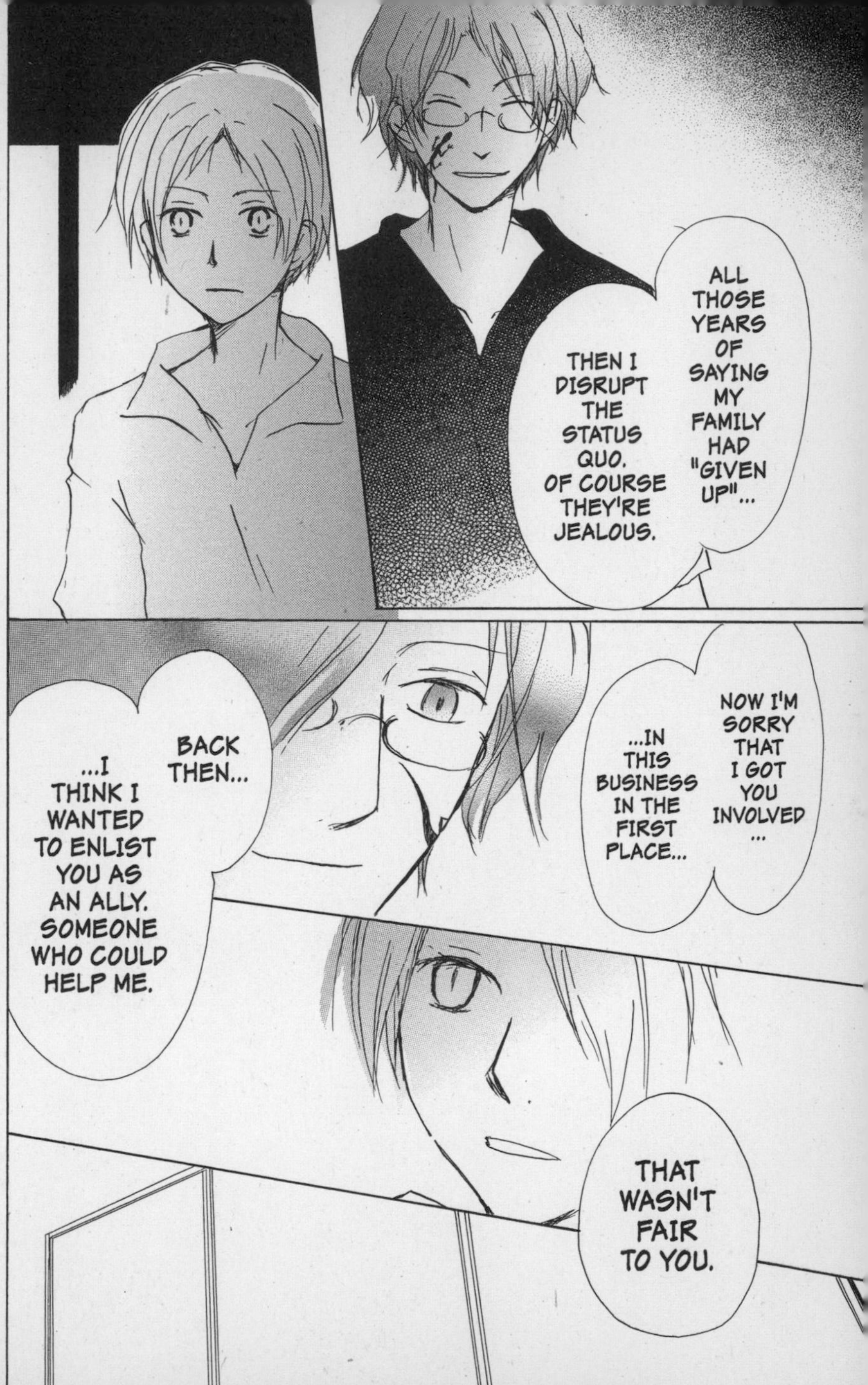
ALL THOSE YEARS OF SAYING MY FAMILY HAD "GIVEN UP"...
THEN I DISRUPT THE STATUS QUO. OF COURSE THEY'RE JEALOUS.
NOW I'M SORRY THAT I GOT YOU INVOLVED ...
...IN THIS BUSINESS IN THE FIRST PLACE...
BACK THEN...
...I THINK I WANTED TO ENLIST YOU AS AN ALLY. SOMEONE WHO COULD HELP ME.
THAT WASN'T FAIR TO YOU.

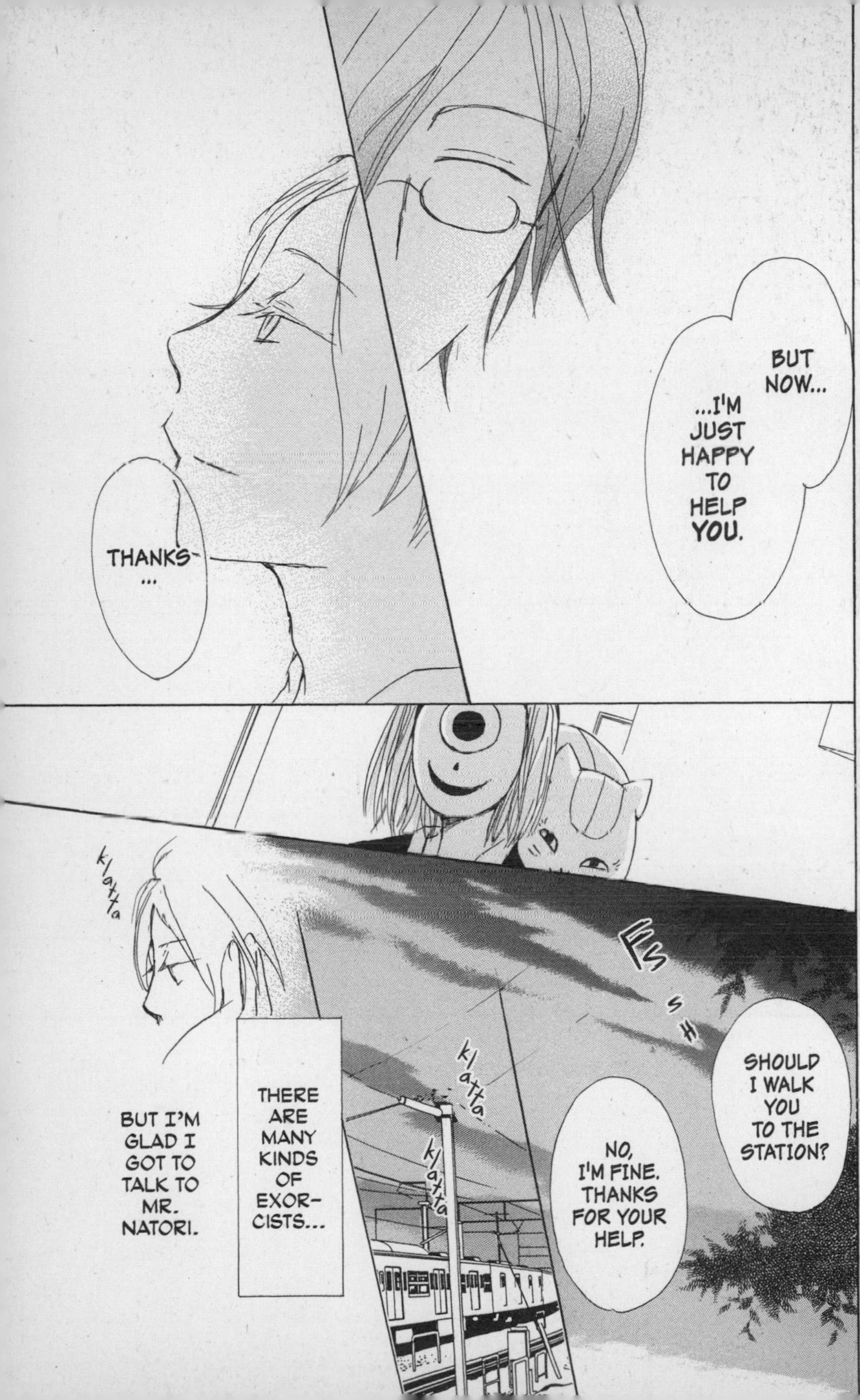
BUT NOW...
...I'M JUST HAPPY TO HELP YOU.
THANKS-...
FSSH
SHOULD I WALK YOU TO THE STATION?
NO, I'M FINE. THANKS FOR YOUR HELP.
klatta klatta
THERE ARE MANY KINDS OF EXOR-CISTS...
BUT I'M GLAD I GOT TO TALK TO MR. NATORI.
klatta

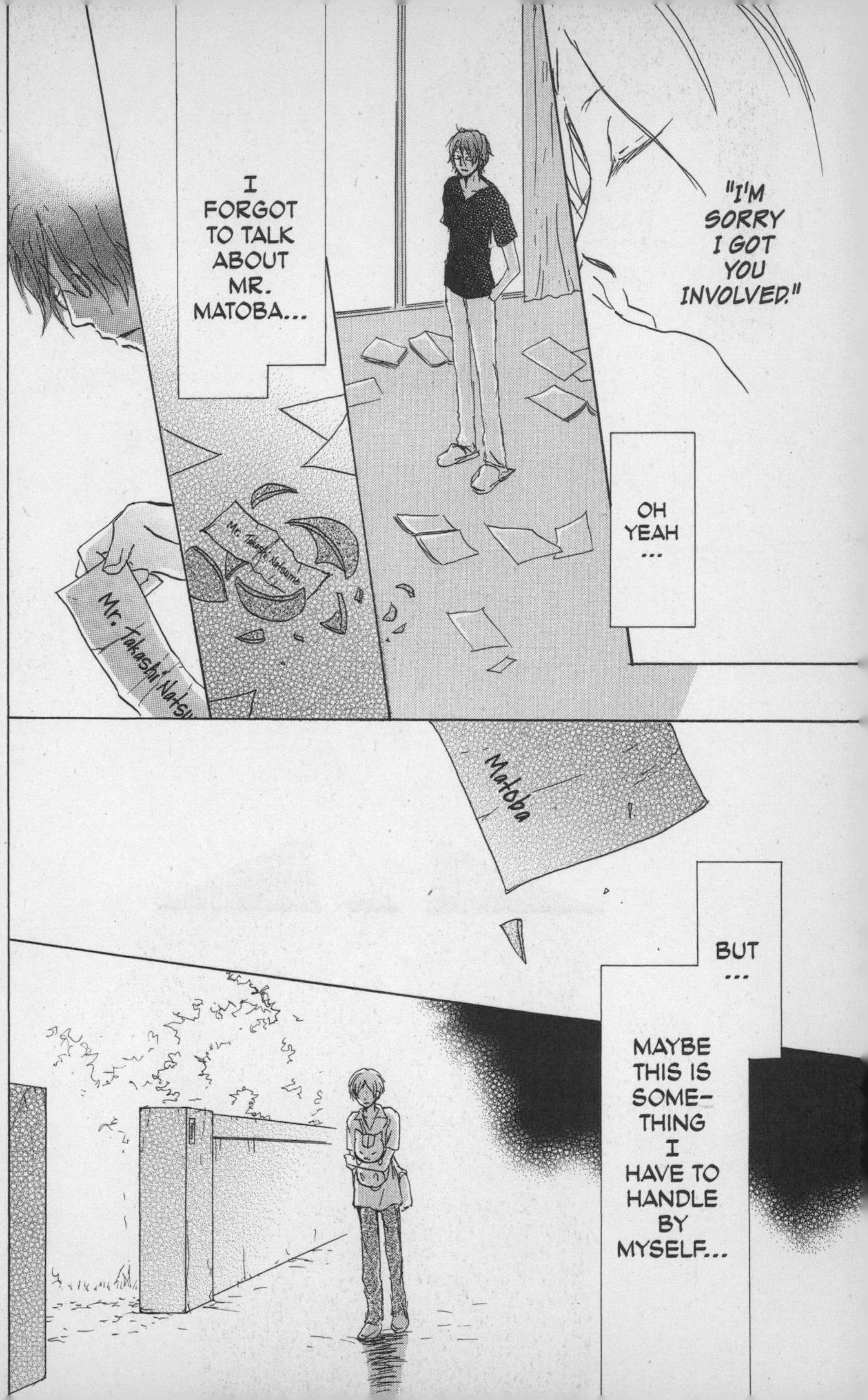
"I'M SORRY I GOT YOU INVOLVED."
OH YEAH...
I FORGOT TO TALK ABOUT MR. MATOBA...
Mr. Takashi Natsume
Matoba
BUT...
MAYBE THIS IS SOME-THING I HAVE TO HANDLE BY MYSELF...

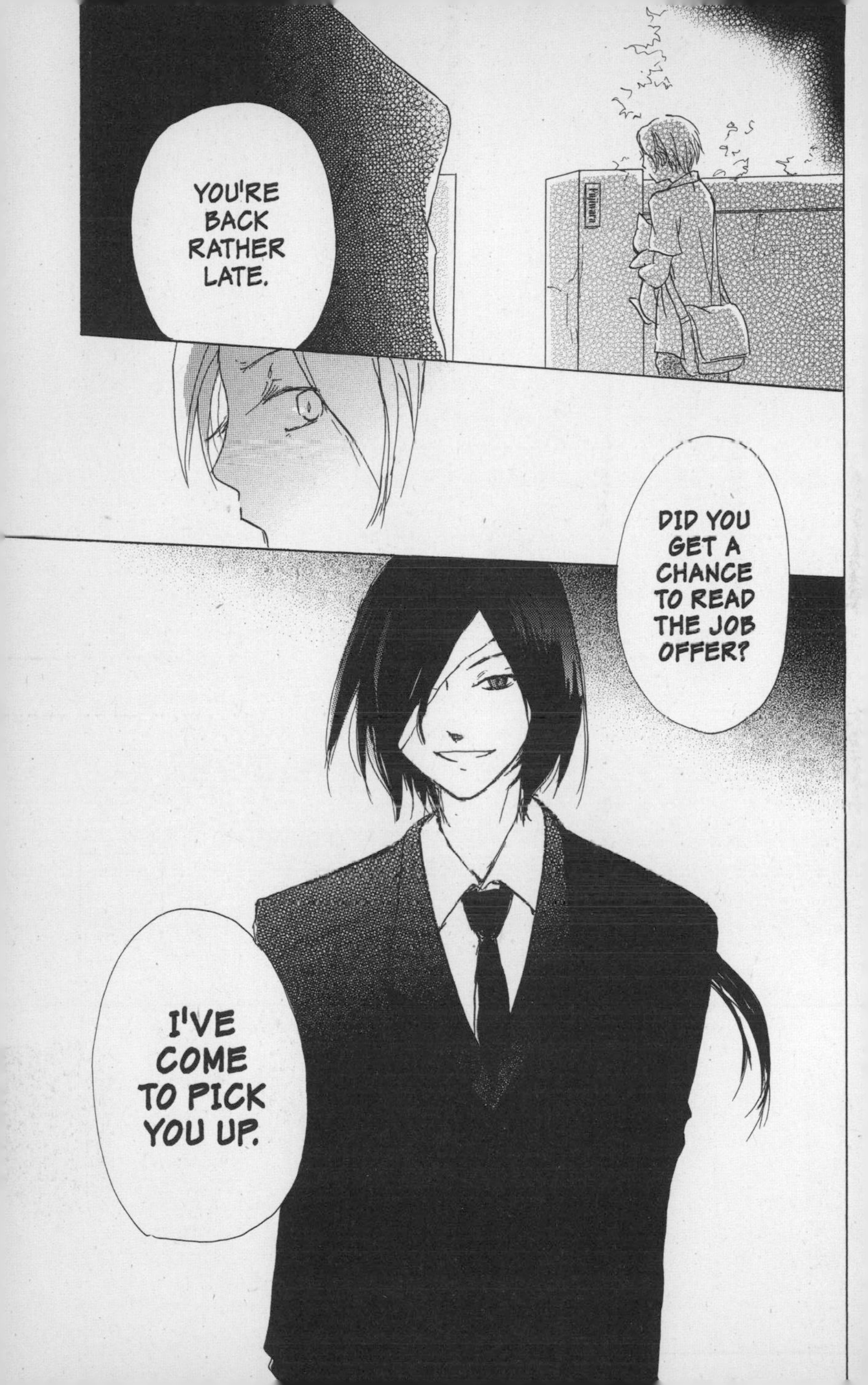
YOU'RE BACK RATHER LATE.
DID YOU GET A CHANCE TO READ THE JOB OFFER?
I'VE COME TO PICK YOU UP.

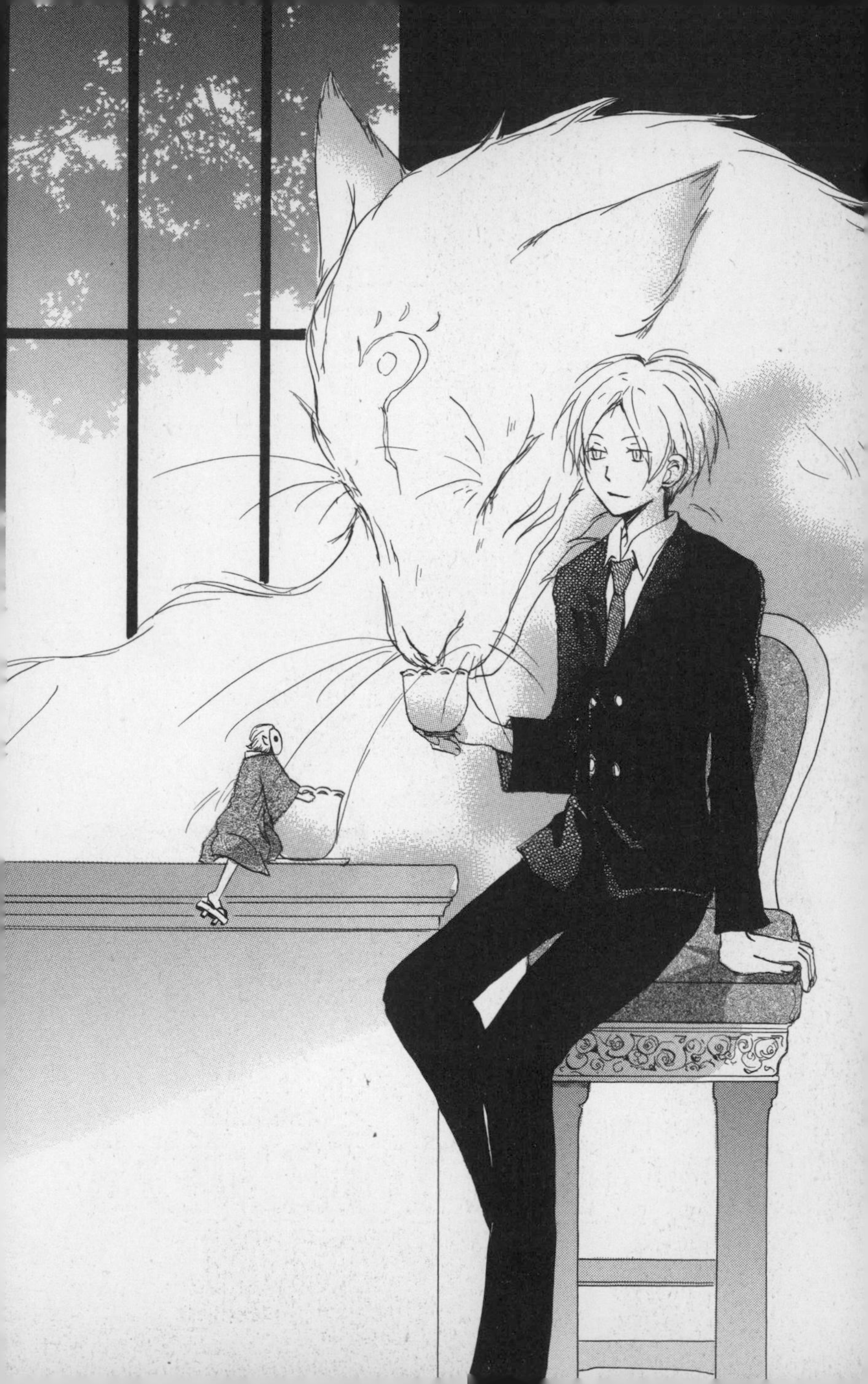

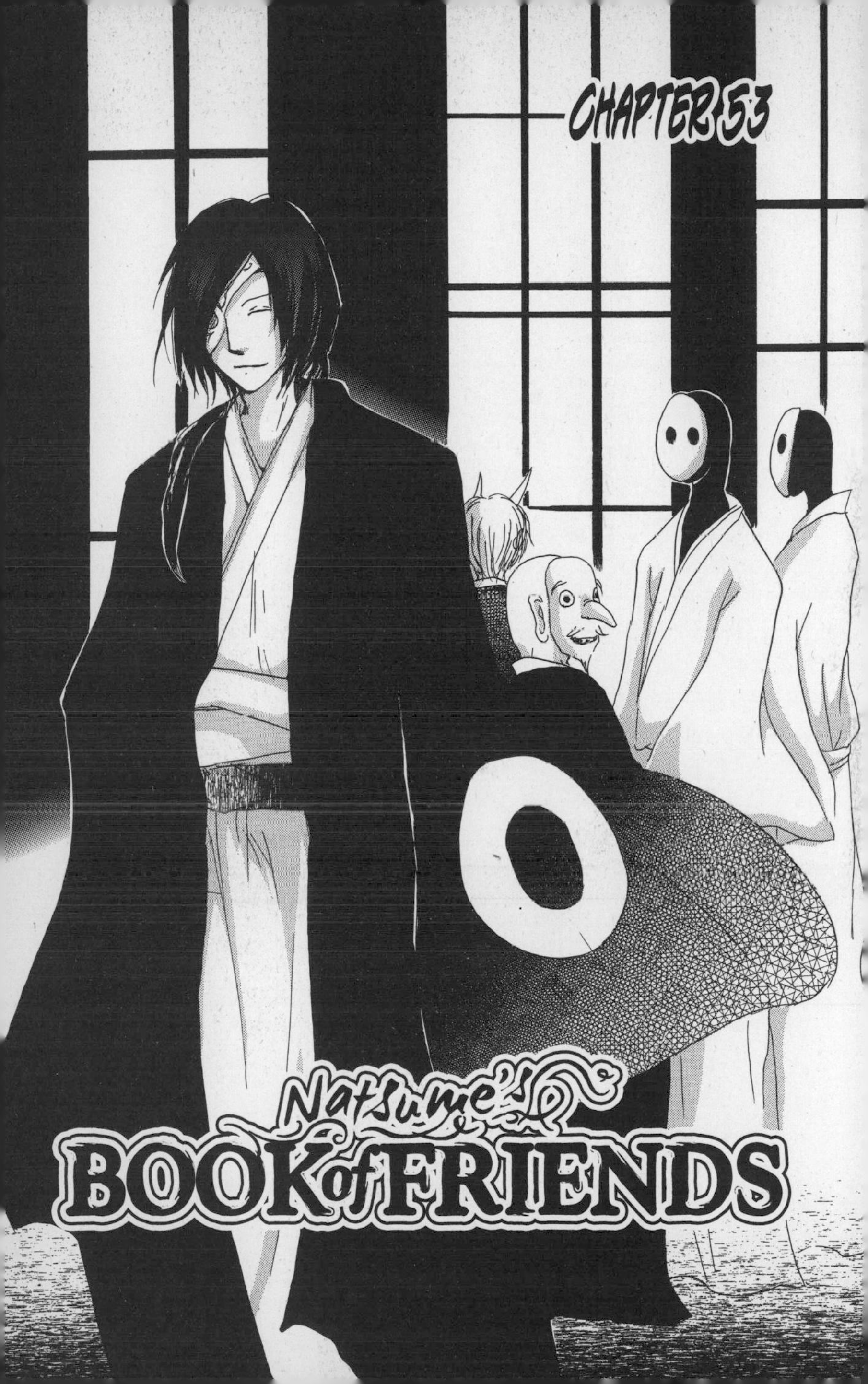
CHAPTER 53
Natsume's
BOOK of FRIENDS

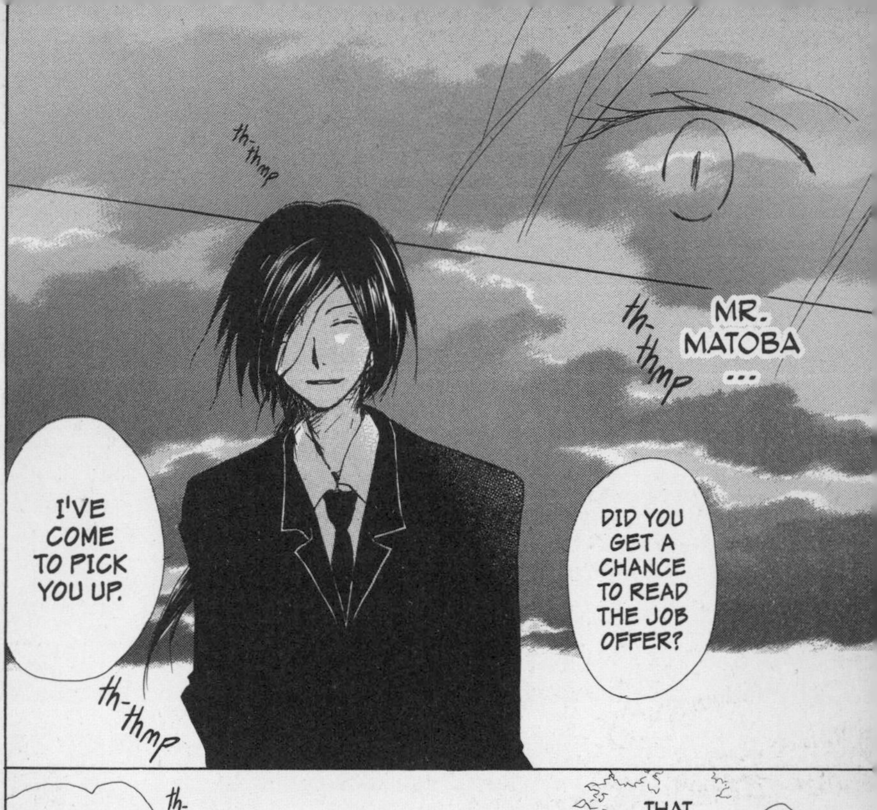
th-thmp
MR. MATOBA ...
th-thmp
DID YOU GET A CHANCE TO READ THE JOB OFFER?
I'VE COME TO PICK YOU UP.
th-thmp
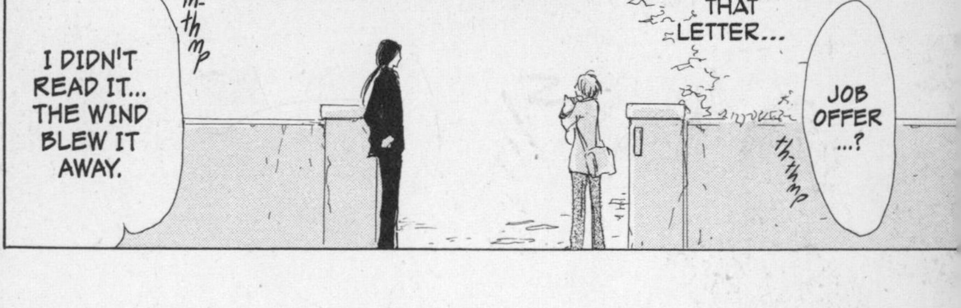
JOB OFFER ...?
th-thmp
THAT LETTER...
th-thmp
I DIDN'T READ IT... THE WIND BLEW IT AWAY.
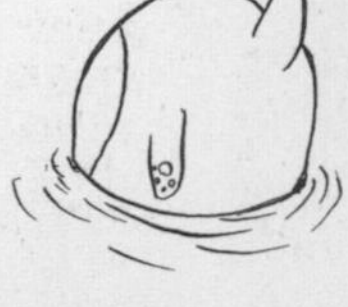

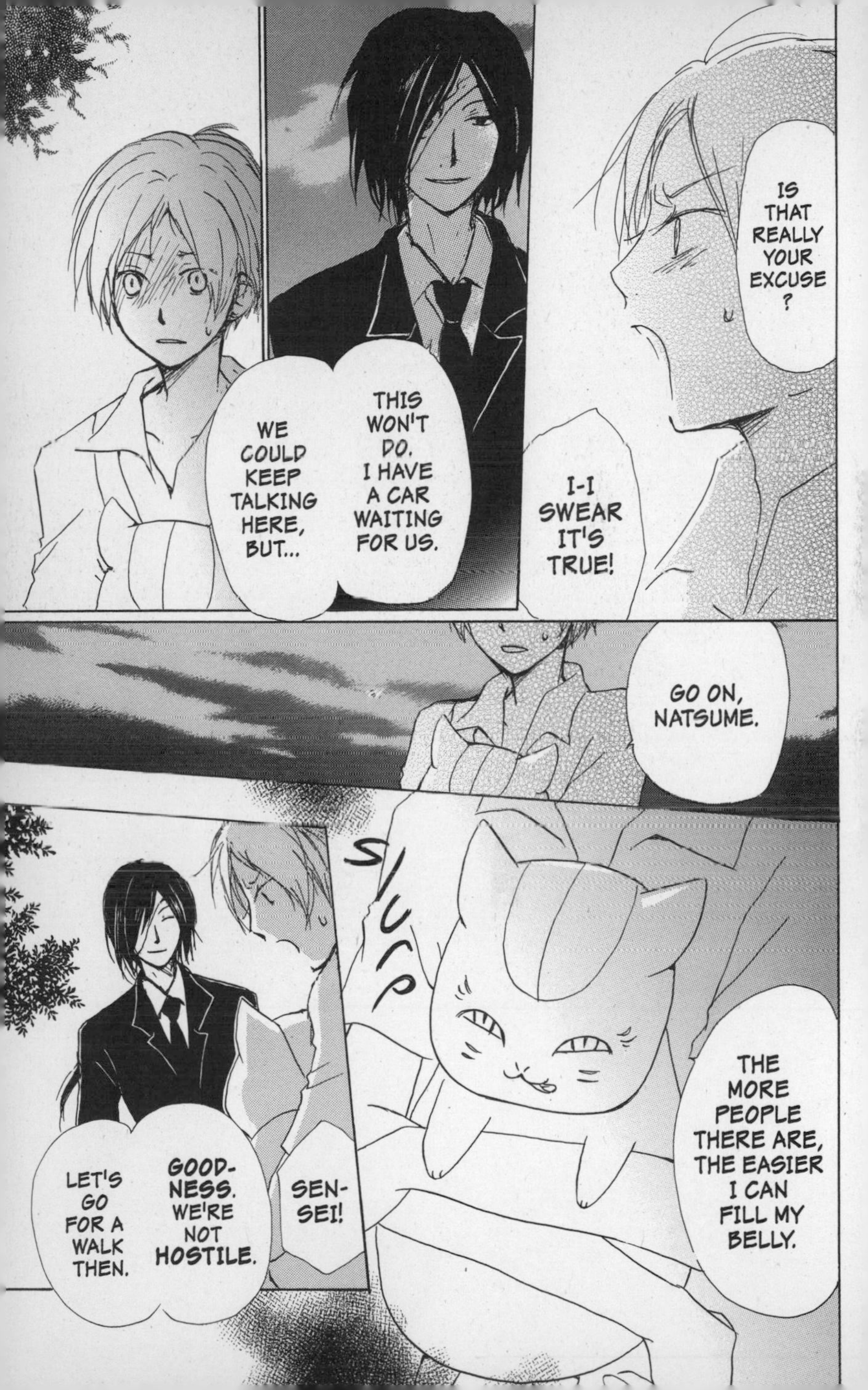
IS THAT REALLY YOUR EXCUSE?
I-I SWEAR IT'S TRUE!
THIS WON'T DO. I HAVE A CAR WAITING FOR US.
WE COULD KEEP TALKING HERE, BUT...
GO ON, NATSUME.
SLURP
THE MORE PEOPLE THERE ARE, THE EASIER I CAN FILL MY BELLY.
SEN-SEI!
GOOD-NESS. WE'RE NOT HOSTILE.
LET'S GO FOR A WALK THEN.

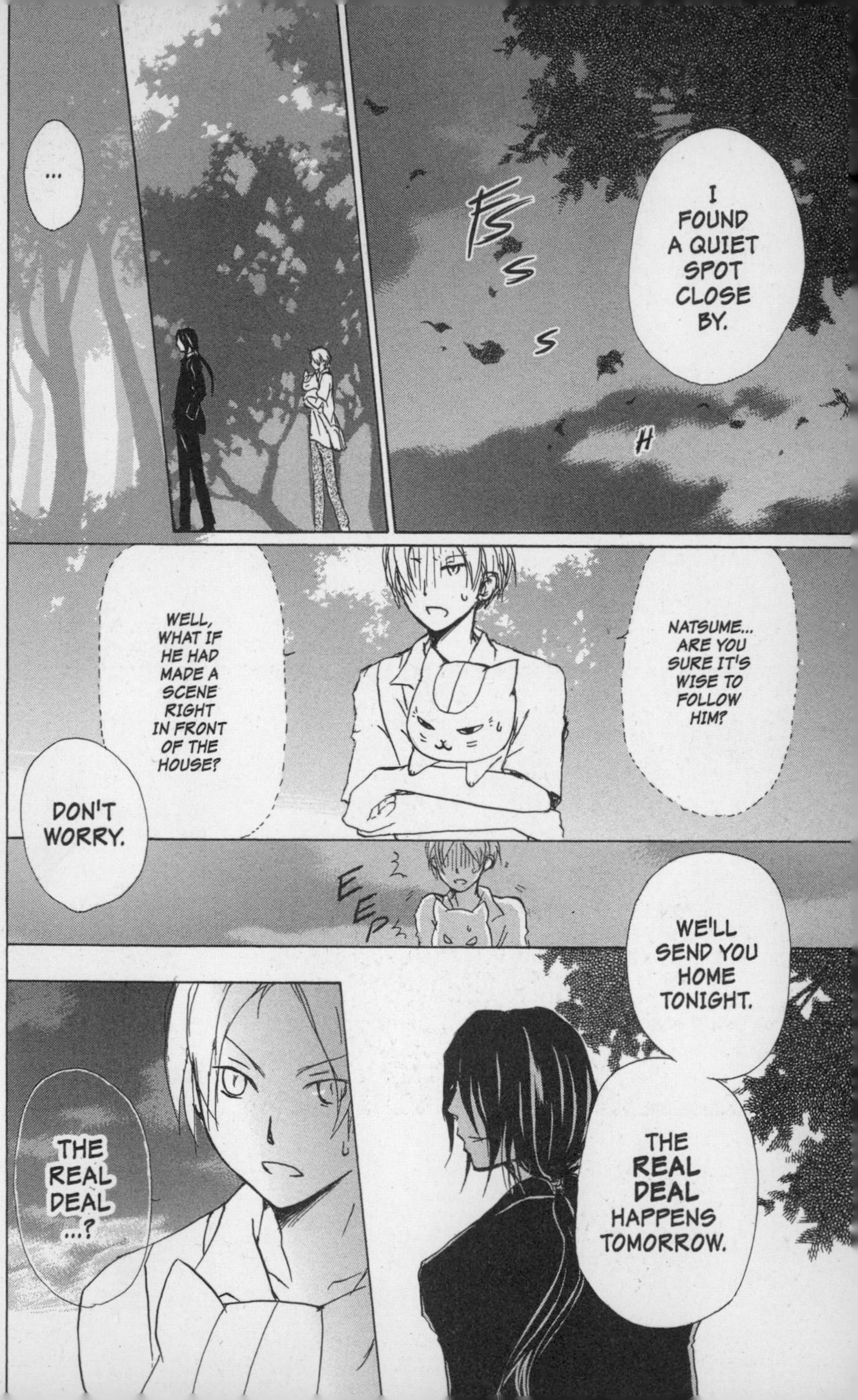
I FOUND A QUIET SPOT CLOSE BY.
FSSSH
...
NATSUME... ARE YOU SURE IT'S WISE TO FOLLOW HIM?
WELL, WHAT IF HE HAD MADE A SCENE RIGHT IN FRONT OF THE HOUSE?
DON'T WORRY.
WE'LL SEND YOU HOME TONIGHT.
EEEP
THE REAL DEAL HAPPENS TOMORROW.
THE REAL DEAL ...?

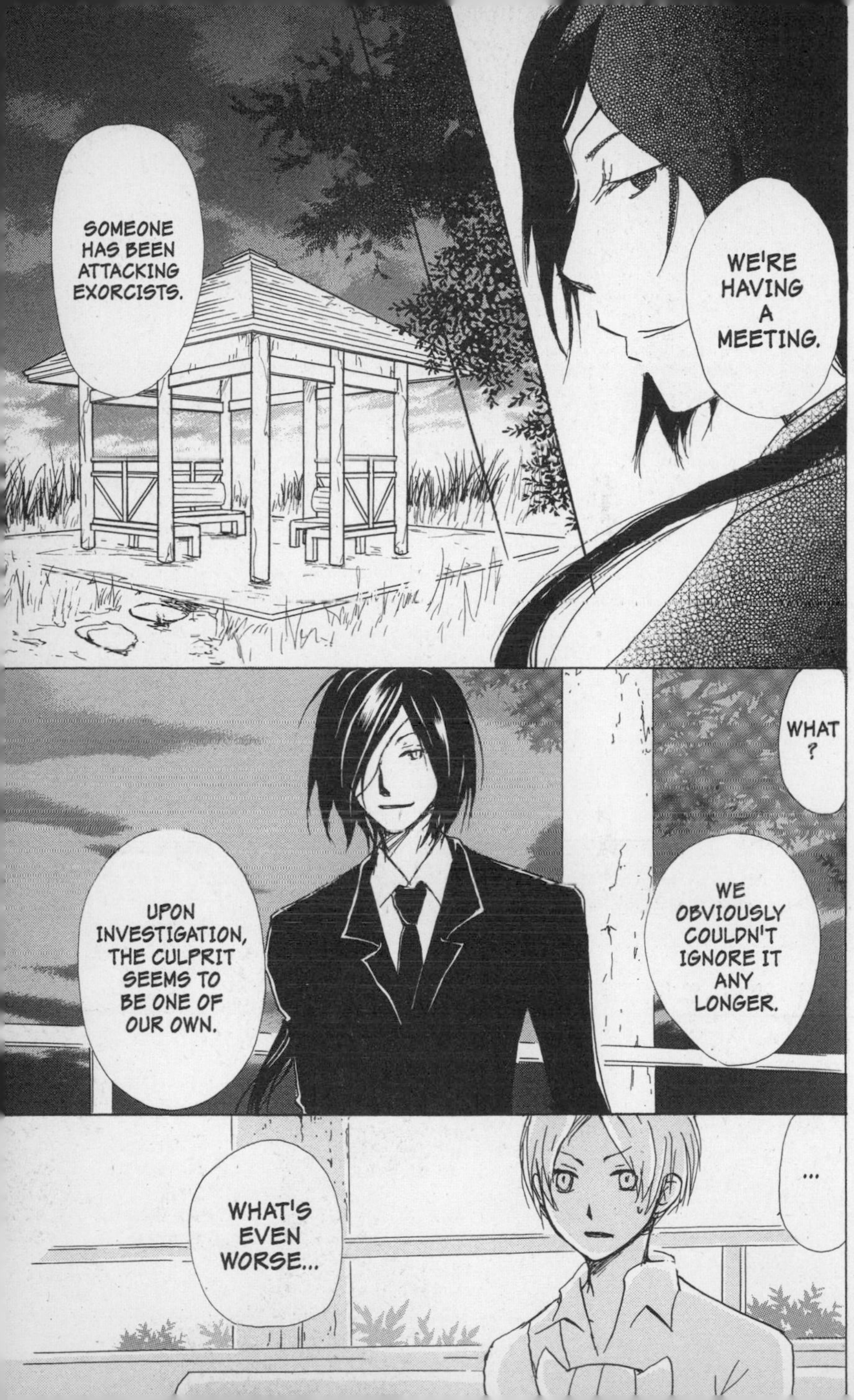
WE'RE HAVING A MEETING.
SOMEONE HAS BEEN ATTACKING EXORCISTS.
WHAT?
WE OBVIOUSLY COULDN'T IGNORE IT ANY LONGER.
UPON INVESTIGATION, THE CULPRIT SEEMS TO BE ONE OF OUR OWN.
...
WHAT'S EVEN WORSE...

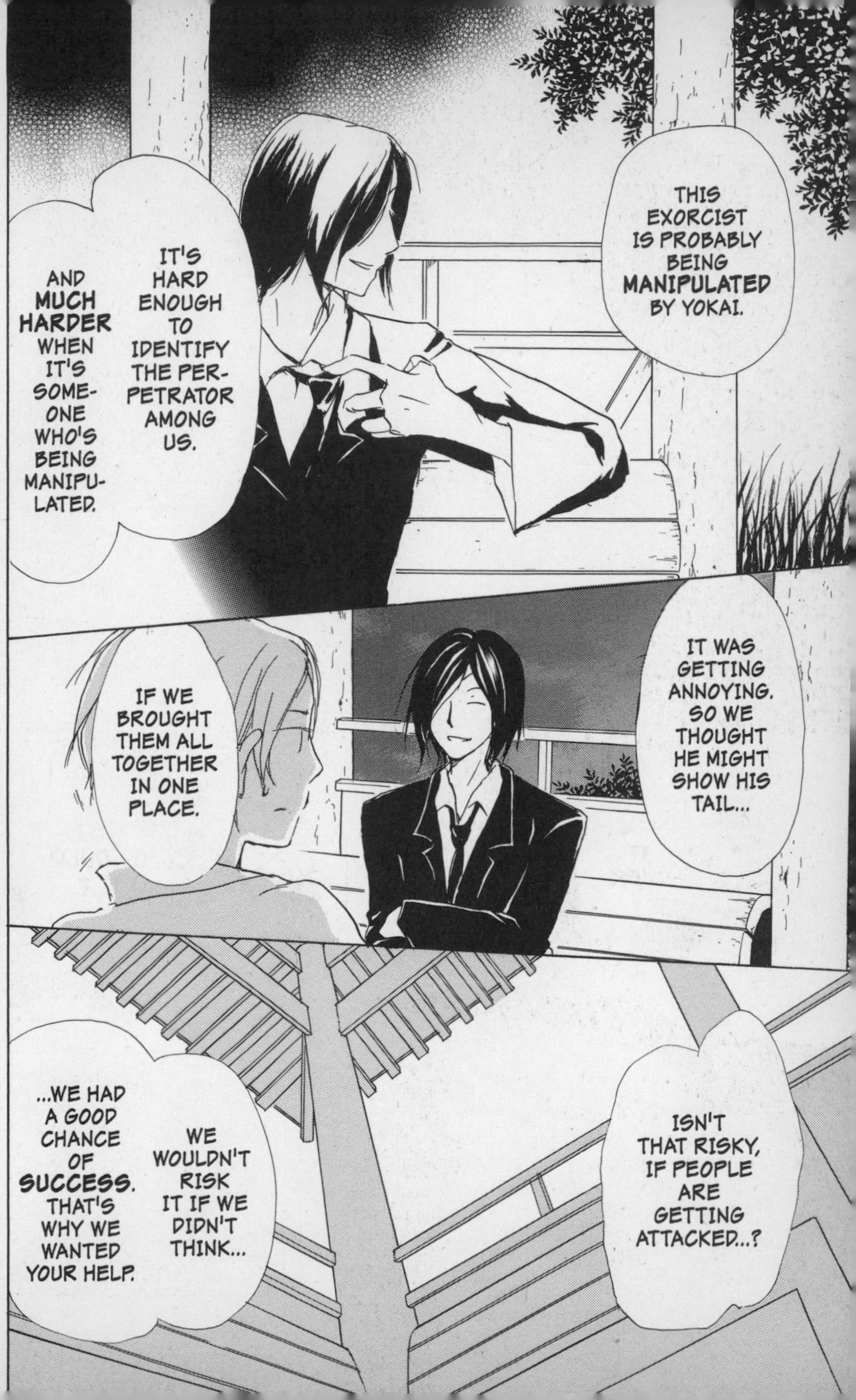
THIS EXORCIST IS PROBABLY BEING MANIPULATED BY YOKAI.
IT'S HARD ENOUGH TO IDENTIFY THE PERPETRATOR AMONG US.
AND MUCH HARDER WHEN IT'S SOMEONE WHO'S BEING MANIPULATED.
IT WAS GETTING ANNOYING. SO WE THOUGHT HE MIGHT SHOW HIS TAIL...
IF WE BROUGHT THEM ALL TOGETHER IN ONE PLACE.
ISN'T THAT RISKY, IF PEOPLE ARE GETTING ATTACKED...?
WE WOULDN'T RISK IT IF WE DIDN'T THINK...
...WE HAD A GOOD CHANCE OF SUCCESS. THAT'S WHY WE WANTED YOUR HELP.

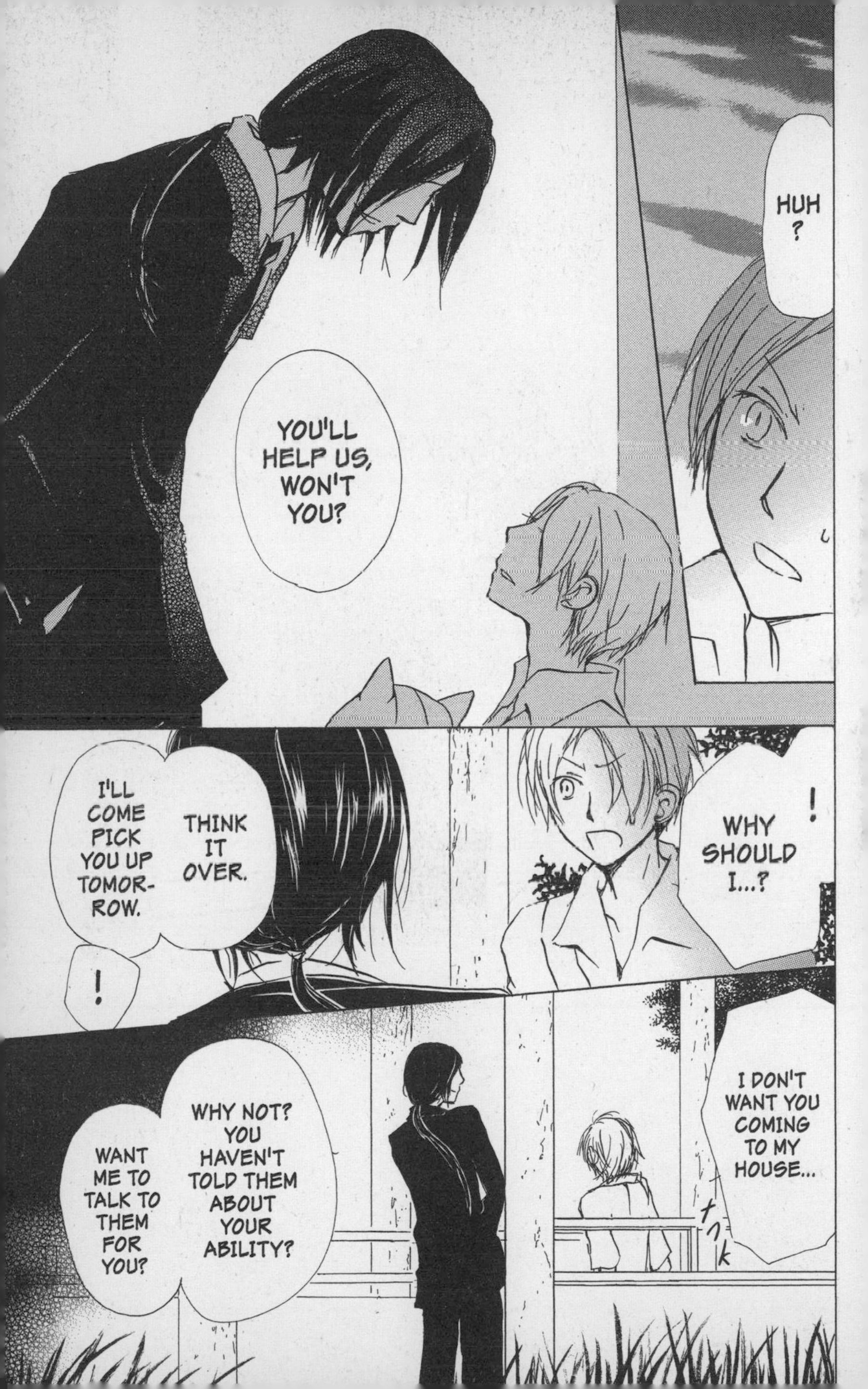
HUH ?
YOU'LL HELP US, WON'T YOU?
!
WHY SHOULD I...?
THINK IT OVER.
I'LL COME PICK YOU UP TOMOR-ROW.
!
I DON'T WANT YOU COMING TO MY HOUSE...
WHY NOT? YOU HAVEN'T TOLD THEM ABOUT YOUR ABILITY?
WANT ME TO TALK TO THEM FOR YOU?

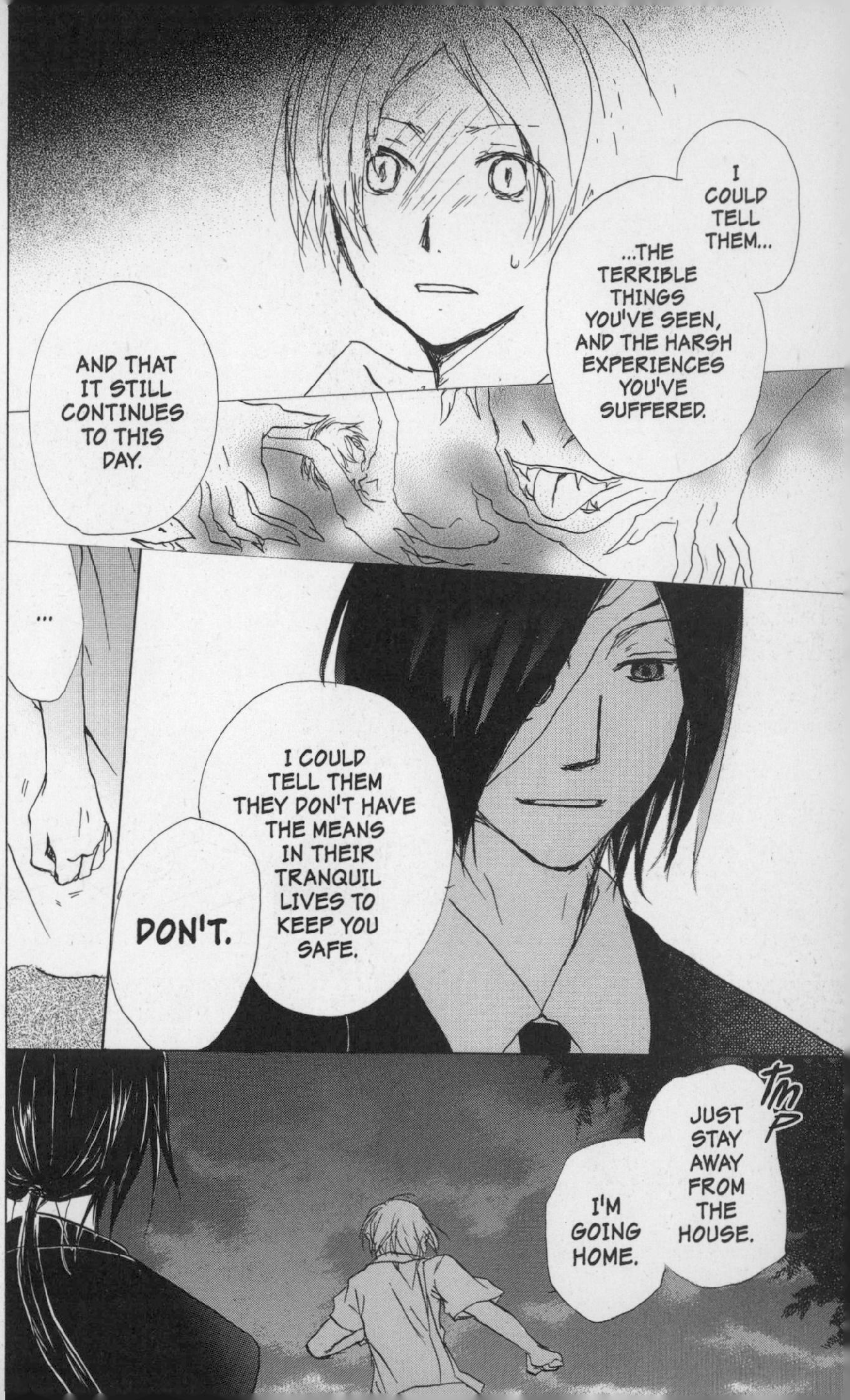
I COULD TELL THEM...
...THE TERRIBLE THINGS YOU'VE SEEN, AND THE HARSH EXPERIENCES YOU'VE SUFFERED.
AND THAT IT STILL CONTINUES TO THIS DAY.
I COULD TELL THEM THEY DON'T HAVE THE MEANS IN THEIR TRANQUIL LIVES TO KEEP YOU SAFE.
DON'T.
...
TMP
JUST STAY AWAY FROM THE HOUSE.
I'M GOING HOME.

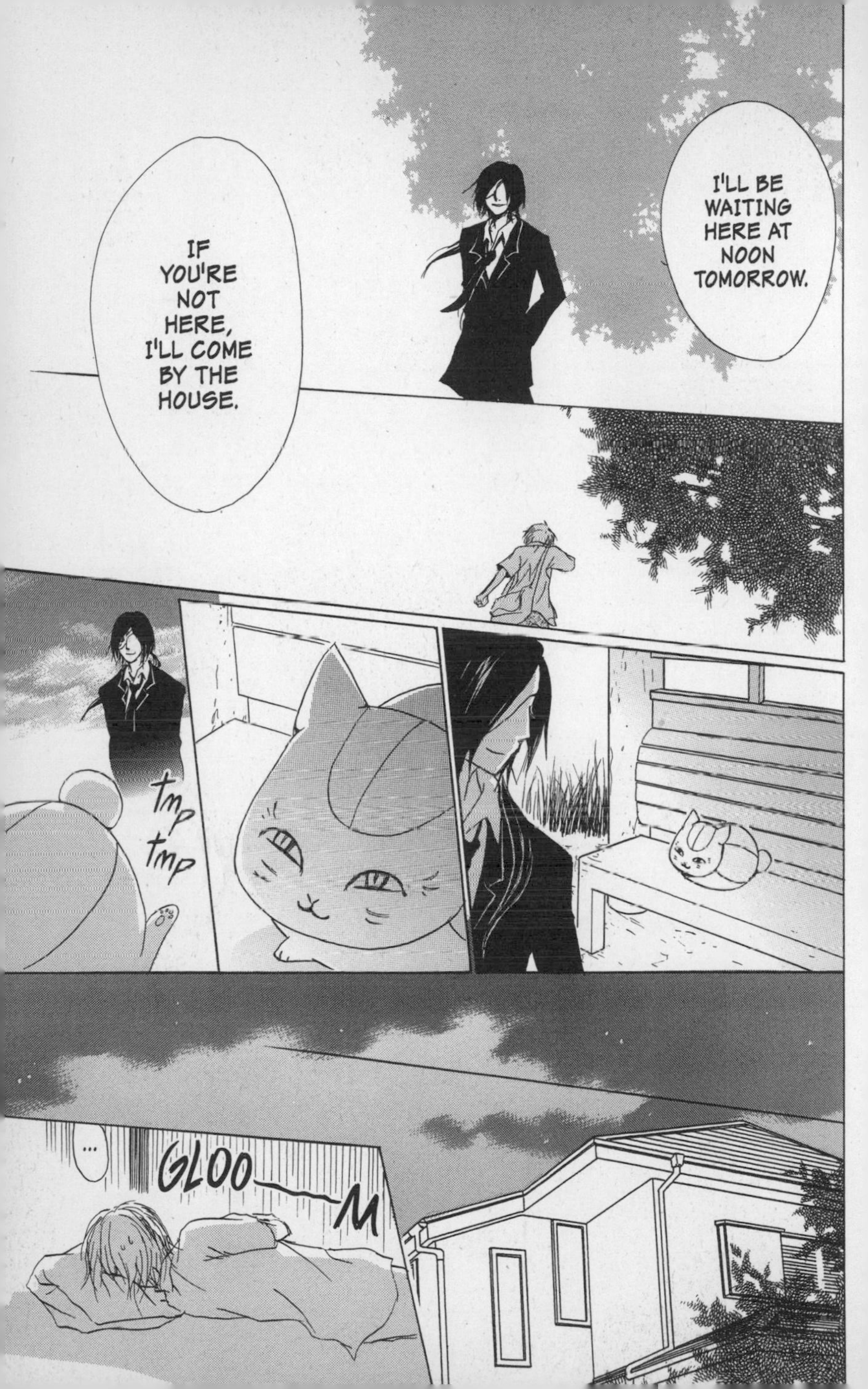
I'LL BE WAITING HERE AT NOON TOMORROW.
IF YOU'RE NOT HERE, I'LL COME BY THE HOUSE.
tmp tmp
...
GLOO--M

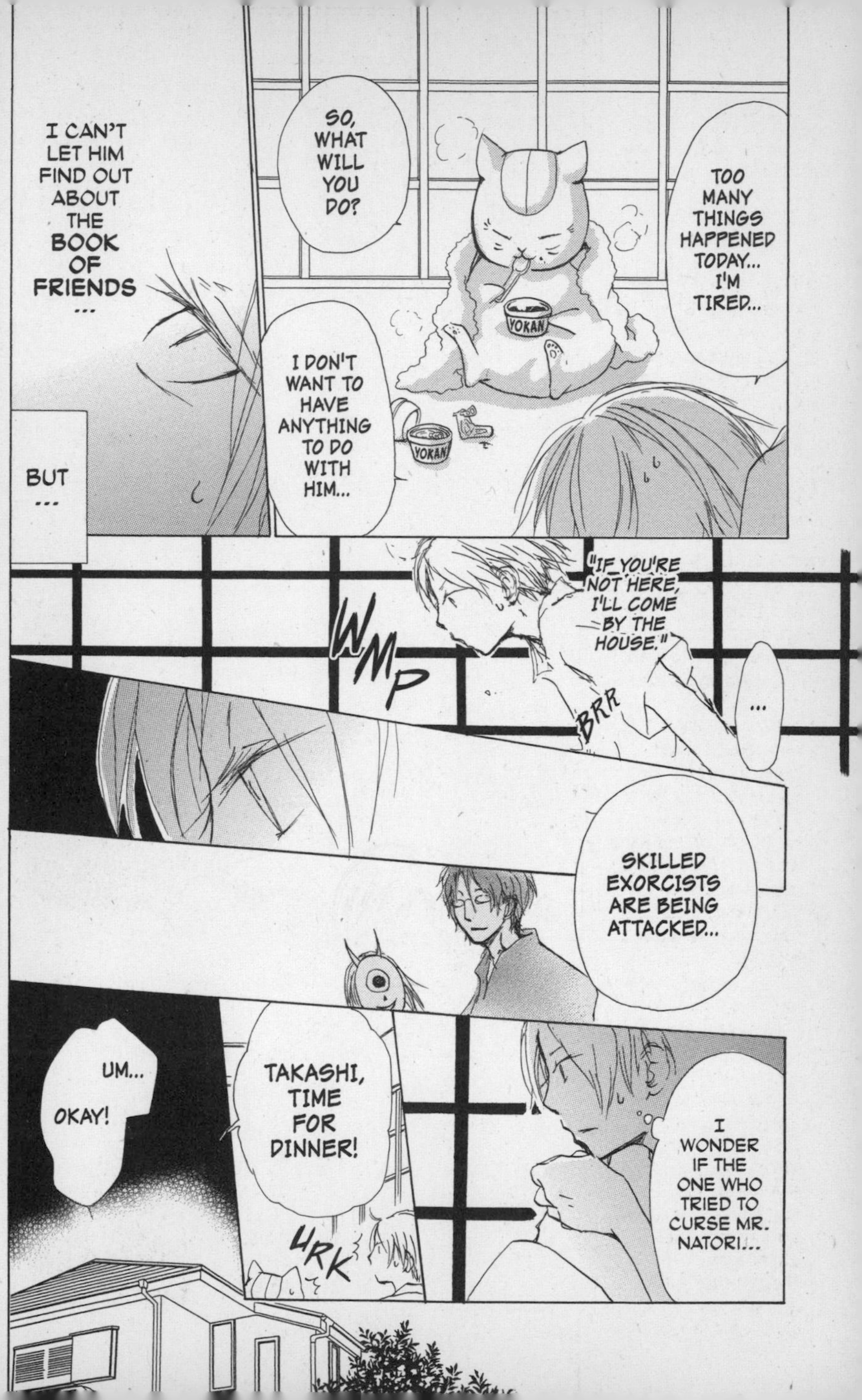
TOO MANY THINGS HAPPENED TODAY... I'M TIRED...
SO, WHAT WILL YOU DO?
YOKAN
I DON'T WANT TO HAVE ANYTHING TO DO WITH HIM...
YOKAN
I CAN'T LET HIM FIND OUT ABOUT THE BOOK OF FRIENDS...
BUT...
"IF YOU'RE NOT HERE, I'LL COME BY THE HOUSE."
WMP
...
BRR
SKILLED EXORCISTS ARE BEING ATTACKED...
I WONDER IF THE ONE WHO TRIED TO CURSE MR. NATORI...
TAKASHI, TIME FOR DINNER!
URK
UM...
OKAY!

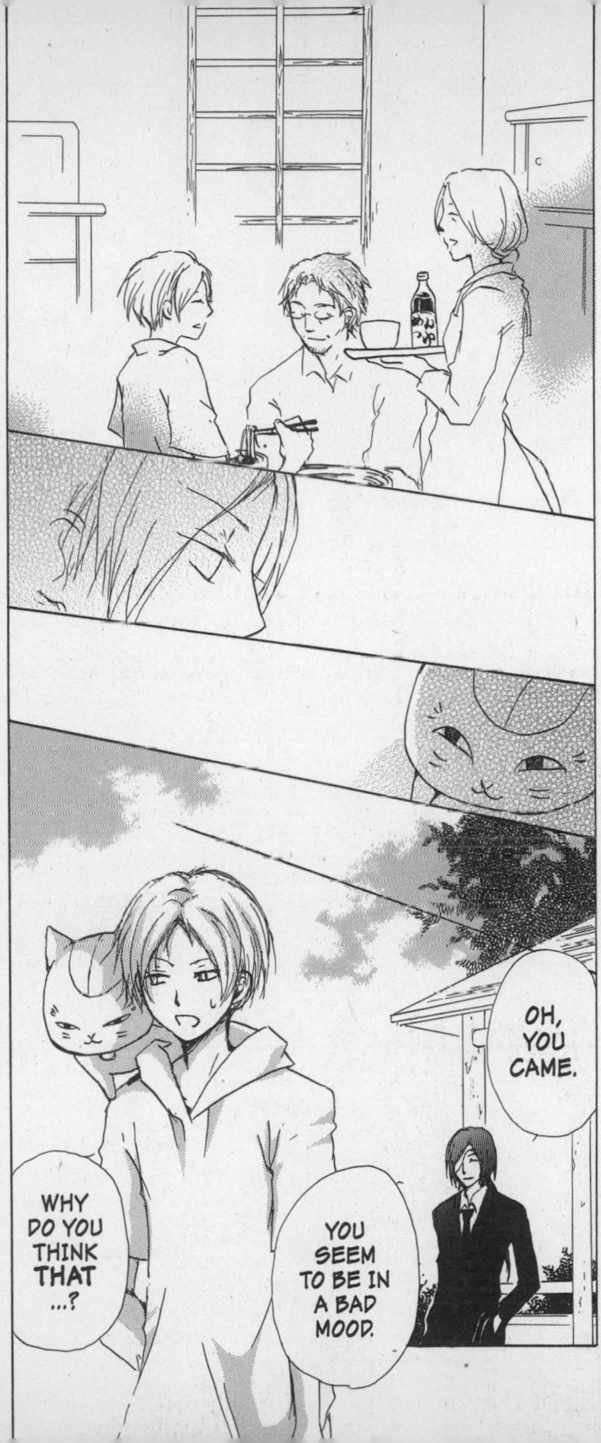
OH, YOU CAME.
YOU SEEM TO BE IN A BAD MOOD.
WHY DO YOU THINK THAT ...?

02

❋"Hotarubi no Mori e"

They made an animated movie out of the short story called "Hotarubi no Mori e" that I wrote a while back. I'd like to thank the movie theaters that showed it and everyone who came to see it.

The same director, staff, composer and artists who worked on the Natsume anime made a beautiful movie about the slow but inevitable and relentless passage of time. I knew it would be embarrassing to cry watching my own work, so I tried hard not to. But I found myself getting teary-eyed over some simple scenes anyway.

I worked on this manga quite a long time ago, but there are a number of devoted fans, so I was a little apprehensive despite my excitement over it being animated. But Director Ohmori and the staff put tender loving care into their work. Please check it out if you get the chance.

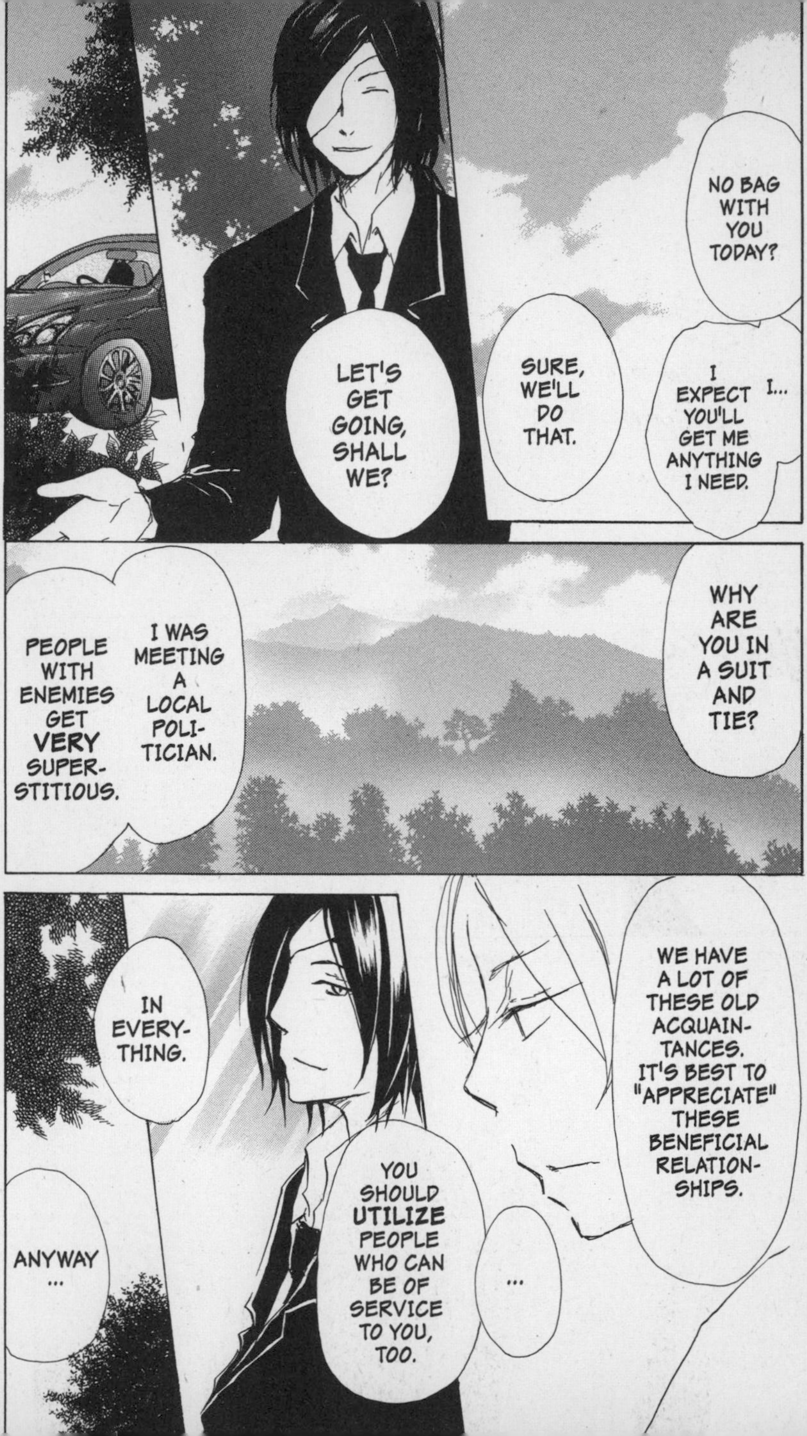
NO BAG WITH YOU TODAY?
I...
I EXPECT YOU'LL GET ME ANYTHING I NEED.
SURE, WE'LL DO THAT.
LET'S GET GOING, SHALL WE?
WHY ARE YOU IN A SUIT AND TIE?
I WAS MEETING A LOCAL POLITICIAN.
PEOPLE WITH ENEMIES GET VERY SUPERSTITIOUS.
IN EVERYTHING.
WE HAVE A LOT OF THESE OLD ACQUAINTANCES. IT'S BEST TO "APPRECIATE" THESE BENEFICIAL RELATIONSHIPS.
YOU SHOULD UTILIZE PEOPLE WHO CAN BE OF SERVICE TO YOU, TOO.
...
ANYWAY...

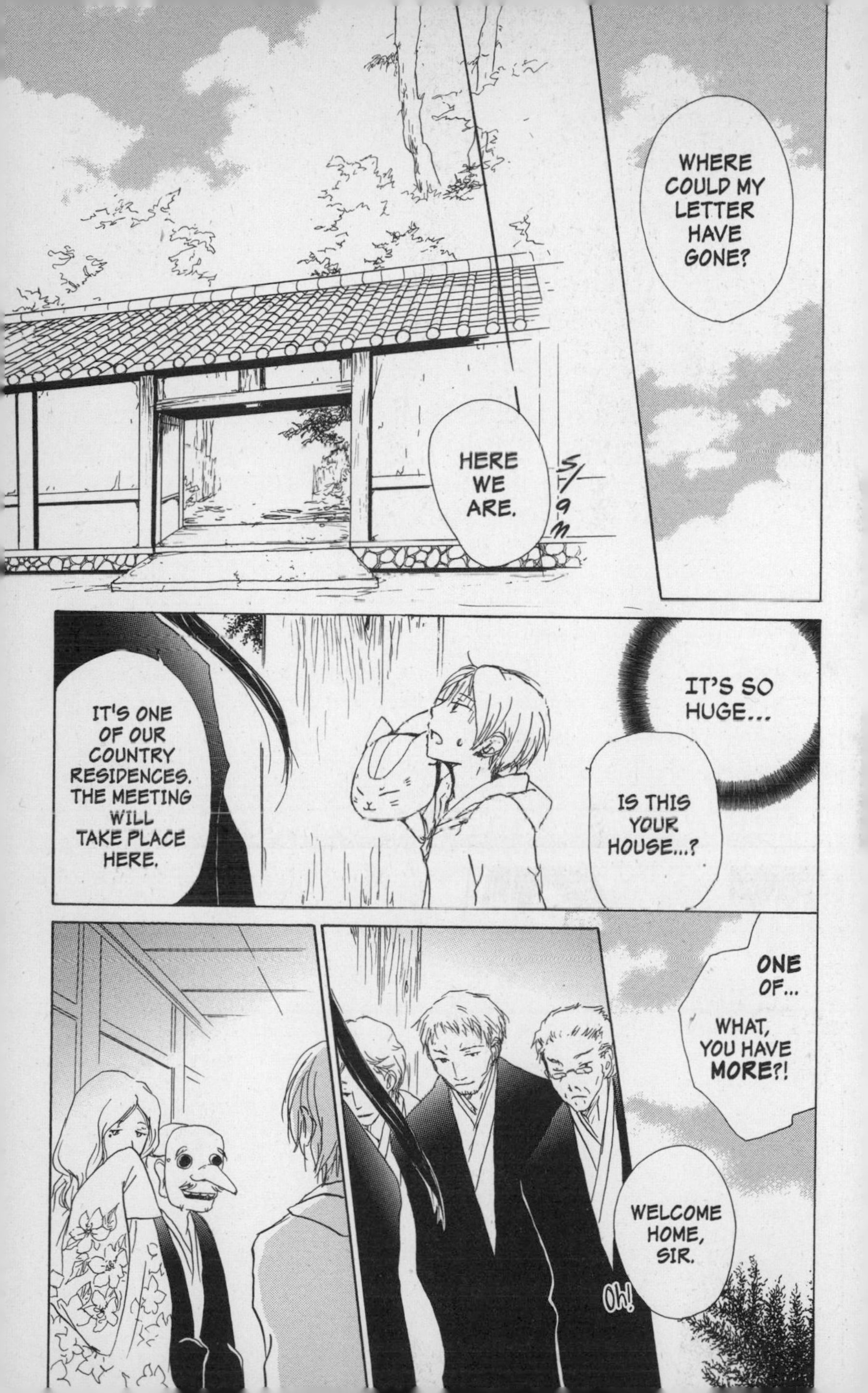
WHERE COULD MY LETTER HAVE GONE?
HERE WE ARE.
IT'S SO HUGE...
IS THIS YOUR HOUSE...?
IT'S ONE OF OUR COUNTRY RESIDENCES. THE MEETING WILL TAKE PLACE HERE.
ONE OF... WHAT, YOU HAVE MORE?!
WELCOME HOME, SIR.
Oh!

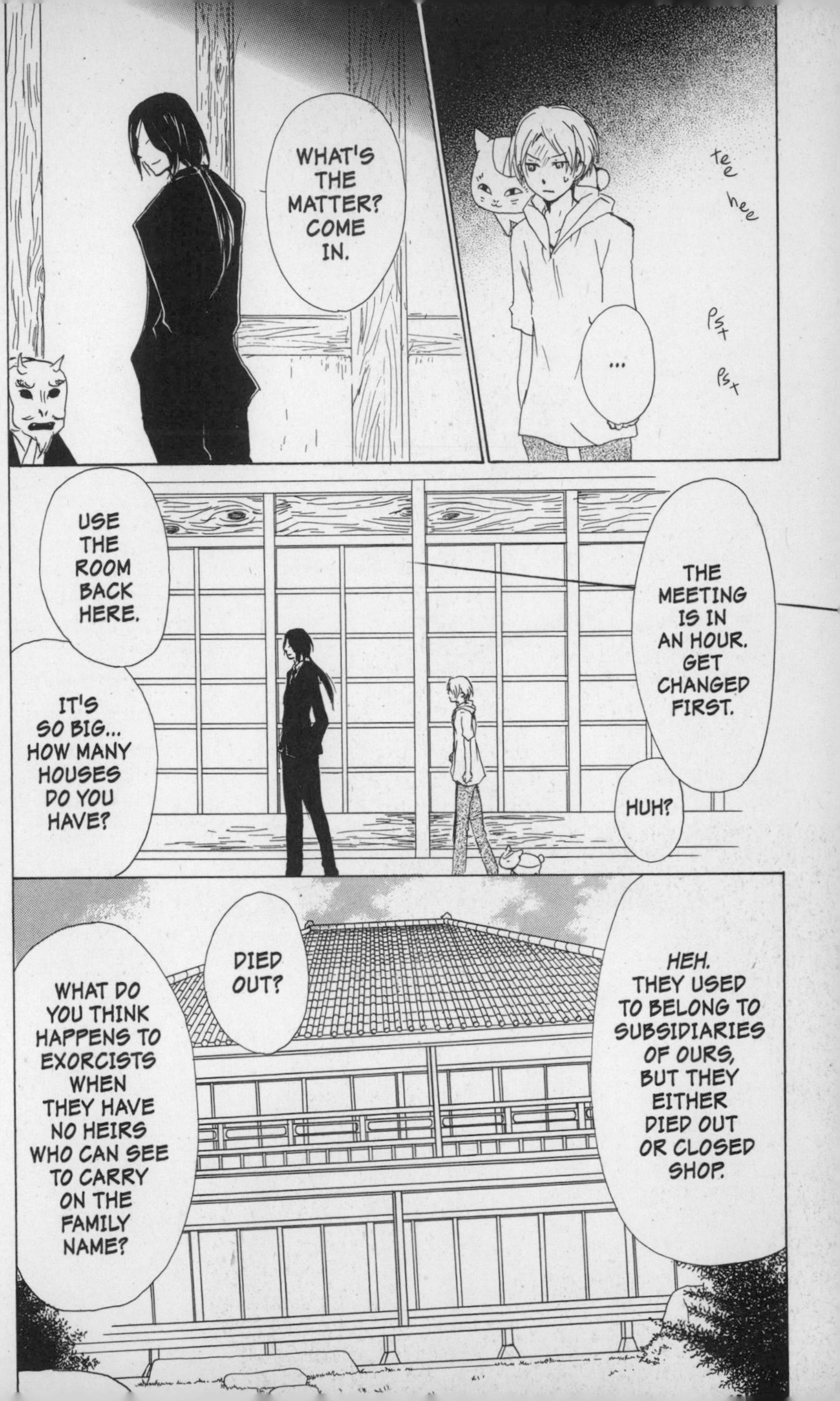
tee hee
...
pst
pst
WHAT'S THE MATTER? COME IN.
THE MEETING IS IN AN HOUR. GET CHANGED FIRST.
USE THE ROOM BACK HERE.
HUH?
IT'S SO BIG... HOW MANY HOUSES DO YOU HAVE?
HEH. THEY USED TO BELONG TO SUBSIDIARIES OF OURS, BUT THEY EITHER DIED OUT OR CLOSED SHOP.
DIED OUT?
WHAT DO YOU THINK HAPPENS TO EXORCISTS WHEN THEY HAVE NO HEIRS WHO CAN SEE TO CARRY ON THE FAMILY NAME?

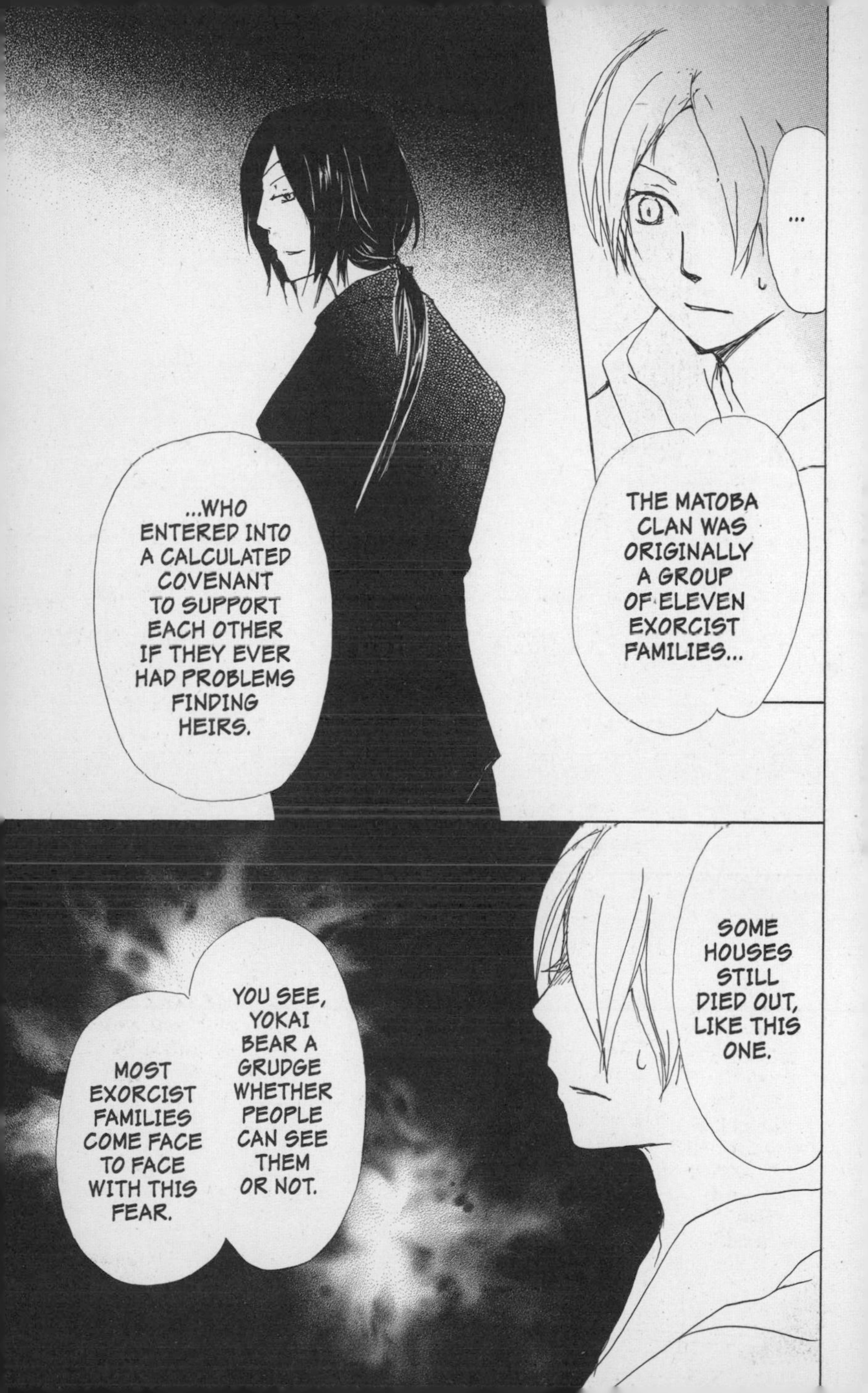
...
THE MATOBA CLAN WAS ORIGINALLY A GROUP OF ELEVEN EXORCIST FAMILIES...
...WHO ENTERED INTO A CALCULATED COVENANT TO SUPPORT EACH OTHER IF THEY EVER HAD PROBLEMS FINDING HEIRS.
SOME HOUSES STILL DIED OUT, LIKE THIS ONE.
YOU SEE, YOKAI BEAR A GRUDGE WHETHER PEOPLE CAN SEE THEM OR NOT.
MOST EXORCIST FAMILIES COME FACE TO FACE WITH THIS FEAR.

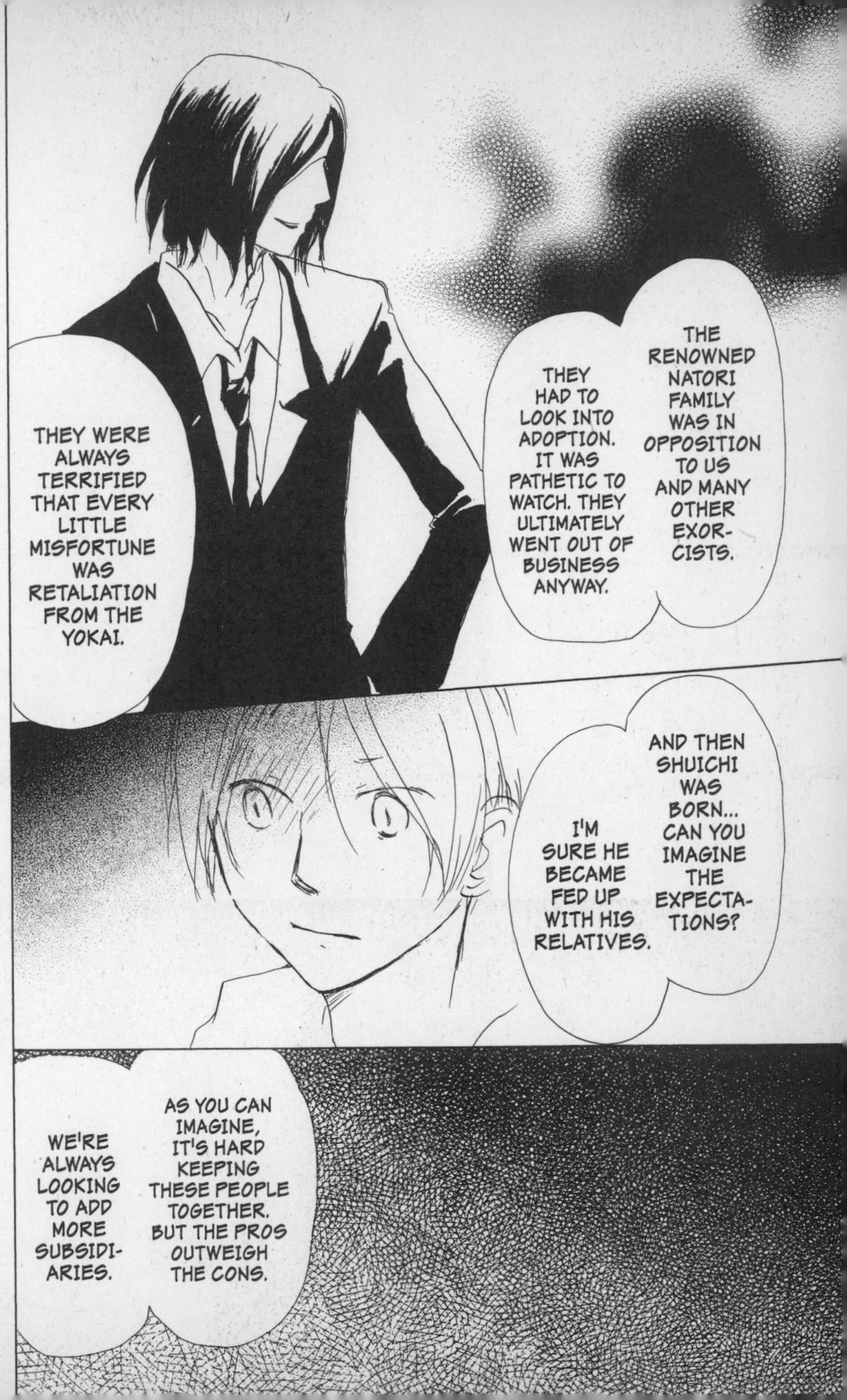
THE RENOWNED NATORI FAMILY WAS IN OPPOSITION TO US AND MANY OTHER EXORCISTS.
THEY HAD TO LOOK INTO ADOPTION. IT WAS PATHETIC TO WATCH. THEY ULTIMATELY WENT OUT OF BUSINESS ANYWAY.
THEY WERE ALWAYS TERRIFIED THAT EVERY LITTLE MISFORTUNE WAS RETALIATION FROM THE YOKAI.
AND THEN SHUICHI WAS BORN... CAN YOU IMAGINE THE EXPECTATIONS?
I'M SURE HE BECAME FED UP WITH HIS RELATIVES.
AS YOU CAN IMAGINE, IT'S HARD KEEPING THESE PEOPLE TOGETHER. BUT THE PROS OUTWEIGH THE CONS.
WE'RE ALWAYS LOOKING TO ADD MORE SUBSIDIARIES.

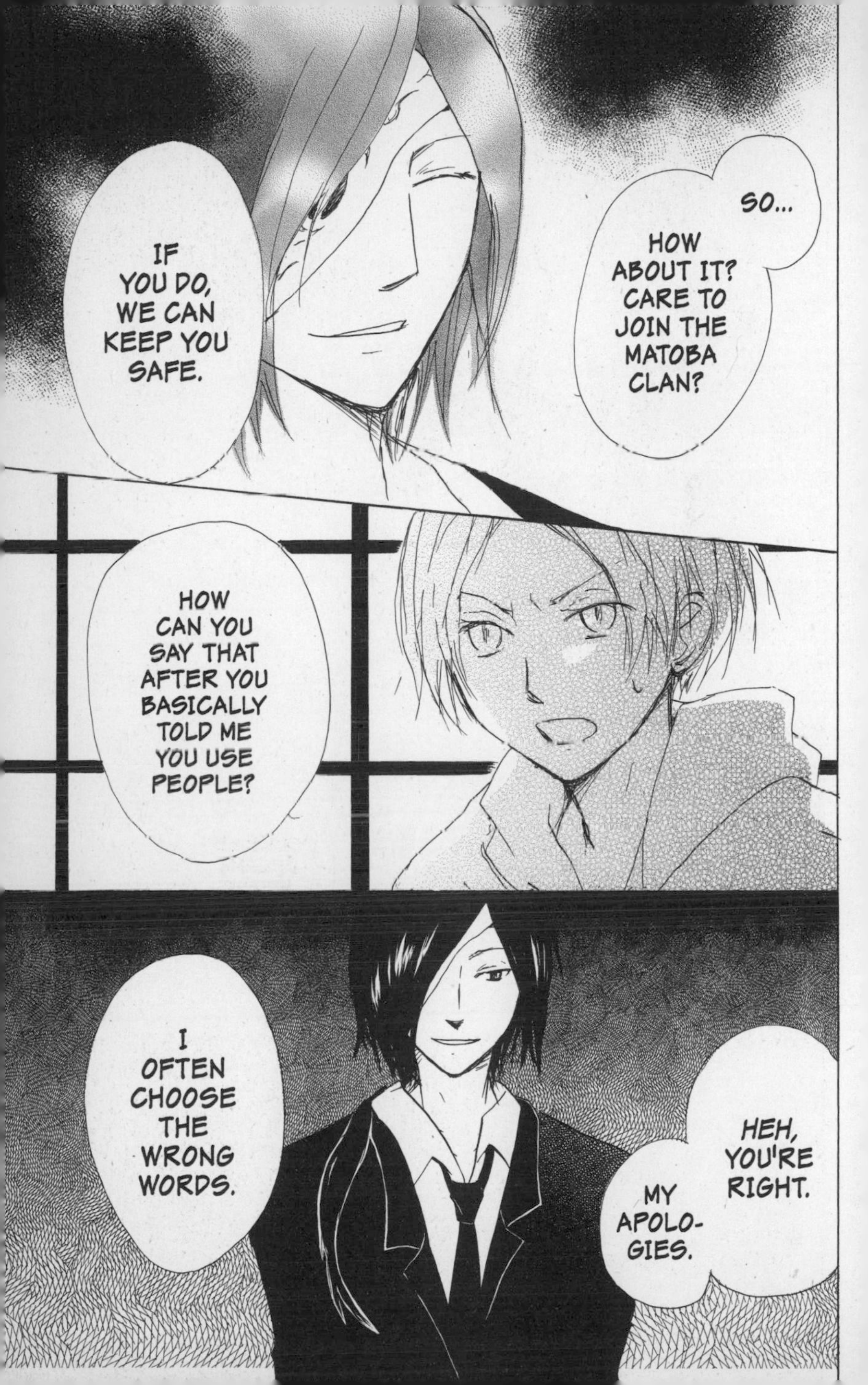
SO... HOW ABOUT IT? CARE TO JOIN THE MATOBA CLAN?
IF YOU DO, WE CAN KEEP YOU SAFE.
HOW CAN YOU SAY THAT AFTER YOU BASICALLY TOLD ME YOU USE PEOPLE?
HEH, YOU'RE RIGHT.
MY APOLOGIES.
I OFTEN CHOOSE THE WRONG WORDS.

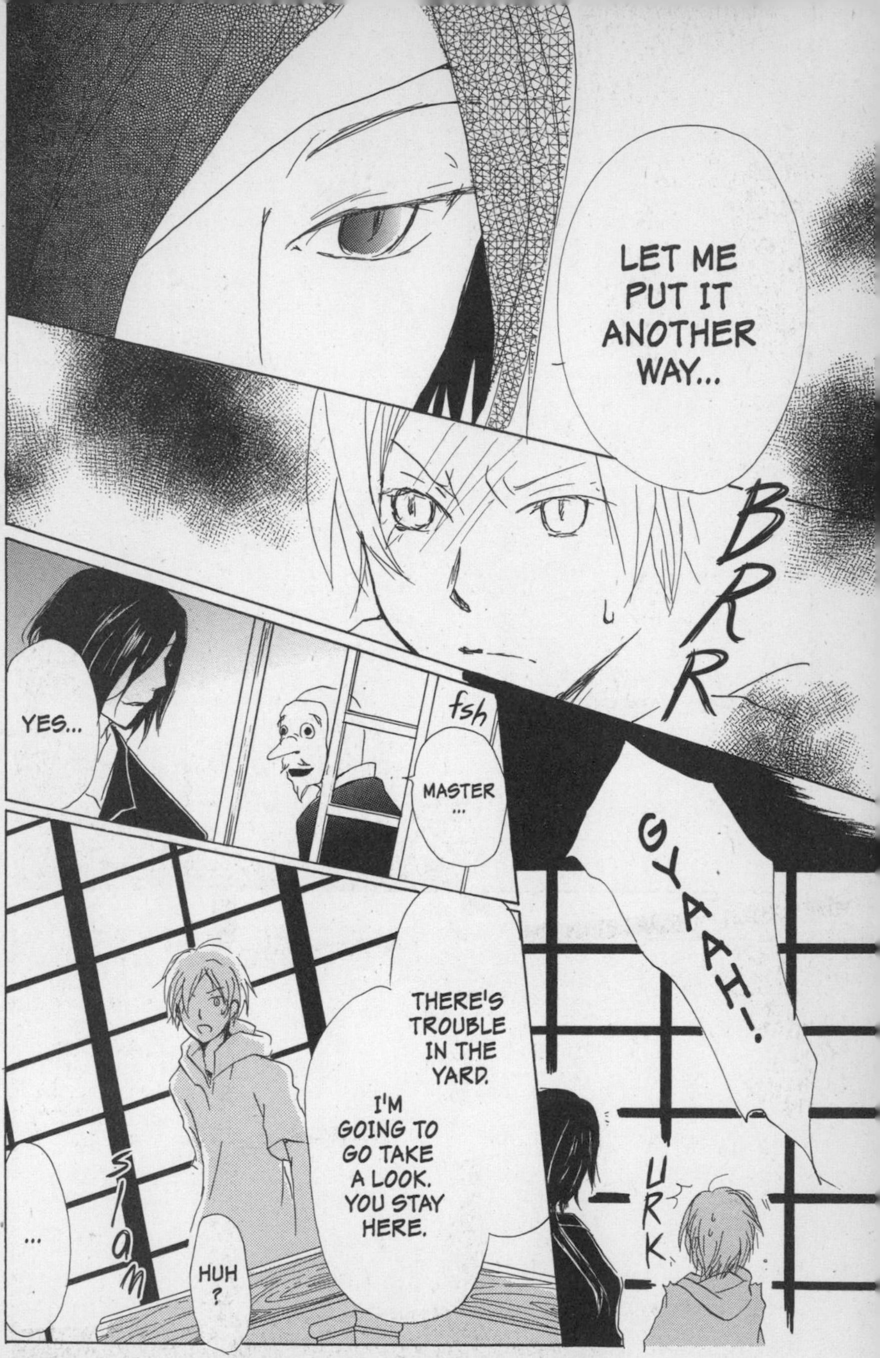
LET ME PUT IT ANOTHER WAY...
BRRR
fsh
MASTER ...
YES...
GYAAH!
URK
THERE'S TROUBLE IN THE YARD.
I'M GOING TO GO TAKE A LOOK. YOU STAY HERE.
HUH ?
slam
...

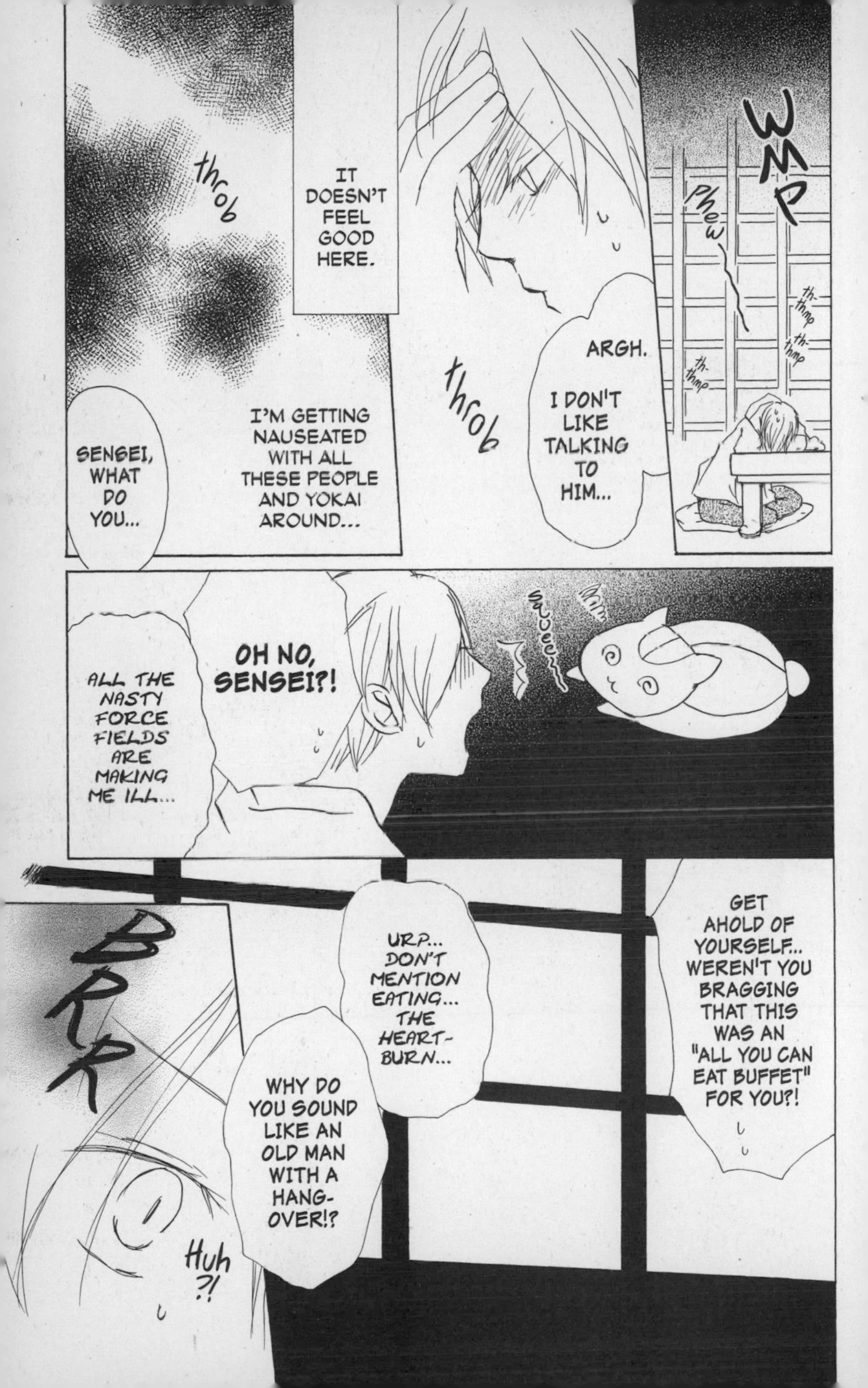
WMP
Phew
th-thmp
th-thmp
th-thmp
ARGH.
I DON'T LIKE TALKING TO HIM...
throb
IT DOESN'T FEEL GOOD HERE.
I'M GETTING NAUSEATED WITH ALL THESE PEOPLE AND YOKAI AROUND...
throb
SENSEI, WHAT DO YOU...
OH NO, SENSEI?!
ALL THE NASTY FORCE FIELDS ARE MAKING ME ILL...
GET AHOLD OF YOURSELF... WEREN'T YOU BRAGGING THAT THIS WAS AN "ALL YOU CAN EAT BUFFET" FOR YOU?!
URP... DON'T MENTION EATING... THE HEART-BURN...
WHY DO YOU SOUND LIKE AN OLD MAN WITH A HANG-OVER!?
BRR
Huh?!

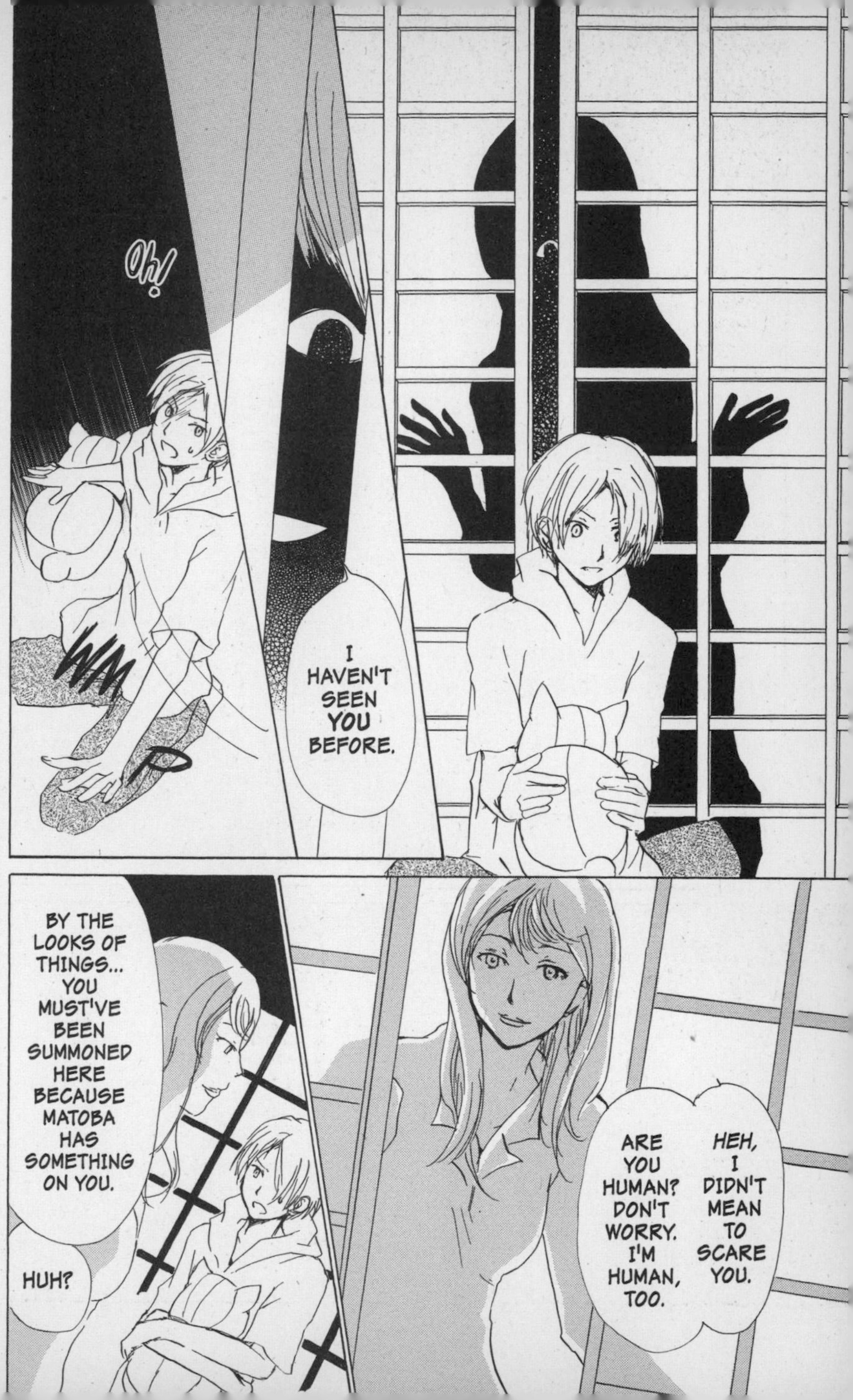
I HAVEN'T SEEN YOU BEFORE.
Oh!
WMP
HEH, I DIDN'T MEAN TO SCARE YOU.
ARE YOU HUMAN? DON'T WORRY. I'M HUMAN, TOO.
BY THE LOOKS OF THINGS... YOU MUST'VE BEEN SUMMONED HERE BECAUSE MATOBA HAS SOMETHING ON YOU.
HUH?

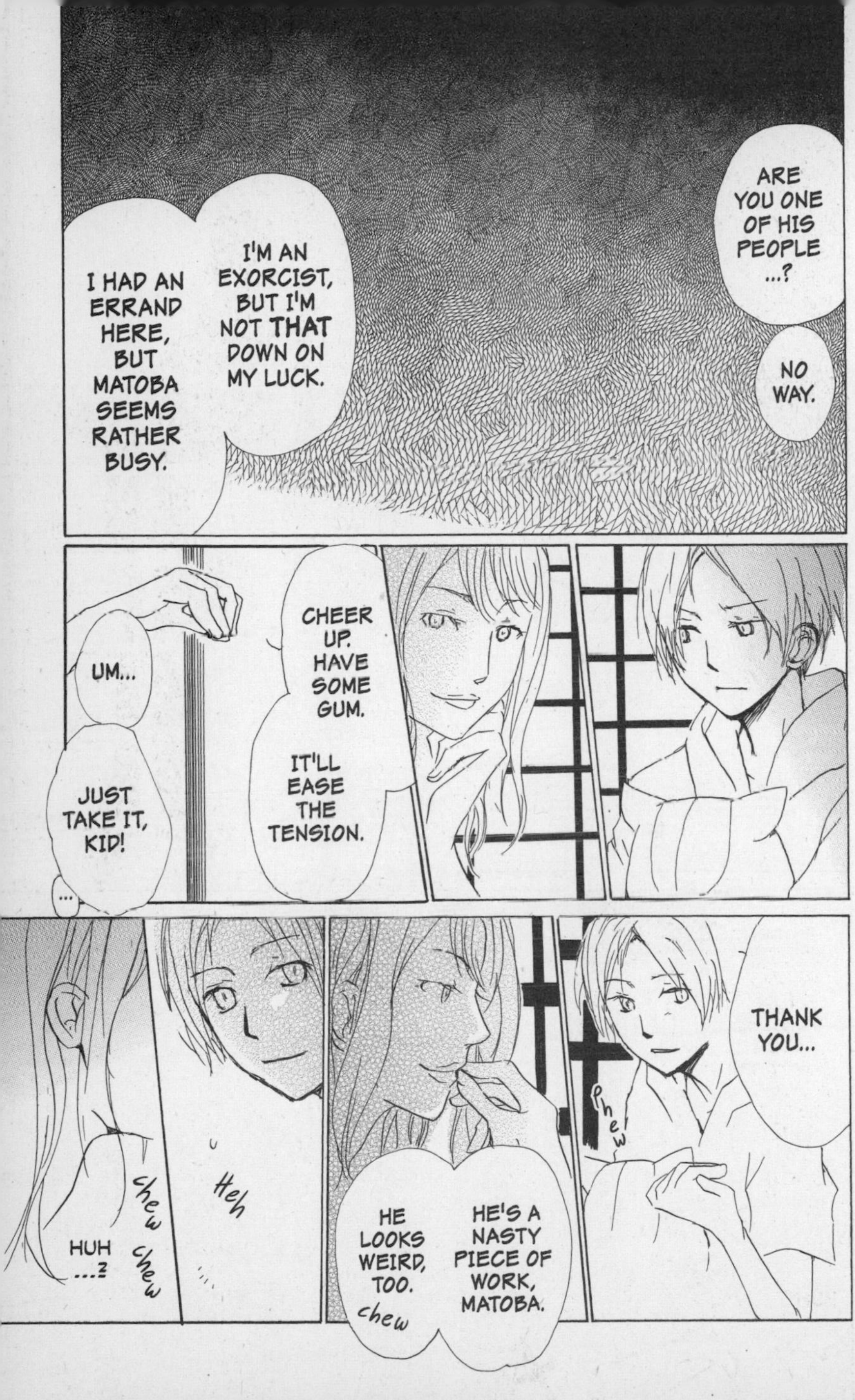
ARE YOU ONE OF HIS PEOPLE ...?
NO WAY.
I'M AN EXORCIST, BUT I'M NOT THAT DOWN ON MY LUCK.
I HAD AN ERRAND HERE, BUT MATOBA SEEMS RATHER BUSY.
CHEER UP. HAVE SOME GUM.
IT'LL EASE THE TENSION.
UM...
JUST TAKE IT, KID!
...
THANK YOU...
phew
HE'S A NASTY PIECE OF WORK, MATOBA.
HE LOOKS WEIRD, TOO.
chew
Heh
chew chew
HUH ...?

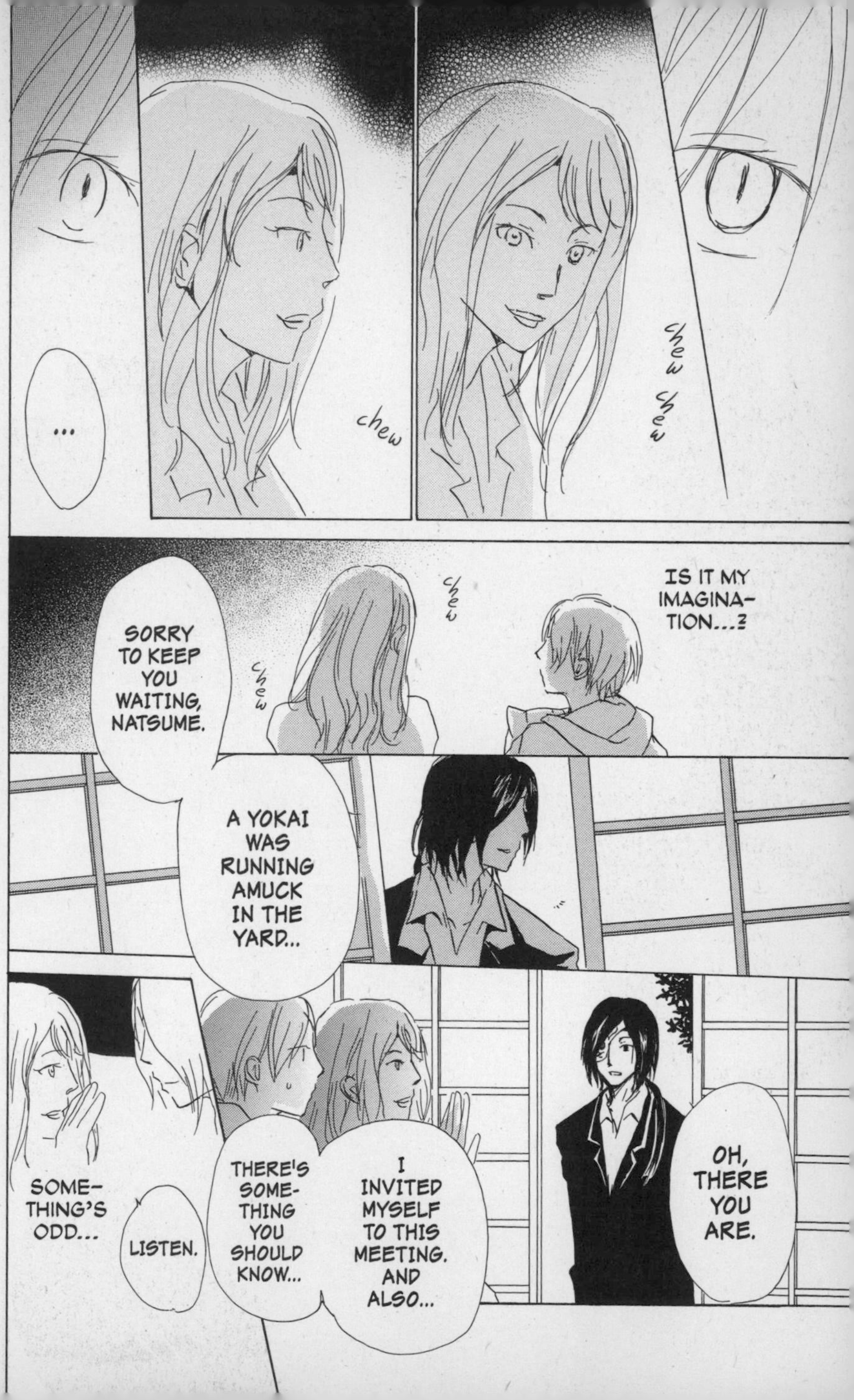
chew chew
chew
...
IS IT MY IMAGINATION...?
chew
chew
SORRY TO KEEP YOU WAITING, NATSUME.
A YOKAI WAS RUNNING AMUCK IN THE YARD...
OH, THERE YOU ARE.
I INVITED MYSELF TO THIS MEETING. AND ALSO...
THERE'S SOMETHING YOU SHOULD KNOW...
LISTEN.
SOMETHING'S ODD...

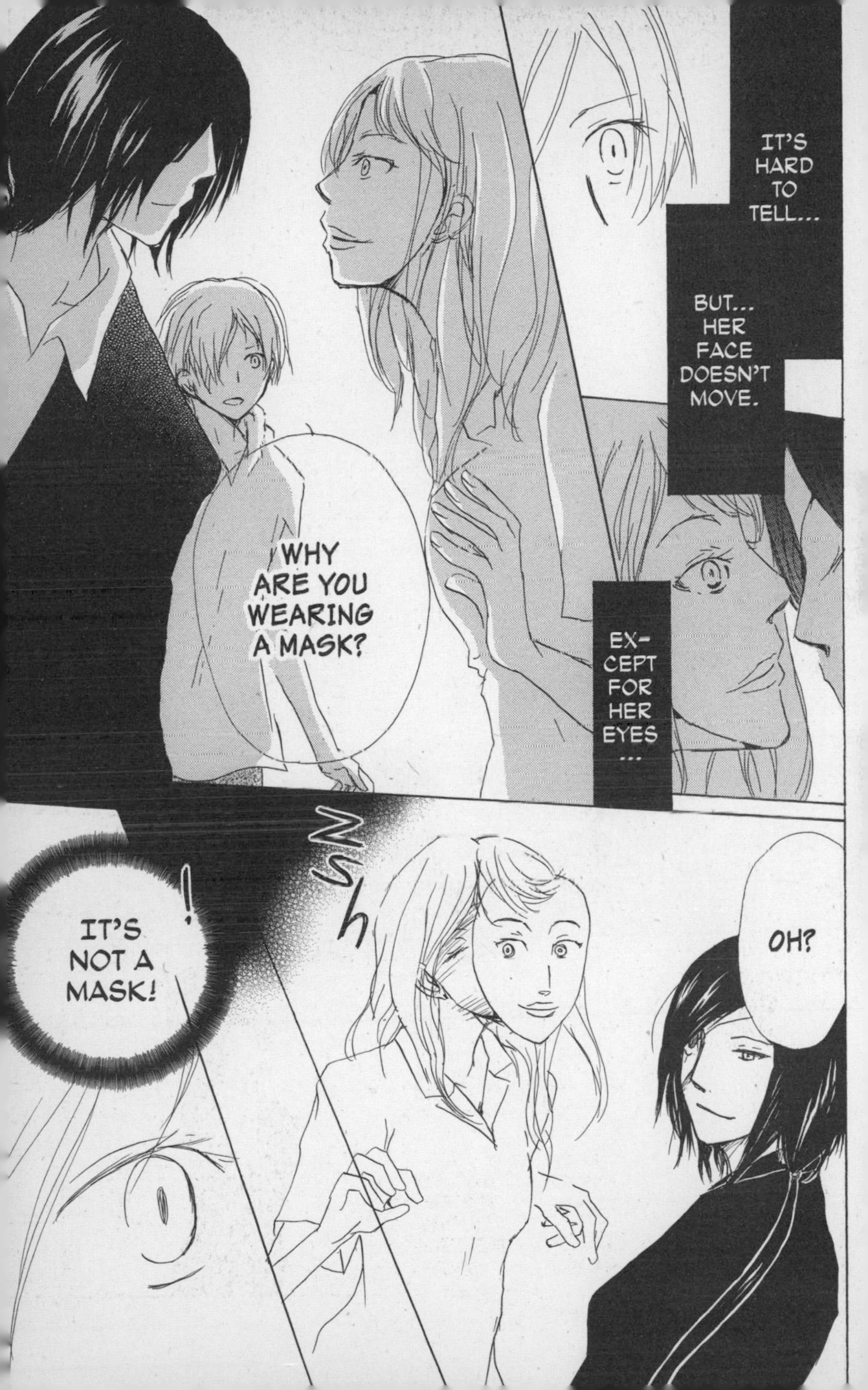
IT'S HARD TO TELL...
BUT... HER FACE DOESN'T MOVE.
EX-CEPT FOR HER EYES...
WHY ARE YOU WEARING A MASK?
OH?
!
IT'S NOT A MASK!

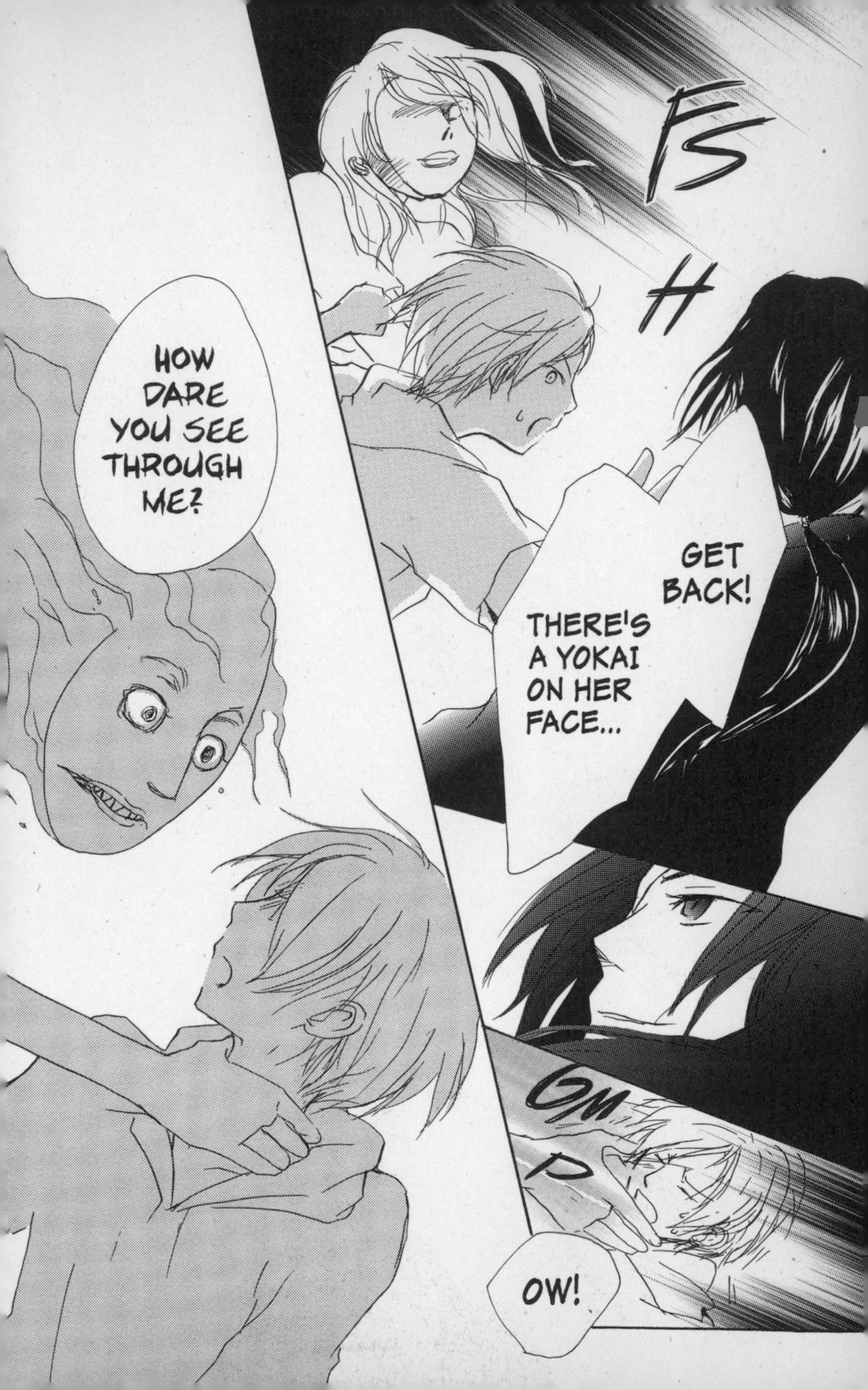
FS
H
GET BACK!
THERE'S A YOKAI ON HER FACE...
GM
P
OW!
HOW DARE YOU SEE THROUGH ME?

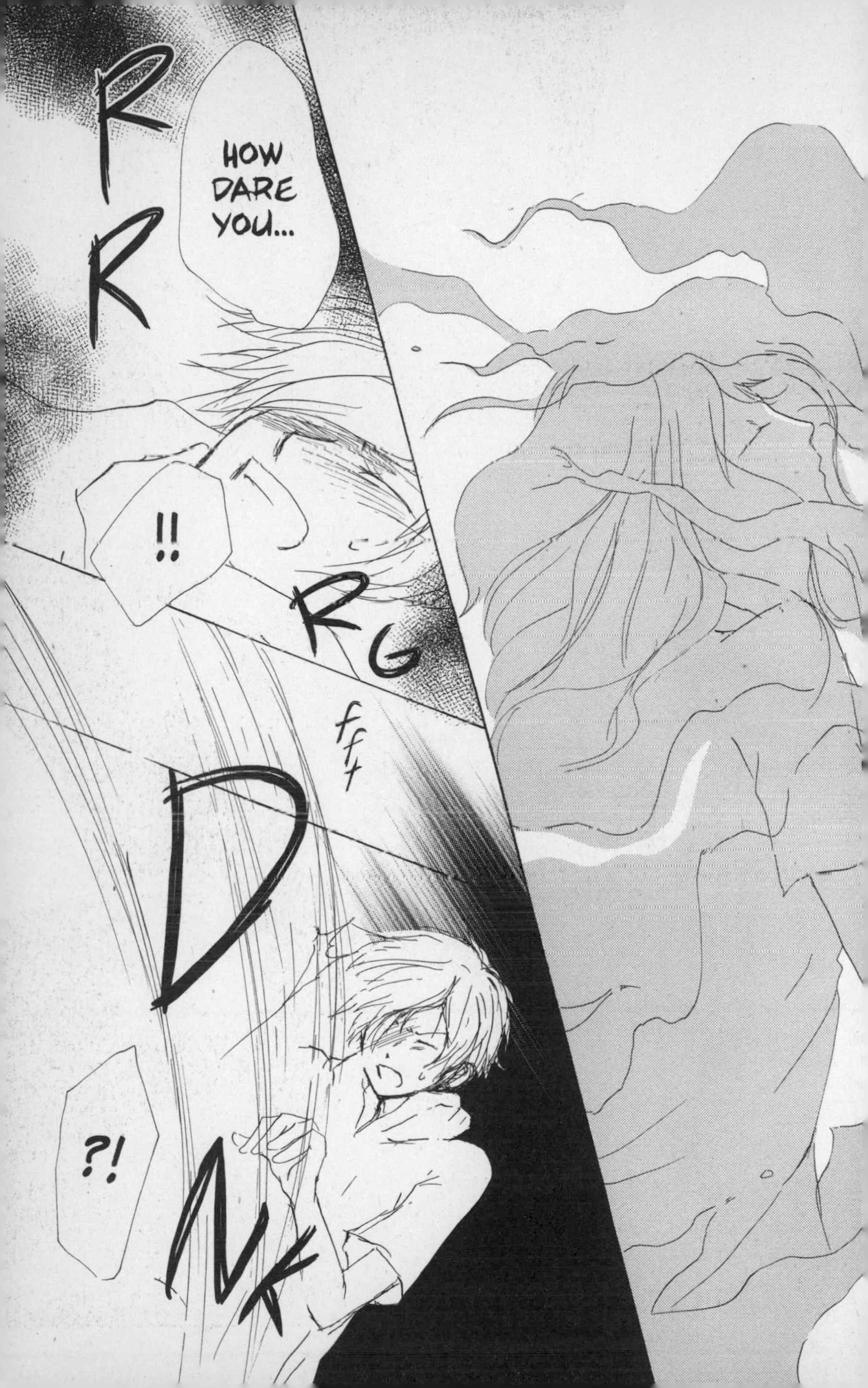
HOW DARE YOU...
RR
!!
RG
fff
D
?!
NK

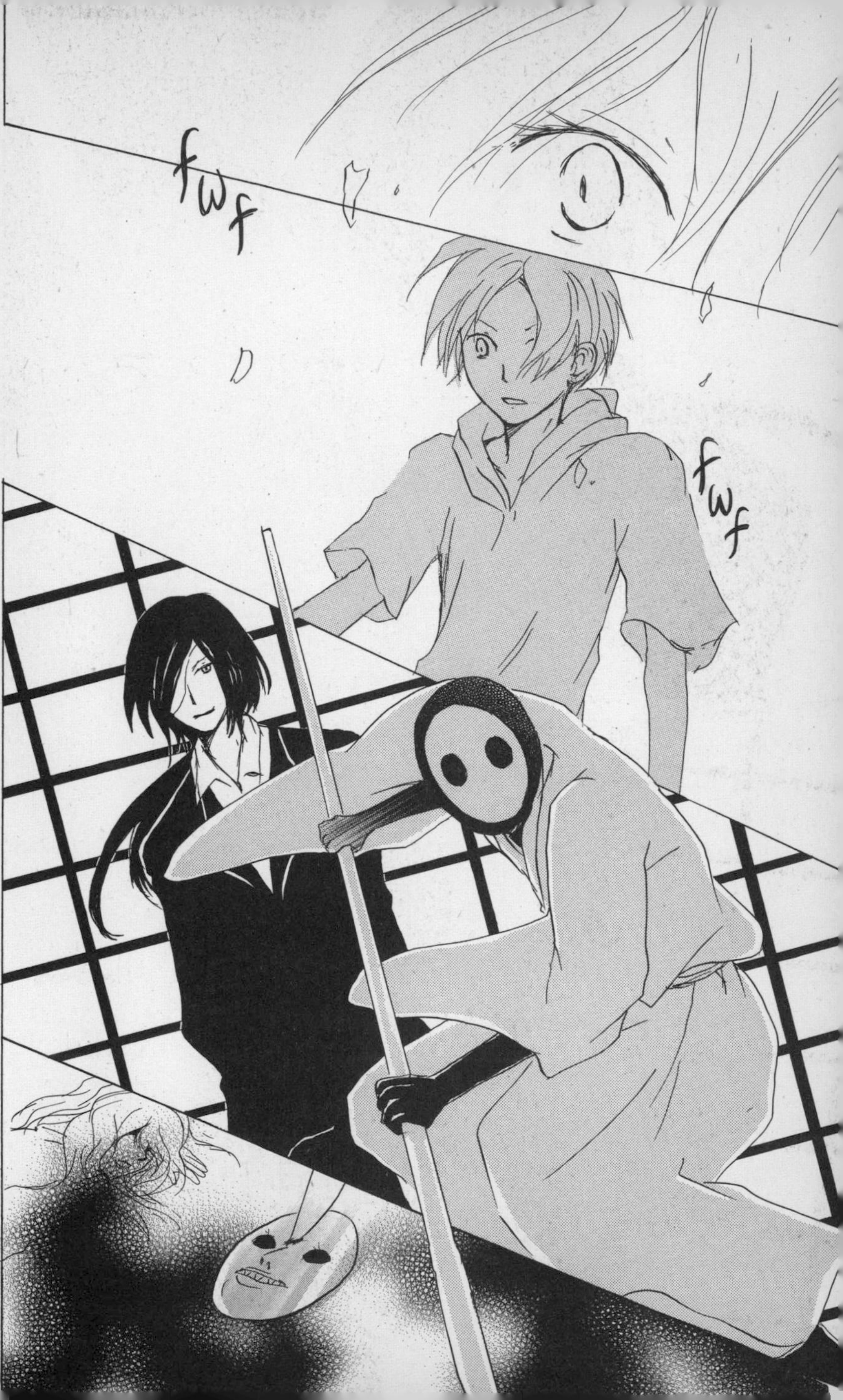
fwf
fwf

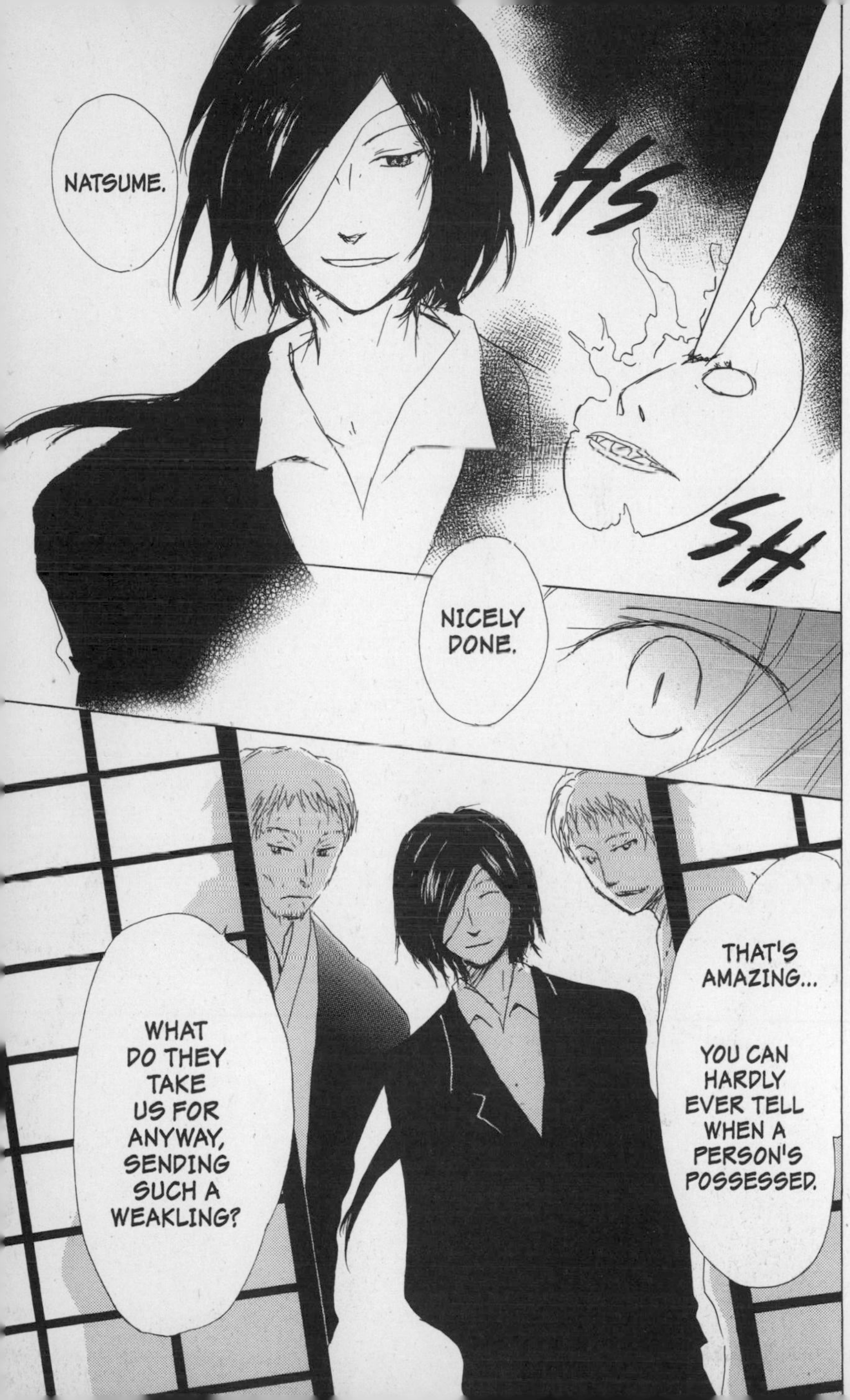
HS
SH
NATSUME.
NICELY DONE.
THAT'S AMAZING...
YOU CAN HARDLY EVER TELL WHEN A PERSON'S POSSESSED.
WHAT DO THEY TAKE US FOR ANYWAY, SENDING SUCH A WEAKLING?

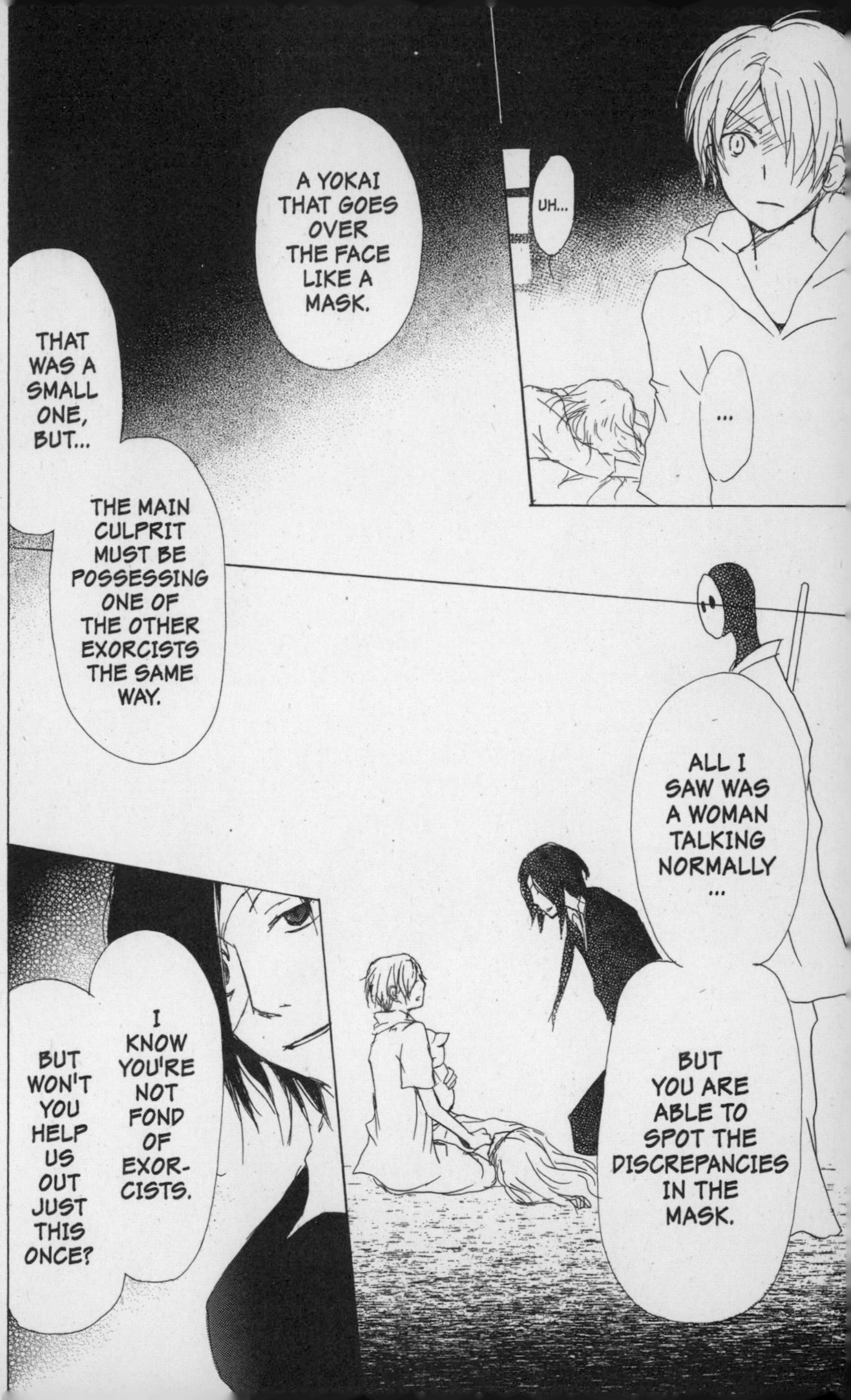
UH...
...
A YOKAI THAT GOES OVER THE FACE LIKE A MASK.
THAT WAS A SMALL ONE, BUT...
THE MAIN CULPRIT MUST BE POSSESSING ONE OF THE OTHER EXORCISTS THE SAME WAY.
ALL I SAW WAS A WOMAN TALKING NORMALLY...
BUT YOU ARE ABLE TO SPOT THE DISCREPANCIES IN THE MASK.
I KNOW YOU'RE NOT FOND OF EXOR-CISTS.
BUT WON'T YOU HELP US OUT JUST THIS ONCE?

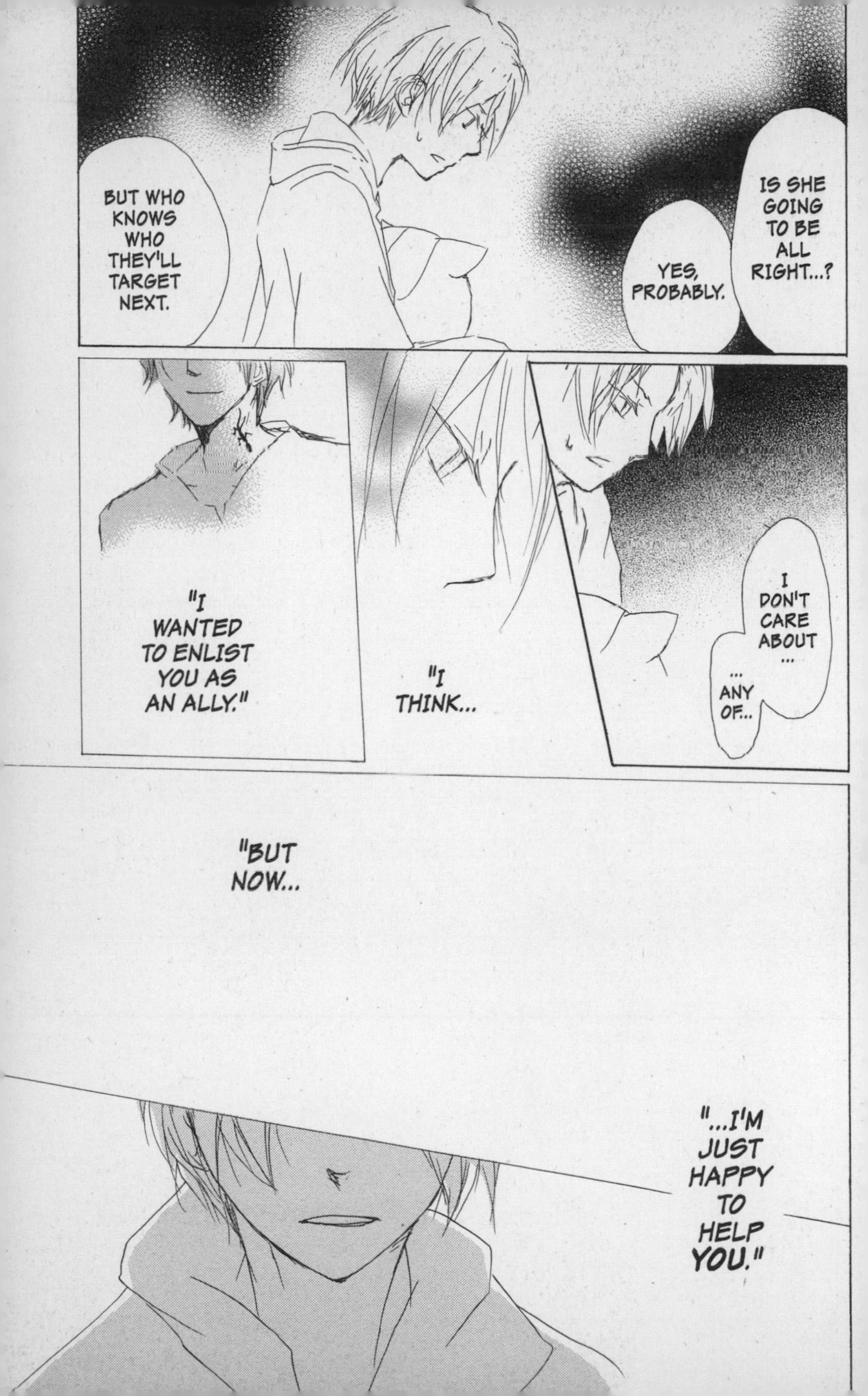
IS SHE GOING TO BE ALL RIGHT...?
YES, PROBABLY.
BUT WHO KNOWS WHO THEY'LL TARGET NEXT.
I DON'T CARE ABOUT ...
... ANY OF...
"I THINK...
"I WANTED TO ENLIST YOU AS AN ALLY."
"BUT NOW...
"...I'M JUST HAPPY TO HELP YOU."

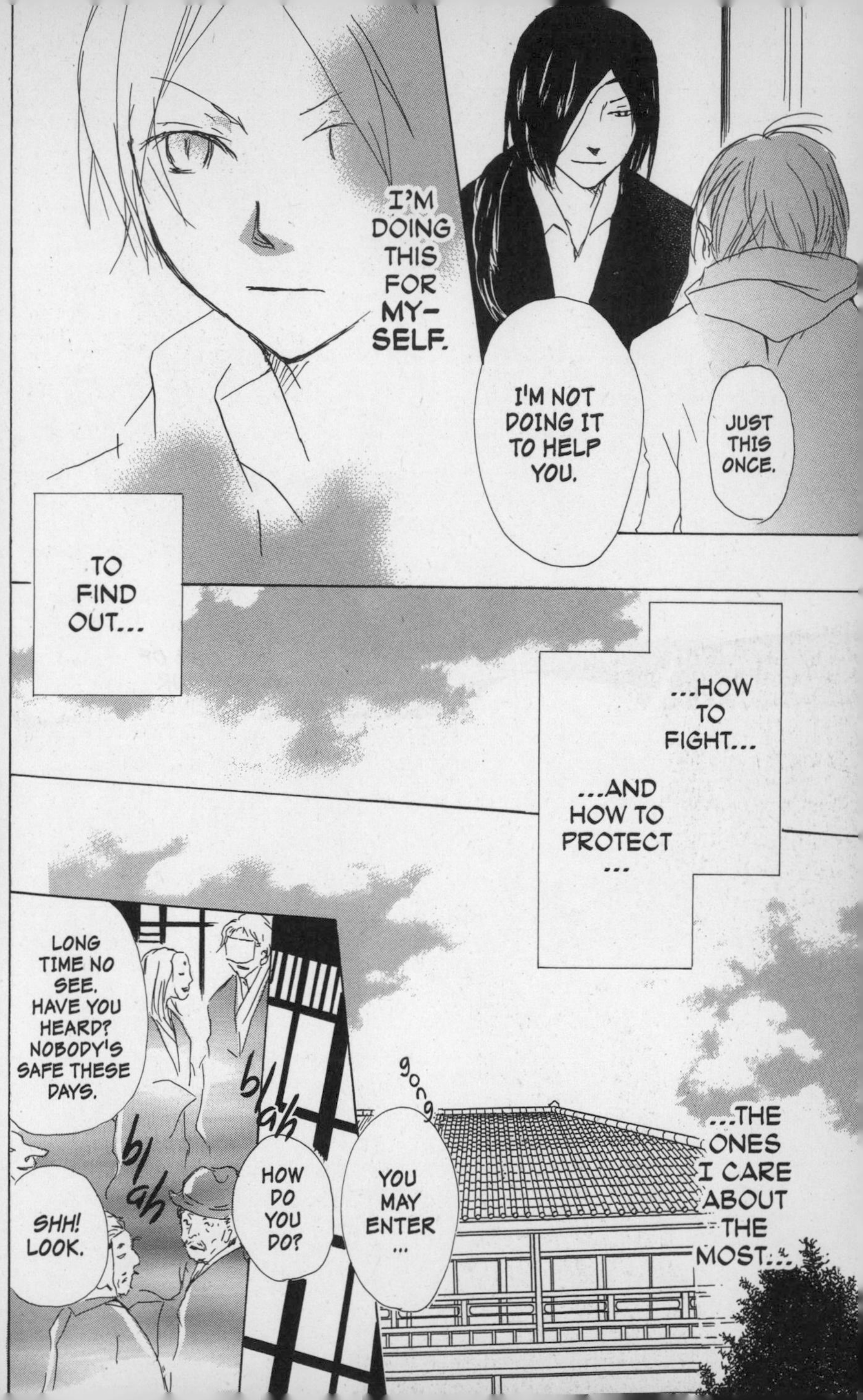
JUST THIS ONCE.
I'M NOT DOING IT TO HELP YOU.
I'M DOING THIS FOR MY-SELF.
TO FIND OUT...
...HOW TO FIGHT...
...AND HOW TO PROTECT...
...THE ONES I CARE ABOUT THE MOST...
gong
YOU MAY ENTER...
HOW DO YOU DO?
blah
blah
LONG TIME NO SEE. HAVE YOU HEARD? NOBODY'S SAFE THESE DAYS.
SHH! LOOK.

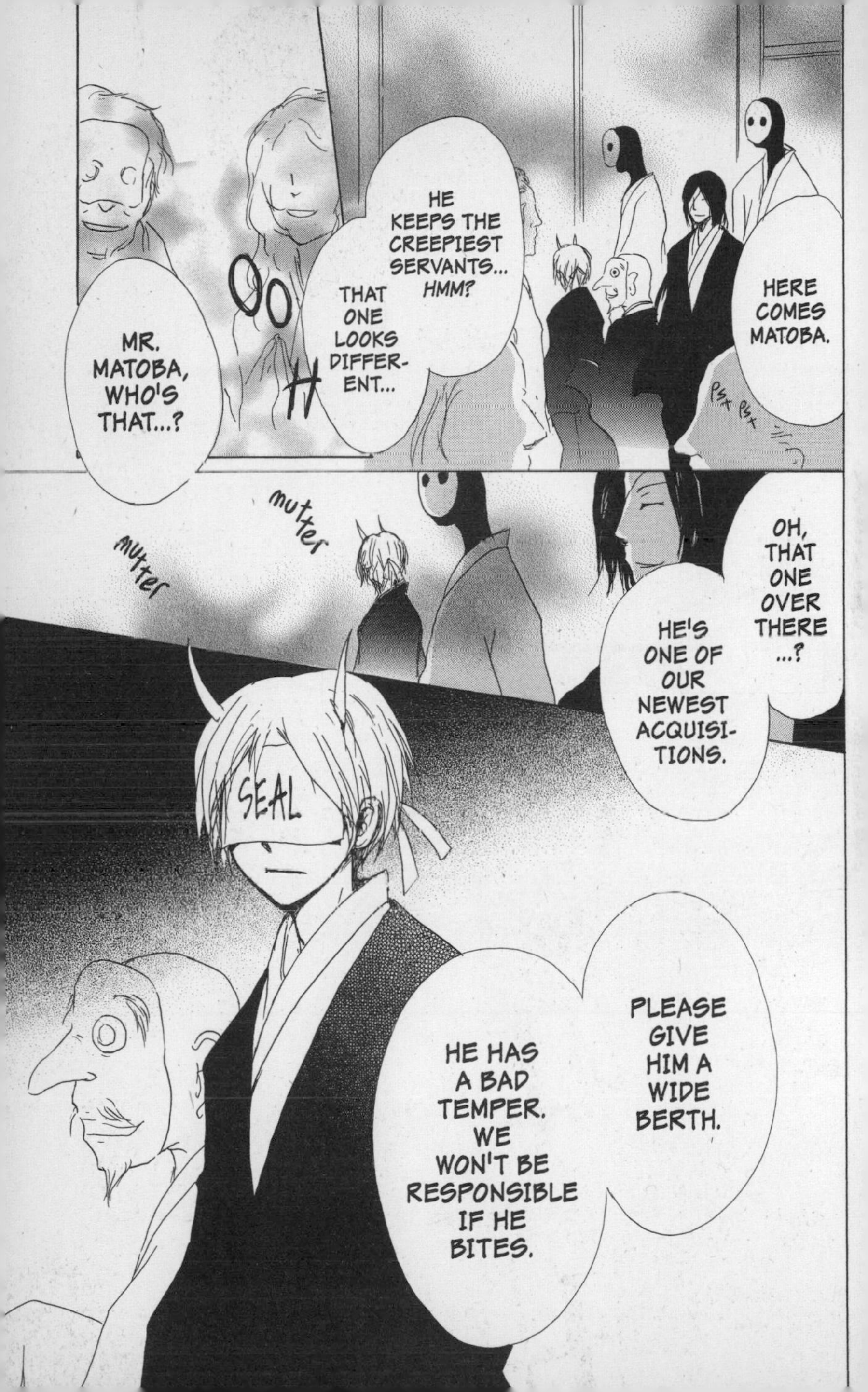
HERE COMES MATOBA.
psx psx
HE KEEPS THE CREEPIEST SERVANTS... HMM?
THAT ONE LOOKS DIFFERENT...
MR. MATOBA, WHO'S THAT...?
OH, THAT ONE OVER THERE...?
HE'S ONE OF OUR NEWEST ACQUISITIONS.
mutter
mutter
SEAL
PLEASE GIVE HIM A WIDE BERTH.
HE HAS A BAD TEMPER. WE WON'T BE RESPONSIBLE IF HE BITES.

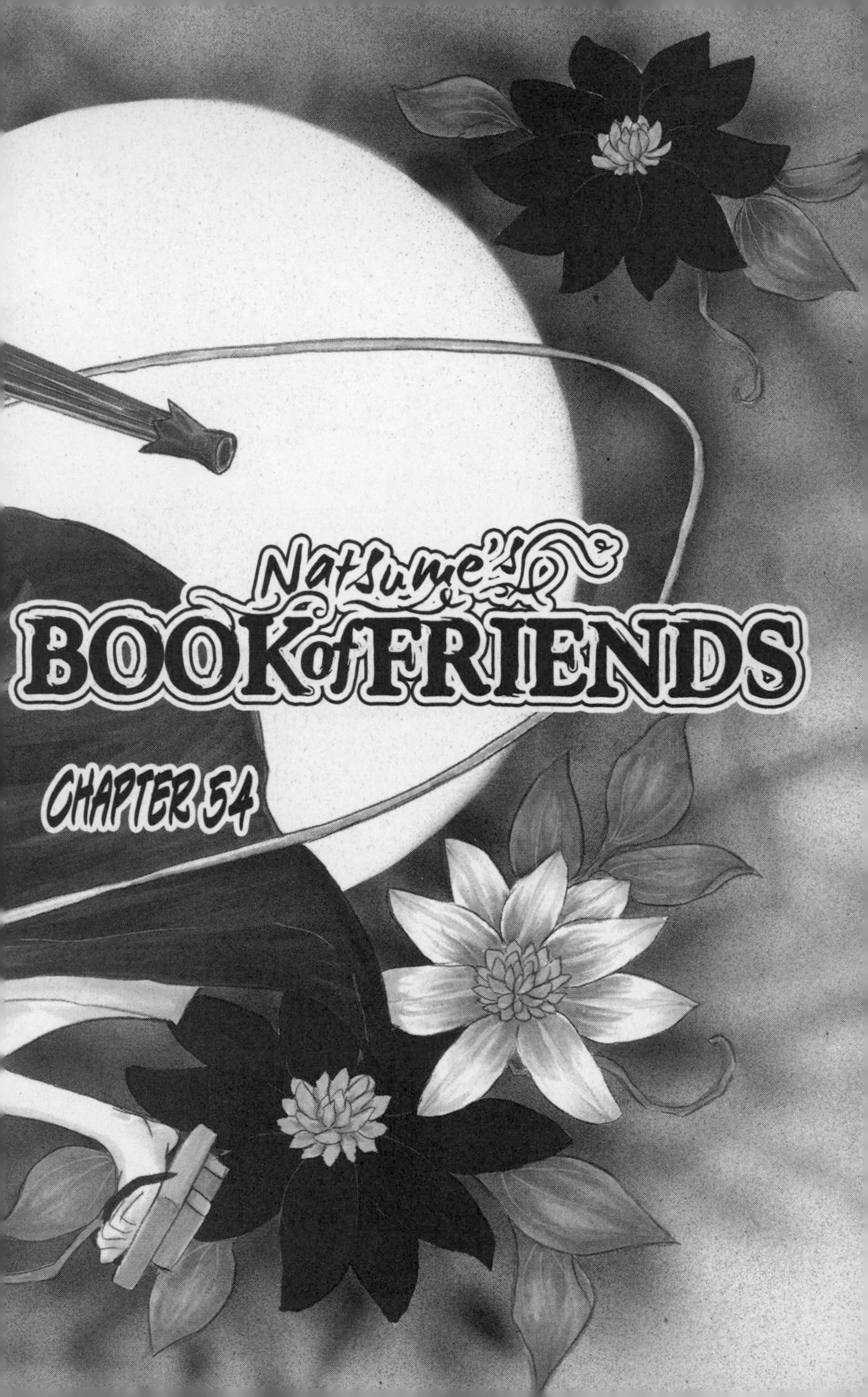
Natsume's
BOOK of FRIENDS
CHAPTER 54

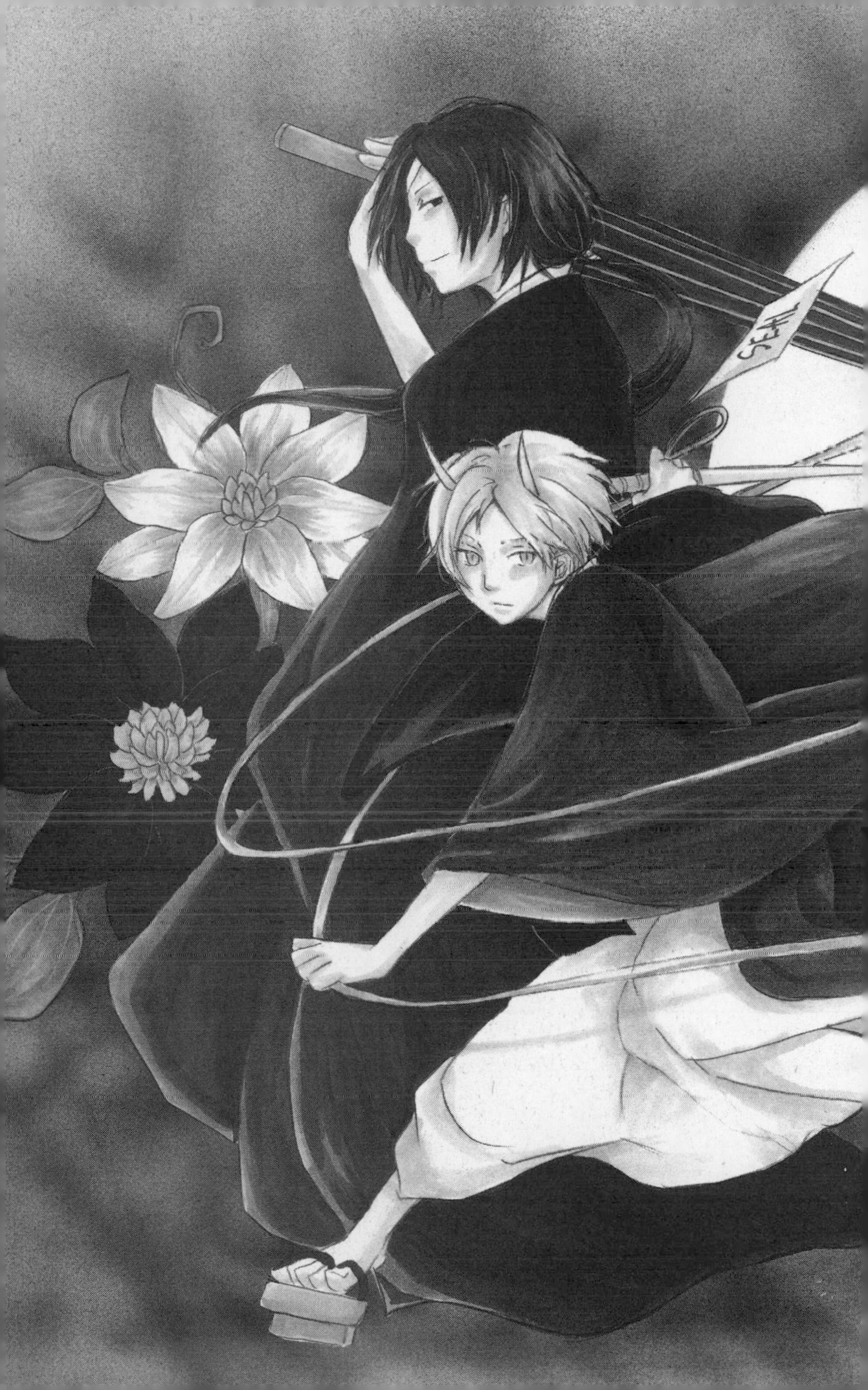

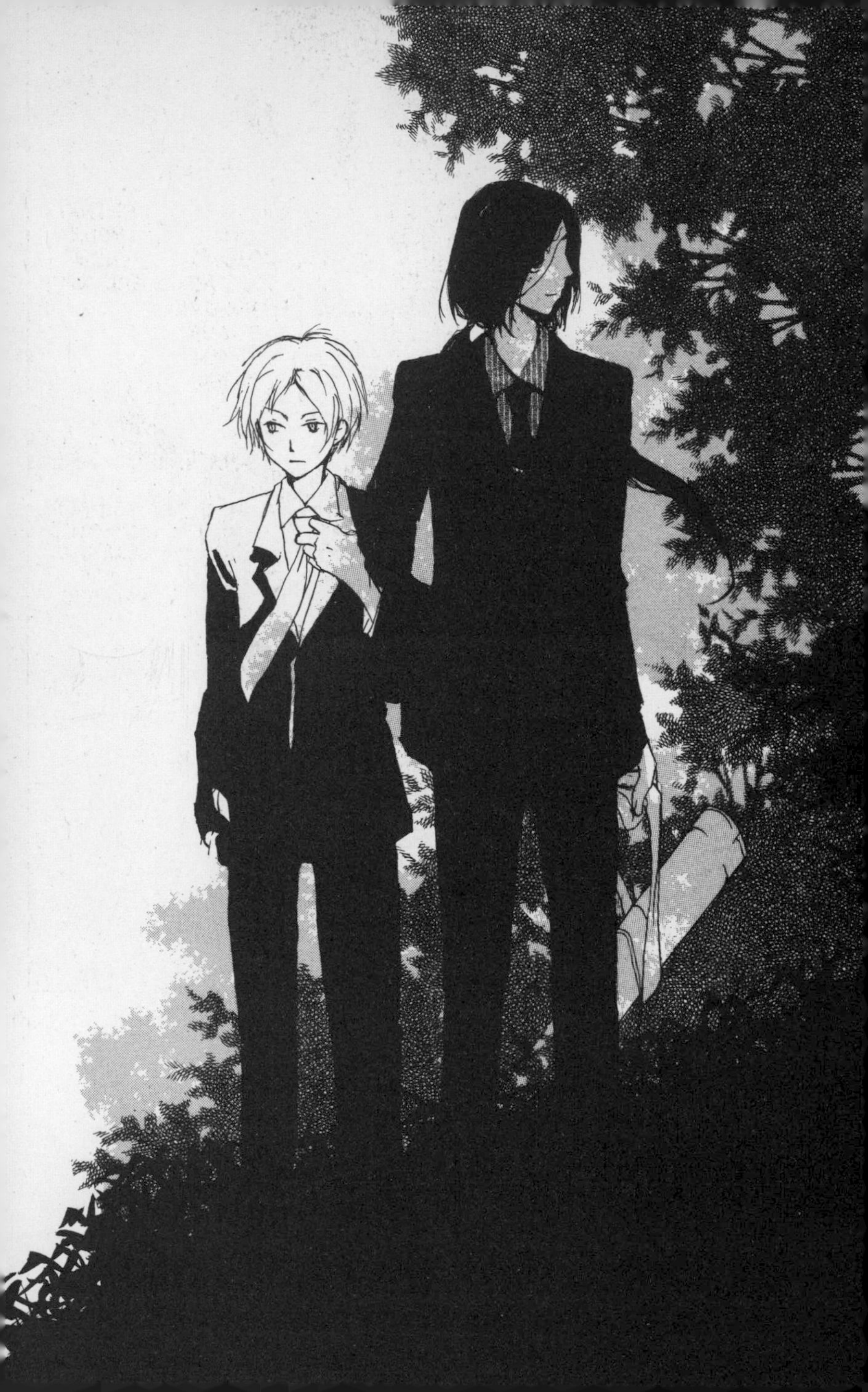

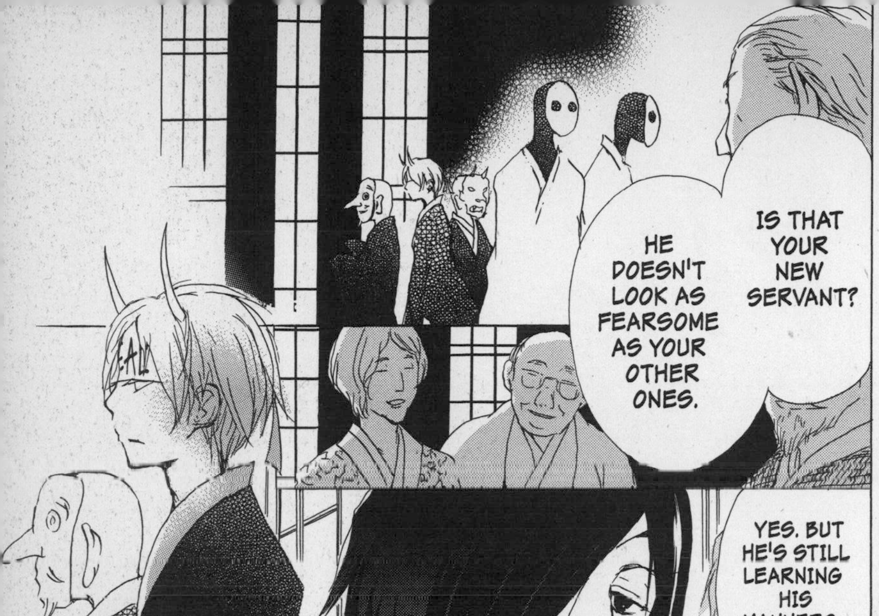
IS THAT YOUR NEW SERVANT?
HE DOESN'T LOOK AS FEARSOME AS YOUR OTHER ONES.
YES. BUT HE'S STILL LEARNING HIS MANNERS.
IF YOU'RE NOT CAREFUL, HE MAY BITE. DON'T SAY I DIDN'T WARN YOU.

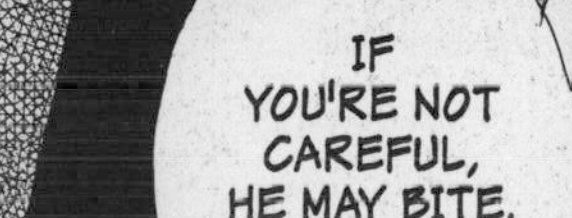

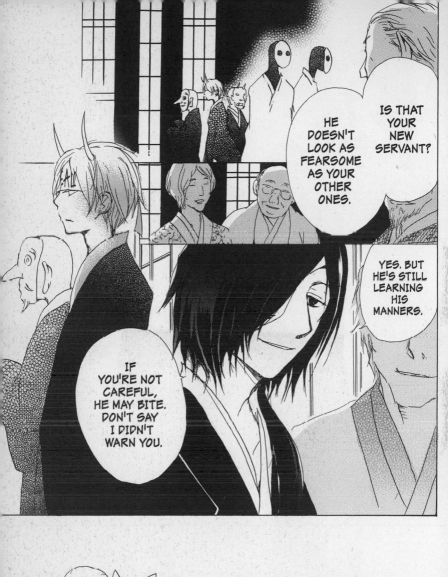

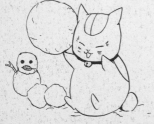

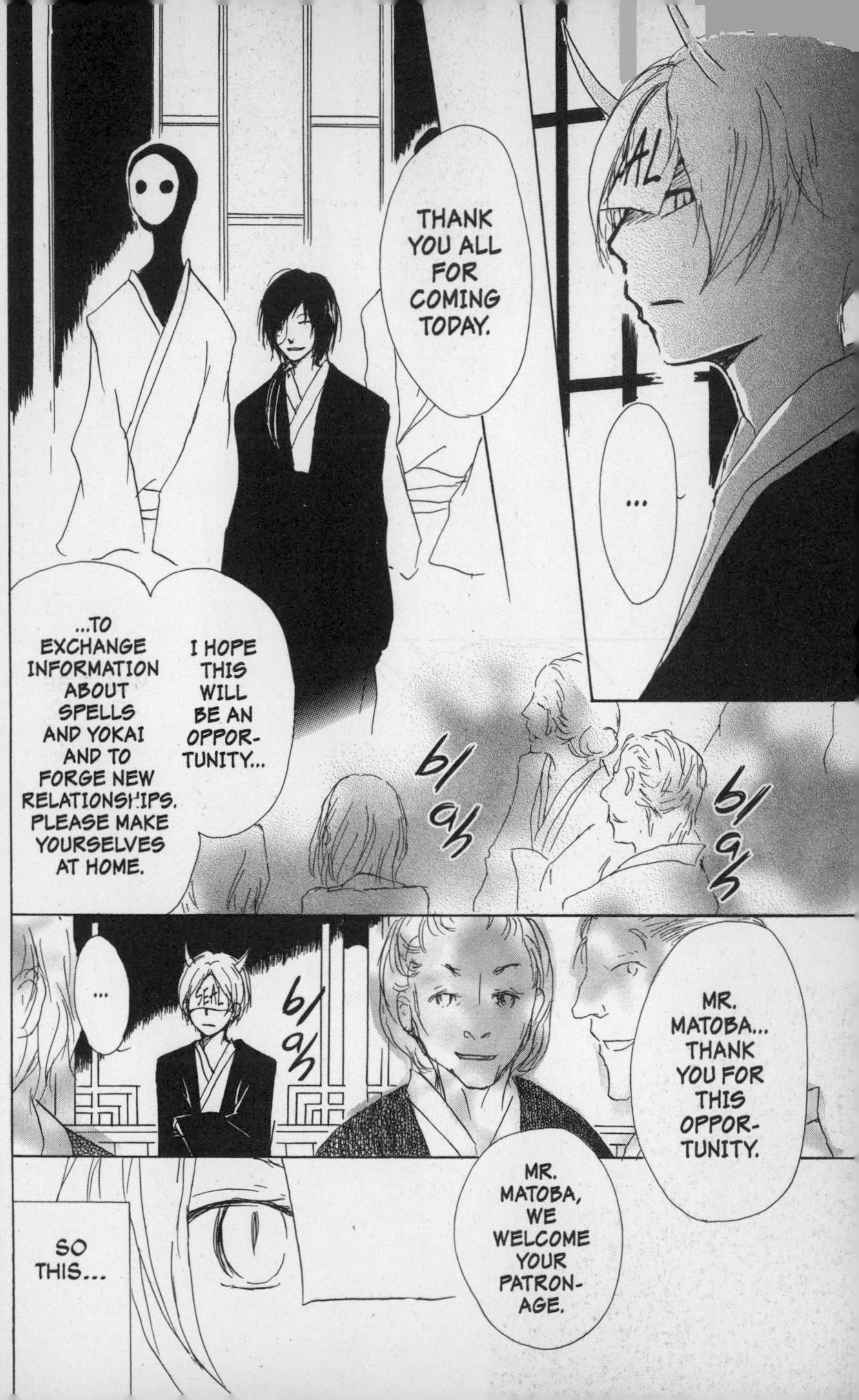
...
THANK YOU ALL FOR COMING TODAY.
I HOPE THIS WILL BE AN OPPORTUNITY...
...TO EXCHANGE INFORMATION ABOUT SPELLS AND YOKAI AND TO FORGE NEW RELATIONSHIPS. PLEASE MAKE YOURSELVES AT HOME.
blah
blah
MR. MATOBA... THANK YOU FOR THIS OPPORTUNITY.
blah
SEAL
...
MR. MATOBA, WE WELCOME YOUR PATRONAGE.
SO THIS...

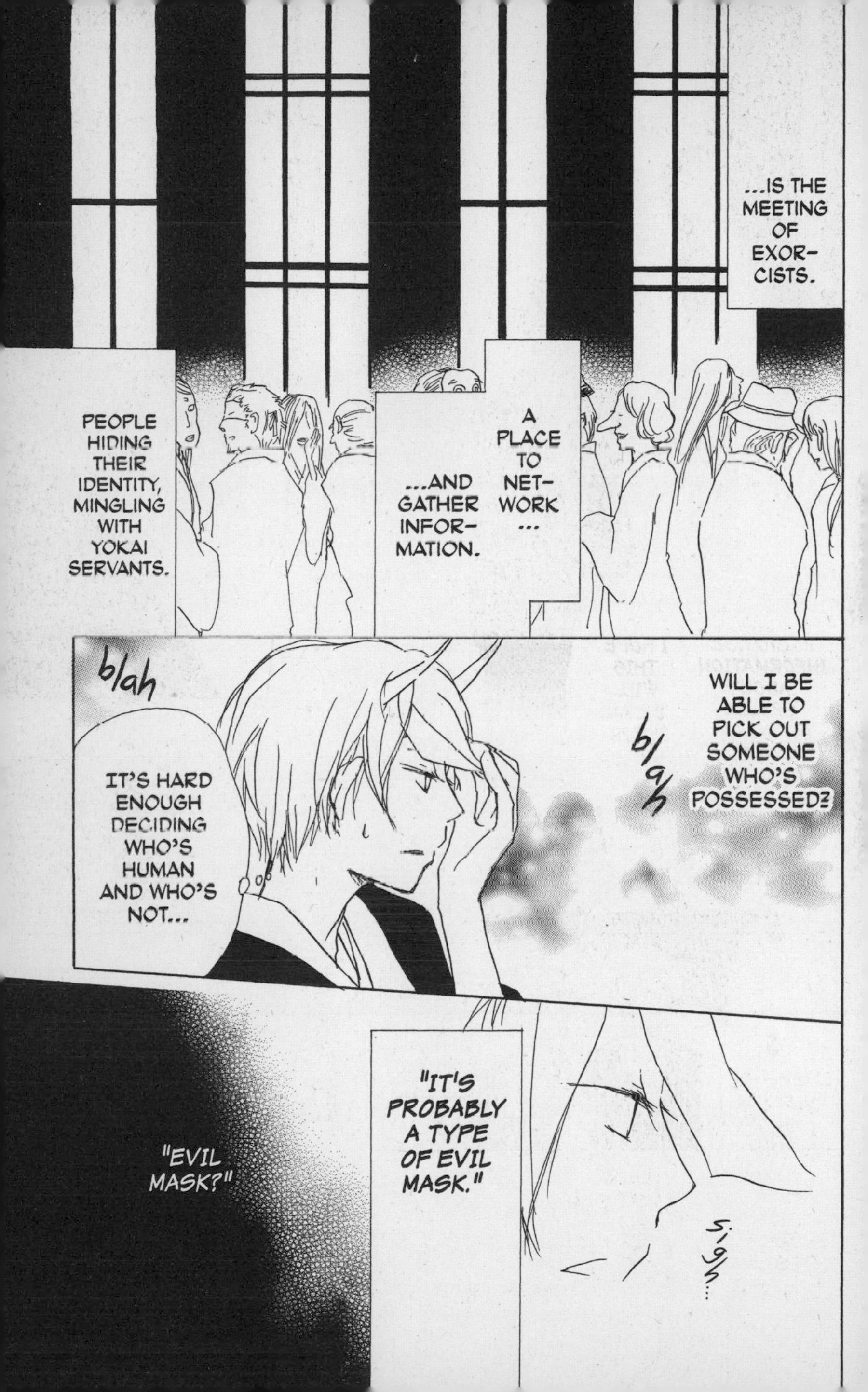
...IS THE MEETING OF EXORCISTS.
A PLACE TO NETWORK...
...AND GATHER INFORMATION.
PEOPLE HIDING THEIR IDENTITY, MINGLING WITH YOKAI SERVANTS.
WILL I BE ABLE TO PICK OUT SOMEONE WHO'S POSSESSED?
blah
blah
IT'S HARD ENOUGH DECIDING WHO'S HUMAN AND WHO'S NOT...
sigh...
"IT'S PROBABLY A TYPE OF EVIL MASK."
"EVIL MASK?"

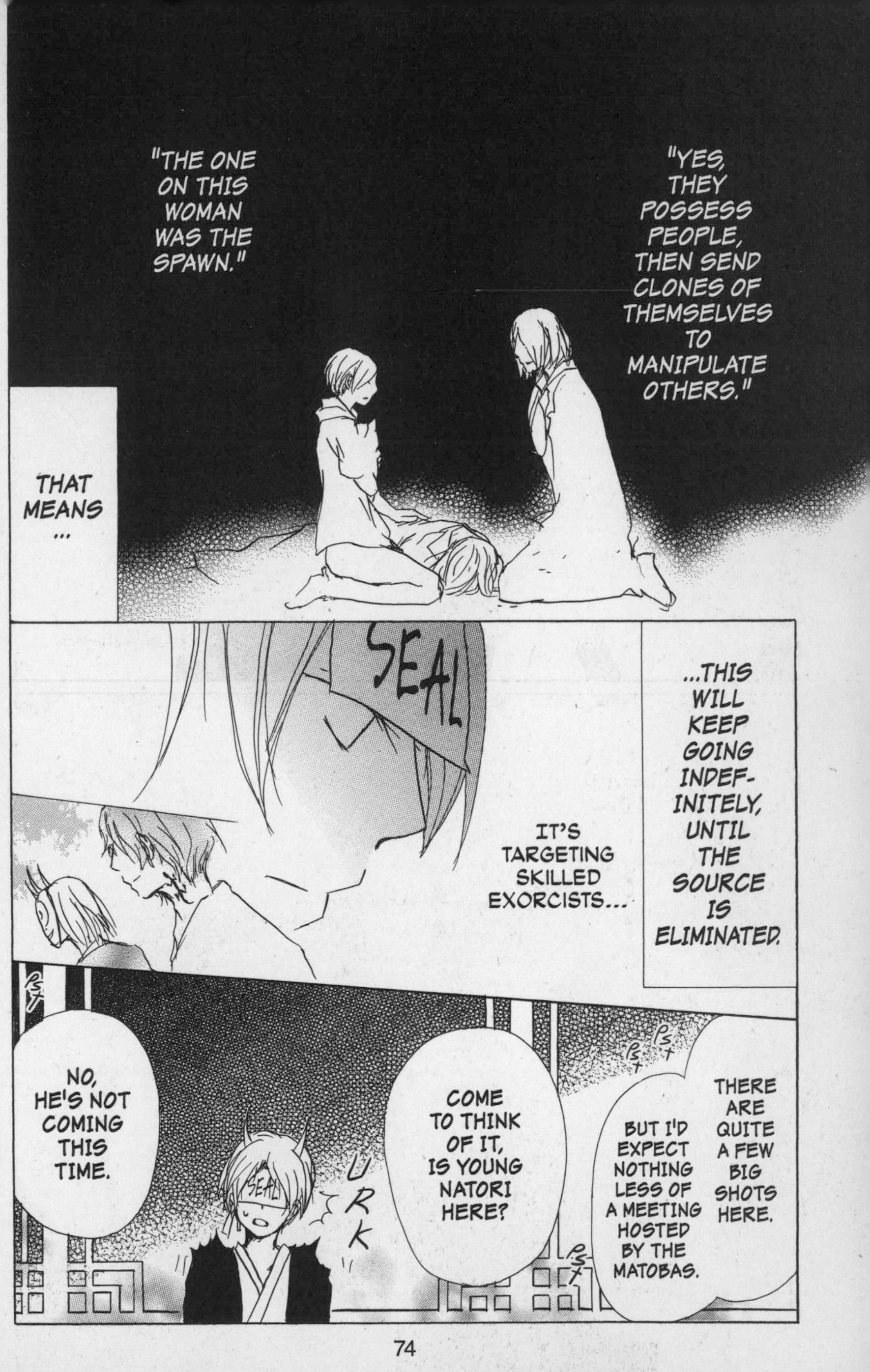
"THE ONE ON THIS WOMAN WAS THE SPAWN."
"YES, THEY POSSESS PEOPLE, THEN SEND CLONES OF THEMSELVES TO MANIPULATE OTHERS."
THAT MEANS ...
...THIS WILL KEEP GOING INDEF-INITELY, UNTIL THE SOURCE IS ELIMINATED.
IT'S TARGETING SKILLED EXORCISTS...
SEAL
Pst
Pst
THERE ARE QUITE A FEW BIG SHOTS HERE.
BUT I'D EXPECT NOTHING LESS OF A MEETING HOSTED BY THE MATOBAS.
Pst
COME TO THINK OF IT, IS YOUNG NATORI HERE?
URK
SEAL
Pst
NO, HE'S NOT COMING THIS TIME.

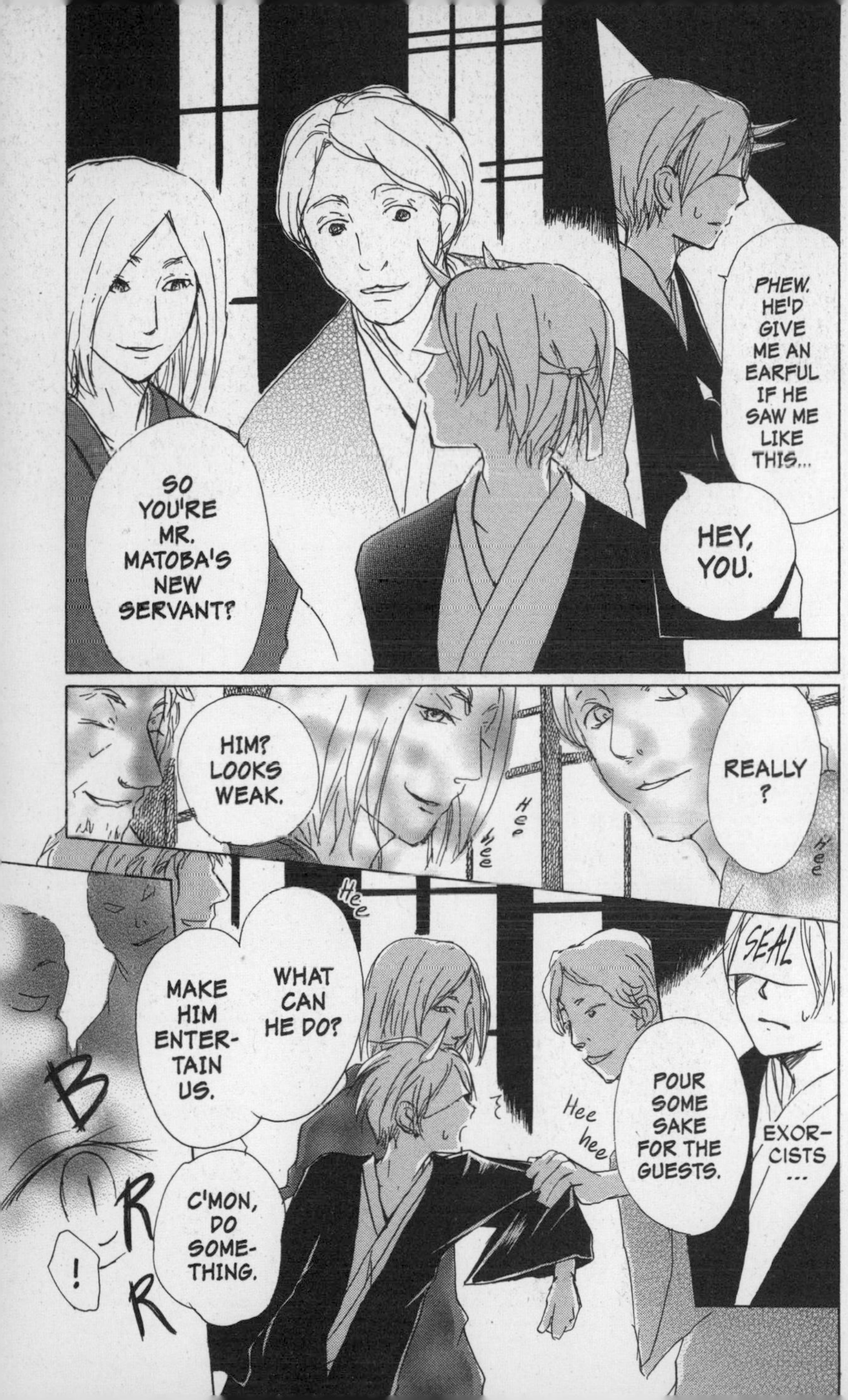
PHEW. HE'D GIVE ME AN EARFUL IF HE SAW ME LIKE THIS...
HEY, YOU.
SO YOU'RE MR. MATOBA'S NEW SERVANT?
REALLY?
hee
Hee hee
HIM? LOOKS WEAK.
SEAL
EXORCISTS...
POUR SOME SAKE FOR THE GUESTS.
Hee hee
WHAT CAN HE DO?
Hee
MAKE HIM ENTERTAIN US.
C'MON, DO SOMETHING.
!
BRR

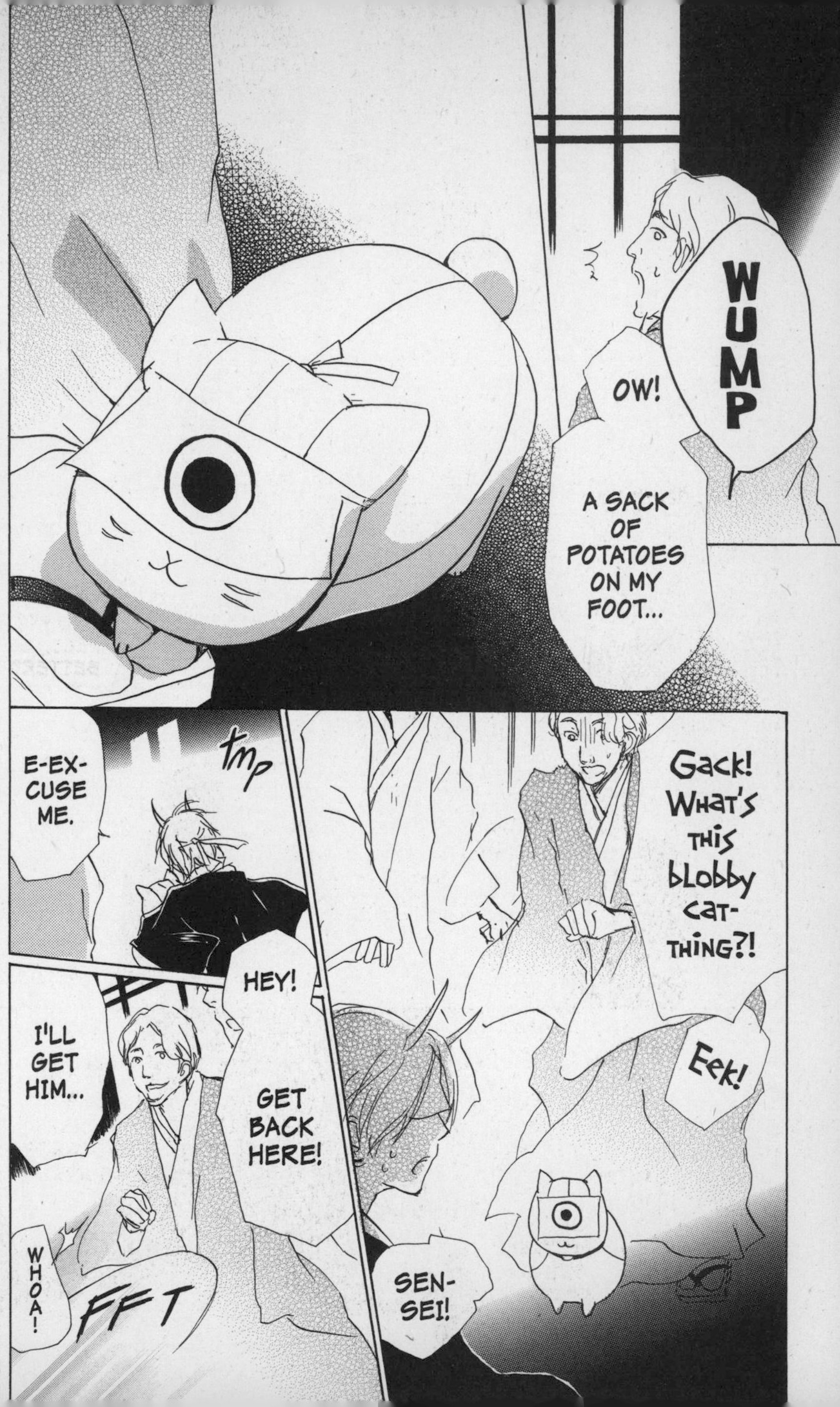
WUMP
OW!
A SACK OF POTATOES ON MY FOOT...
Gack! What's this blobby cat-thing?!
Eek!
SEN-SEI!
E-EX-CUSE ME.
tmp
HEY!
GET BACK HERE!
I'LL GET HIM...
WHOA!
FFT

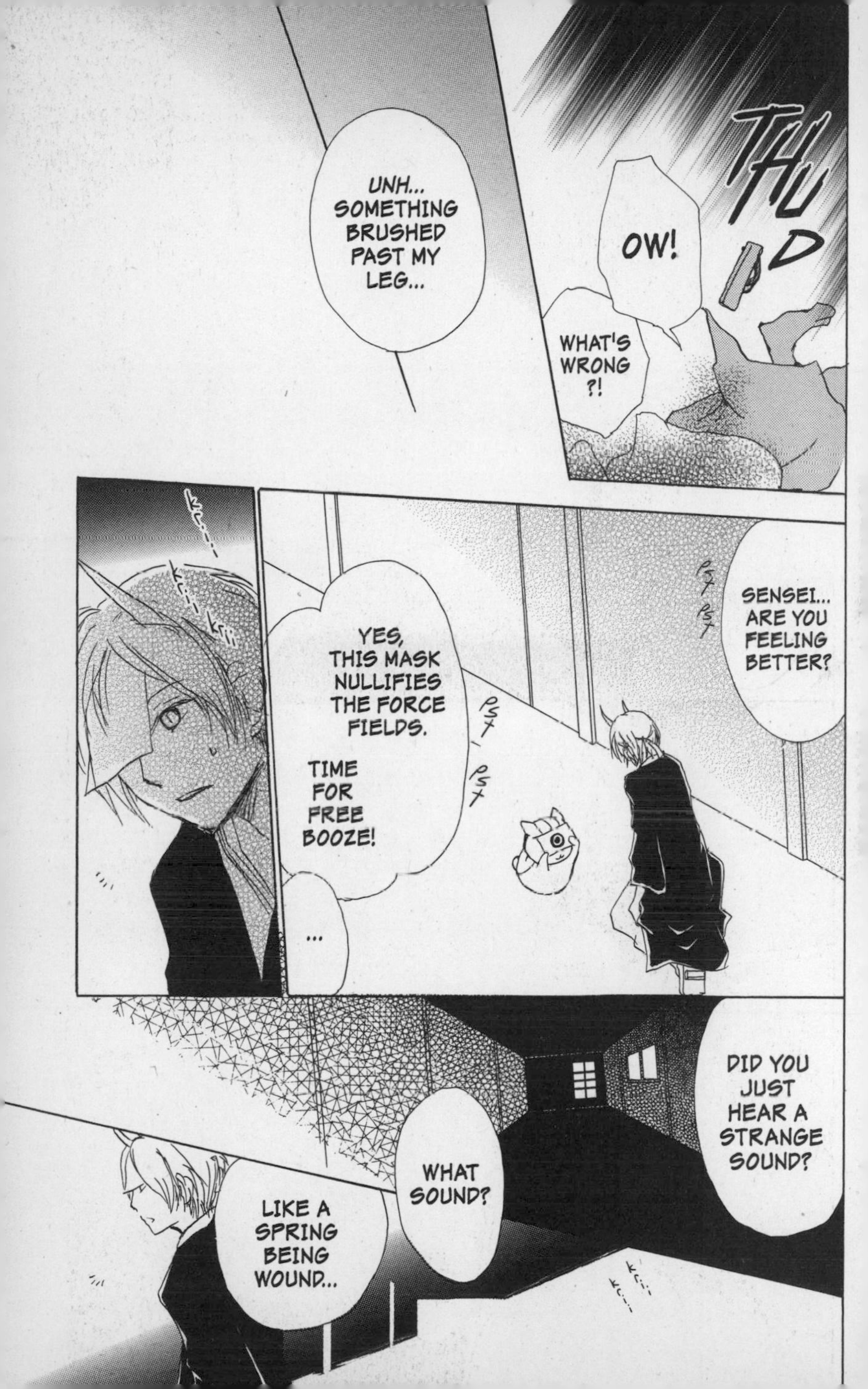
THUD
OW!
WHAT'S WRONG?!
UNH... SOMETHING BRUSHED PAST MY LEG...
SENSEI... ARE YOU FEELING BETTER?
YES, THIS MASK NULLIFIES THE FORCE FIELDS.
TIME FOR FREE BOOZE!
...
DID YOU JUST HEAR A STRANGE SOUND?
WHAT SOUND?
LIKE A SPRING BEING WOUND...

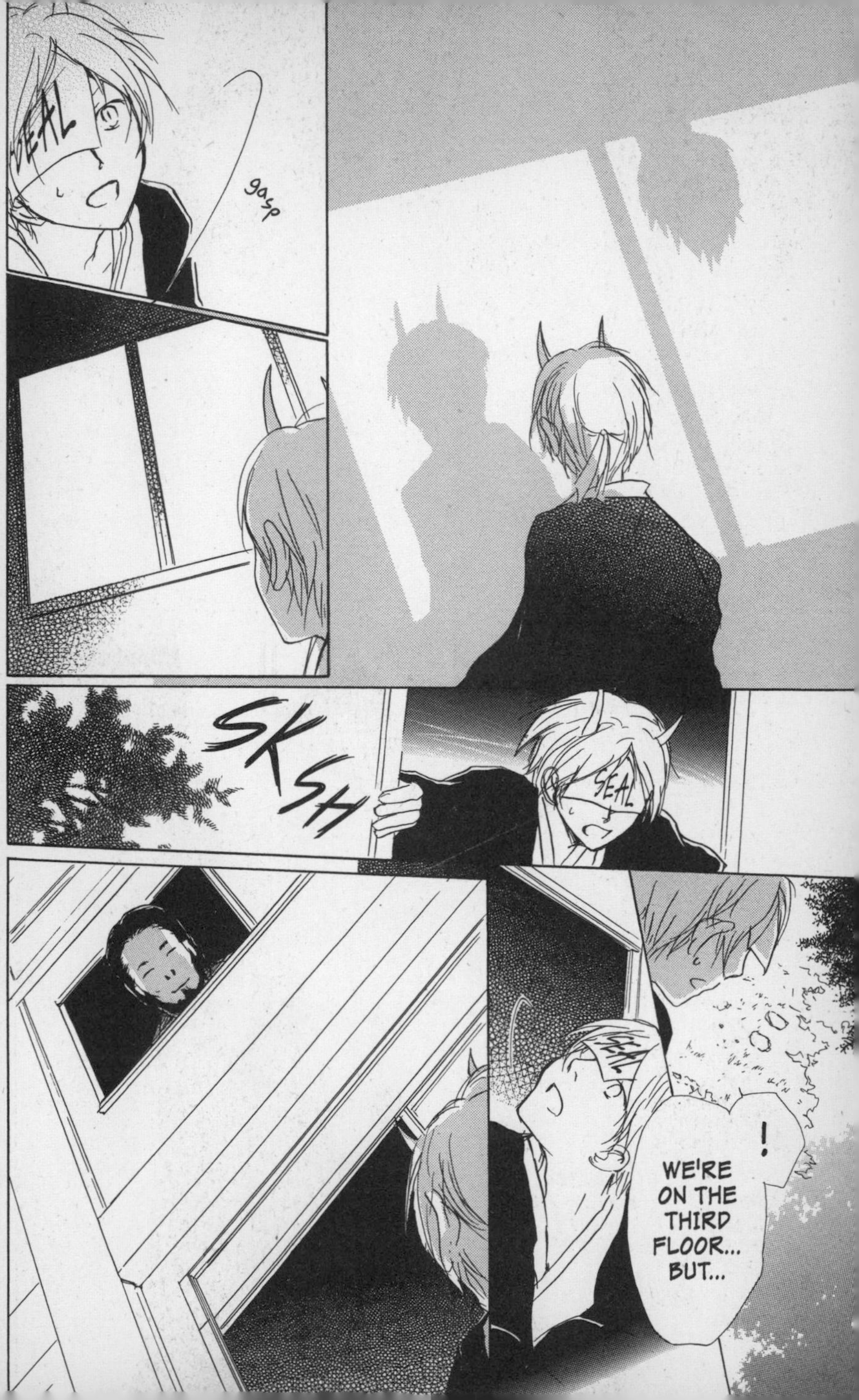
SEAL
gasp
SKSH
SEAL
SEAL
!
WE'RE ON THE THIRD FLOOR... BUT...

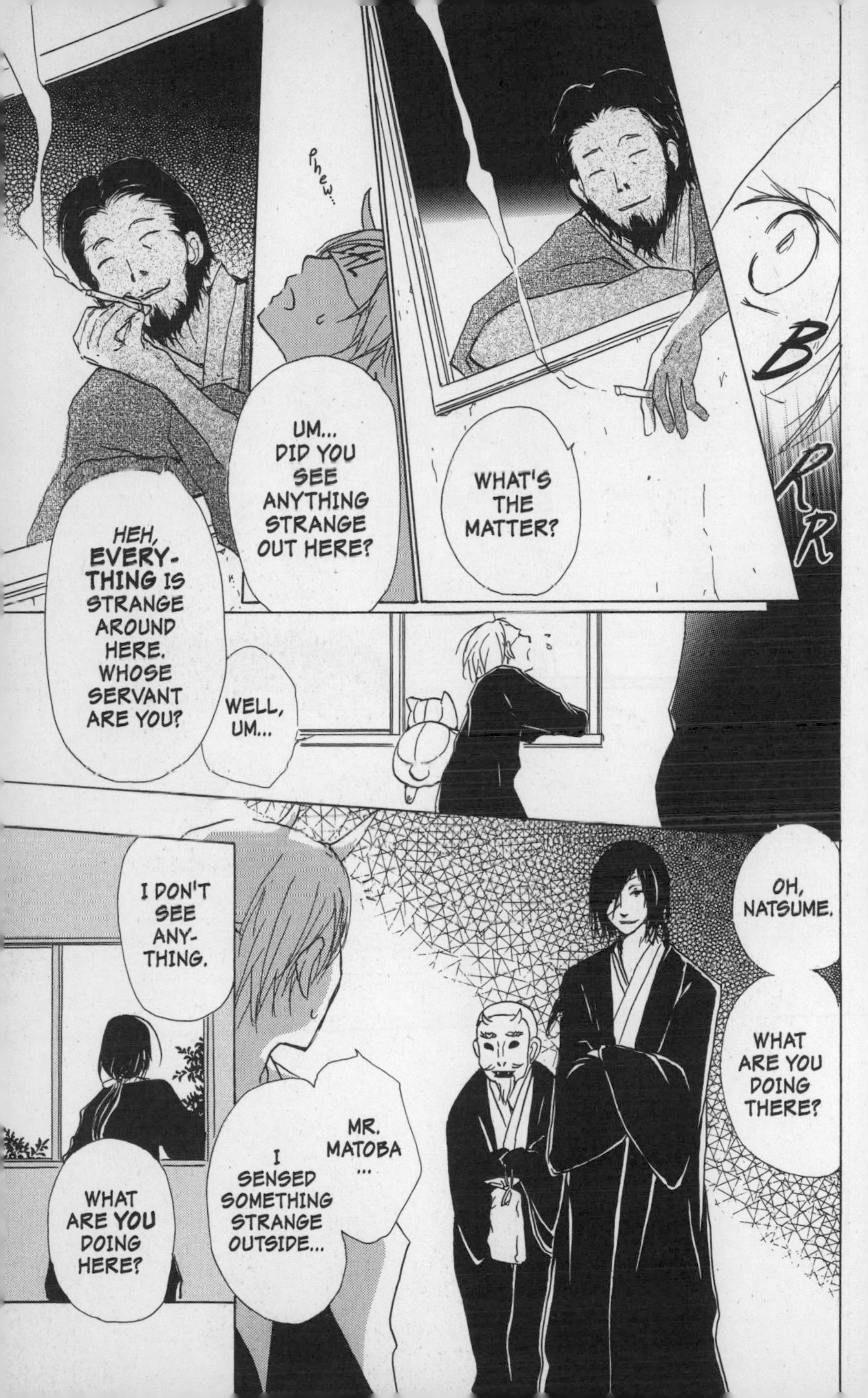
BRRR
WHAT'S THE MATTER?
Phew...
UM... DID YOU SEE ANYTHING STRANGE OUT HERE?
HEH, EVERYTHING IS STRANGE AROUND HERE. WHOSE SERVANT ARE YOU?
WELL, UM...
OH, NATSUME.
WHAT ARE YOU DOING THERE?
MR. MATOBA...
I SENSED SOMETHING STRANGE OUTSIDE...
I DON'T SEE ANYTHING.
WHAT ARE YOU DOING HERE?

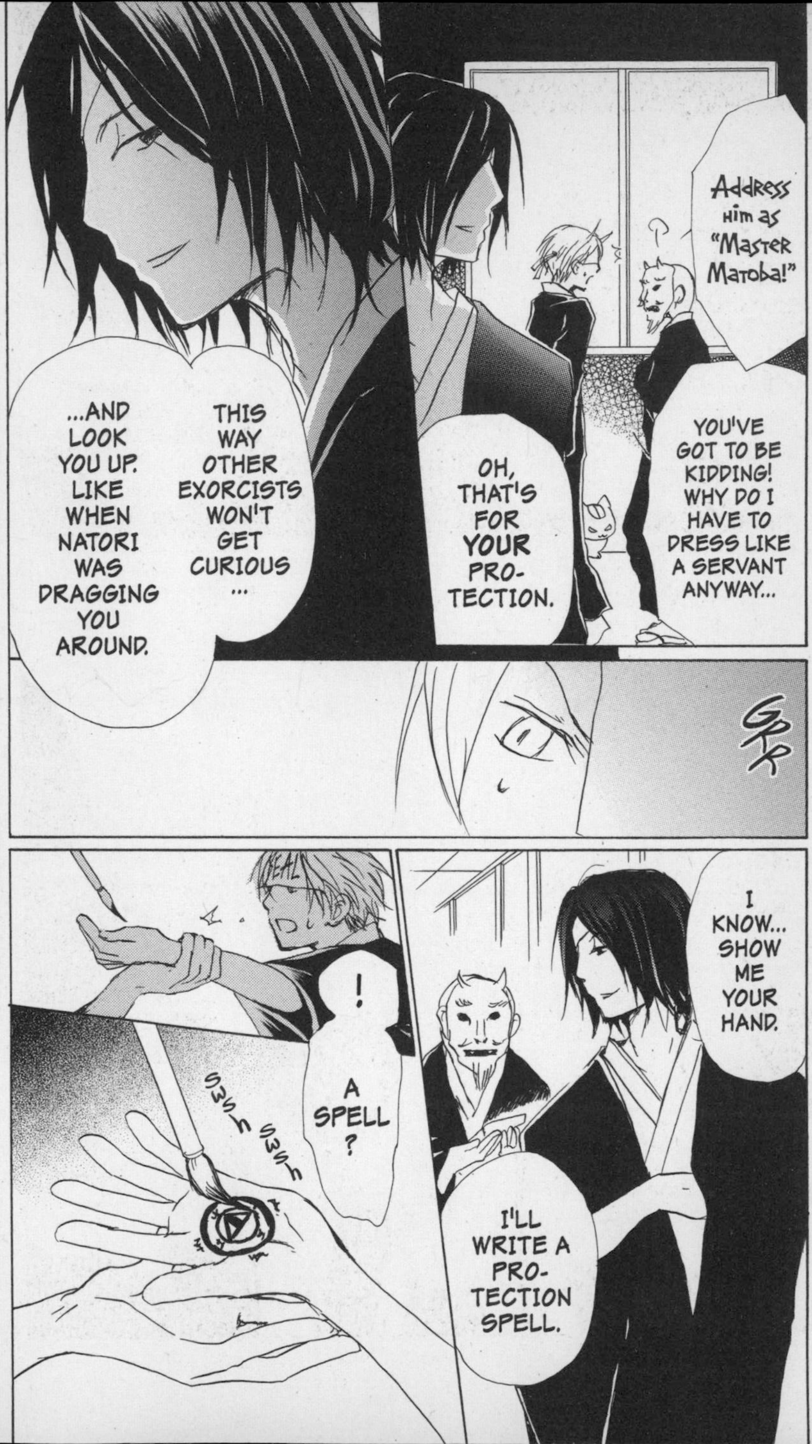
Address him as "Master Matoba!"
YOU'VE GOT TO BE KIDDING! WHY DO I HAVE TO DRESS LIKE A SERVANT ANYWAY...
OH, THAT'S FOR YOUR PROTECTION.
THIS WAY OTHER EXORCISTS WON'T GET CURIOUS...
...AND LOOK YOU UP. LIKE WHEN NATORI WAS DRAGGING YOU AROUND.
GRR
I KNOW... SHOW ME YOUR HAND.
I'LL WRITE A PROTECTION SPELL.
SEAL
!
A SPELL?
SWSH SWSH

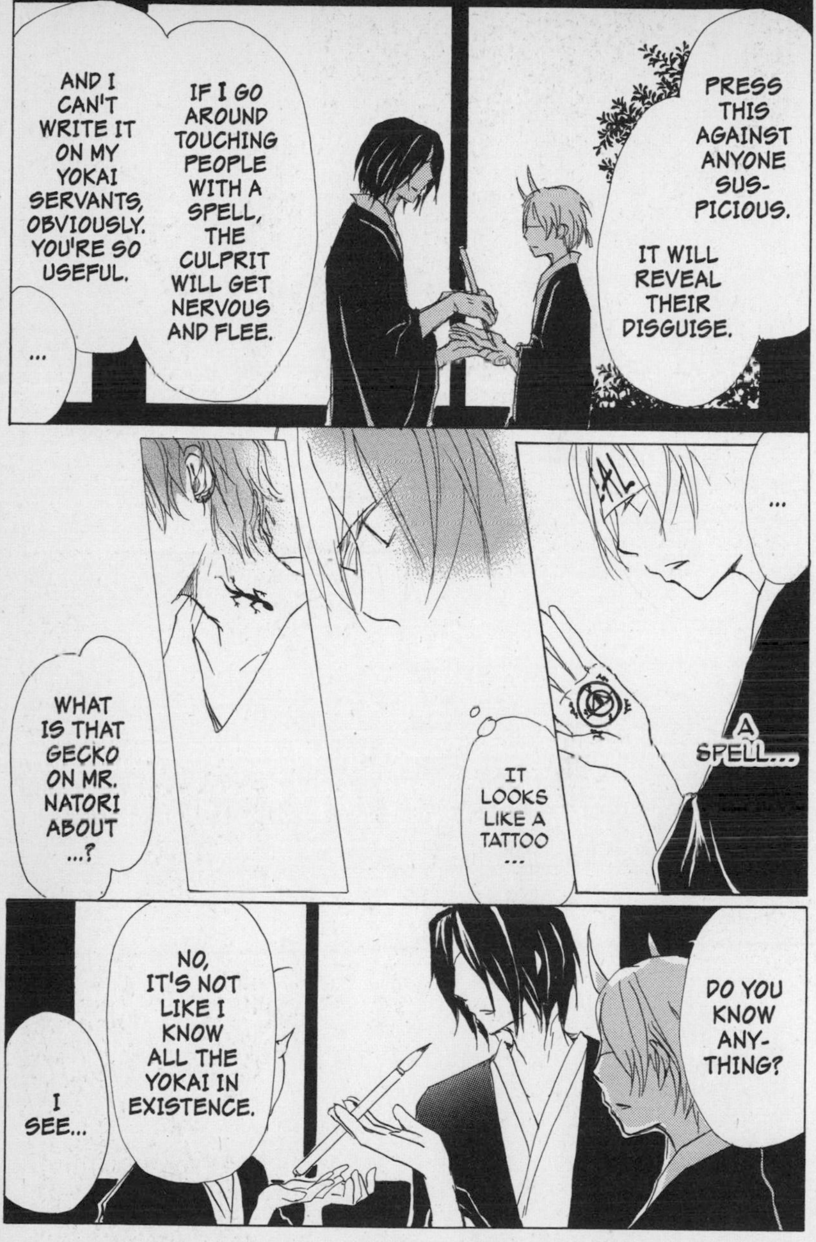
PRESS THIS AGAINST ANYONE SUS-PICIOUS.
IT WILL REVEAL THEIR DISGUISE.
IF I GO AROUND TOUCHING PEOPLE WITH A SPELL, THE CULPRIT WILL GET NERVOUS AND FLEE.
AND I CAN'T WRITE IT ON MY YOKAI SERVANTS, OBVIOUSLY. YOU'RE SO USEFUL.
...
...
A SPELL...
IT LOOKS LIKE A TATTOO ...
WHAT IS THAT GECKO ON MR. NATORI ABOUT ...?
DO YOU KNOW ANY-THING?
NO, IT'S NOT LIKE I KNOW ALL THE YOKAI IN EXISTENCE.
I SEE...

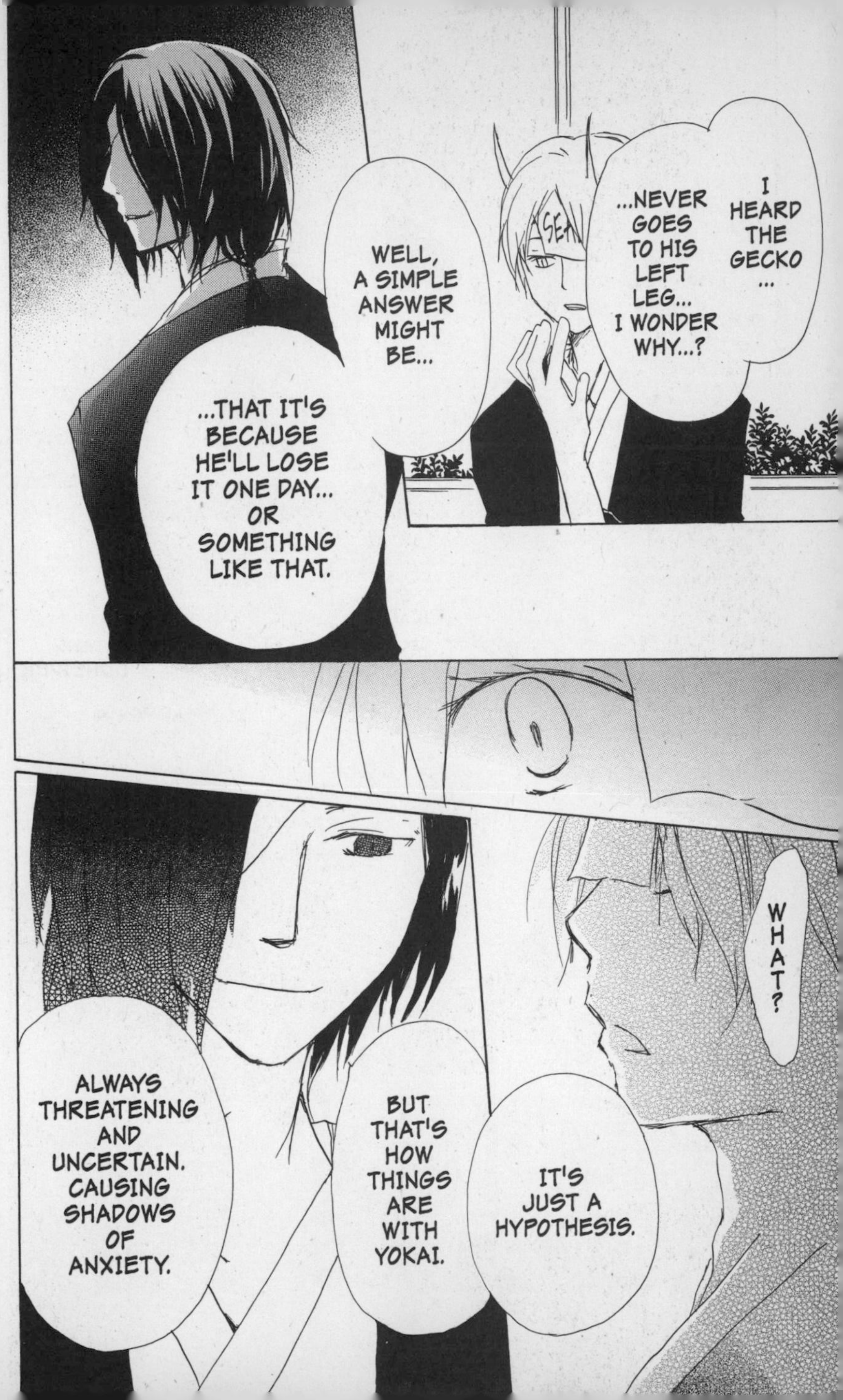
I HEARD THE GECKO ...
...NEVER GOES TO HIS LEFT LEG... I WONDER WHY...?
WELL, A SIMPLE ANSWER MIGHT BE...
...THAT IT'S BECAUSE HE'LL LOSE IT ONE DAY... OR SOMETHING LIKE THAT.
WHAT?
IT'S JUST A HYPOTHESIS.
BUT THAT'S HOW THINGS ARE WITH YOKAI.
ALWAYS THREATENING AND UNCERTAIN. CAUSING SHADOWS OF ANXIETY.

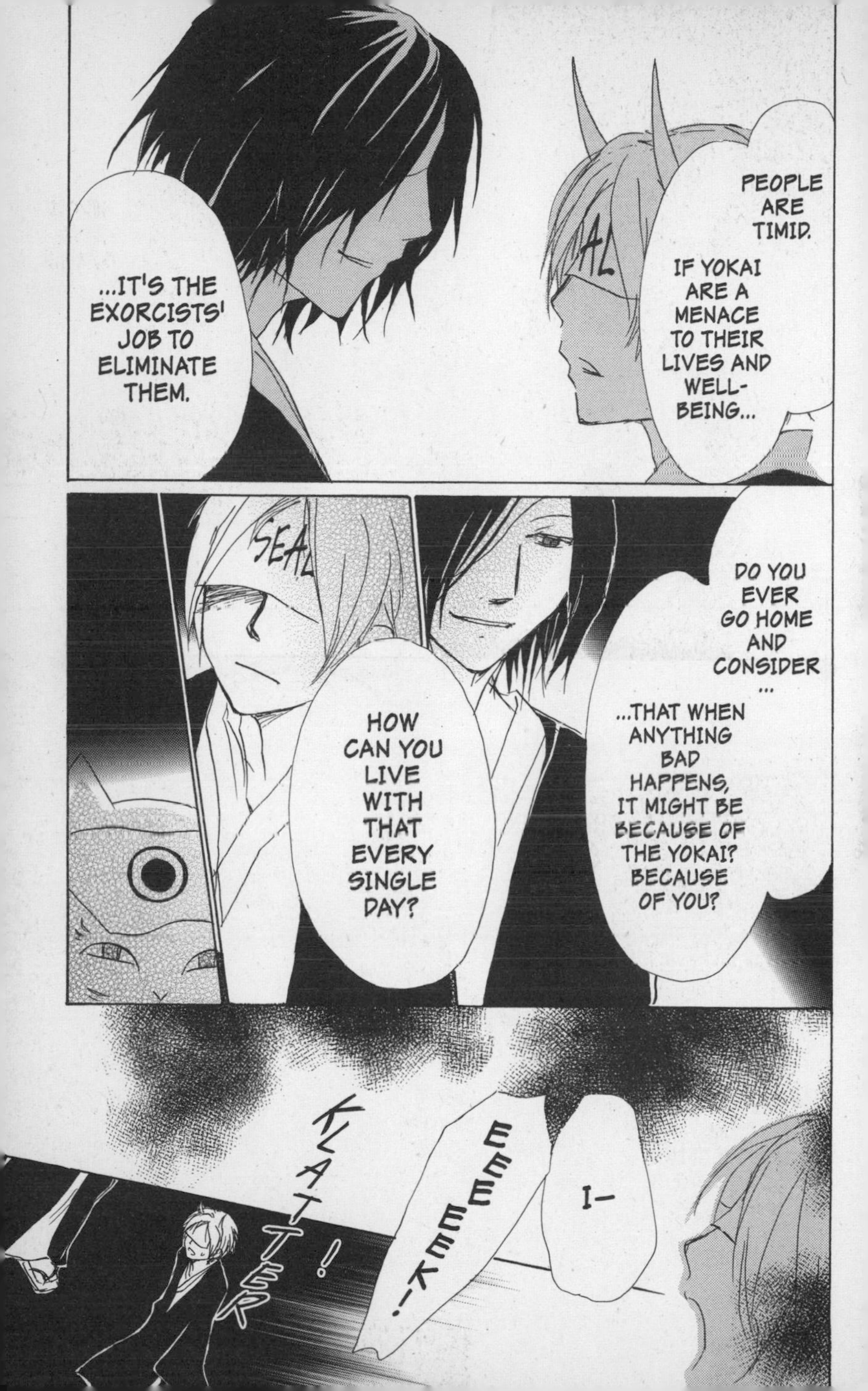
PEOPLE ARE TIMID.
IF YOKAI ARE A MENACE TO THEIR LIVES AND WELL-BEING...
...IT'S THE EXORCISTS' JOB TO ELIMINATE THEM.
DO YOU EVER GO HOME AND CONSIDER...
...THAT WHEN ANYTHING BAD HAPPENS, IT MIGHT BE BECAUSE OF THE YOKAI? BECAUSE OF YOU?
HOW CAN YOU LIVE WITH THAT EVERY SINGLE DAY?
I—
EEEEEEK!
KLATTER!

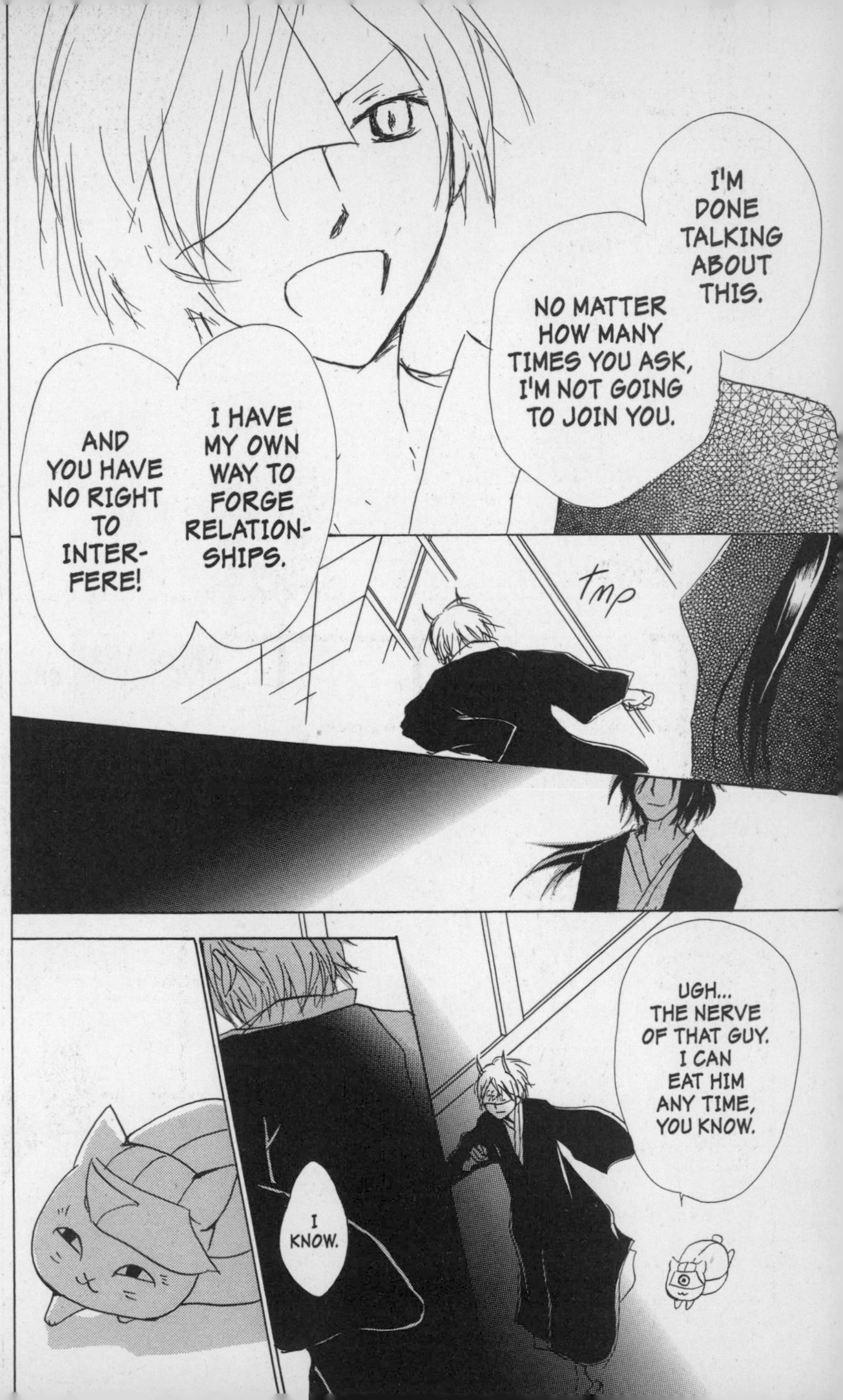
I'M DONE TALKING ABOUT THIS.
NO MATTER HOW MANY TIMES YOU ASK, I'M NOT GOING TO JOIN YOU.
I HAVE MY OWN WAY TO FORGE RELATION-SHIPS.
AND YOU HAVE NO RIGHT TO INTER-FERE!
TMP
UGH... THE NERVE OF THAT GUY. I CAN EAT HIM ANY TIME, YOU KNOW.
I KNOW.

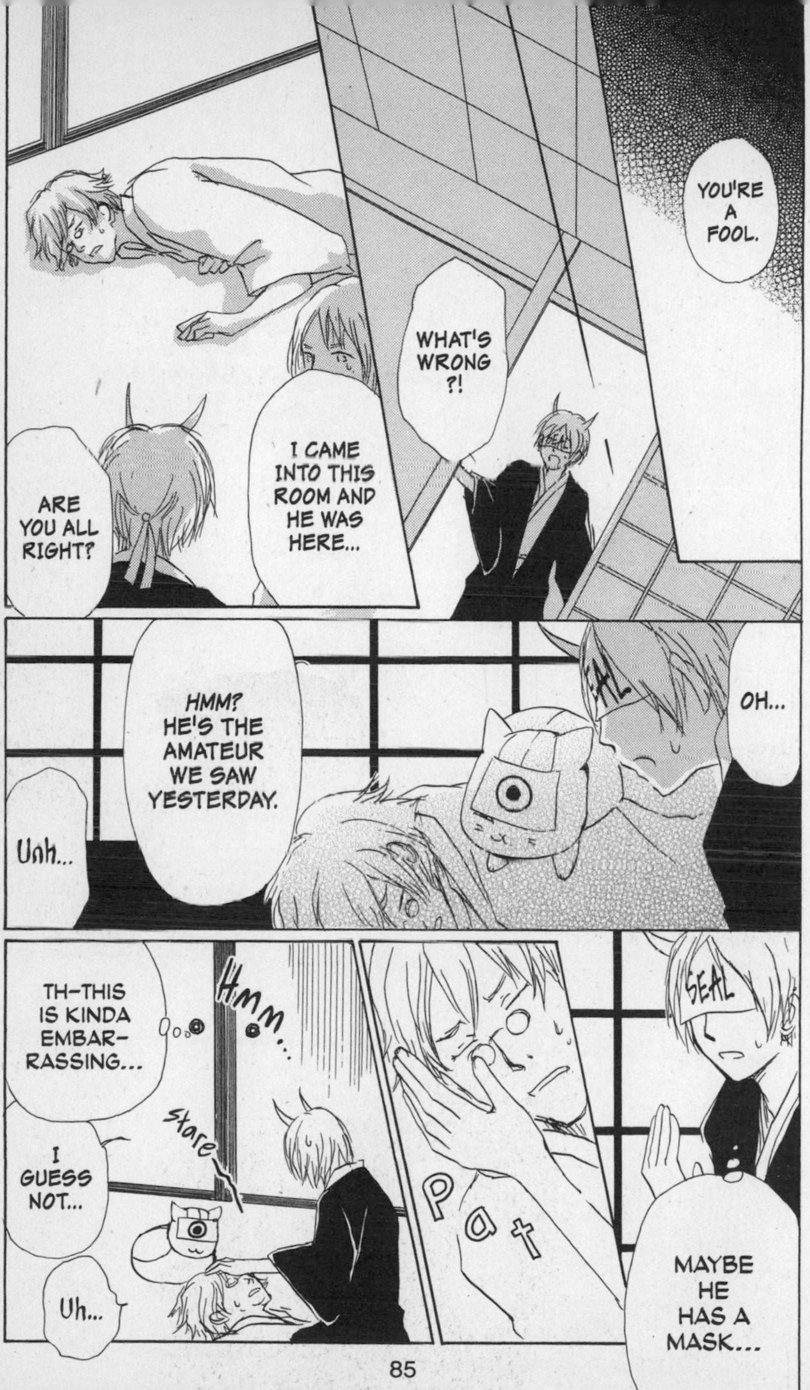
YOU'RE A FOOL.
WHAT'S WRONG?!
SEAL
I CAME INTO THIS ROOM AND HE WAS HERE...
ARE YOU ALL RIGHT?
OH...
SEAL
HMM? HE'S THE AMATEUR WE SAW YESTERDAY.
Unh...
SEAL
MAYBE HE HAS A MASK...
Pat
Hmm...
TH-THIS IS KINDA EMBARRASSING...
stare
I GUESS NOT...
Uh...

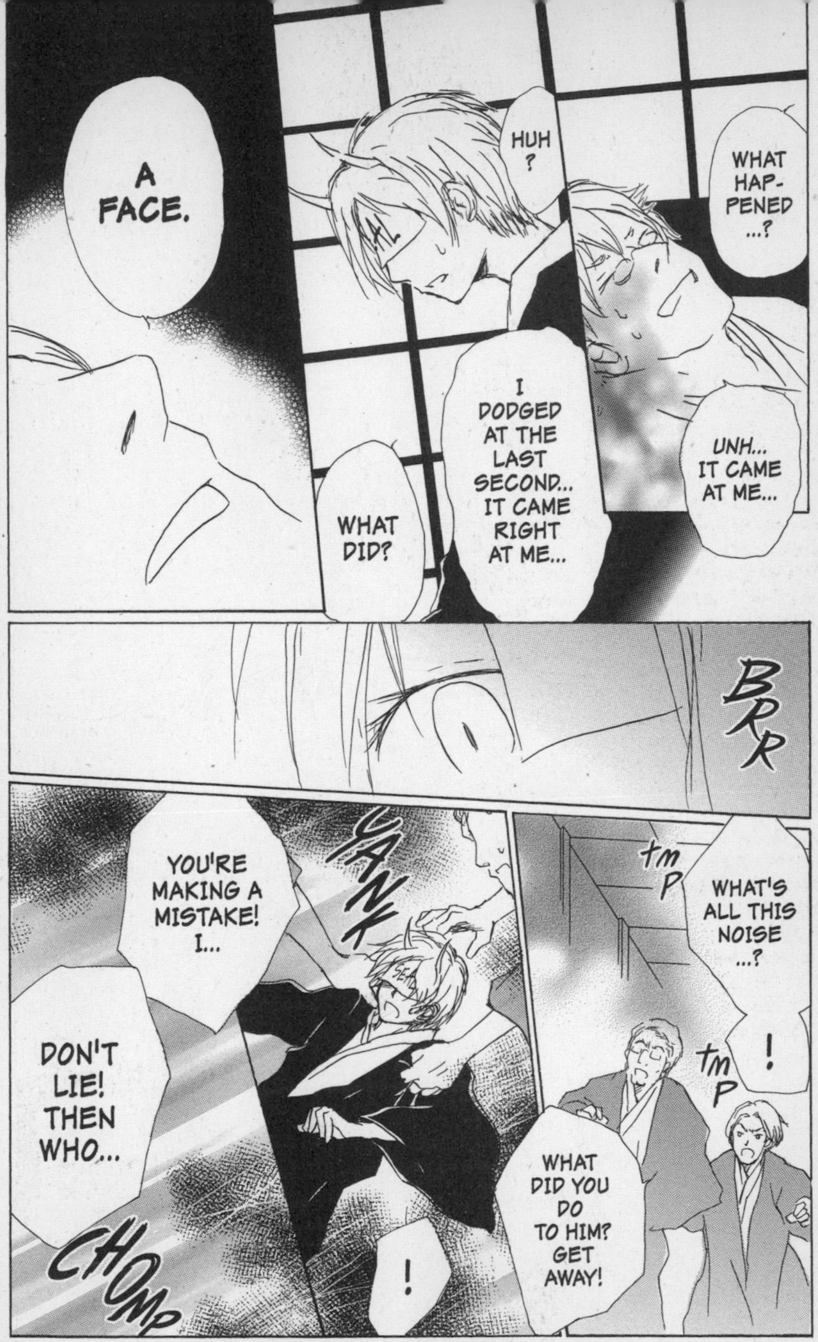
WHAT HAP-PENED ...?
HUH ?
UNH... IT CAME AT ME...
I DODGED AT THE LAST SECOND... IT CAME RIGHT AT ME...
WHAT DID?
A FACE.
BRRR
tmp
WHAT'S ALL THIS NOISE ...?
!
tmp
WHAT DID YOU DO TO HIM? GET AWAY!
YANK
YOU'RE MAKING A MISTAKE! I...
DON'T LIE! THEN WHO...
!
CHOMP

03

❋Nishimura

I think the first impression Nishimura gets of somebody like Natsume is, "I don't like this guy." But he's curious about things he doesn't like—his personality is such that he wants to figure out what he doesn't like about it. This might get him in trouble sometimes. I think of him as a man of action. I imagine him coming into conflicts with some older students, whereas Kitamoto is the type to respect his seniors. That was my impression from the beginning. On the other hand, if someone shows vulnerability, Nishimura resolves to help out. He's probably the most softhearted person in this manga.

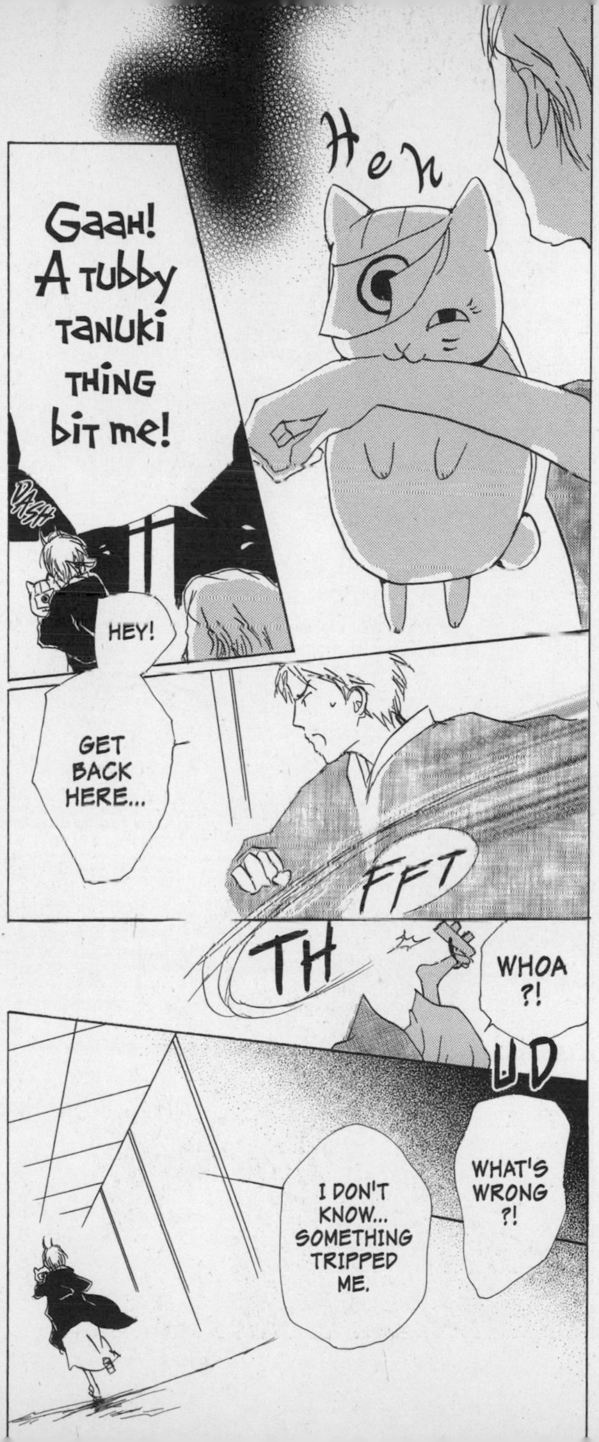

Heh
Gaah! A tubby tanuki thing bit me!
HEY!
GET BACK HERE...
FFT
TH
WHOA ?!
UD
WHAT'S WRONG ?!
I DON'T KNOW... SOMETHING TRIPPED ME.

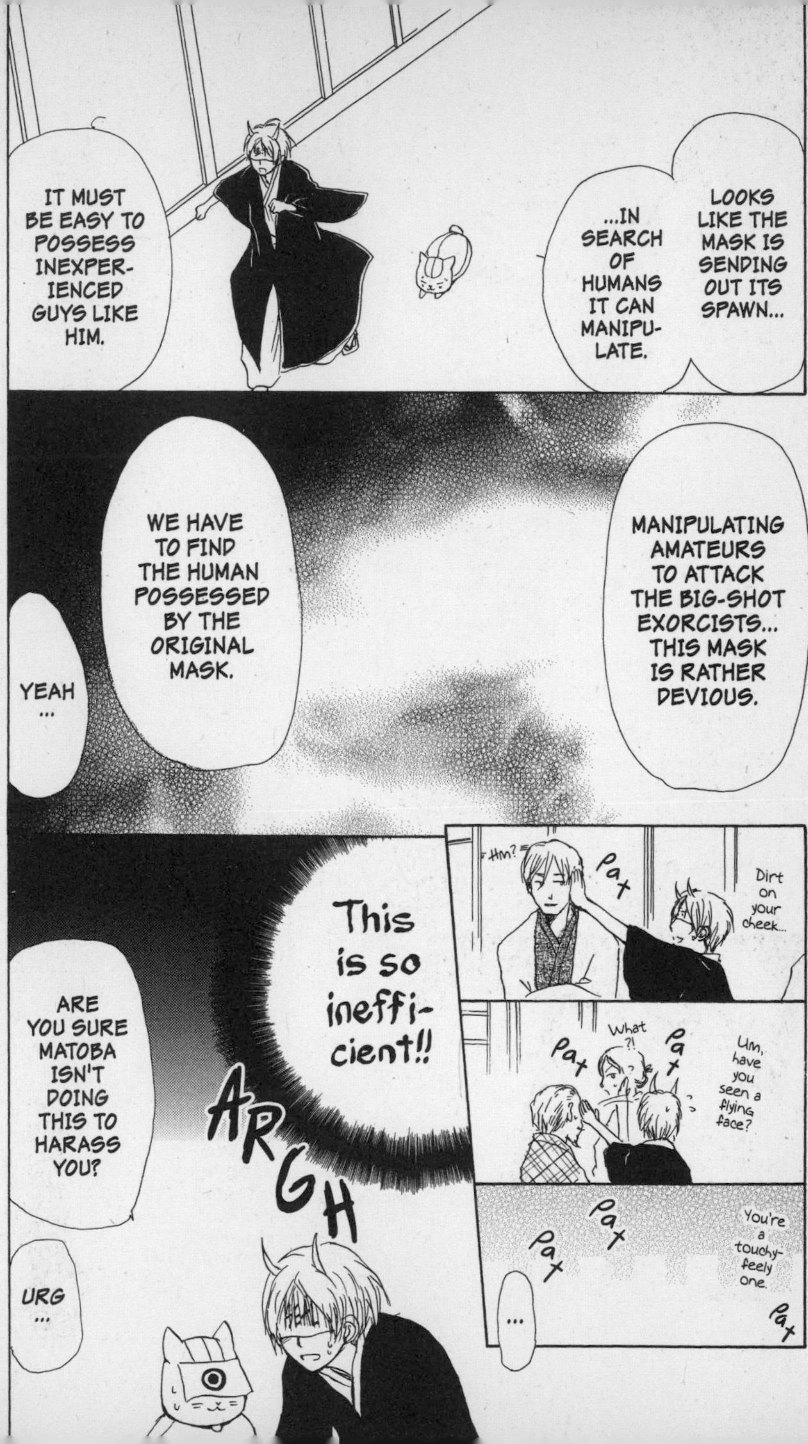
LOOKS LIKE THE MASK IS SENDING OUT ITS SPAWN...
...IN SEARCH OF HUMANS IT CAN MANIPULATE.
IT MUST BE EASY TO POSSESS INEXPERIENCED GUYS LIKE HIM.
MANIPULATING AMATEURS TO ATTACK THE BIG-SHOT EXORCISTS... THIS MASK IS RATHER DEVIOUS.
WE HAVE TO FIND THE HUMAN POSSESSED BY THE ORIGINAL MASK.
YEAH...
Dirt on your cheek...
Pat
Hm?
Um, have you seen a flying face?
Pat
What?!
Pat
You're a touchy-feely one.
Pat
Pat
...
Pat
This is so inefficient!!
ARE YOU SURE MATOBA ISN'T DOING THIS TO HARASS YOU?
ARGH
URG...

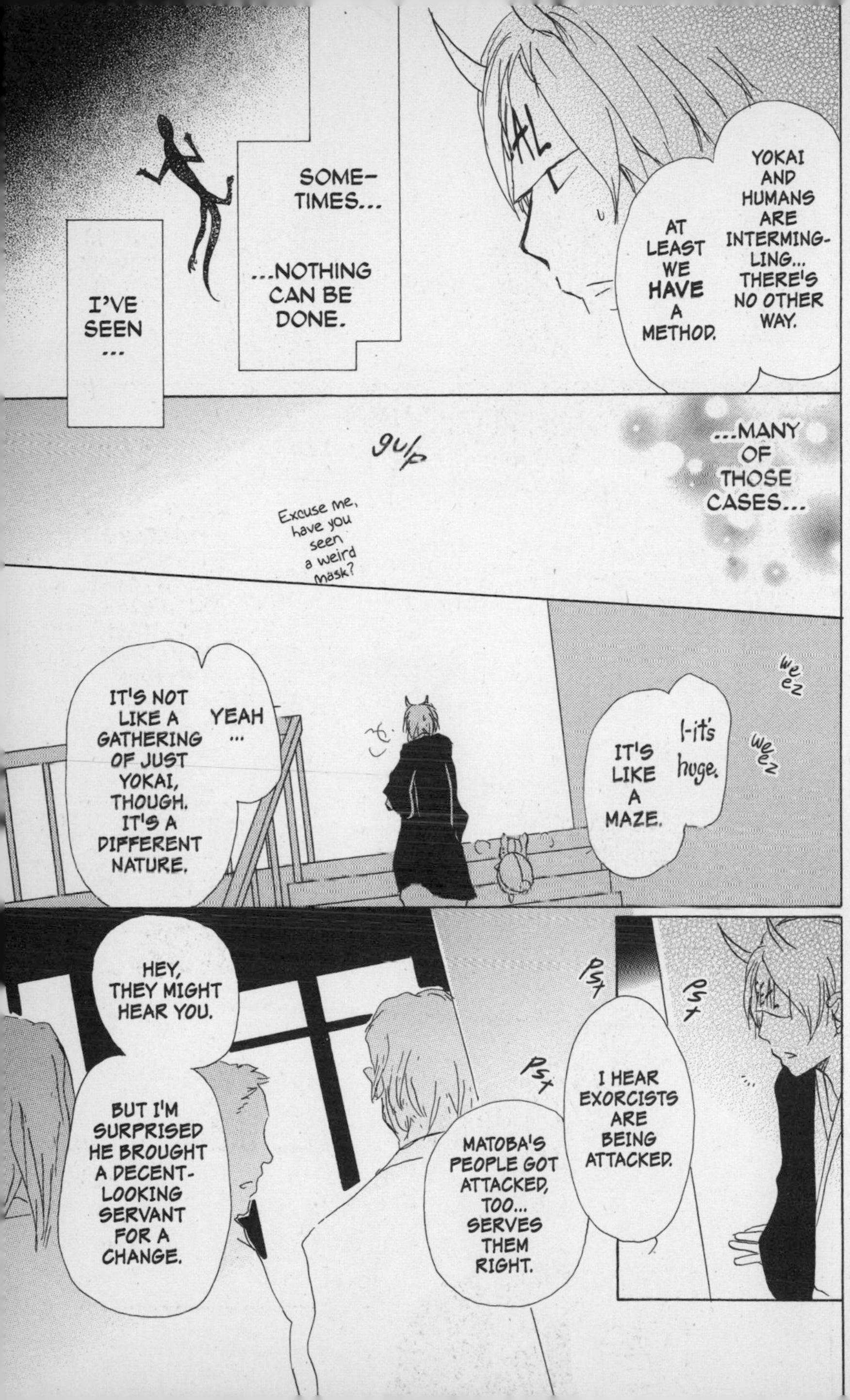

YOKAI AND HUMANS ARE INTERMINGLING... THERE'S NO OTHER WAY.
AT LEAST WE HAVE A METHOD.
SOME-TIMES...
...NOTHING CAN BE DONE.
I'VE SEEN ...
...MANY OF THOSE CASES...
gulp
Excuse me, have you seen a weird mask?
weez
weez
I-it's huge.
IT'S LIKE A MAZE.
YEAH ...
IT'S NOT LIKE A GATHERING OF JUST YOKAI, THOUGH. IT'S A DIFFERENT NATURE.
Pst
Pst
Pst
I HEAR EXORCISTS ARE BEING ATTACKED.
MATOBA'S PEOPLE GOT ATTACKED, TOO... SERVES THEM RIGHT.
HEY, THEY MIGHT HEAR YOU.
BUT I'M SURPRISED HE BROUGHT A DECENT-LOOKING SERVANT FOR A CHANGE.

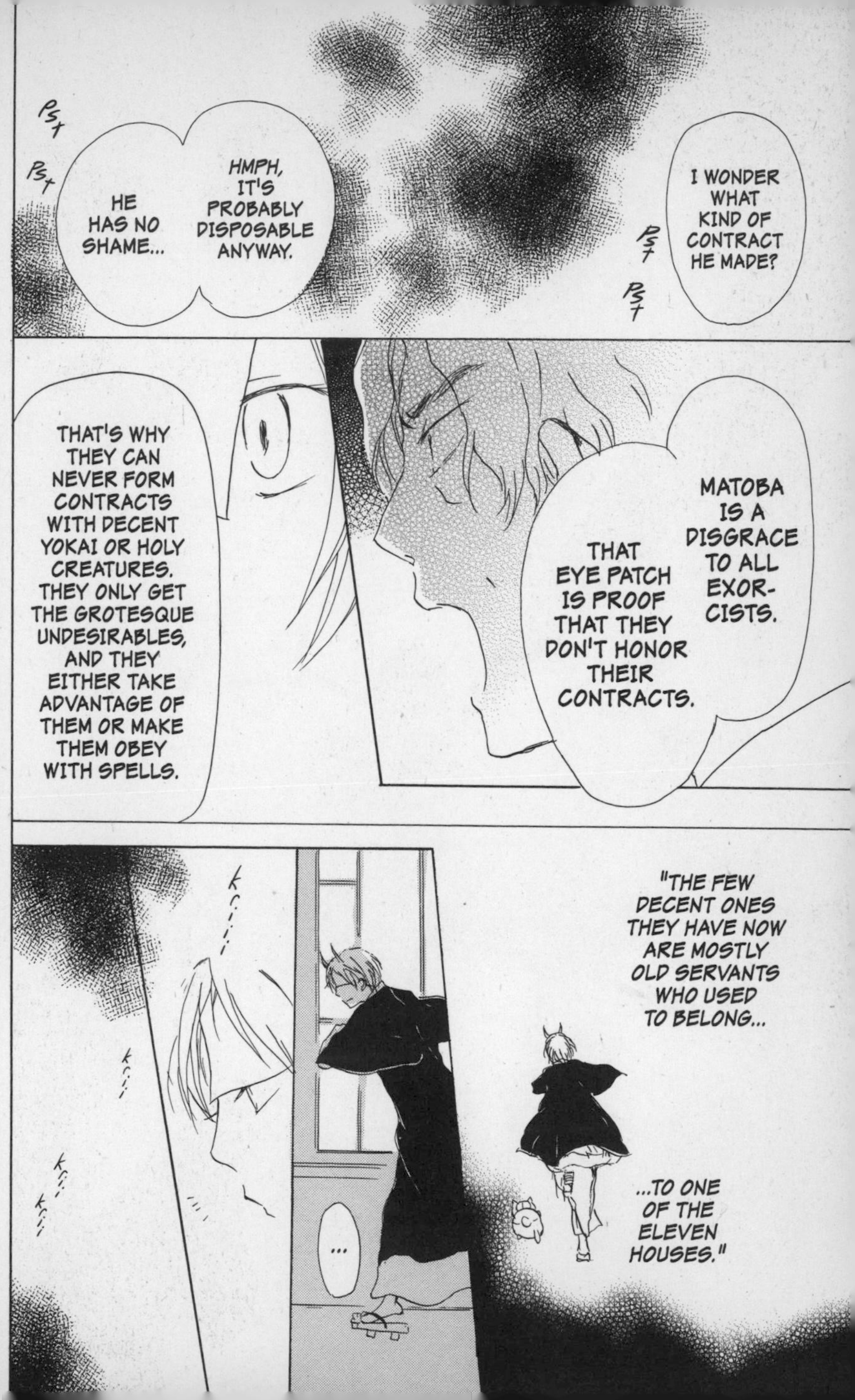
Pst
Pst
I WONDER WHAT KIND OF CONTRACT HE MADE?
Pst
Pst
HMPH, IT'S PROBABLY DISPOSABLE ANYWAY.
HE HAS NO SHAME...
MATOBA IS A DISGRACE TO ALL EXOR-CISTS.
THAT EYE PATCH IS PROOF THAT THEY DON'T HONOR THEIR CONTRACTS.
THAT'S WHY THEY CAN NEVER FORM CONTRACTS WITH DECENT YOKAI OR HOLY CREATURES. THEY ONLY GET THE GROTESQUE UNDESIRABLES, AND THEY EITHER TAKE ADVANTAGE OF THEM OR MAKE THEM OBEY WITH SPELLS.
"THE FEW DECENT ONES THEY HAVE NOW ARE MOSTLY OLD SERVANTS WHO USED TO BELONG...
...TO ONE OF THE ELEVEN HOUSES."
...
Kri
Kri
Kri
Kri

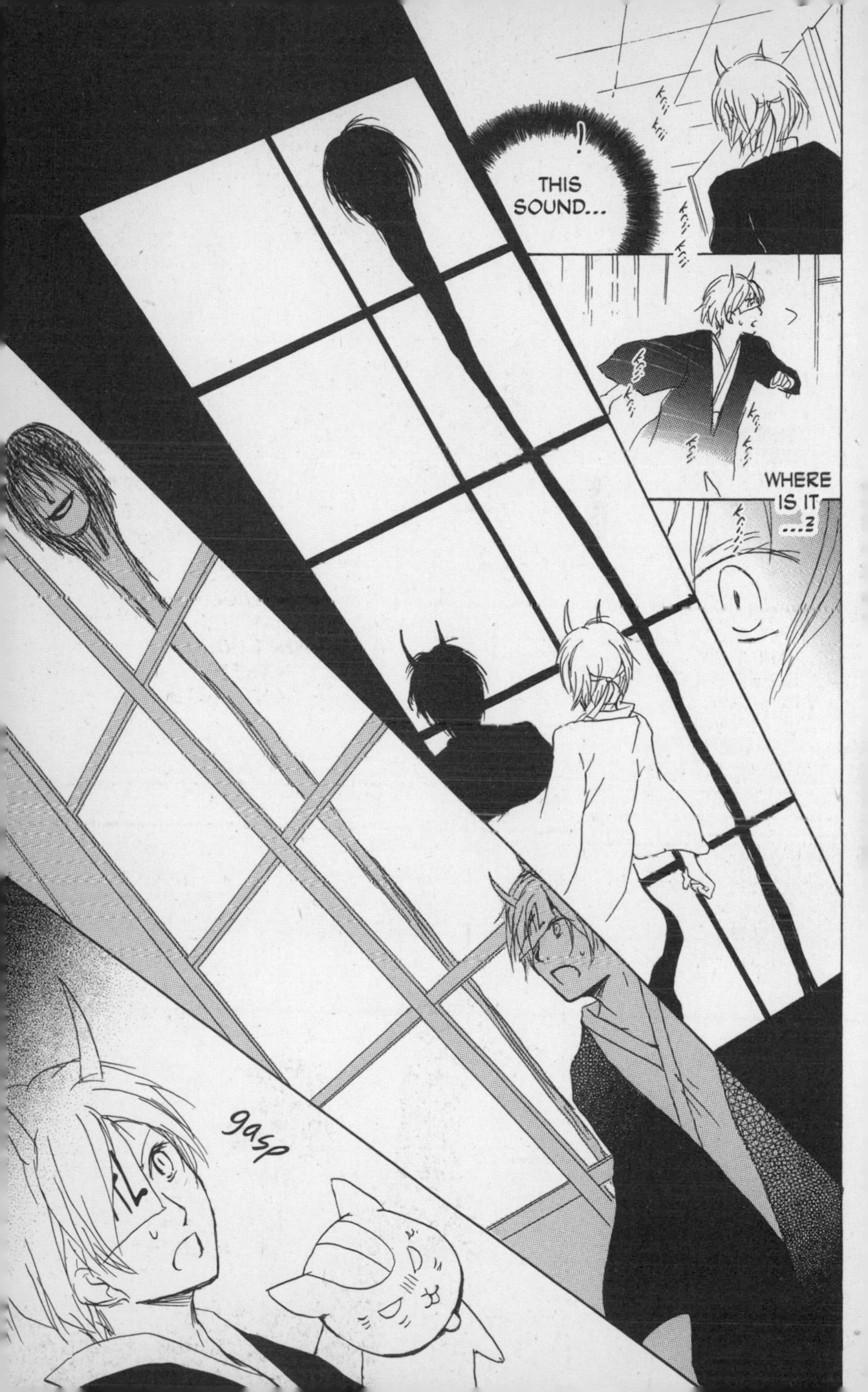

kriii
kriii
!
THIS SOUND...
kriii
kriii
kriii
WHERE IS IT ...?
gasp

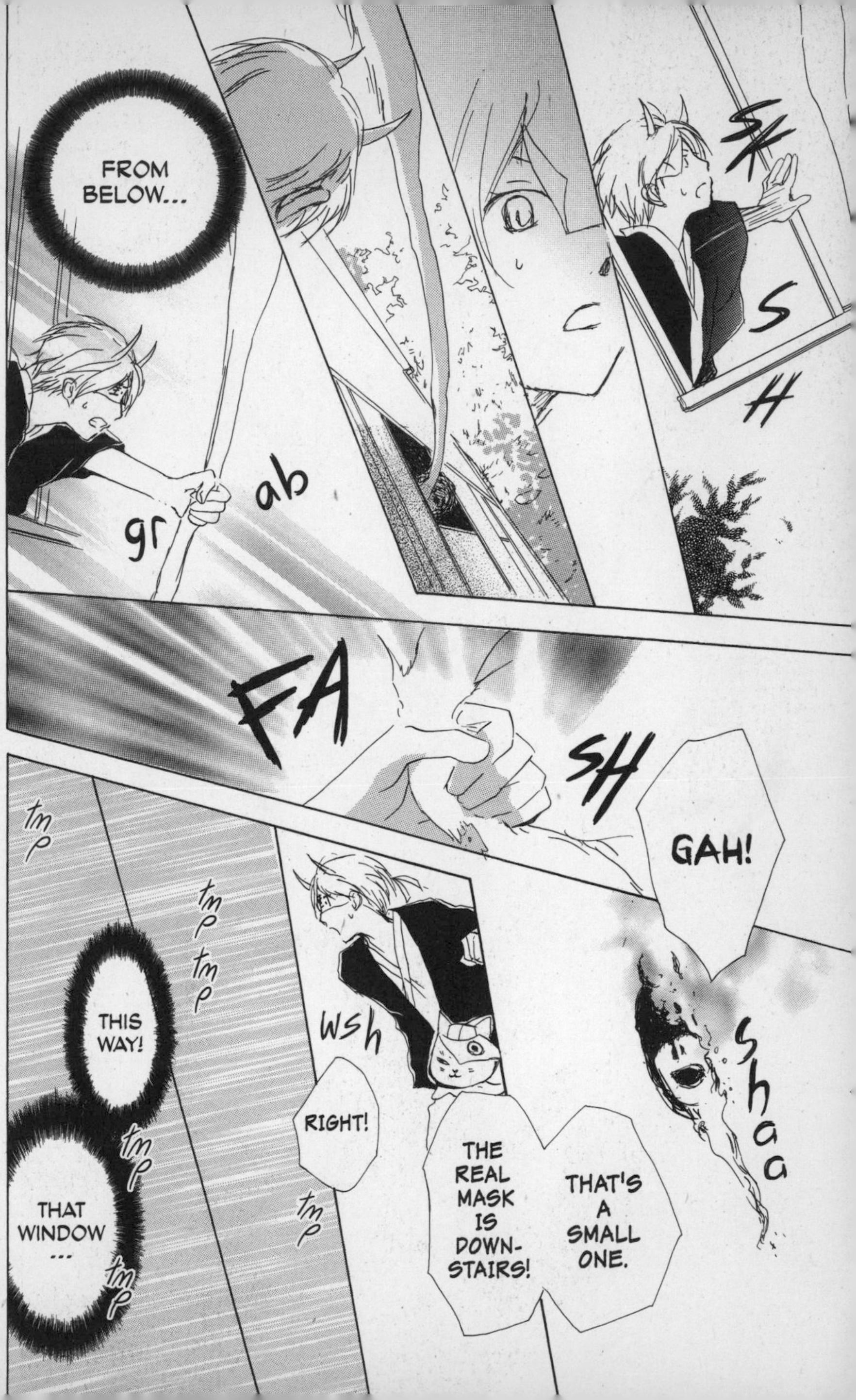
SKSH
FROM BELOW...
gr ab
FA SH
GAH!
Shaa
THAT'S A SMALL ONE.
THE REAL MASK IS DOWN-STAIRS!
RIGHT!
wsh
tmp
tmp tmp
THIS WAY!
tmp
tmp
THAT WINDOW ...
tmp

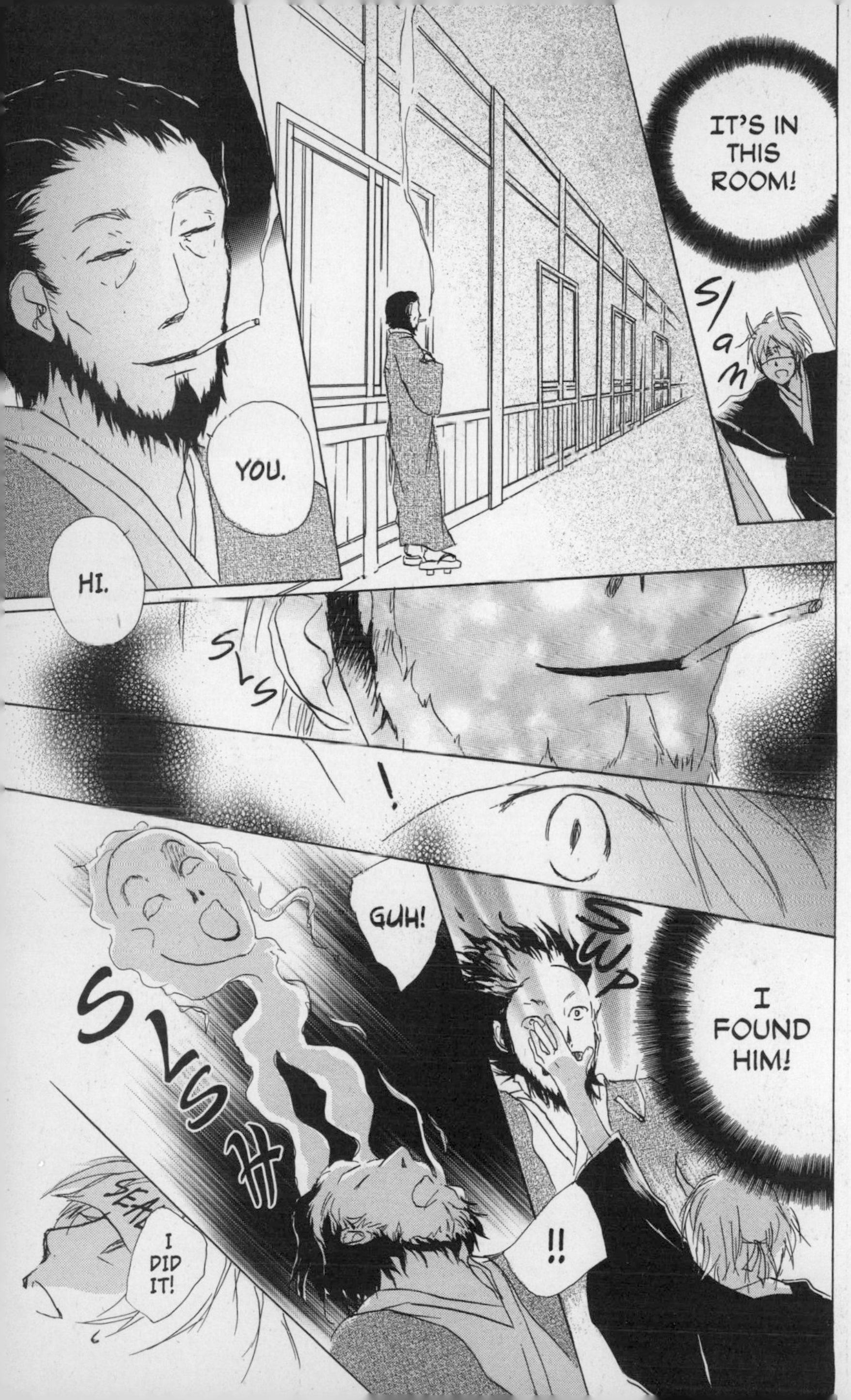
IT'S IN THIS ROOM!
SLAM
YOU.
HI.
SLS
!
I FOUND HIM!
SWP
GUH!
!!
I DID IT!

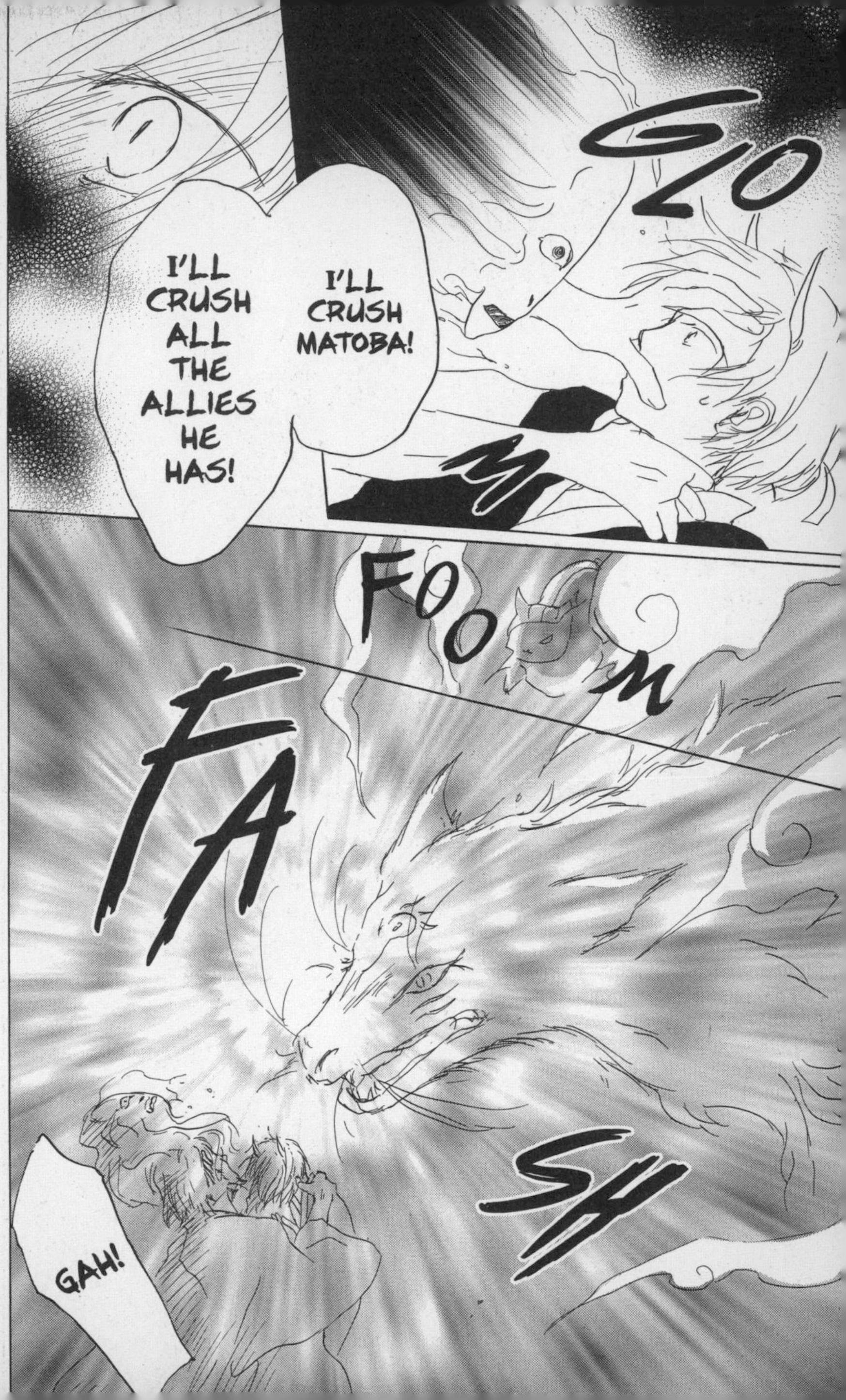
I'LL CRUSH MATOBA!
I'LL CRUSH ALL THE ALLIES HE HAS!
FOOM
FA
SH
GAH!

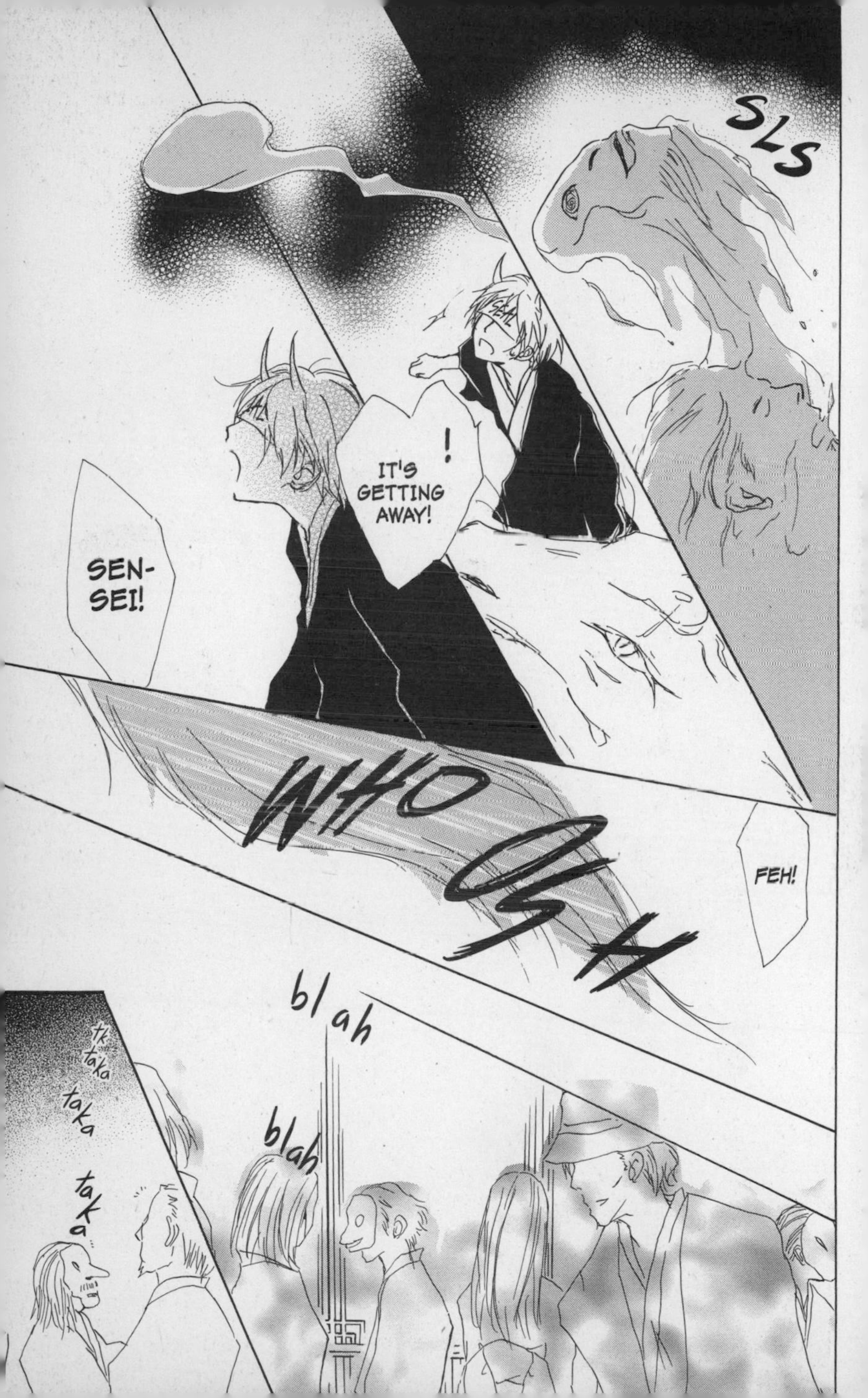
SLS
!
IT'S GETTING AWAY!
SEN-SEI!
FEH!
WHOOSH
blah
blah
tk taka
taka
taka...

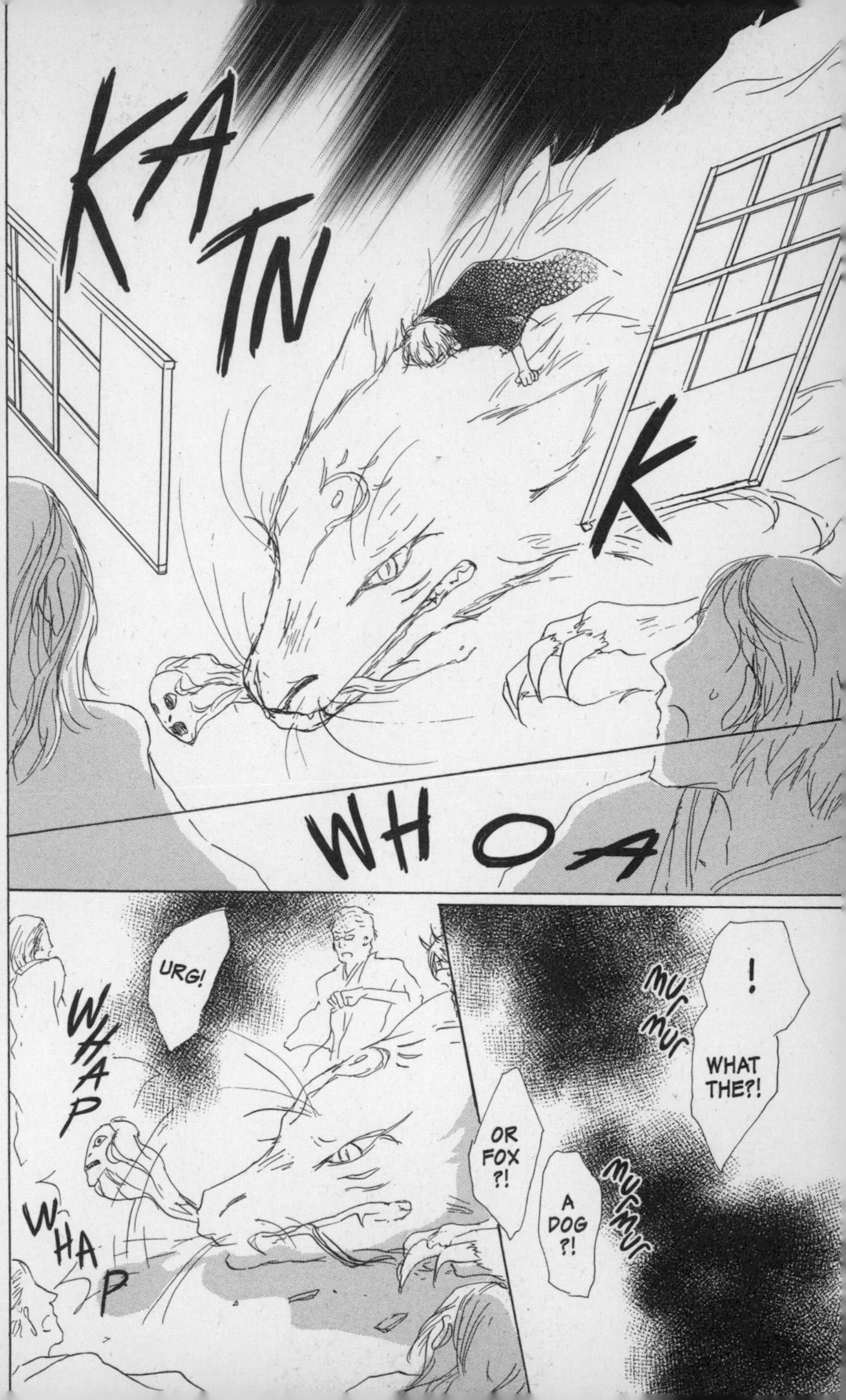
KA TN K
WHOA
!
WHAT THE?!
mur mur
URG!
WHAP
OR FOX ?!
A DOG ?!
mur mur
WHAP

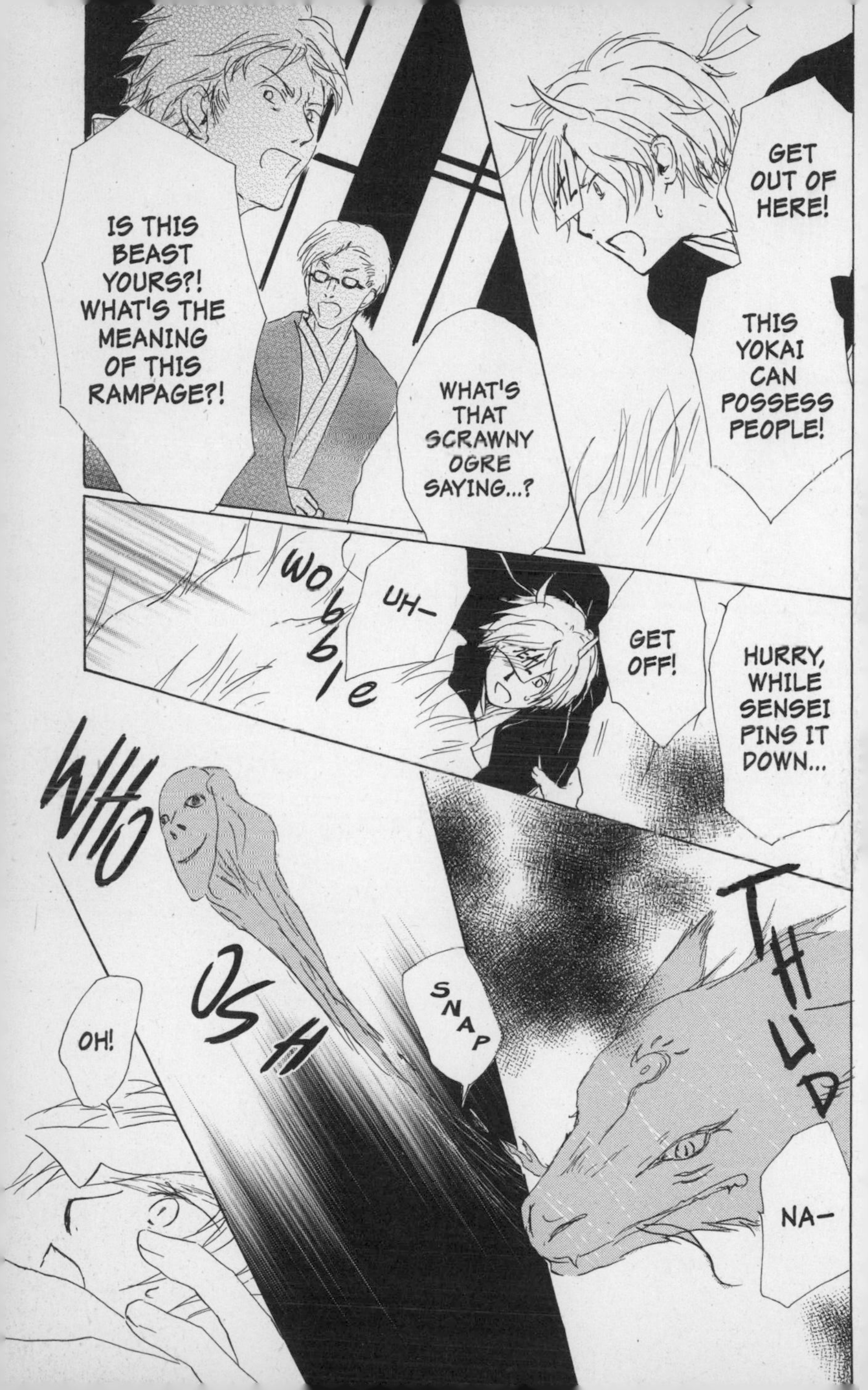

GET OUT OF HERE!
THIS YOKAI CAN POSSESS PEOPLE!
WHAT'S THAT SCRAWNY OGRE SAYING...?
IS THIS BEAST YOURS?! WHAT'S THE MEANING OF THIS RAMPAGE?!
HURRY, WHILE SENSEI PINS IT DOWN...
GET OFF!
UH-
wobble
THUD
NA-
SNAP
WHOOSH
OH!

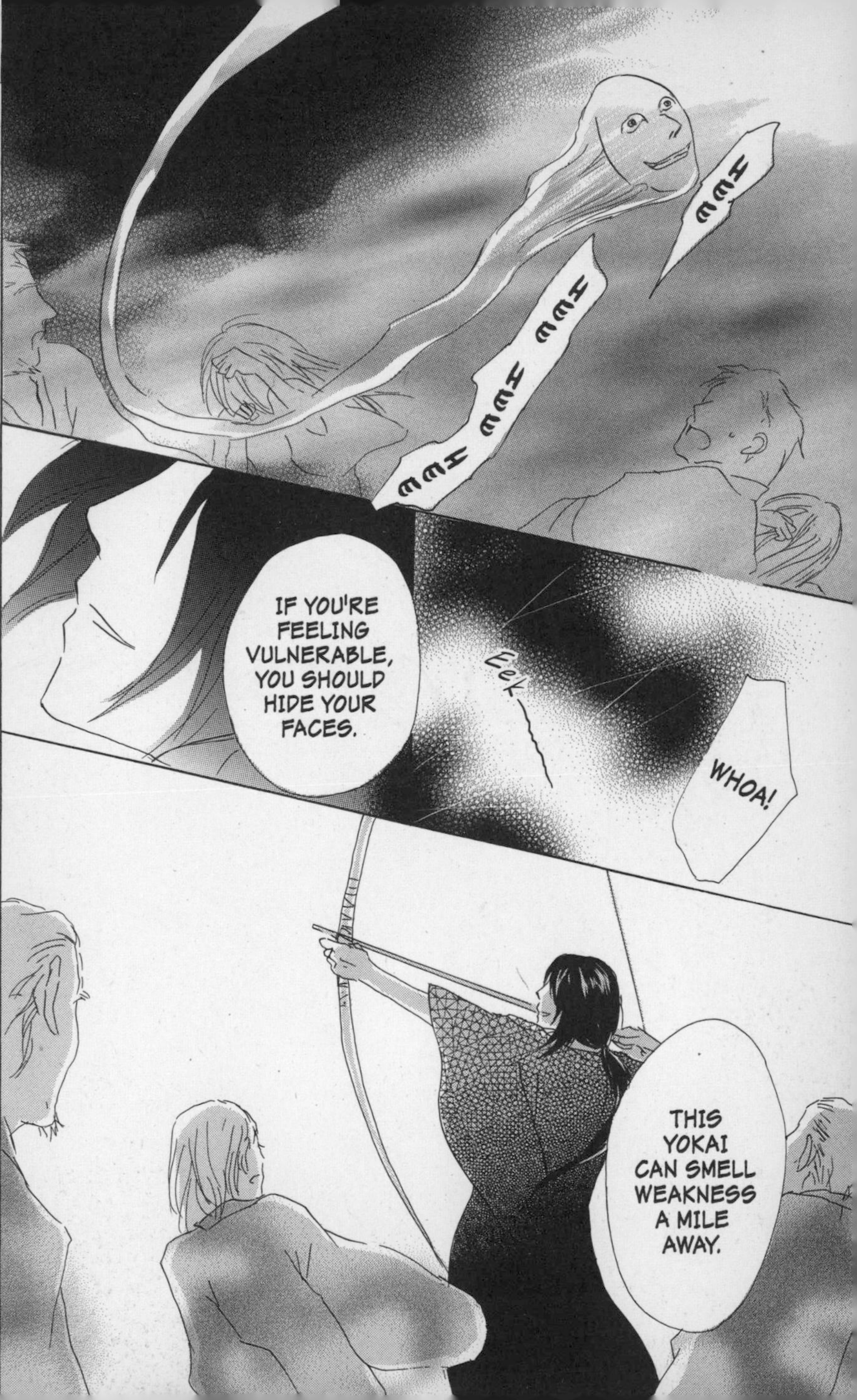
HEE
HEE HEE HEE
Eek—
WHOA!
IF YOU'RE FEELING VULNERABLE, YOU SHOULD HIDE YOUR FACES.
THIS YOKAI CAN SMELL WEAKNESS A MILE AWAY.

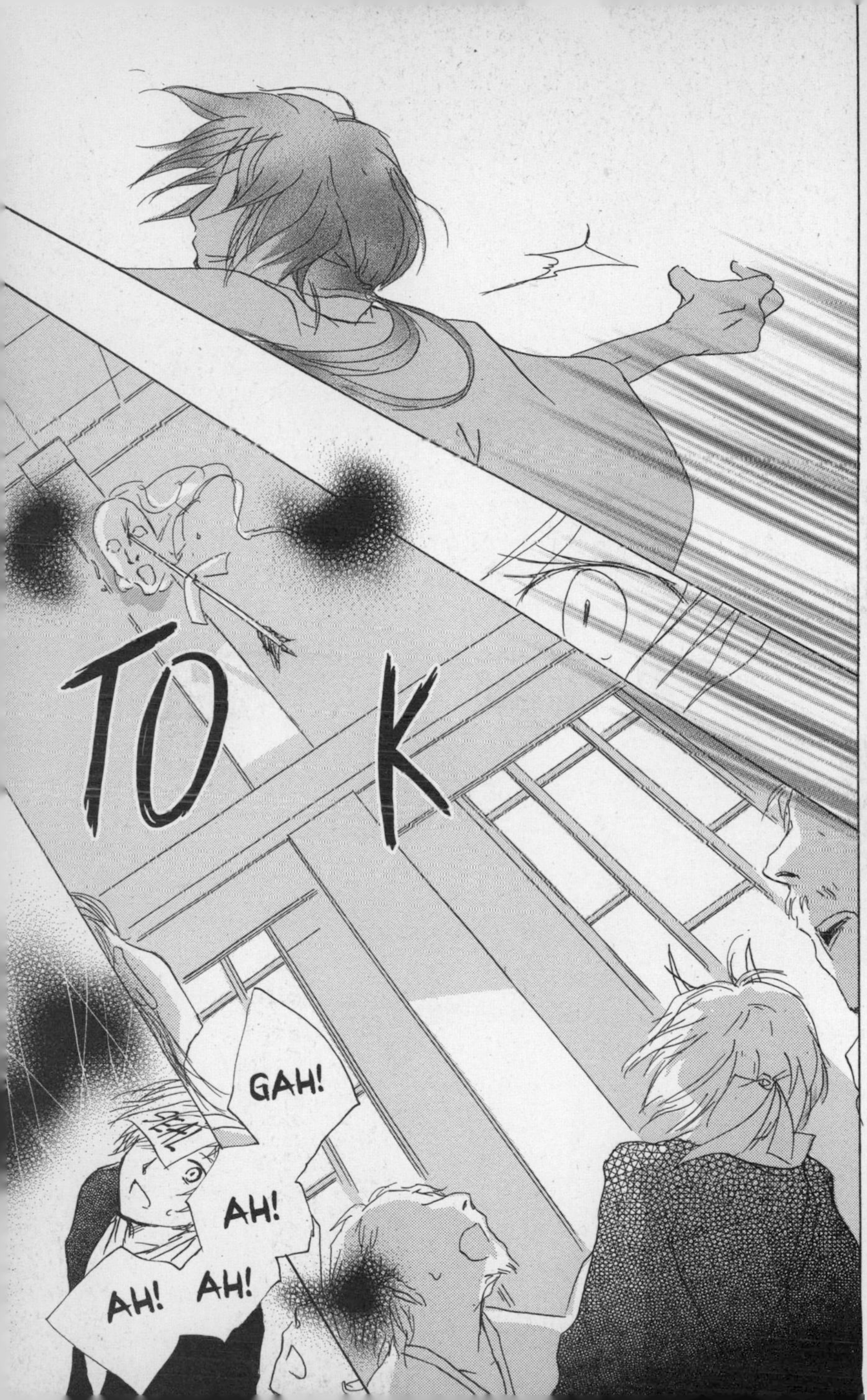
TOK
GAH!
SEAL
AH!
AH!
AH!

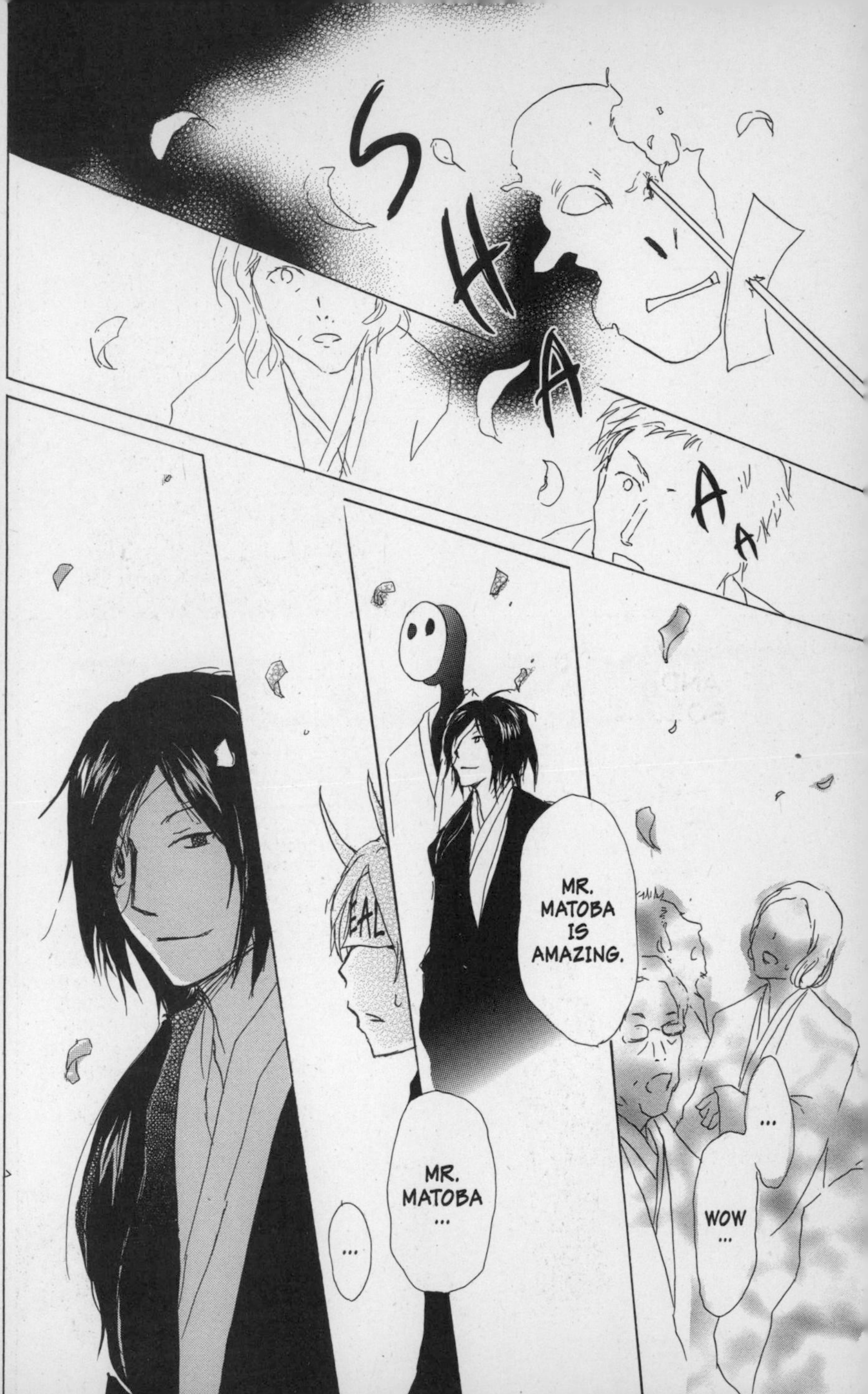
SHA
AA
MR. MATOBA IS AMAZING.
...
WOW ...
MR. MATOBA ...
...

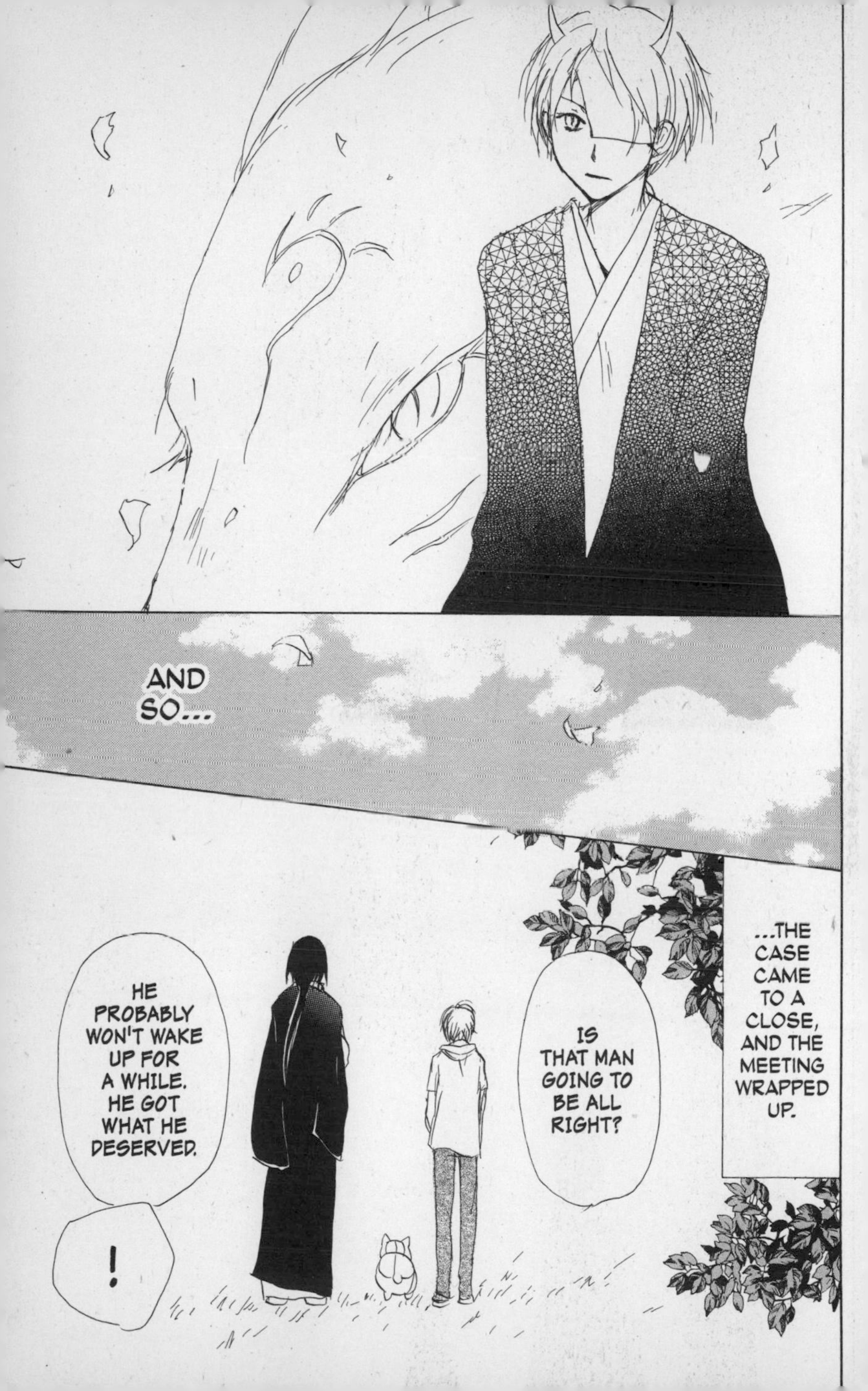
AND SO...
...THE CASE CAME TO A CLOSE, AND THE MEETING WRAPPED UP.
IS THAT MAN GOING TO BE ALL RIGHT?
HE PROBABLY WON'T WAKE UP FOR A WHILE. HE GOT WHAT HE DESERVED.
!

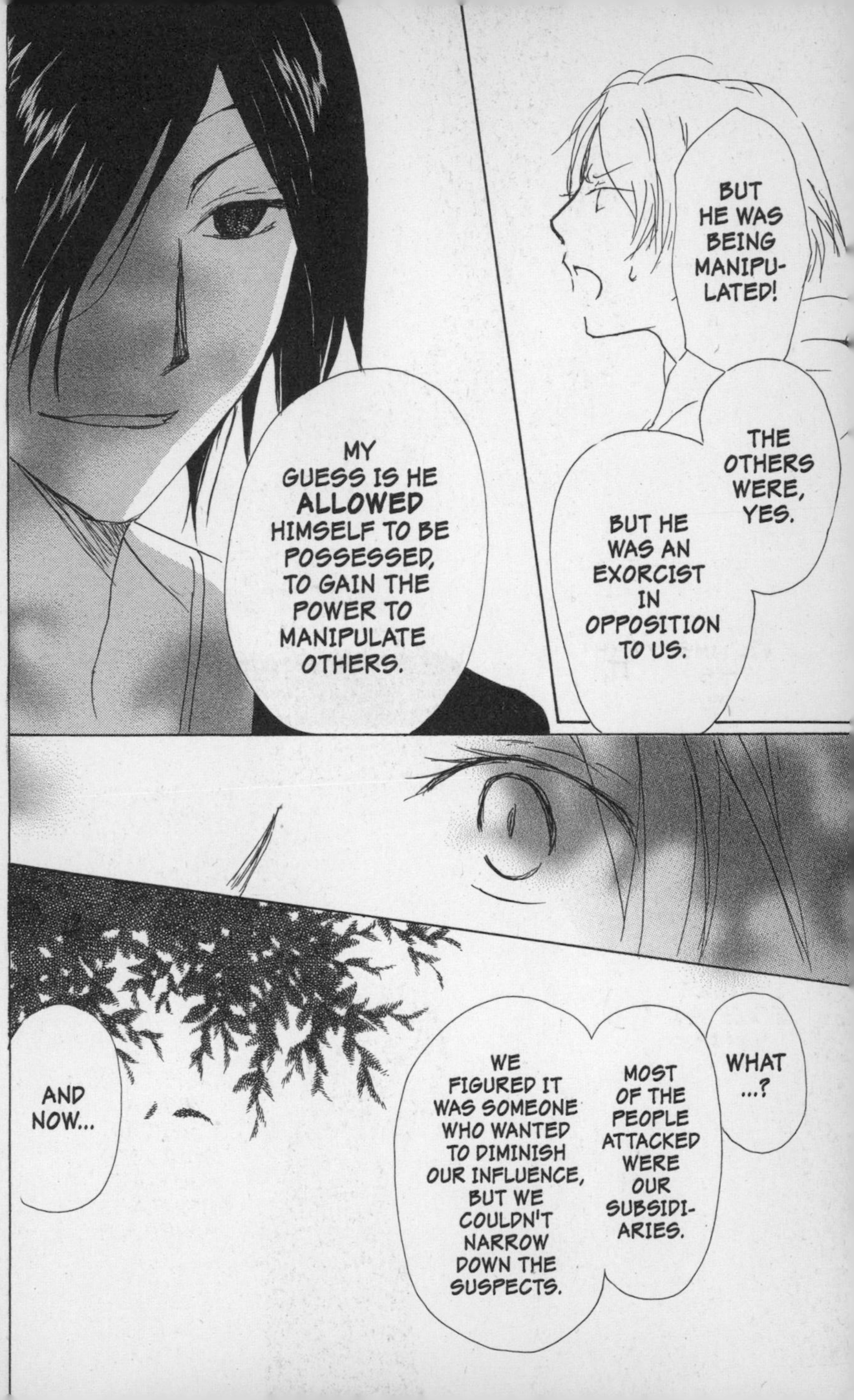
BUT HE WAS BEING MANIPULATED!
THE OTHERS WERE, YES.
BUT HE WAS AN EXORCIST IN OPPOSITION TO US.
MY GUESS IS HE **ALLOWED** HIMSELF TO BE POSSESSED, TO GAIN THE POWER TO MANIPULATE OTHERS.
WHAT ...?
MOST OF THE PEOPLE ATTACKED WERE OUR SUBSIDIARIES.
WE FIGURED IT WAS SOMEONE WHO WANTED TO DIMINISH OUR INFLUENCE, BUT WE COULDN'T NARROW DOWN THE SUSPECTS.
AND NOW...

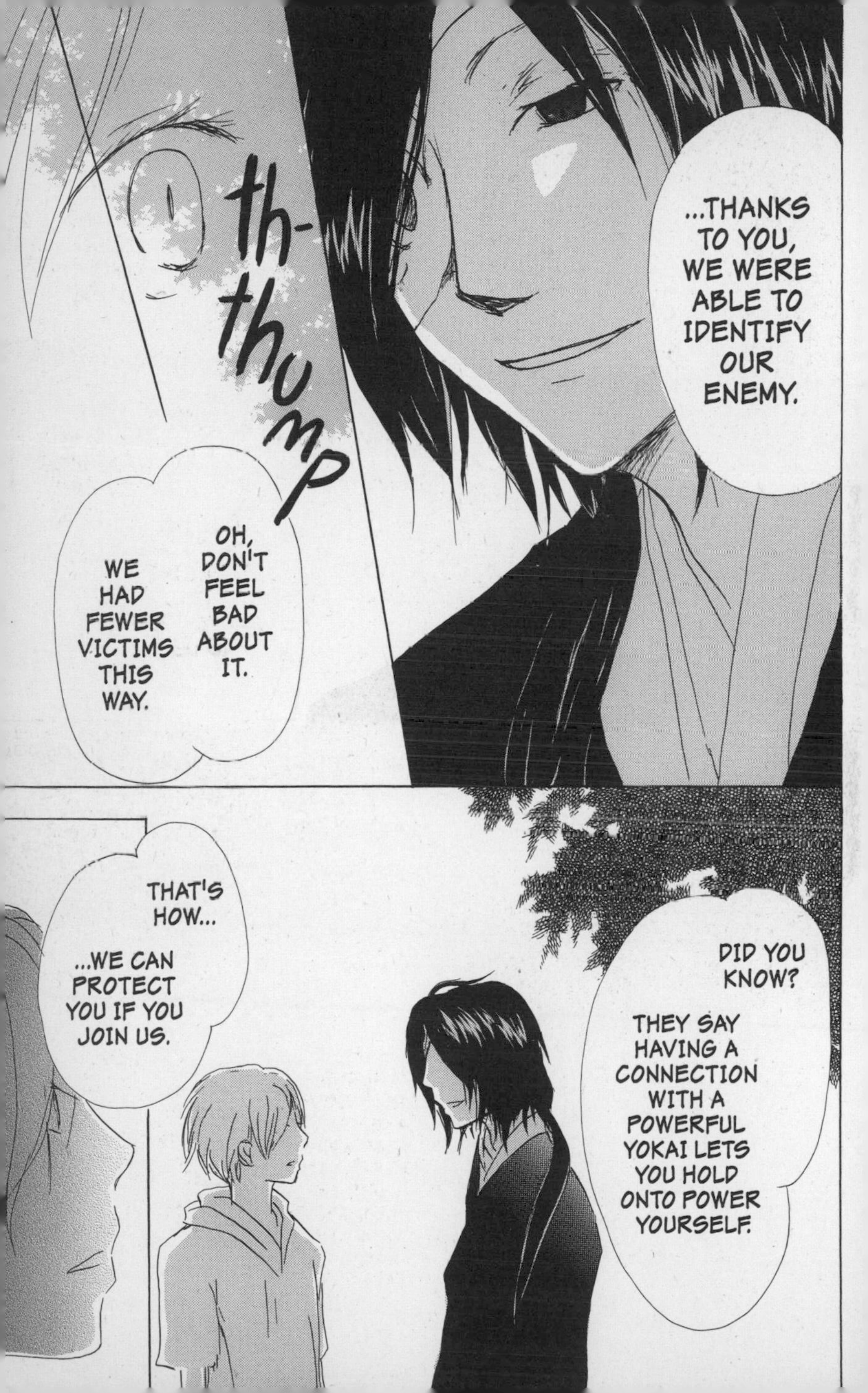
...THANKS TO YOU, WE WERE ABLE TO IDENTIFY OUR ENEMY.
th-thump
OH, DON'T FEEL BAD ABOUT IT.
WE HAD FEWER VICTIMS THIS WAY.
DID YOU KNOW?
THEY SAY HAVING A CONNECTION WITH A POWERFUL YOKAI LETS YOU HOLD ONTO POWER YOURSELF.
THAT'S HOW...
...WE CAN PROTECT YOU IF YOU JOIN US.

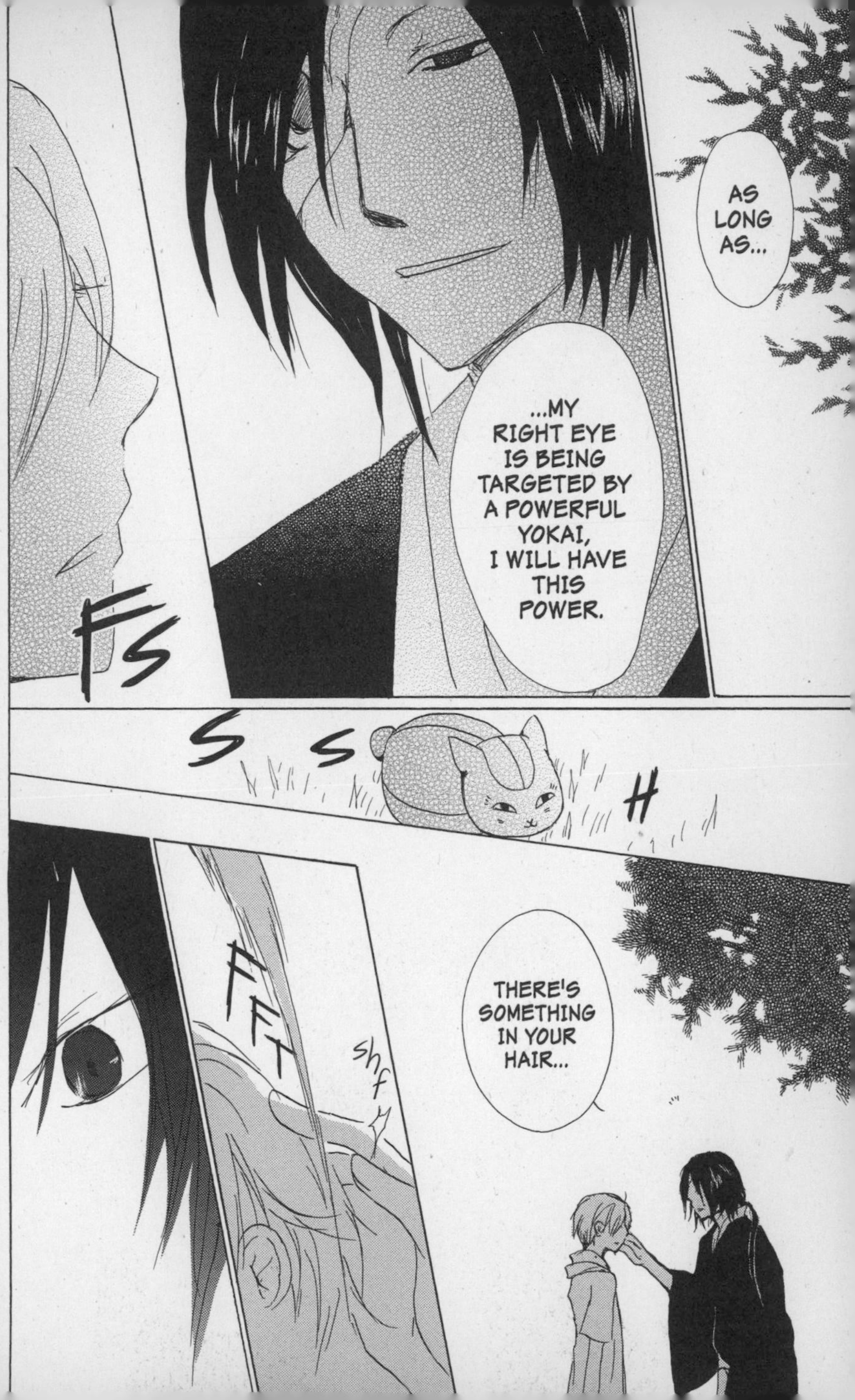
AS LONG AS...
...MY RIGHT EYE IS BEING TARGETED BY A POWERFUL YOKAI, I WILL HAVE THIS POWER.
FS
SSSH
THERE'S SOMETHING IN YOUR HAIR...
FFFT
shfy

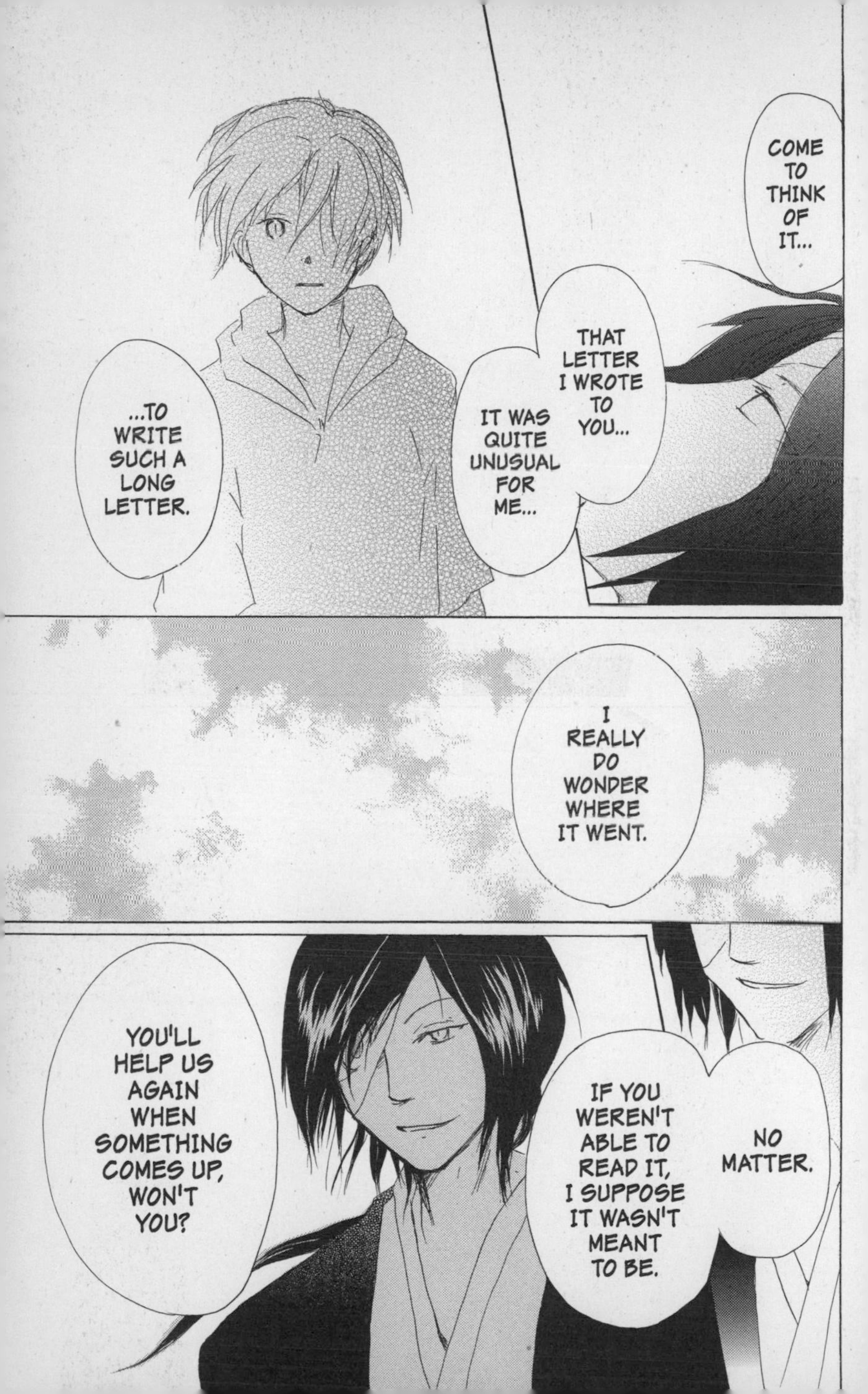
COME TO THINK OF IT...
THAT LETTER I WROTE TO YOU...
IT WAS QUITE UNUSUAL FOR ME...
...TO WRITE SUCH A LONG LETTER.
I REALLY DO WONDER WHERE IT WENT.
NO MATTER.
IF YOU WEREN'T ABLE TO READ IT, I SUPPOSE IT WASN'T MEANT TO BE.
YOU'LL HELP US AGAIN WHEN SOMETHING COMES UP, WON'T YOU?

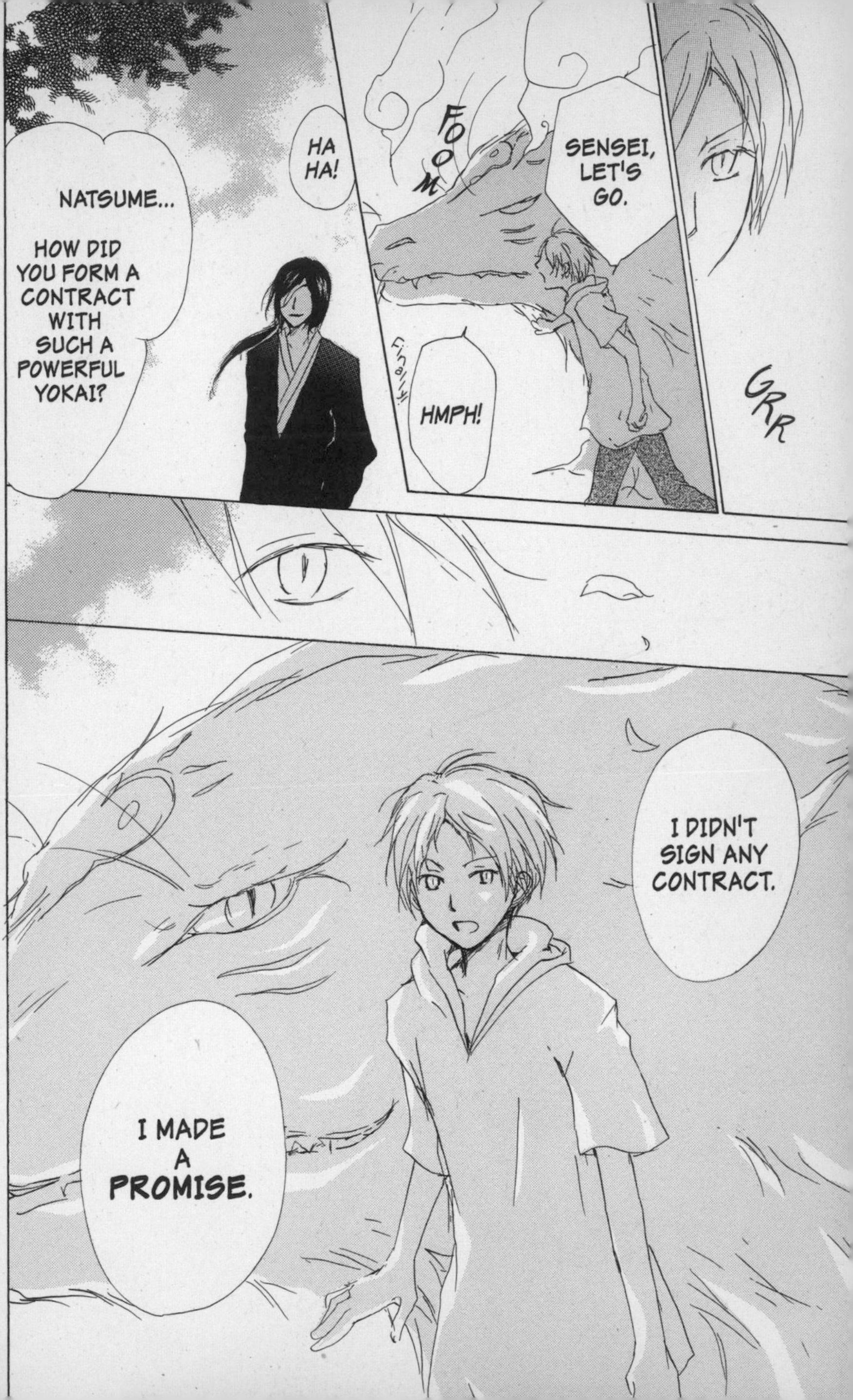
GRR
SENSEI, LET'S GO.
FOOM
HA HA!
Finally!
HMPH!
NATSUME...
HOW DID YOU FORM A CONTRACT WITH SUCH A POWERFUL YOKAI?
I DIDN'T SIGN ANY CONTRACT.
I MADE A PROMISE.

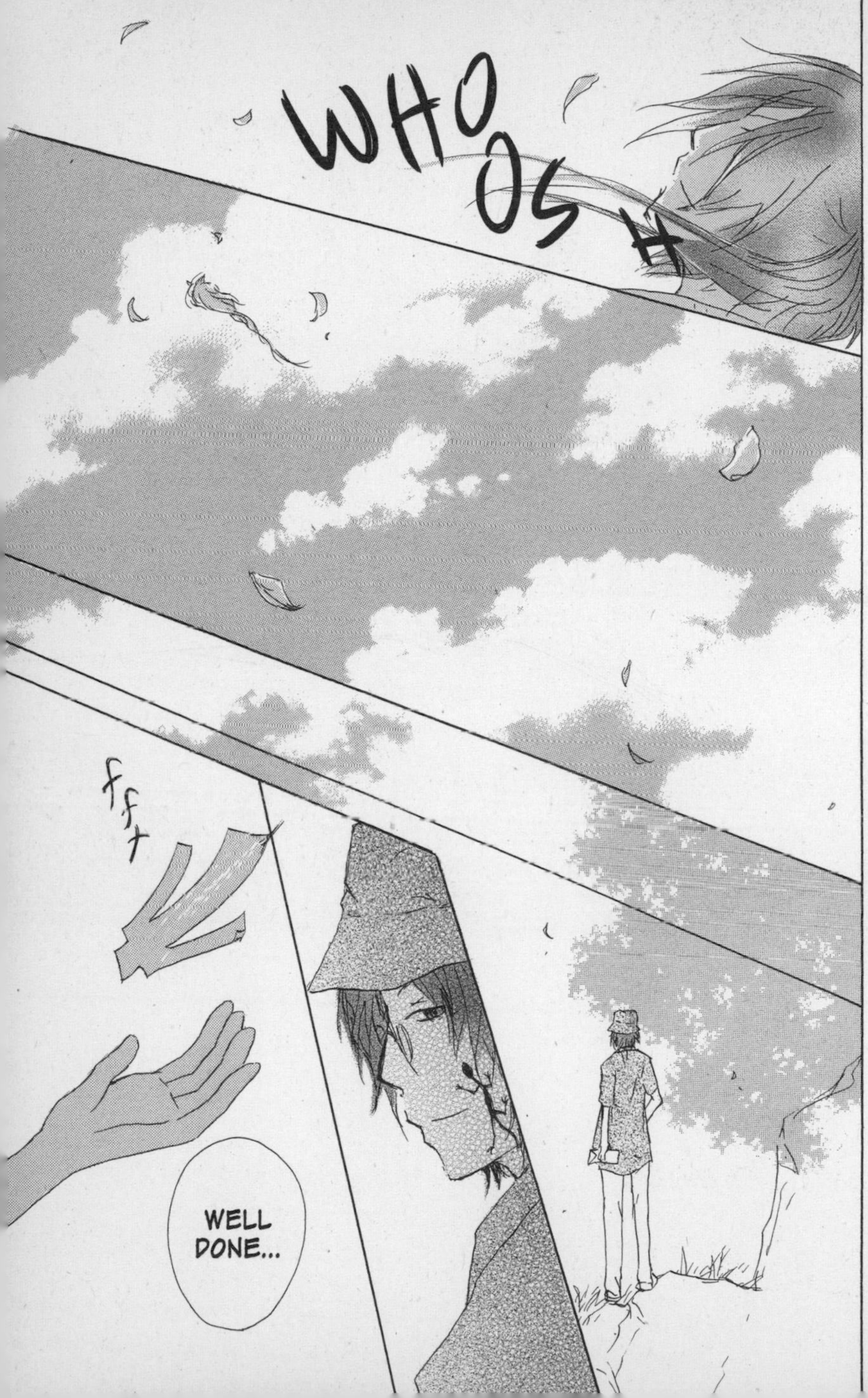
WHOOSH
fft
WELL DONE...

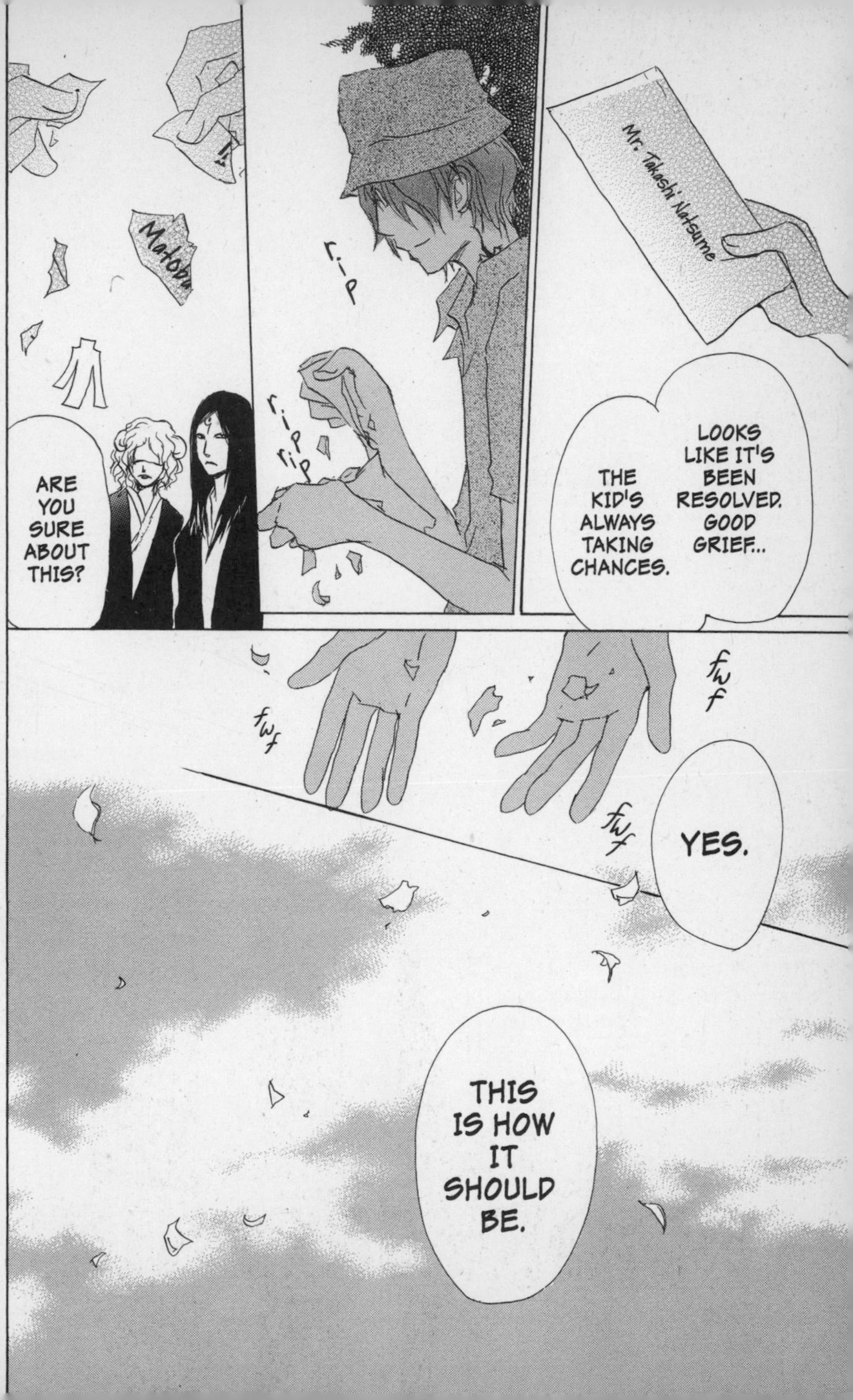
Mr. Takashi Natsume
LOOKS LIKE IT'S BEEN RESOLVED. GOOD GRIEF...
THE KID'S ALWAYS TAKING CHANCES.
rip
rip rip
ARE YOU SURE ABOUT THIS?
fwf
fwf
fwf
YES.
THIS IS HOW IT SHOULD BE.

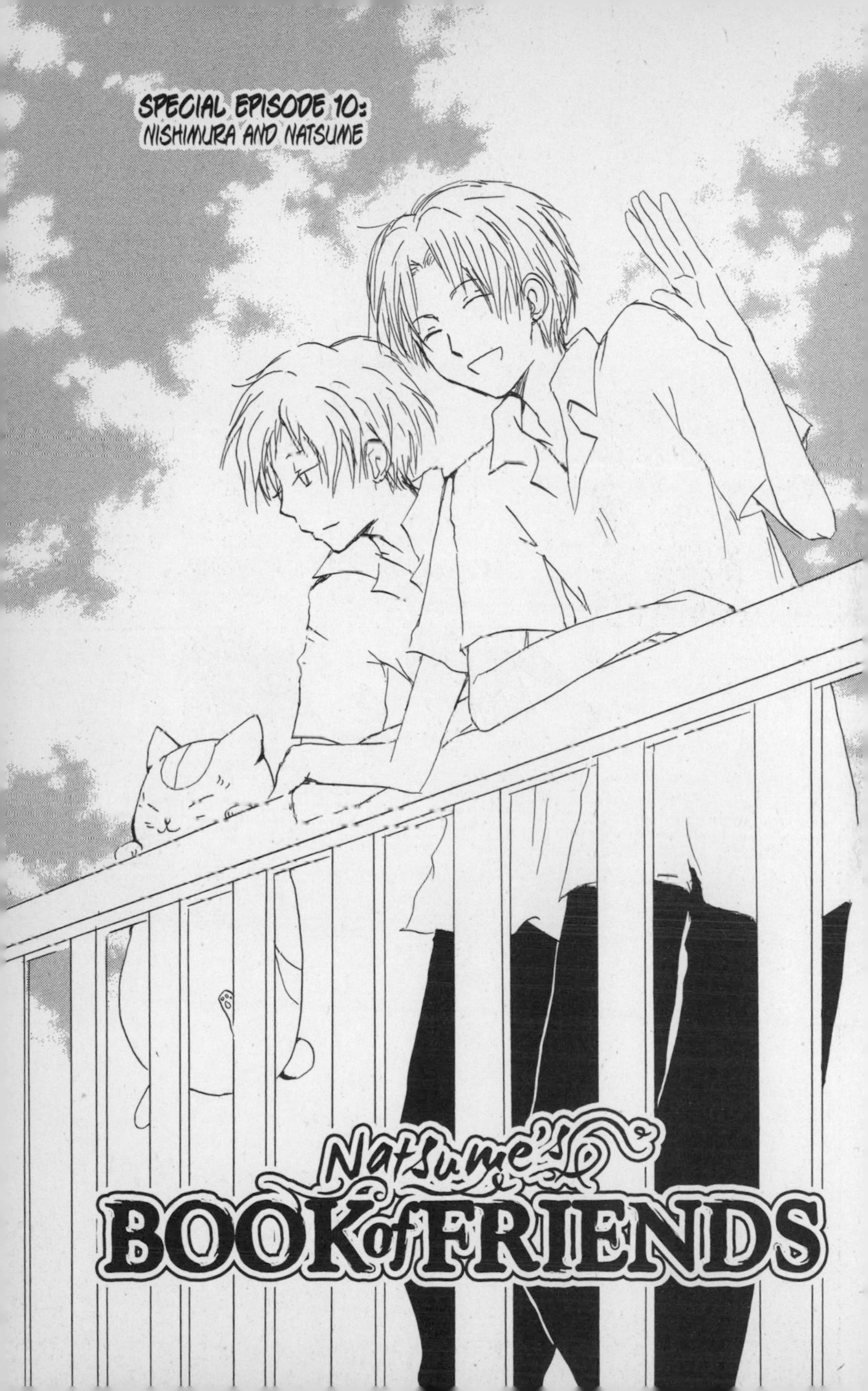
SPECIAL EPISODE 10:
NISHIMURA AND NATSUME
Natsume's
BOOK of FRIENDS

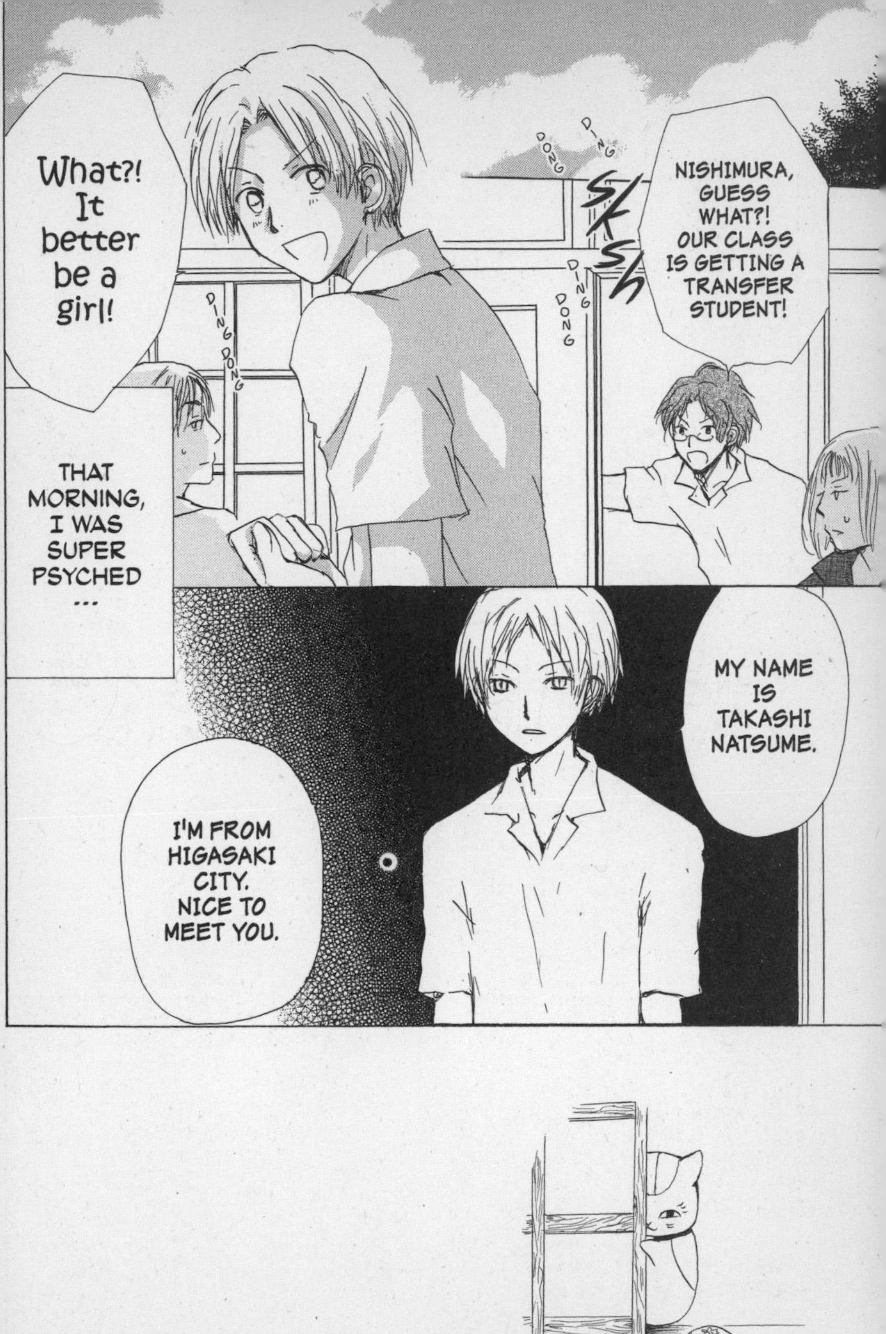
NISHIMURA, GUESS WHAT?! OUR CLASS IS GETTING A TRANSFER STUDENT!
DING DONG
SKSH
DING DONG
DING DONG
What?! It better be a girl!
THAT MORNING, I WAS SUPER PSYCHED ...
MY NAME IS TAKASHI NATSUME.
I'M FROM HIGASAKI CITY. NICE TO MEET YOU.

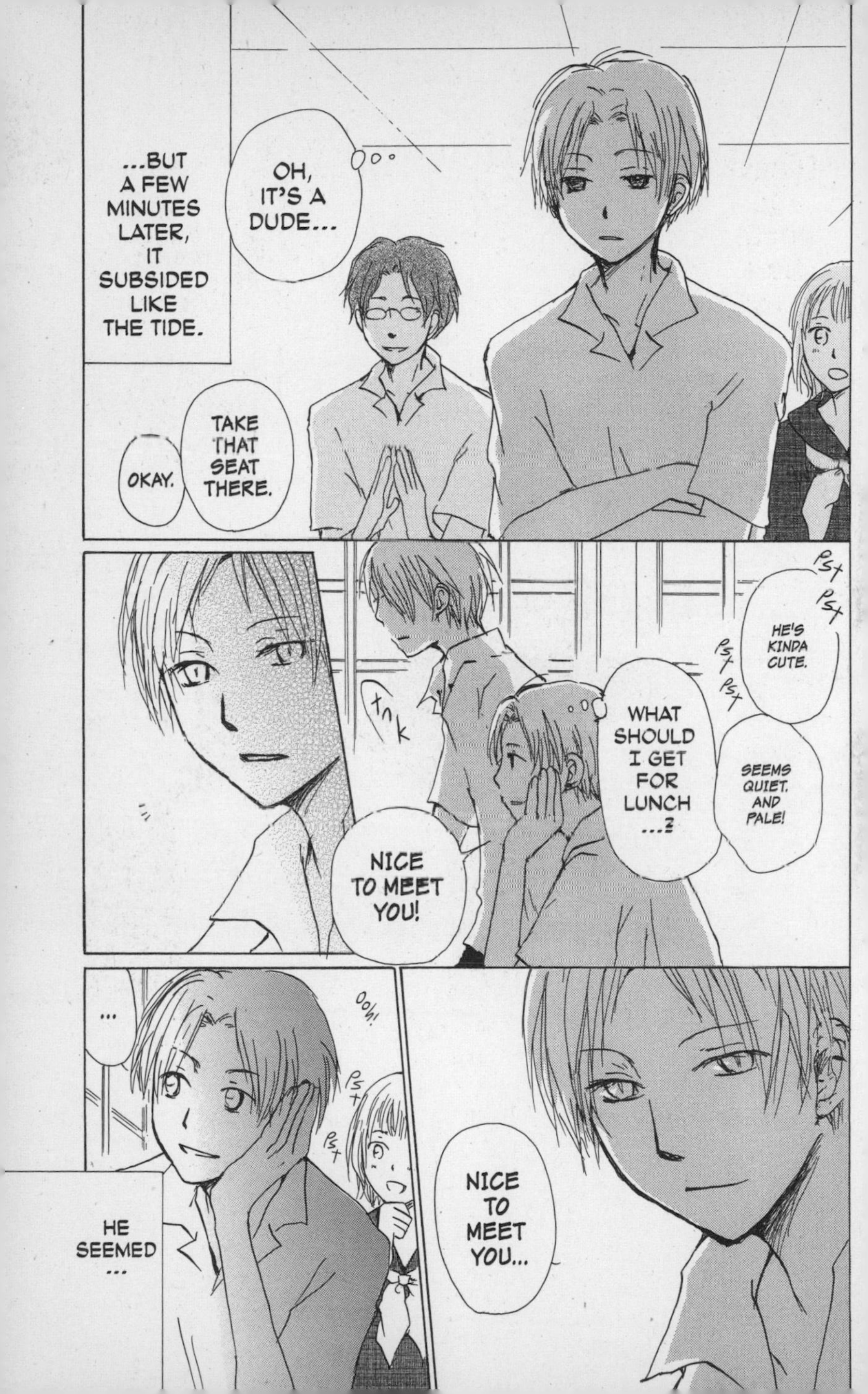
OH, IT'S A DUDE...
...BUT A FEW MINUTES LATER, IT SUBSIDED LIKE THE TIDE.
TAKE THAT SEAT THERE.
OKAY.
Psst Psst
HE'S KINDA CUTE.
Psst Psst
SEEMS QUIET. AND PALE!
WHAT SHOULD I GET FOR LUNCH ...?
tnk
NICE TO MEET YOU!
NICE TO MEET YOU...
Ooh!
Psst
Psst
...
HE SEEMED ...

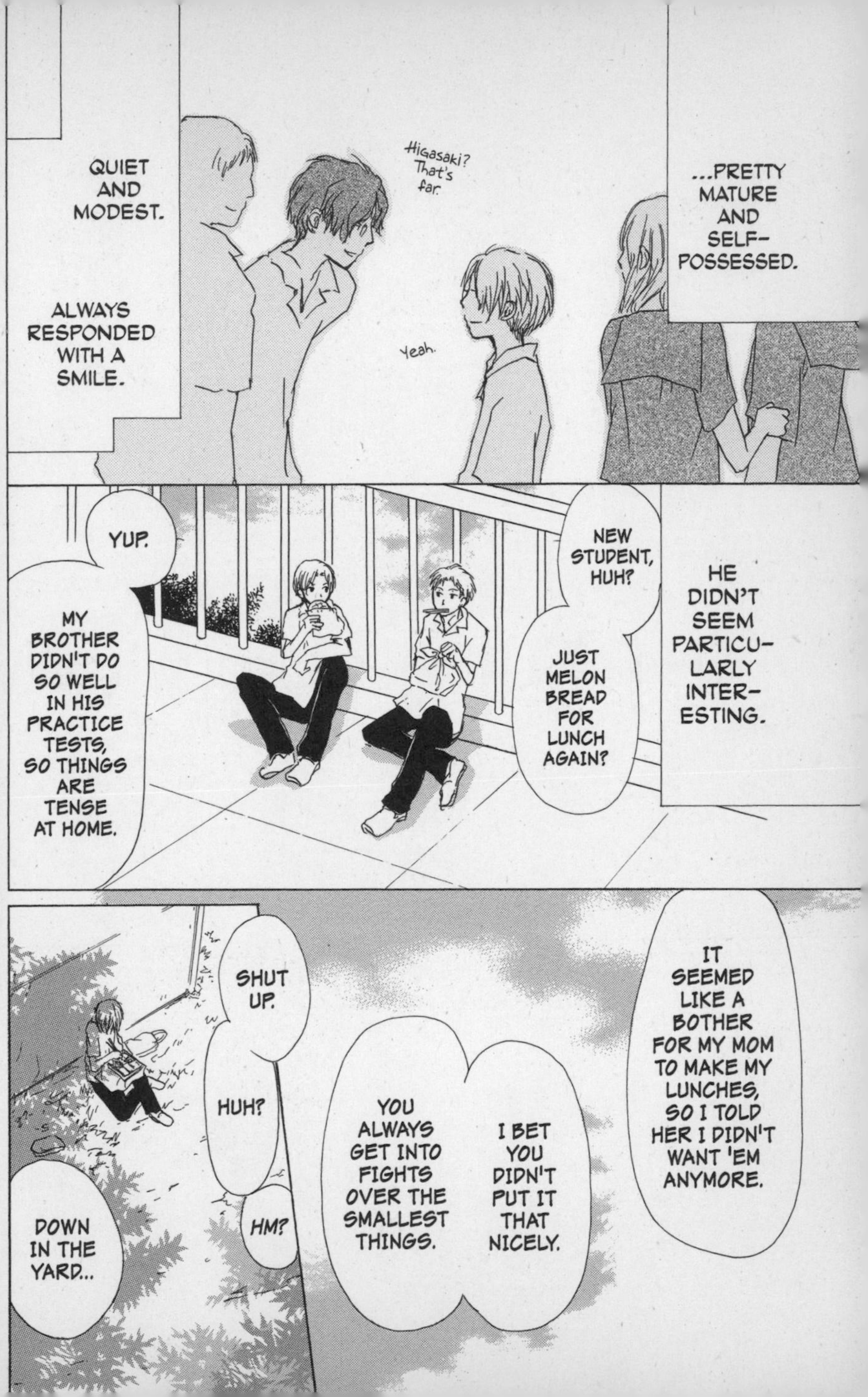
...PRETTY MATURE AND SELF-POSSESSED.
Higasaki? That's far.
Yeah.
QUIET AND MODEST.
ALWAYS RESPONDED WITH A SMILE.
HE DIDN'T SEEM PARTICU-LARLY INTER-ESTING.
NEW STUDENT, HUH?
JUST MELON BREAD FOR LUNCH AGAIN?
YUP.
MY BROTHER DIDN'T DO SO WELL IN HIS PRACTICE TESTS, SO THINGS ARE TENSE AT HOME.
IT SEEMED LIKE A BOTHER FOR MY MOM TO MAKE MY LUNCHES, SO I TOLD HER I DIDN'T WANT 'EM ANYMORE.
I BET YOU DIDN'T PUT IT THAT NICELY.
YOU ALWAYS GET INTO FIGHTS OVER THE SMALLEST THINGS.
SHUT UP.
HUH?
HM?
DOWN IN THE YARD...

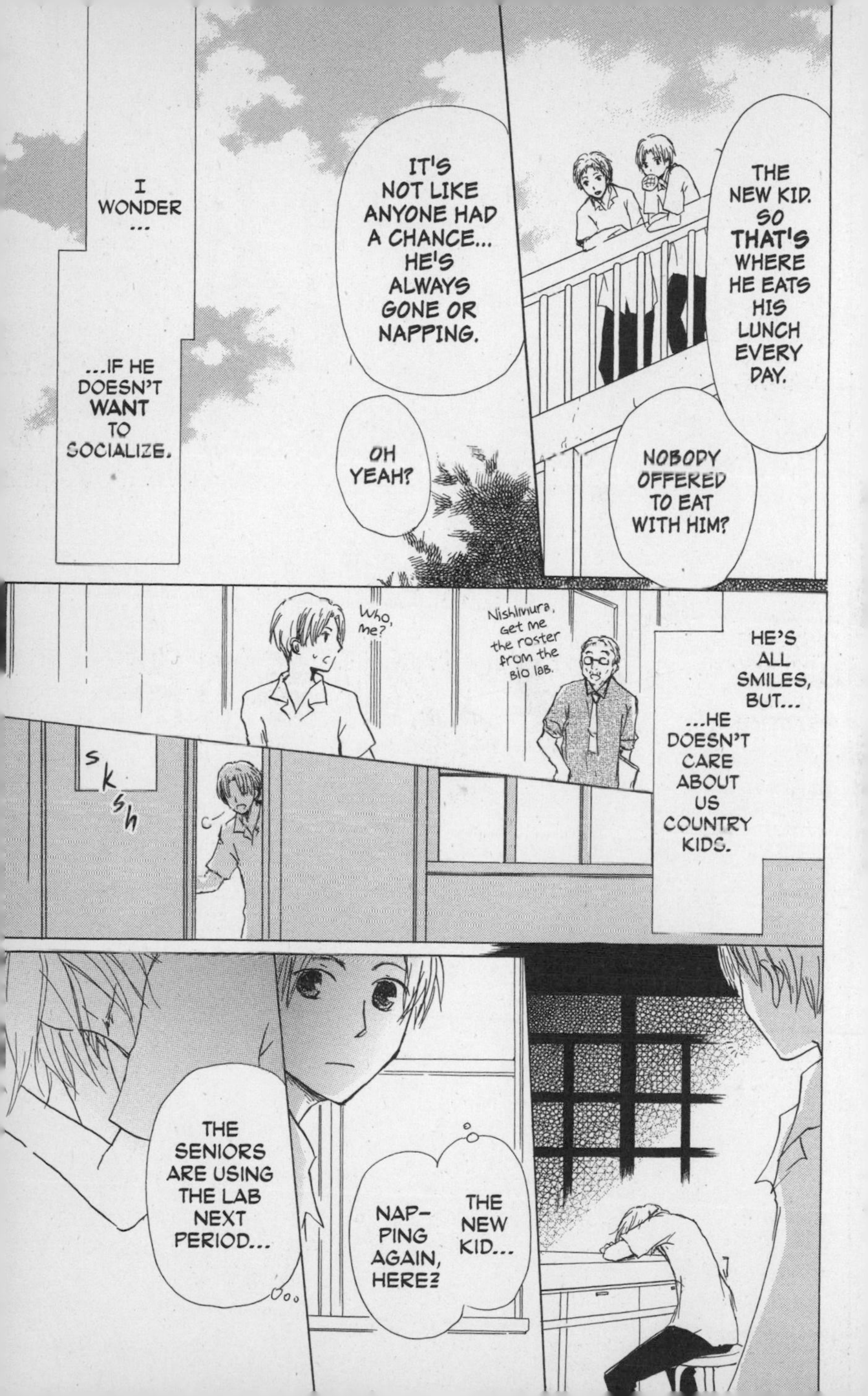
THE NEW KID. SO THAT'S WHERE HE EATS HIS LUNCH EVERY DAY.
NOBODY OFFERED TO EAT WITH HIM?
IT'S NOT LIKE ANYONE HAD A CHANCE... HE'S ALWAYS GONE OR NAPPING.
OH YEAH?
I WONDER ...
...IF HE DOESN'T WANT TO SOCIALIZE.
HE'S ALL SMILES, BUT...
...HE DOESN'T CARE ABOUT US COUNTRY KIDS.
Nishimura, get me the roster from the bio lab.
Who, me?
sksh
THE NEW KID...
NAP-PING AGAIN, HERE?
THE SENIORS ARE USING THE LAB NEXT PERIOD...

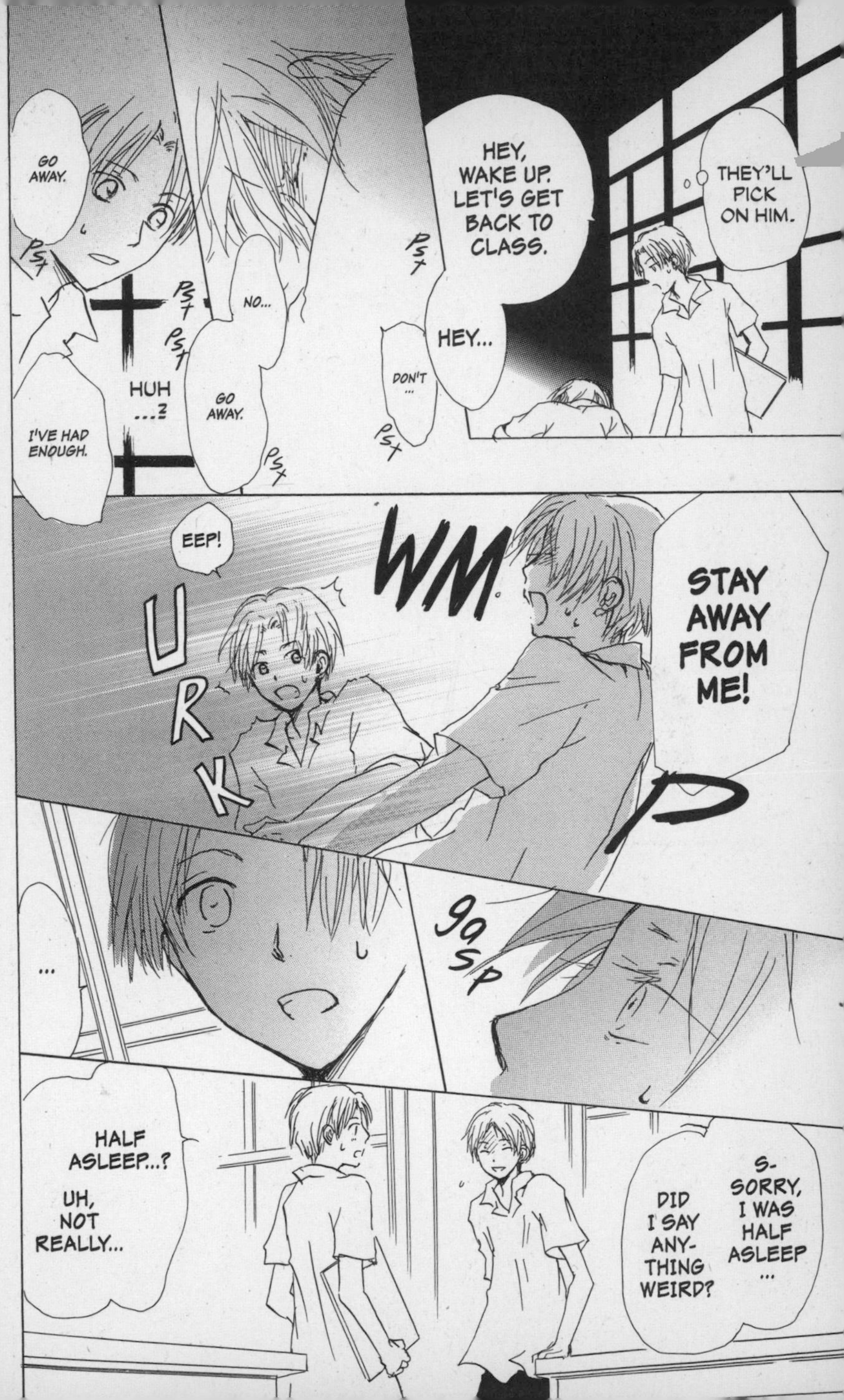
THEY'LL PICK ON HIM.
HEY, WAKE UP. LET'S GET BACK TO CLASS.
PST
HEY...
DON'T...
PST
NO...
PST
PST
GO AWAY.
PST
GO AWAY.
PST
HUH...?
I'VE HAD ENOUGH.
STAY AWAY FROM ME!
WMP
EEP!
URK
gasp
...
S-SORRY, I WAS HALF ASLEEP...
DID I SAY ANY-THING WEIRD?
HALF ASLEEP...?
UH, NOT REALLY...

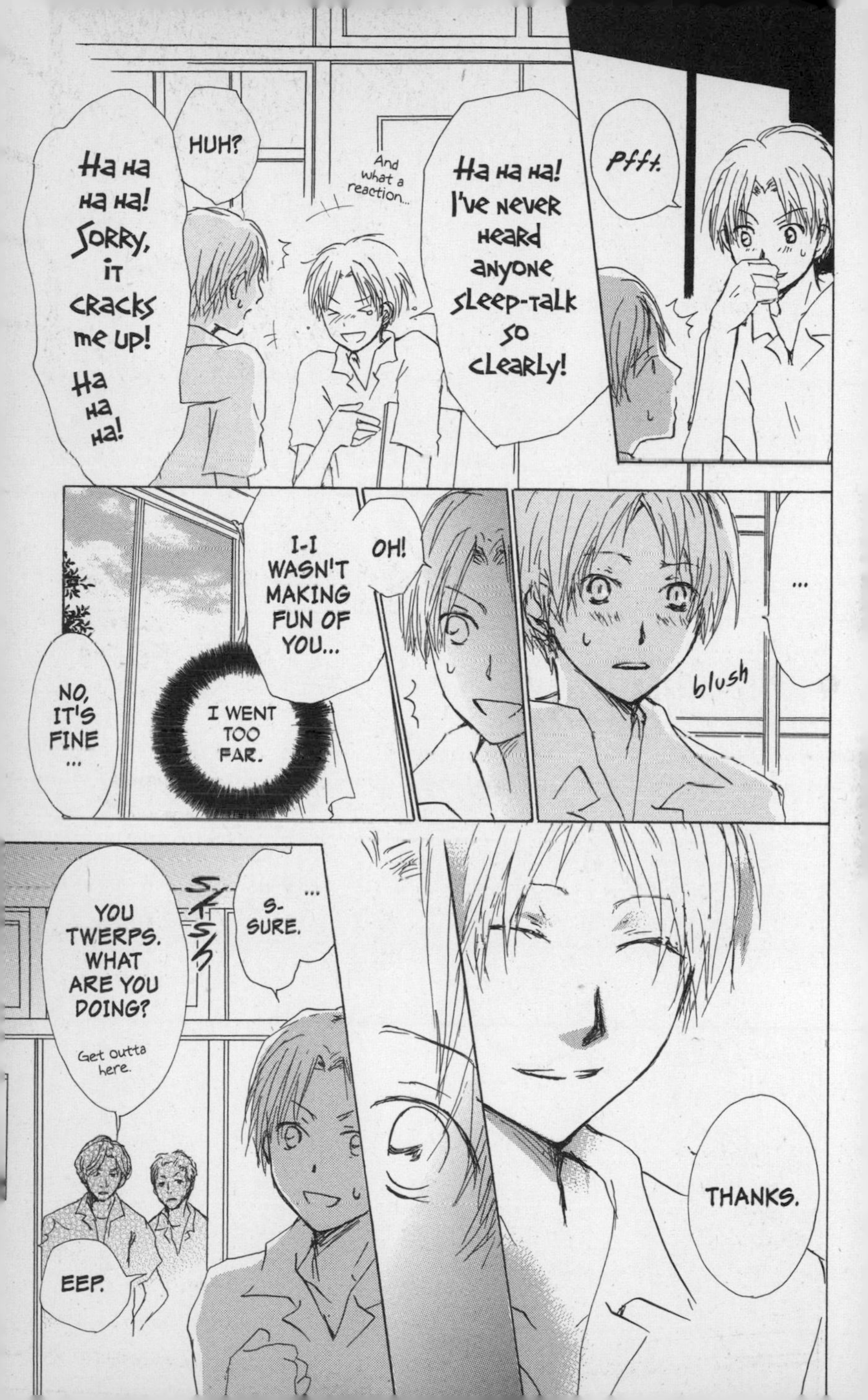
Pfft.
Ha ha ha! I've never heard anyone sleep-talk so clearly!
And what a reaction...
HUH?
Ha ha ha ha! Sorry, it cracks me up!
Ha ha ha!
...
blush
OH!
I-I WASN'T MAKING FUN OF YOU...
I WENT TOO FAR.
NO, IT'S FINE ...
THANKS.
... S-SURE.
YOU TWERPS. WHAT ARE YOU DOING?
Get outta here.
EEP.

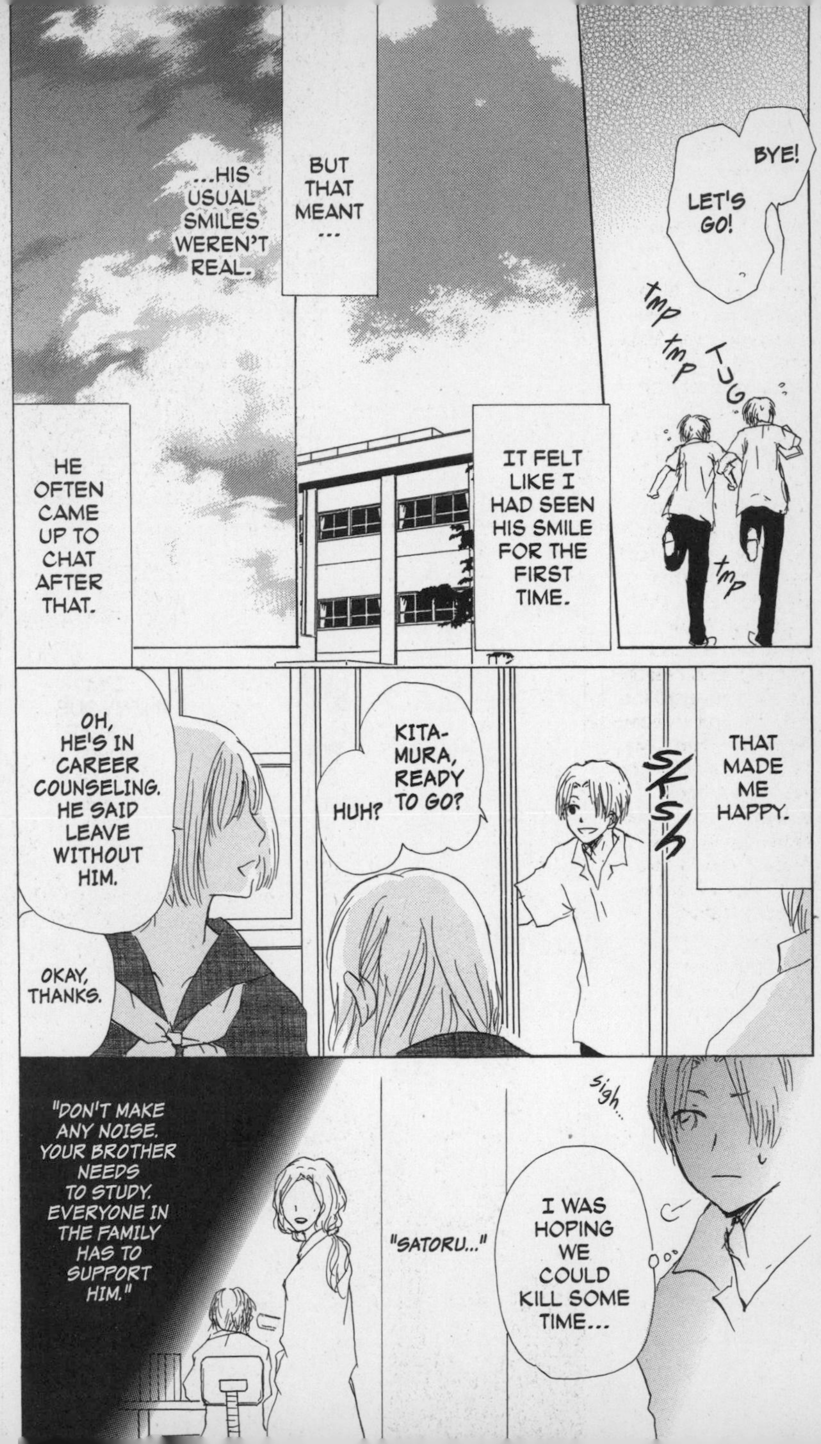
BYE!
LET'S GO!
tmp tmp
TUG
tmp
IT FELT LIKE I HAD SEEN HIS SMILE FOR THE FIRST TIME.
BUT THAT MEANT...
...HIS USUAL SMILES WEREN'T REAL.
HE OFTEN CAME UP TO CHAT AFTER THAT.
THAT MADE ME HAPPY.
SKSH
KITA-MURA, READY TO GO?
HUH?
OH, HE'S IN CAREER COUNSELING. HE SAID LEAVE WITHOUT HIM.
OKAY, THANKS.
sigh...
I WAS HOPING WE COULD KILL SOME TIME...
"SATORU..."
"DON'T MAKE ANY NOISE. YOUR BROTHER NEEDS TO STUDY. EVERYONE IN THE FAMILY HAS TO SUPPORT HIM."

04

❋Kitamoto

He's used to being conscientious. He thinks you can solve problems without getting angry or getting into a confrontation. That's what Natsume respects about Kitamoto. Kitamoto, on the other hand, likes Nishimura for his free-spirited nature. Kitamoto's a little awkward because he unconsciously feels responsible for everything. He has that in common with Natsume. I created Kitamoto hoping he could be someone who could hang out with Natsume without the two of them feeling nervous.

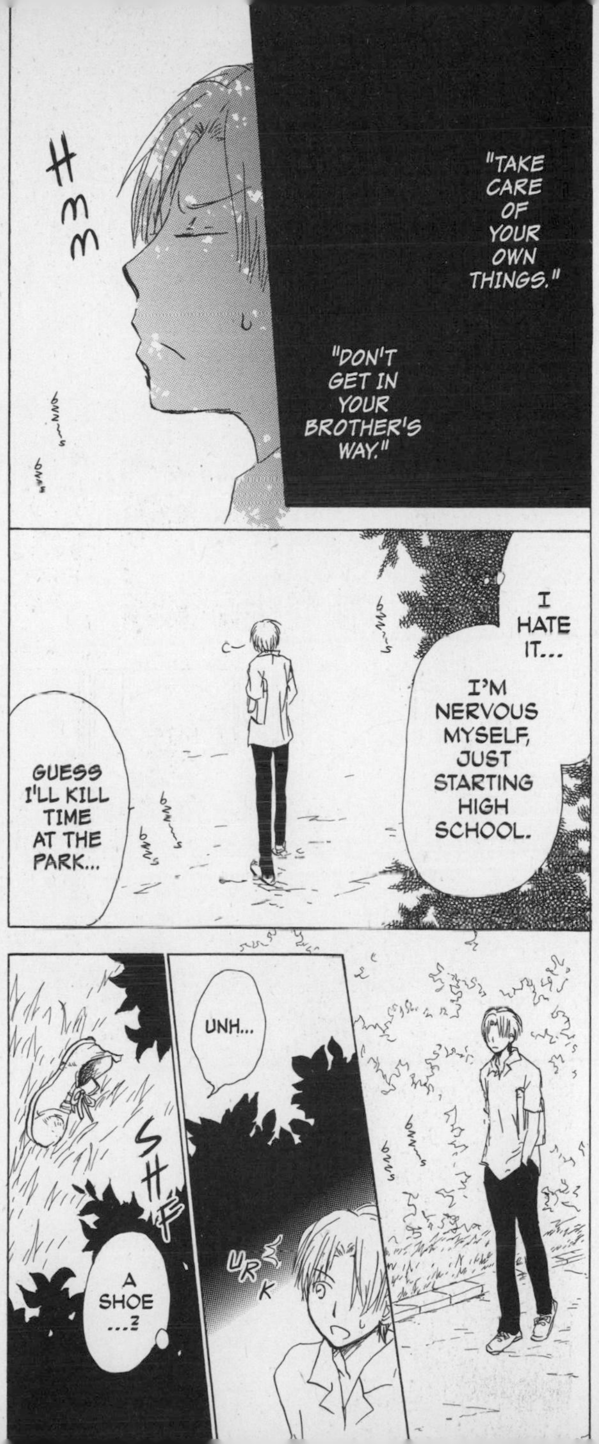
"TAKE CARE OF YOUR OWN THINGS."
"DON'T GET IN YOUR BROTHER'S WAY."
HMM
I HATE IT...
I'M NERVOUS MYSELF, JUST STARTING HIGH SCHOOL.
GUESS I'LL KILL TIME AT THE PARK...
UNH...
URK
SHF
A SHOE ...?

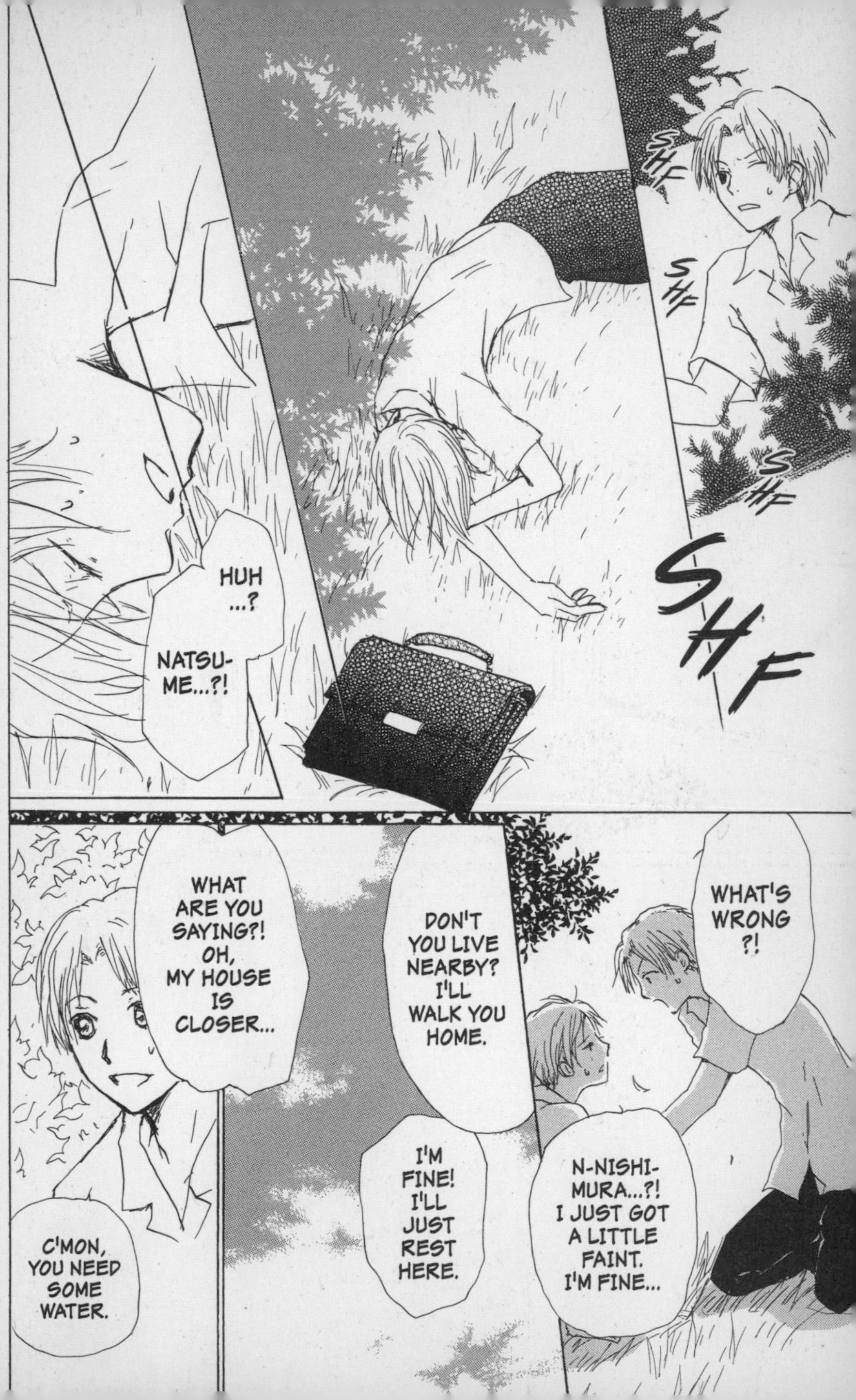
SHF
SHF
SHF
SHF
HUH ...?
NATSU-ME...?!
WHAT'S WRONG?!
N-NISHIMURA...?! I JUST GOT A LITTLE FAINT. I'M FINE...
DON'T YOU LIVE NEARBY? I'LL WALK YOU HOME.
I'M FINE! I'LL JUST REST HERE.
WHAT ARE YOU SAYING?! OH, MY HOUSE IS CLOSER...
C'MON, YOU NEED SOME WATER.

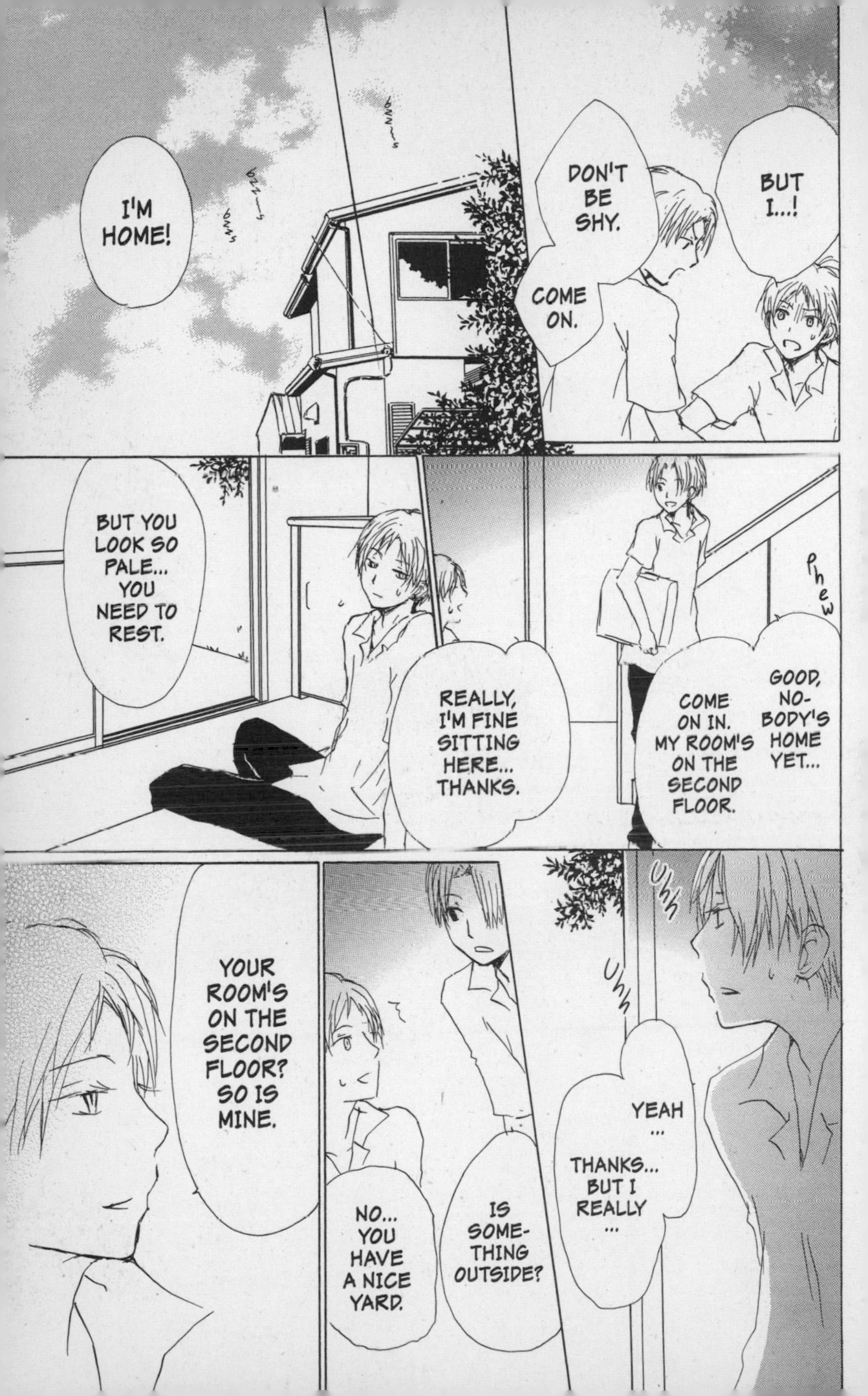
BUT I...!
DON'T BE SHY.
COME ON.
I'M HOME!
Phew
GOOD, NO-BODY'S HOME YET...
COME ON IN. MY ROOM'S ON THE SECOND FLOOR.
REALLY, I'M FINE SITTING HERE... THANKS.
BUT YOU LOOK SO PALE... YOU NEED TO REST.
Uhh
Uhh
YEAH ...
THANKS... BUT I REALLY ...
IS SOME-THING OUTSIDE?
NO... YOU HAVE A NICE YARD.
YOUR ROOM'S ON THE SECOND FLOOR? SO IS MINE.

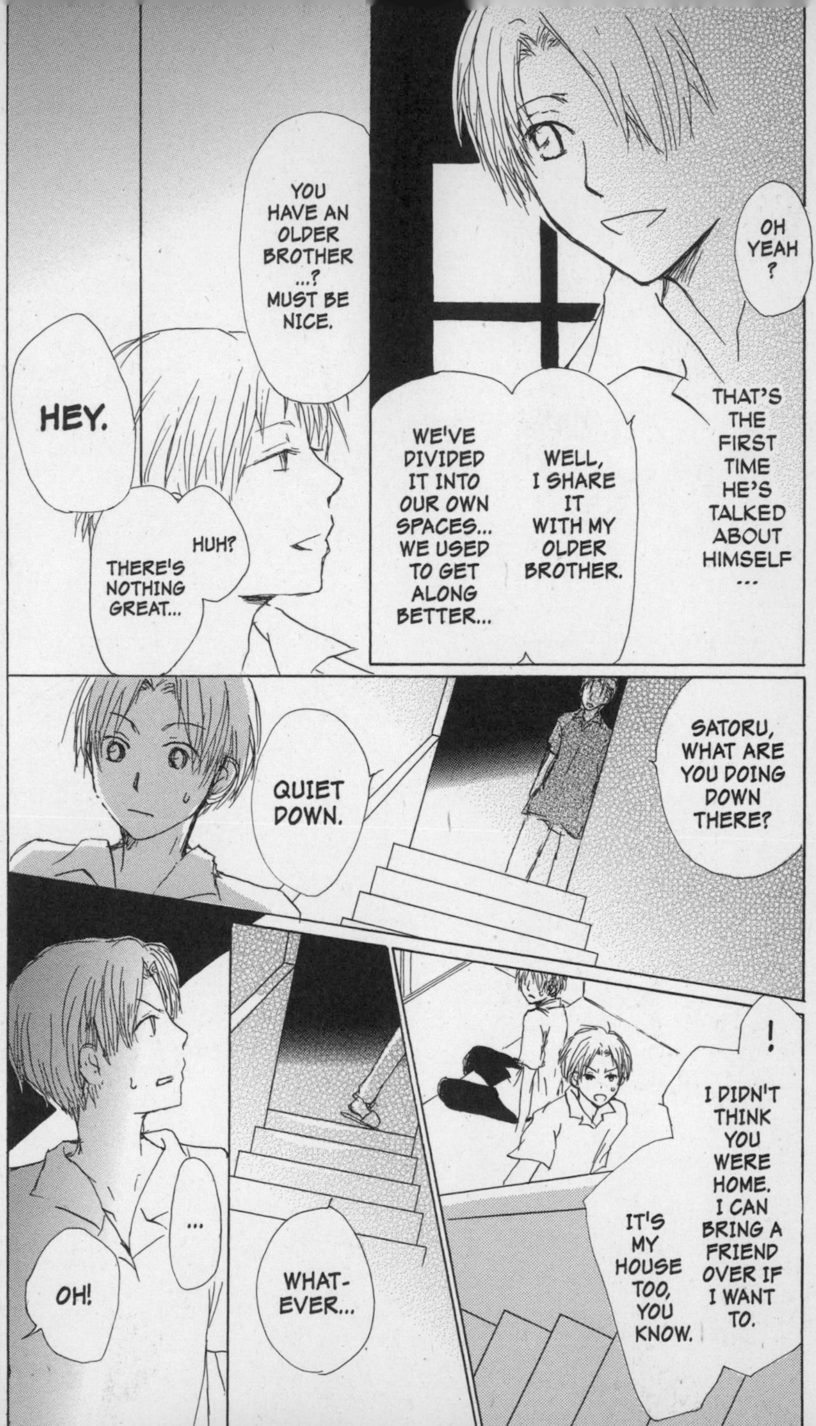
OH YEAH?
THAT'S THE FIRST TIME HE'S TALKED ABOUT HIMSELF...
WELL, I SHARE IT WITH MY OLDER BROTHER.
WE'VE DIVIDED IT INTO OUR OWN SPACES... WE USED TO GET ALONG BETTER...
YOU HAVE AN OLDER BROTHER...? MUST BE NICE.
HUH? THERE'S NOTHING GREAT...
HEY.
SATORU, WHAT ARE YOU DOING DOWN THERE?
QUIET DOWN.
!
I DIDN'T THINK YOU WERE HOME. I CAN BRING A FRIEND OVER IF I WANT TO.
IT'S MY HOUSE TOO, YOU KNOW.
WHAT-EVER...
...
OH!

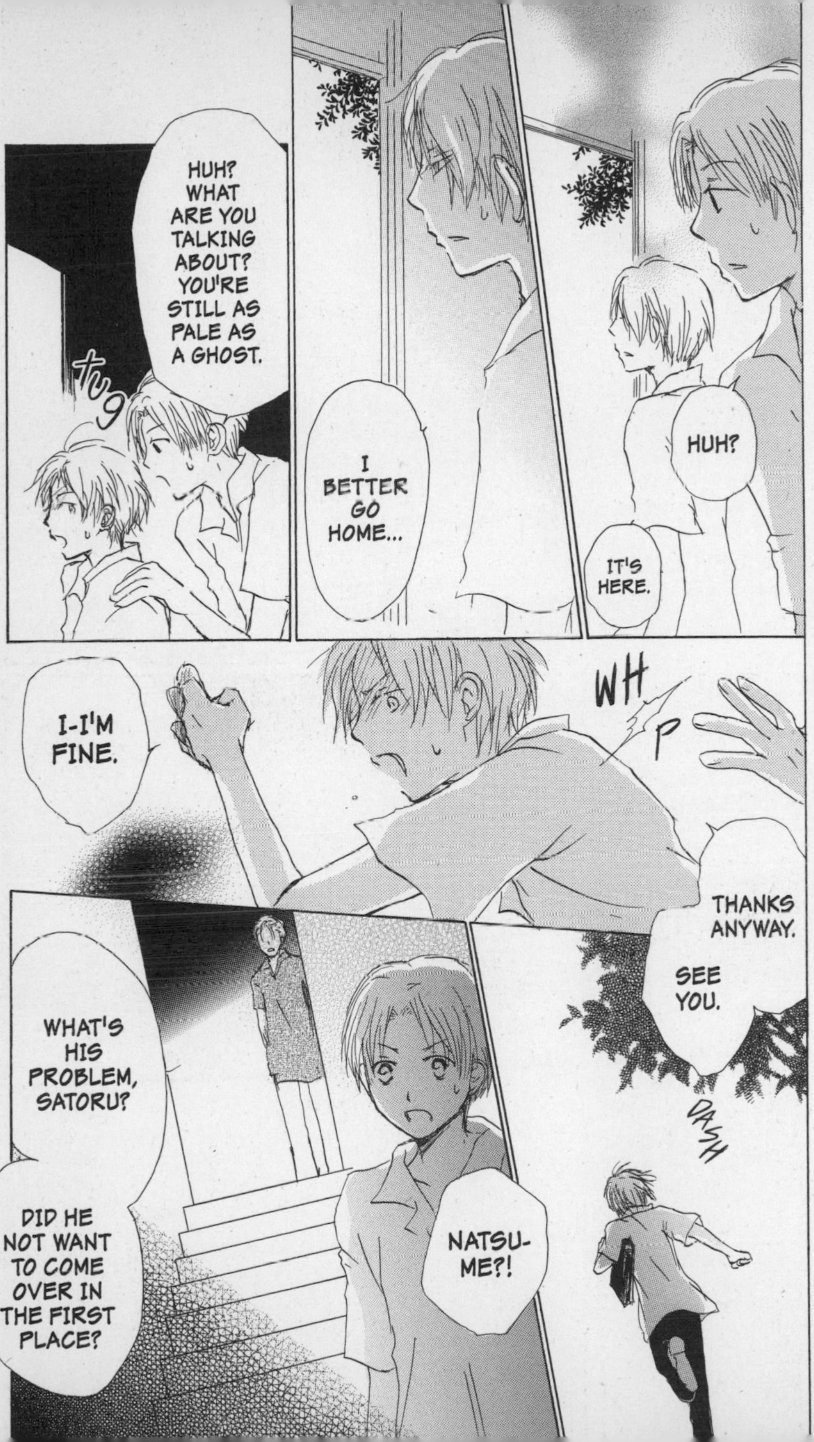
HUH?
IT'S HERE.
I BETTER GO HOME...
TUG
HUH? WHAT ARE YOU TALKING ABOUT? YOU'RE STILL AS PALE AS A GHOST.
WHP
I-I'M FINE.
THANKS ANYWAY.
SEE YOU.
DASH
NATSU-ME?!
WHAT'S HIS PROBLEM, SATORU?
DID HE NOT WANT TO COME OVER IN THE FIRST PLACE?

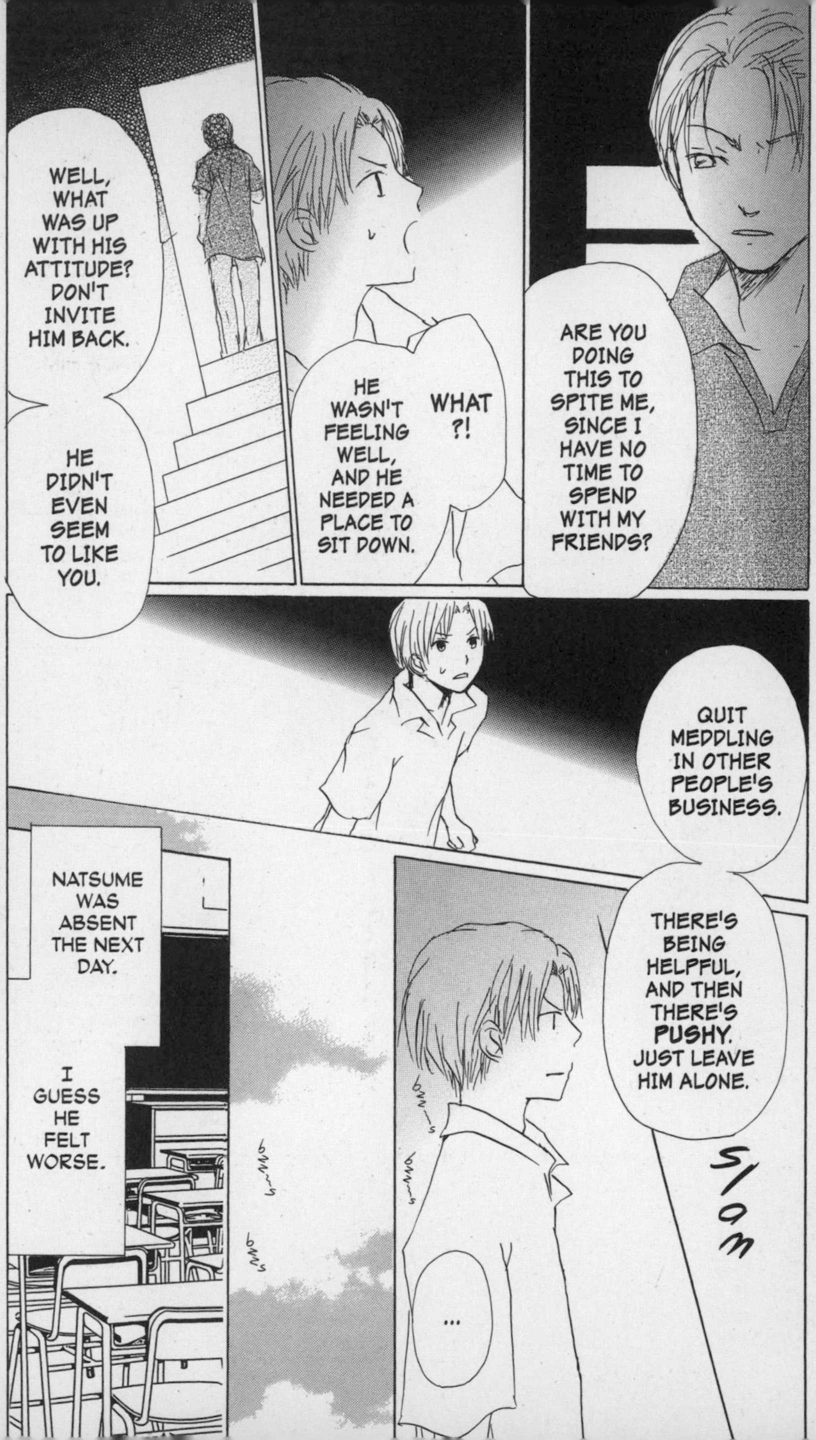
ARE YOU DOING THIS TO SPITE ME, SINCE I HAVE NO TIME TO SPEND WITH MY FRIENDS?
WHAT?!
HE WASN'T FEELING WELL, AND HE NEEDED A PLACE TO SIT DOWN.
WELL, WHAT WAS UP WITH HIS ATTITUDE? DON'T INVITE HIM BACK.
HE DIDN'T EVEN SEEM TO LIKE YOU.
QUIT MEDDLING IN OTHER PEOPLE'S BUSINESS.
THERE'S BEING HELPFUL, AND THEN THERE'S PUSHY. JUST LEAVE HIM ALONE.
SLAM
...
NATSUME WAS ABSENT THE NEXT DAY.
I GUESS HE FELT WORSE.

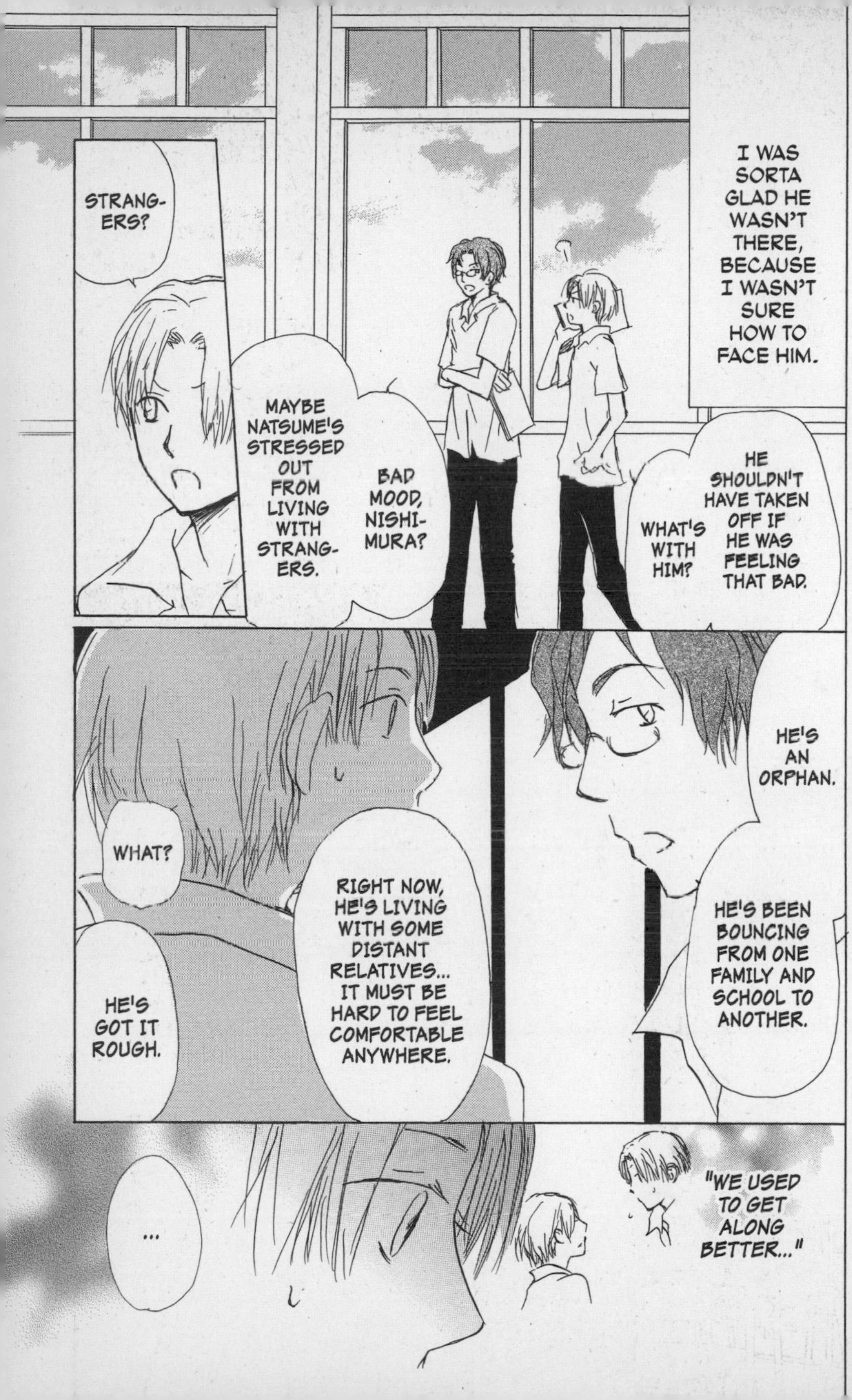
I WAS SORTA GLAD HE WASN'T THERE, BECAUSE I WASN'T SURE HOW TO FACE HIM.
HE SHOULDN'T HAVE TAKEN OFF IF HE WAS FEELING THAT BAD.
WHAT'S WITH HIM?
BAD MOOD, NISHIMURA?
MAYBE NATSUME'S STRESSED OUT FROM LIVING WITH STRANGERS.
STRANGERS?
HE'S AN ORPHAN.
HE'S BEEN BOUNCING FROM ONE FAMILY AND SCHOOL TO ANOTHER.
WHAT?
RIGHT NOW, HE'S LIVING WITH SOME DISTANT RELATIVES... IT MUST BE HARD TO FEEL COMFORTABLE ANYWHERE.
HE'S GOT IT ROUGH.
"WE USED TO GET ALONG BETTER..."
...

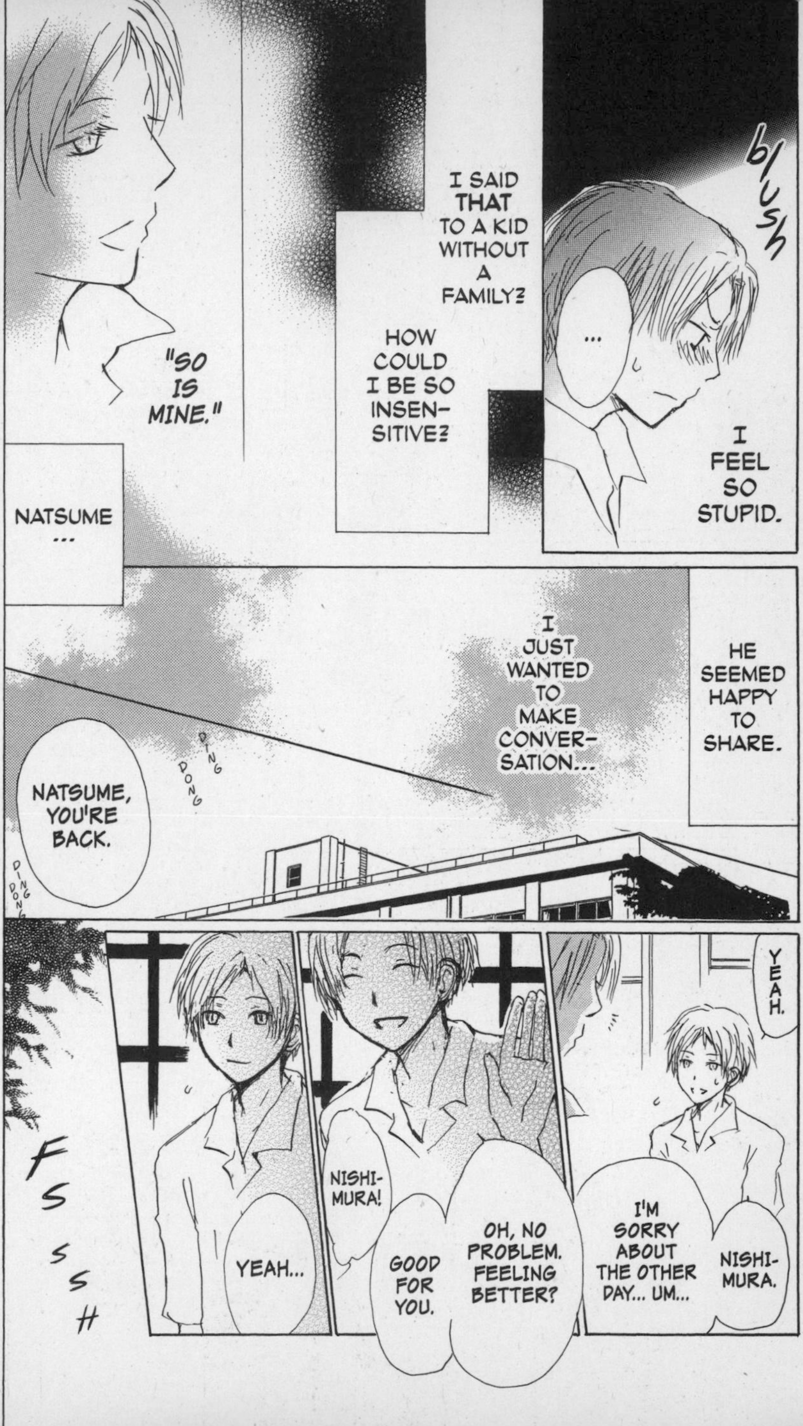
blush
...
I FEEL SO STUPID.
I SAID THAT TO A KID WITHOUT A FAMILY?
HOW COULD I BE SO INSENSITIVE?
"SO IS MINE."
NATSUME...
HE SEEMED HAPPY TO SHARE.
I JUST WANTED TO MAKE CONVERSATION...
DING DONG
NATSUME, YOU'RE BACK.
DING DONG
YEAH.
NISHI-MURA.
I'M SORRY ABOUT THE OTHER DAY... UM...
OH, NO PROBLEM. FEELING BETTER?
NISHI-MURA!
GOOD FOR YOU.
YEAH...
FSSSH

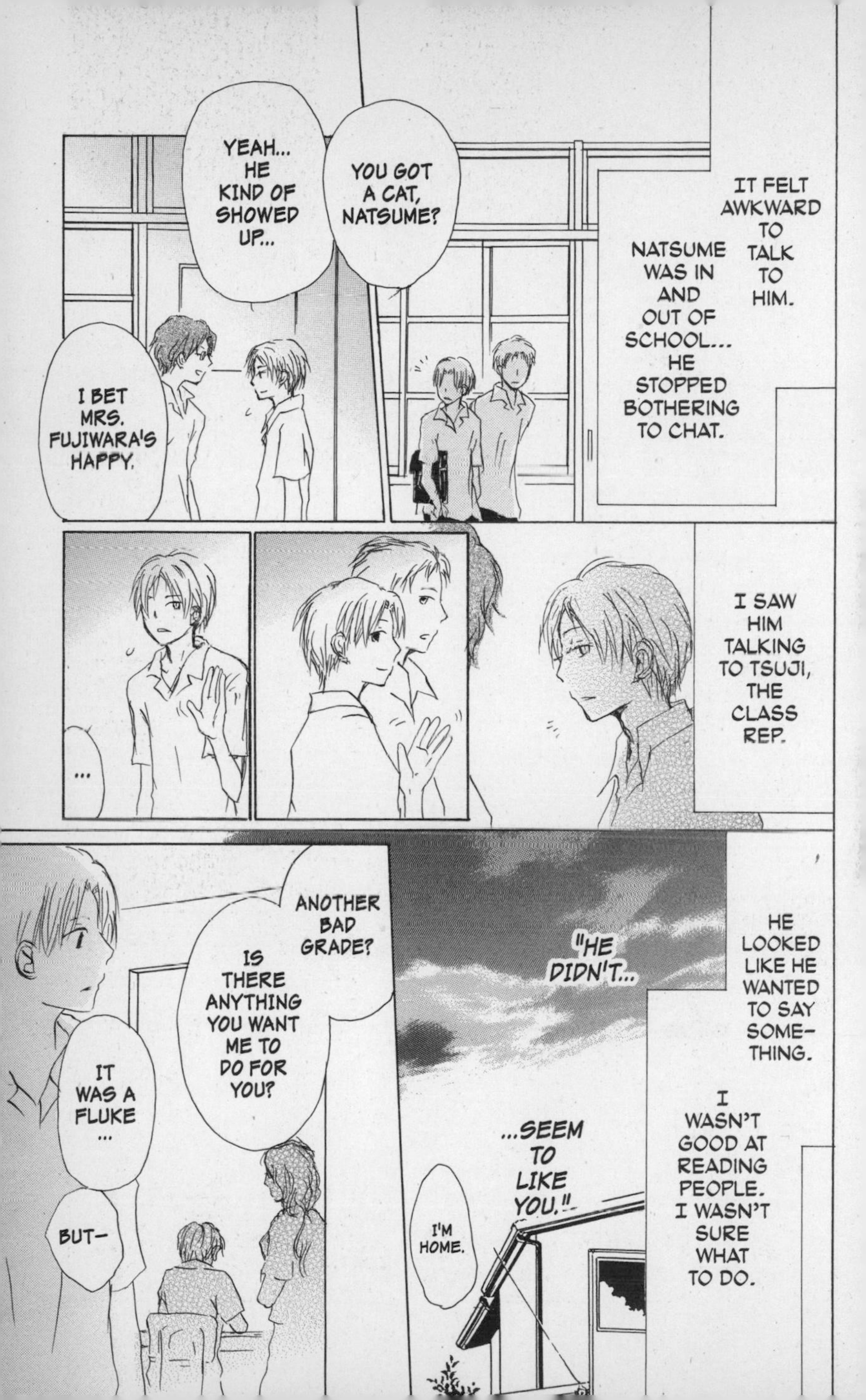
IT FELT AWKWARD TO TALK TO HIM.
NATSUME WAS IN AND OUT OF SCHOOL... HE STOPPED BOTHERING TO CHAT.
YOU GOT A CAT, NATSUME?
YEAH... HE KIND OF SHOWED UP...
I BET MRS. FUJIWARA'S HAPPY.
I SAW HIM TALKING TO TSUJI, THE CLASS REP.
...
HE LOOKED LIKE HE WANTED TO SAY SOME-THING.
I WASN'T GOOD AT READING PEOPLE. I WASN'T SURE WHAT TO DO.
"HE DIDN'T...
...SEEM TO LIKE YOU."
I'M HOME.
ANOTHER BAD GRADE?
IS THERE ANYTHING YOU WANT ME TO DO FOR YOU?
IT WAS A FLUKE...
BUT—

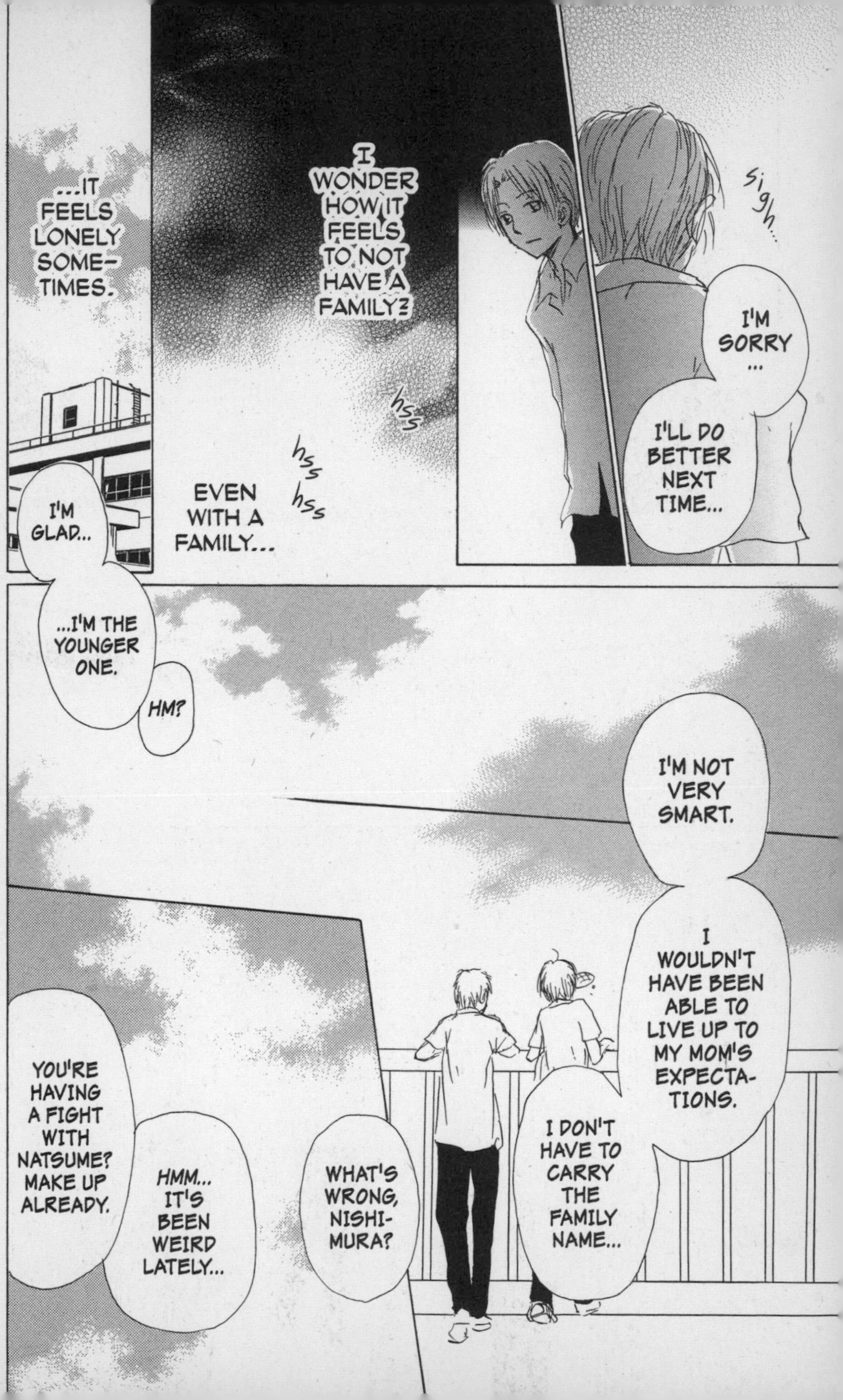
sigh...
I'M SORRY...
I'LL DO BETTER NEXT TIME...
I WONDER HOW IT FEELS TO NOT HAVE A FAMILY?
hss
hss hss
EVEN WITH A FAMILY...
...IT FEELS LONELY SOMETIMES.
I'M GLAD...
...I'M THE YOUNGER ONE.
HM?
I'M NOT VERY SMART.
I WOULDN'T HAVE BEEN ABLE TO LIVE UP TO MY MOM'S EXPECTATIONS.
I DON'T HAVE TO CARRY THE FAMILY NAME...
WHAT'S WRONG, NISHIMURA?
HMM... IT'S BEEN WEIRD LATELY...
YOU'RE HAVING A FIGHT WITH NATSUME? MAKE UP ALREADY.

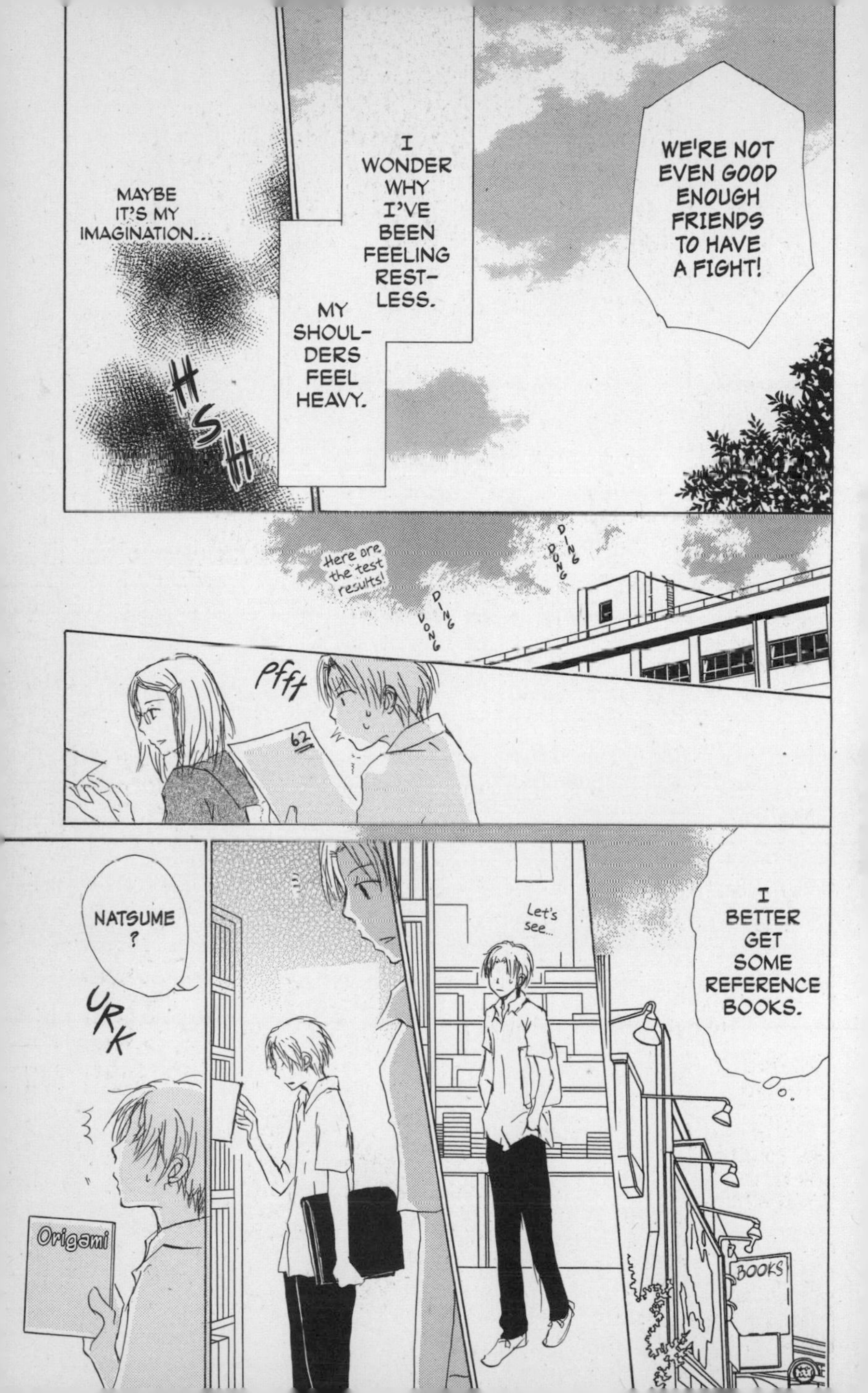
WE'RE NOT EVEN GOOD ENOUGH FRIENDS TO HAVE A FIGHT!
I WONDER WHY I'VE BEEN FEELING REST-LESS.
MY SHOUL-DERS FEEL HEAVY.
MAYBE IT'S MY IMAGINATION...
HSH
DING DONG
DING DONG
Here are the test results!
Pfft
62
I BETTER GET SOME REFERENCE BOOKS.
Let's see...
BOOKS
NATSUME?
URK
Origami

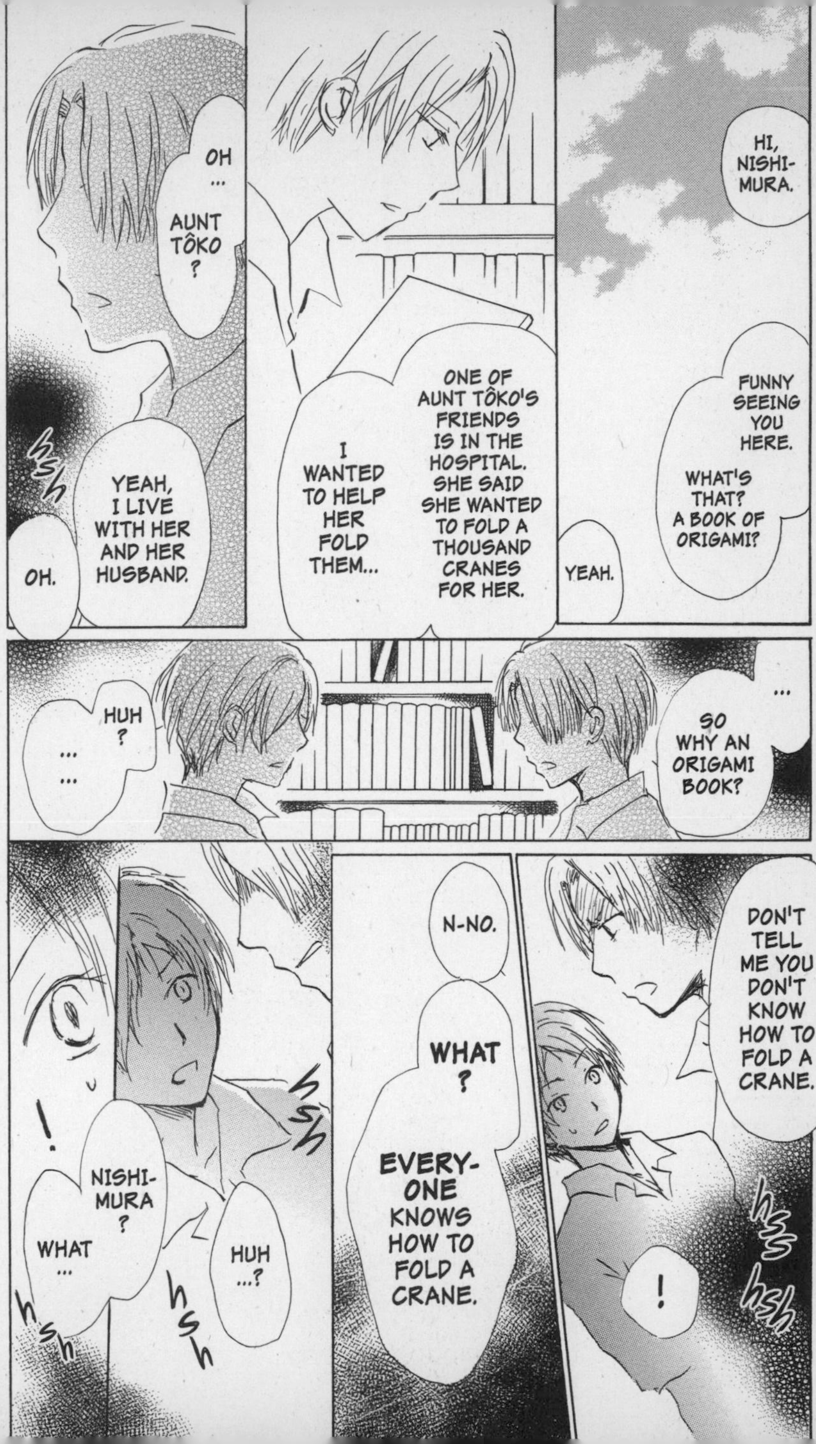
HI, NISHI-MURA.
FUNNY SEEING YOU HERE.
WHAT'S THAT? A BOOK OF ORIGAMI?
YEAH.
ONE OF AUNT TÔKO'S FRIENDS IS IN THE HOSPITAL. SHE SAID SHE WANTED TO FOLD A THOUSAND CRANES FOR HER.
I WANTED TO HELP HER FOLD THEM...
OH ...
AUNT TÔKO ?
YEAH, I LIVE WITH HER AND HER HUSBAND.
hsh
OH.
...
SO WHY AN ORIGAMI BOOK?
HUH ?
... ...
DON'T TELL ME YOU DON'T KNOW HOW TO FOLD A CRANE.
hss hsh
!
N-NO.
WHAT ?
EVERY-ONE KNOWS HOW TO FOLD A CRANE.
hsh
!
NISHI-MURA ?
WHAT ...
HUH ...?
hsh
hsh

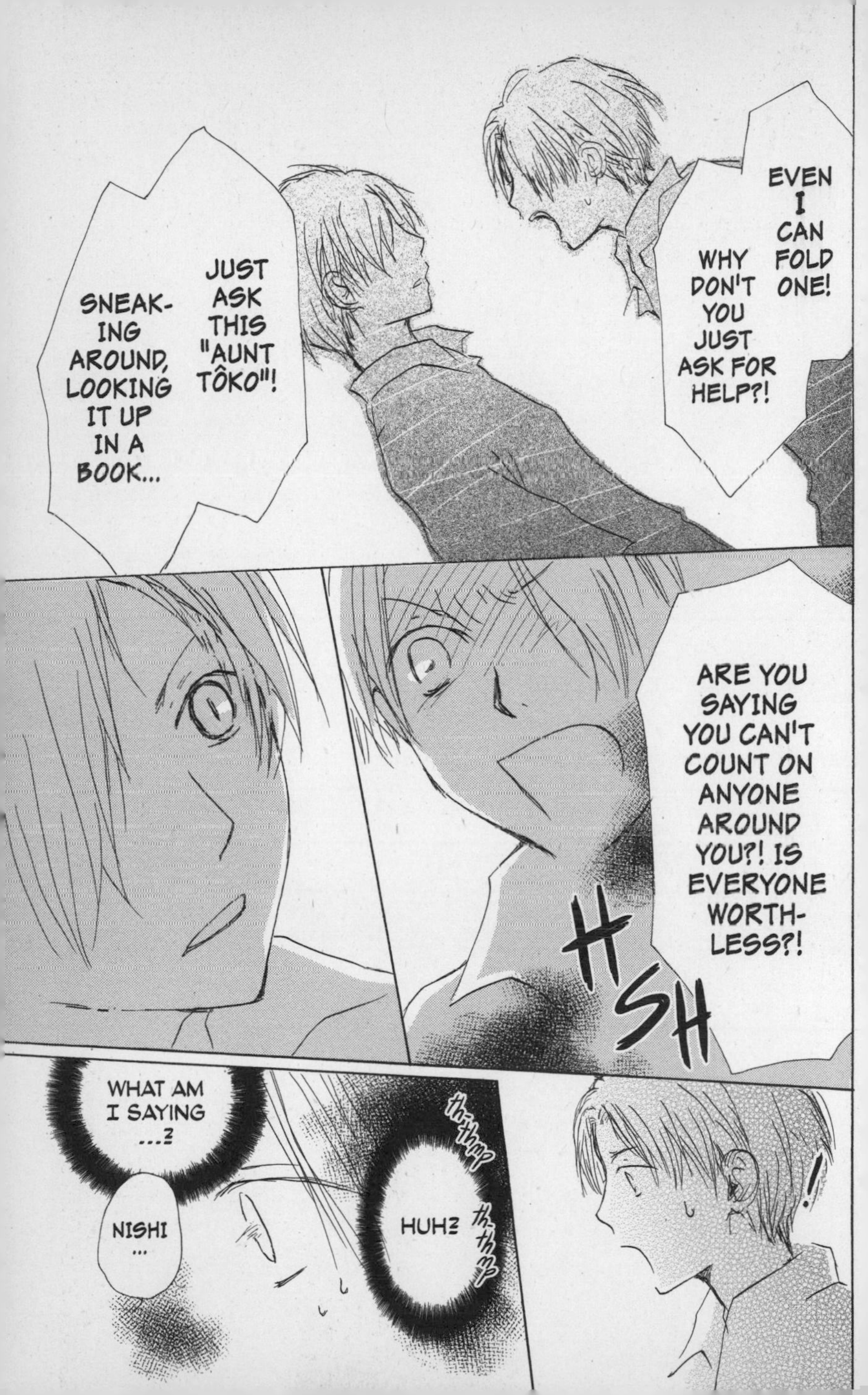
EVEN I CAN FOLD ONE!
WHY DON'T YOU JUST ASK FOR HELP?!
JUST ASK THIS "AUNT TÔKO"!
SNEAK-ING AROUND, LOOKING IT UP IN A BOOK...
ARE YOU SAYING YOU CAN'T COUNT ON ANYONE AROUND YOU?! IS EVERYONE WORTH-LESS?!
HSH
!
th-thmp
th-thmp
HUH?
WHAT AM I SAYING ...?
NISHI ...

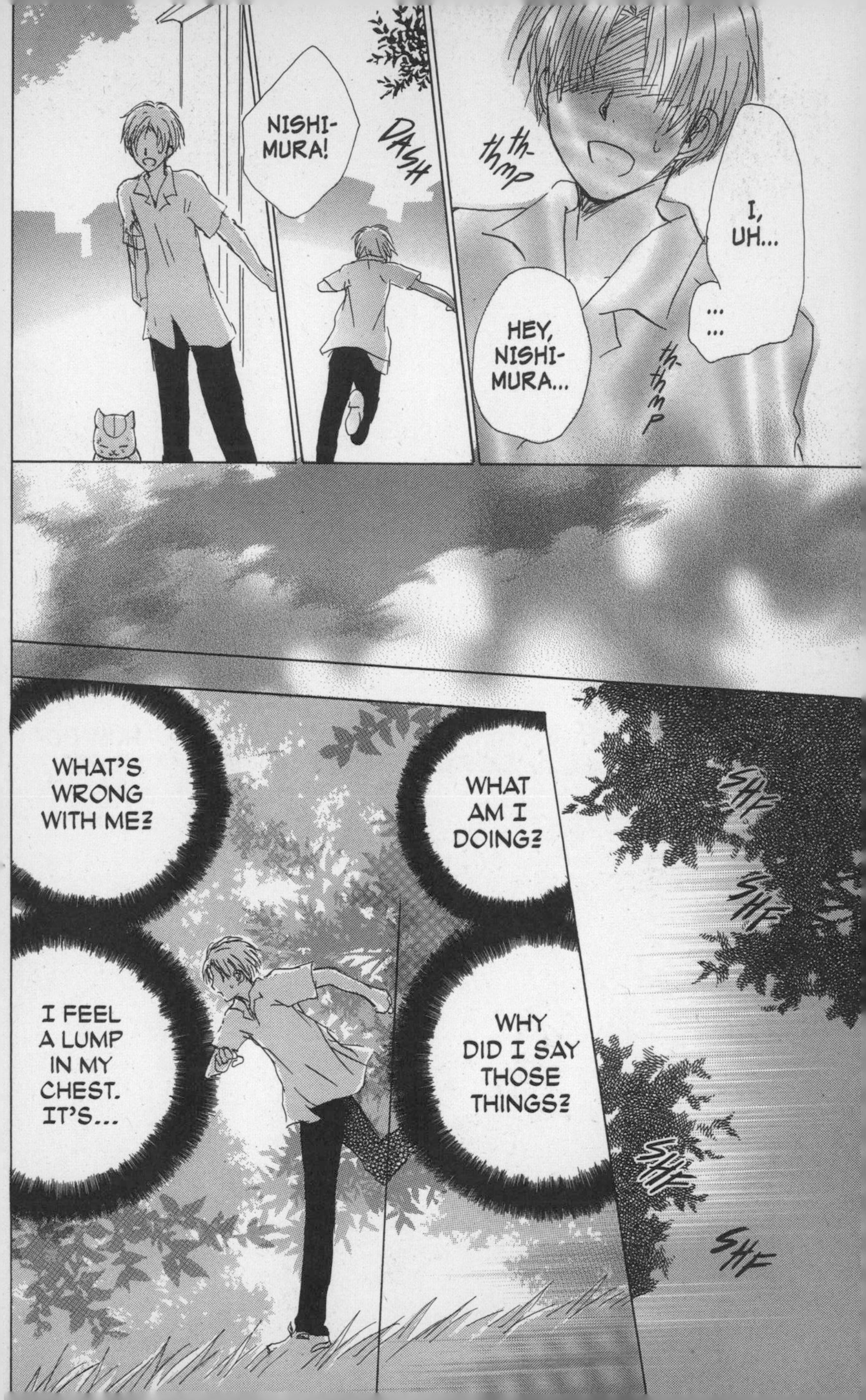
I, UH...
... ...
th-thmp
HEY, NISHI-MURA...
th-thmp
DASH
NISHI-MURA!
SHF
SHF
SHF
SHF
WHAT AM I DOING?
WHAT'S WRONG WITH ME?
WHY DID I SAY THOSE THINGS?
I FEEL A LUMP IN MY CHEST. IT'S...

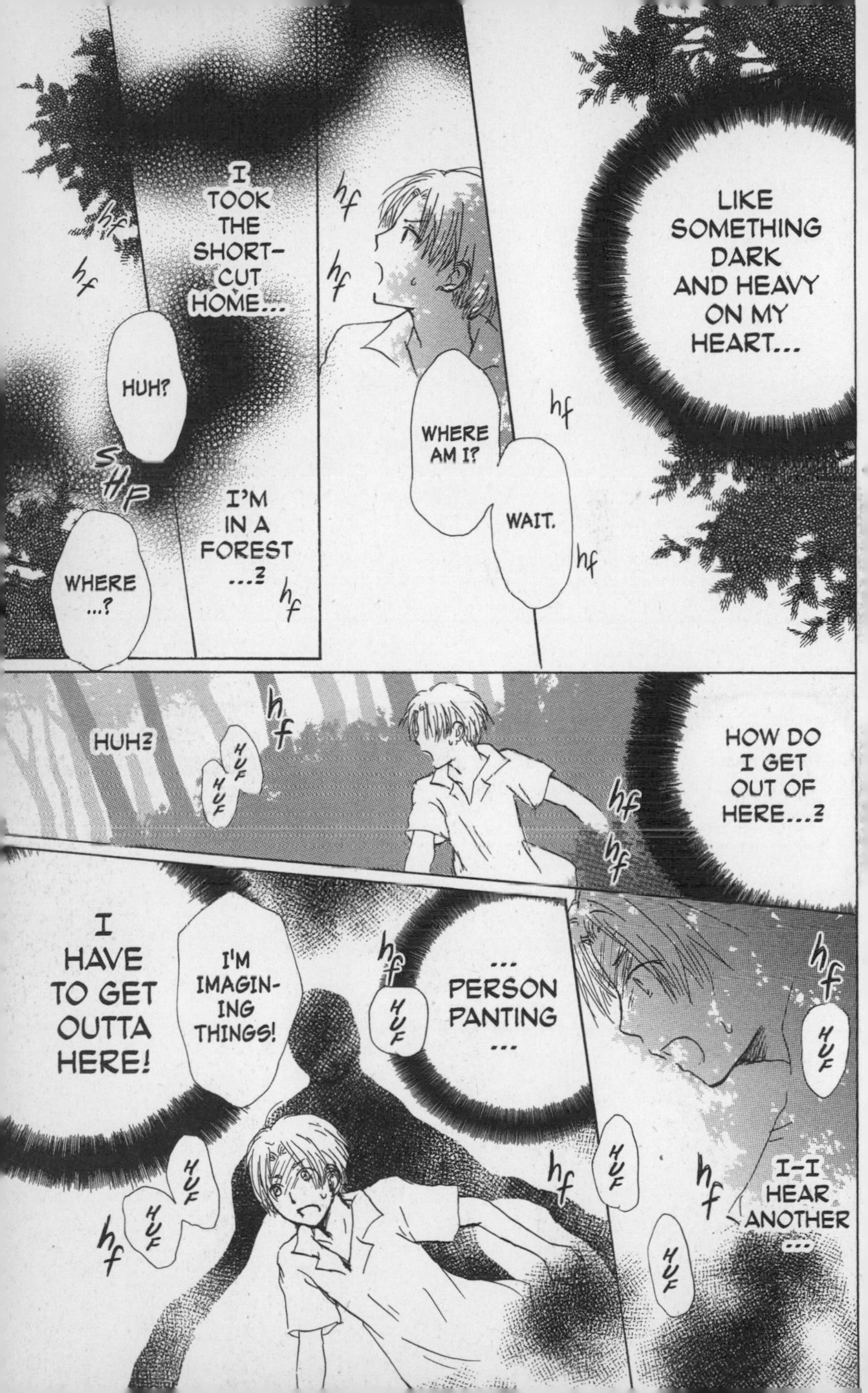
LIKE SOMETHING DARK AND HEAVY ON MY HEART...
hf
hf
WHERE AM I?
WAIT.
hf
hf
I TOOK THE SHORT-CUT HOME...
hf
hf
HUH?
SHF
WHERE ...?
I'M IN A FOREST ...?!
hf
HOW DO I GET OUT OF HERE...?!
hf
hf
hf
HUF
HUF
HUH?!
hf
HUF
I-I HEAR ANOTHER ...
hf
HUF
HUF
... PERSON PANTING ...
hf
HUF
I'M IMAGIN-ING THINGS!
I HAVE TO GET OUTTA HERE!
HUF
HUF
hf

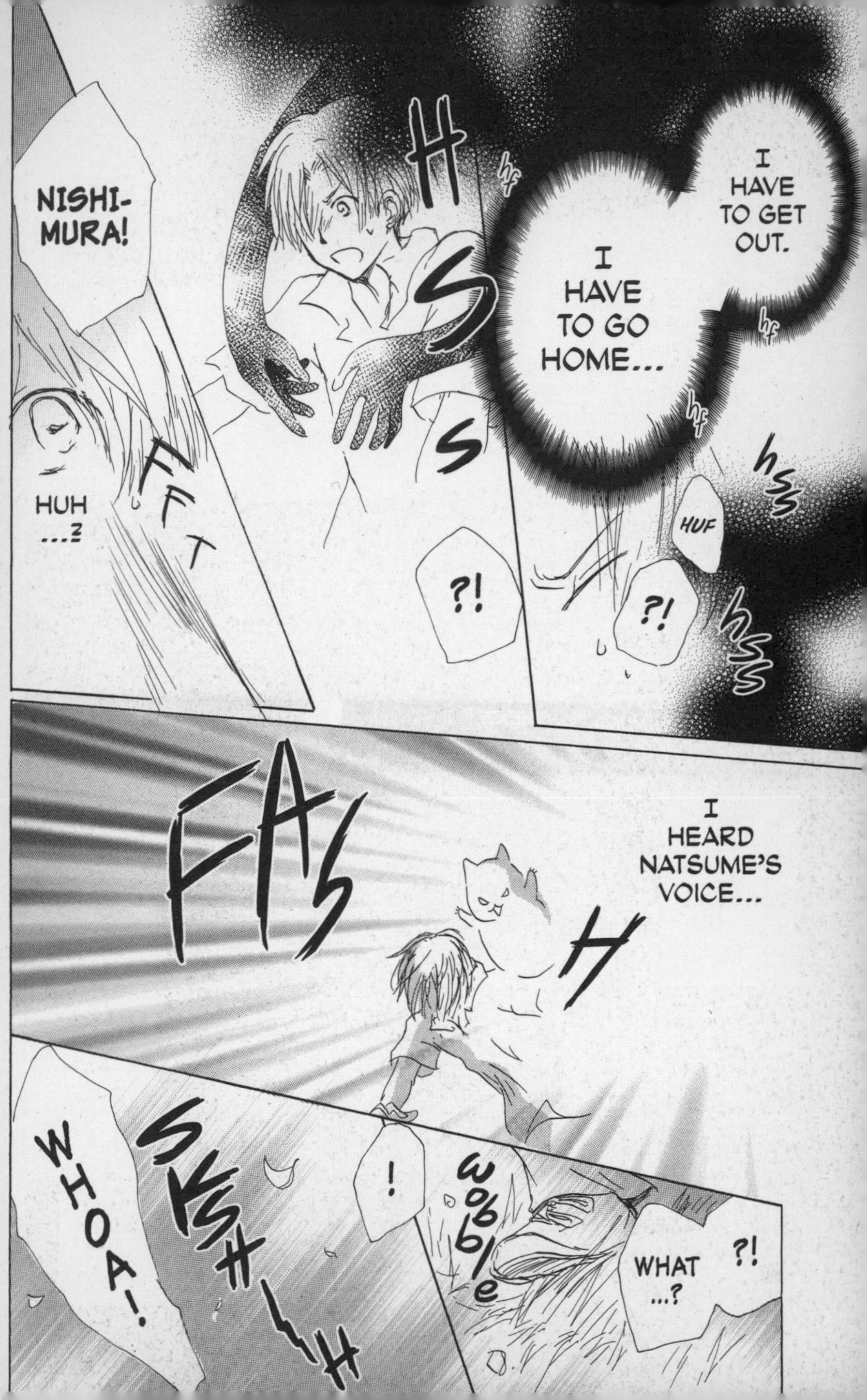
I HAVE TO GET OUT.
I HAVE TO GO HOME...
hf
hf
HUF
hss
hss
?!
HS
hf
S
?!
NISHI-MURA!
HUH...?
FFT
I HEARD NATSUME'S VOICE...
FASH
?!
WHAT...?
wobble
!
SKSHH
WHOA!

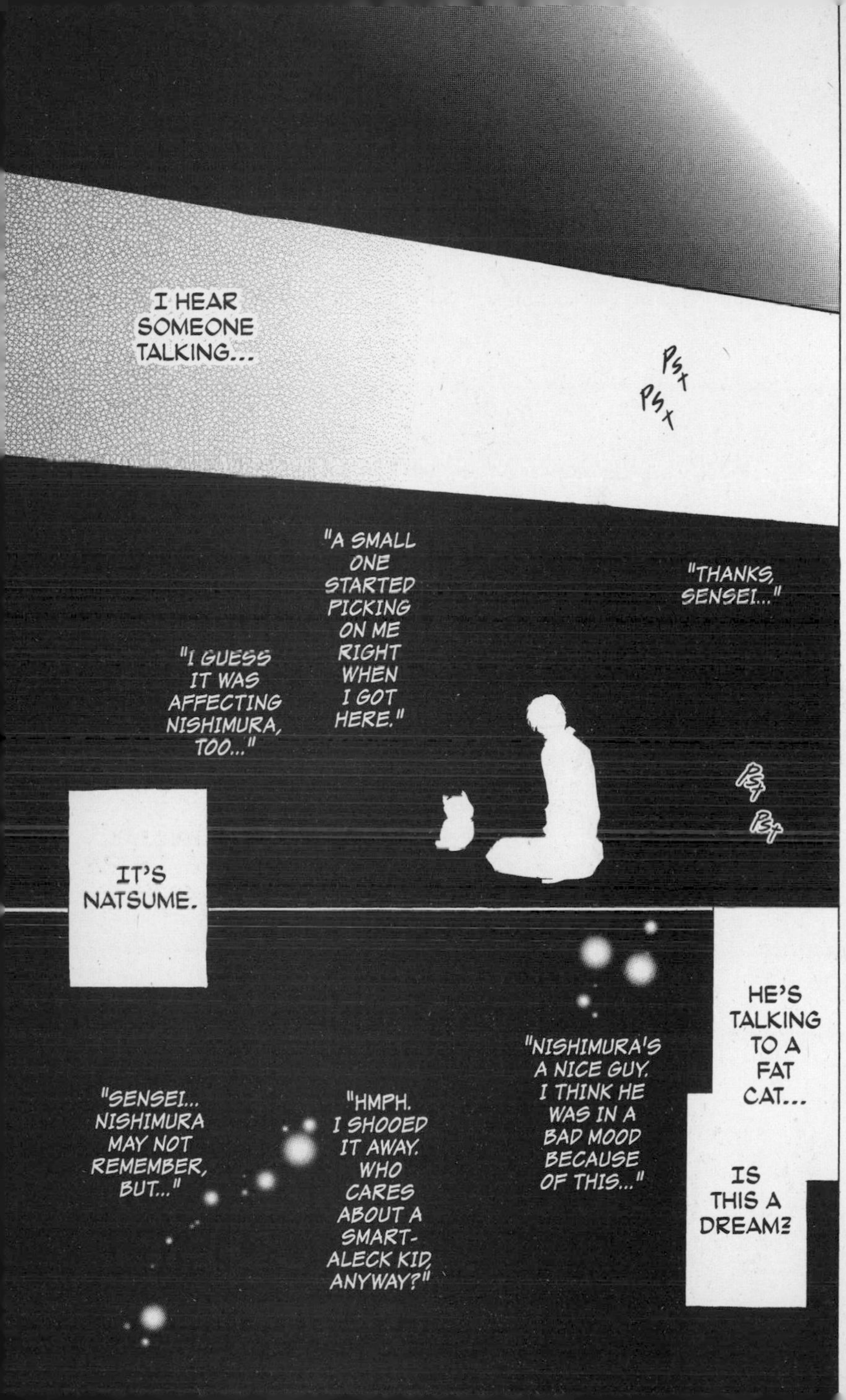
I HEAR SOMEONE TALKING...
Pst Pst
"THANKS, SENSEI..."
"A SMALL ONE STARTED PICKING ON ME RIGHT WHEN I GOT HERE."
"I GUESS IT WAS AFFECTING NISHIMURA, TOO..."
Pst Pst
IT'S NATSUME.
HE'S TALKING TO A FAT CAT...
IS THIS A DREAM?
"NISHIMURA'S A NICE GUY. I THINK HE WAS IN A BAD MOOD BECAUSE OF THIS..."
"HMPH. I SHOOED IT AWAY. WHO CARES ABOUT A SMART-ALECK KID, ANYWAY?"
"SENSEI... NISHIMURA MAY NOT REMEMBER, BUT..."

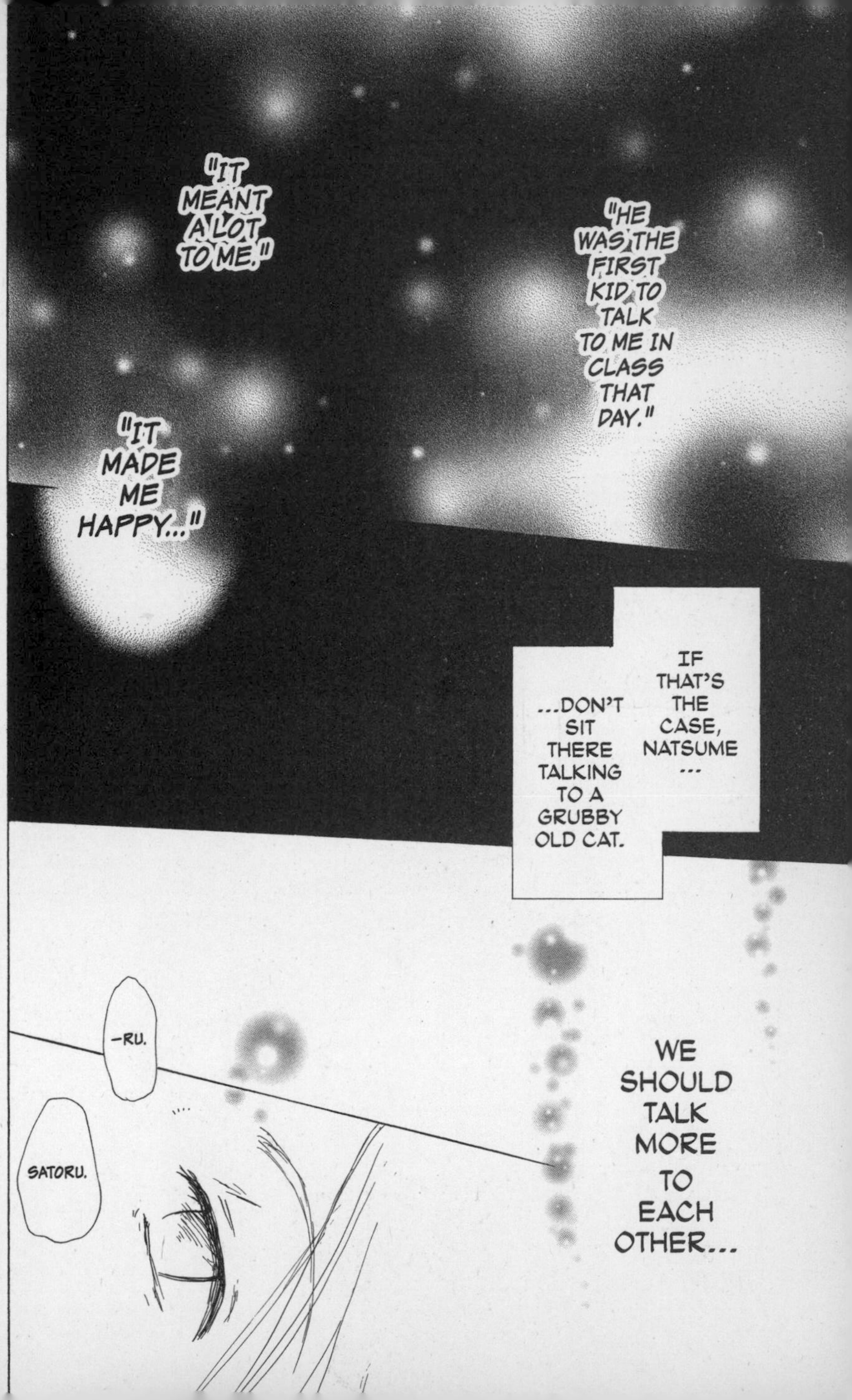
"HE WAS THE FIRST KID TO TALK TO ME IN CLASS THAT DAY."
"IT MEANT A LOT TO ME."
"IT MADE ME HAPPY..."
IF THAT'S THE CASE, NATSUME...
...DON'T SIT THERE TALKING TO A GRUBBY OLD CAT.
WE SHOULD TALK MORE TO EACH OTHER...
-RU.
...
SATORU.

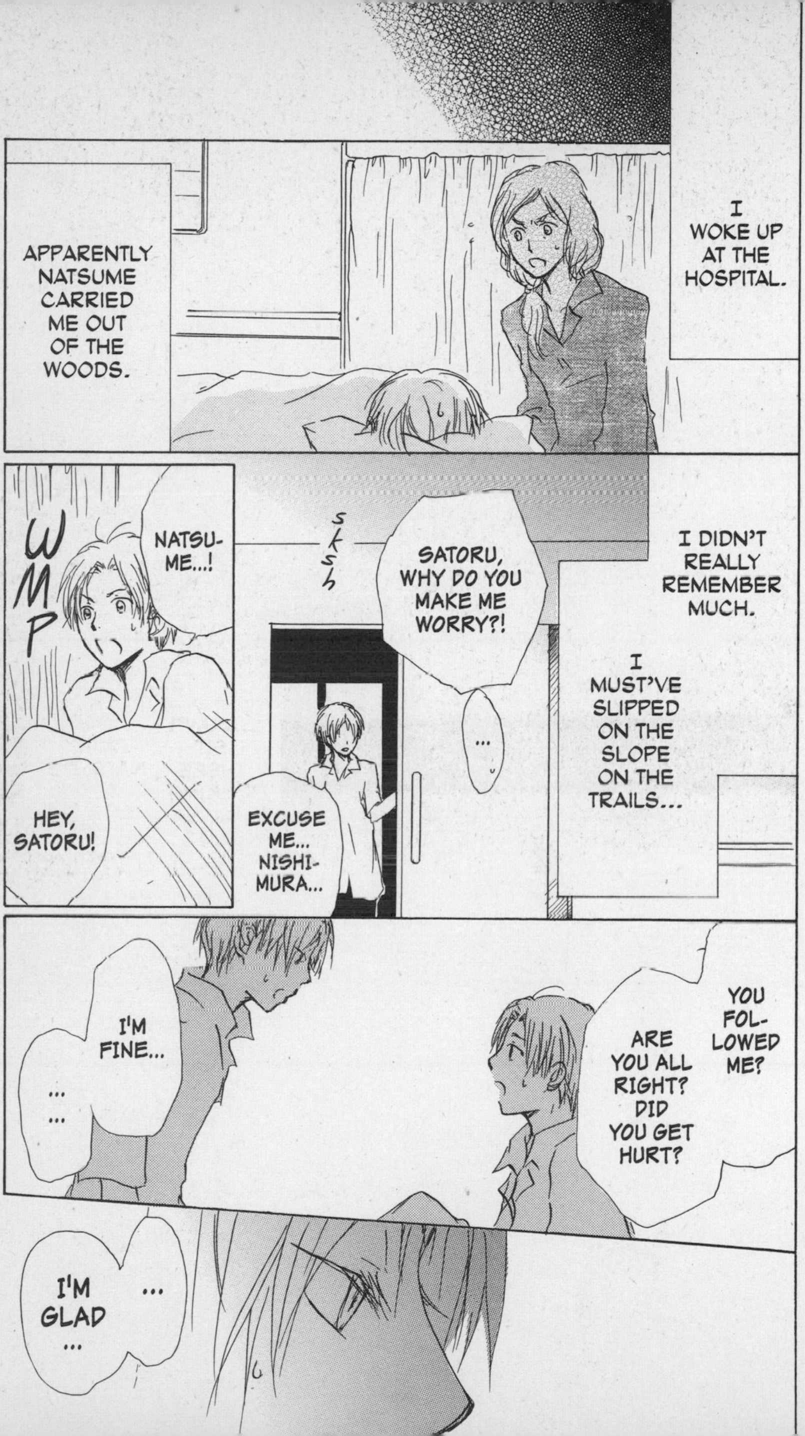
I WOKE UP AT THE HOSPITAL.
APPARENTLY NATSUME CARRIED ME OUT OF THE WOODS.
I DIDN'T REALLY REMEMBER MUCH.
I MUST'VE SLIPPED ON THE SLOPE ON THE TRAILS...
SATORU, WHY DO YOU MAKE ME WORRY?!
SKSH
...
EXCUSE ME... NISHIMURA...
NATSUME...!
WMP
HEY, SATORU!
YOU FOLLOWED ME?
ARE YOU ALL RIGHT? DID YOU GET HURT?
I'M FINE...
......
...
I'M GLAD...

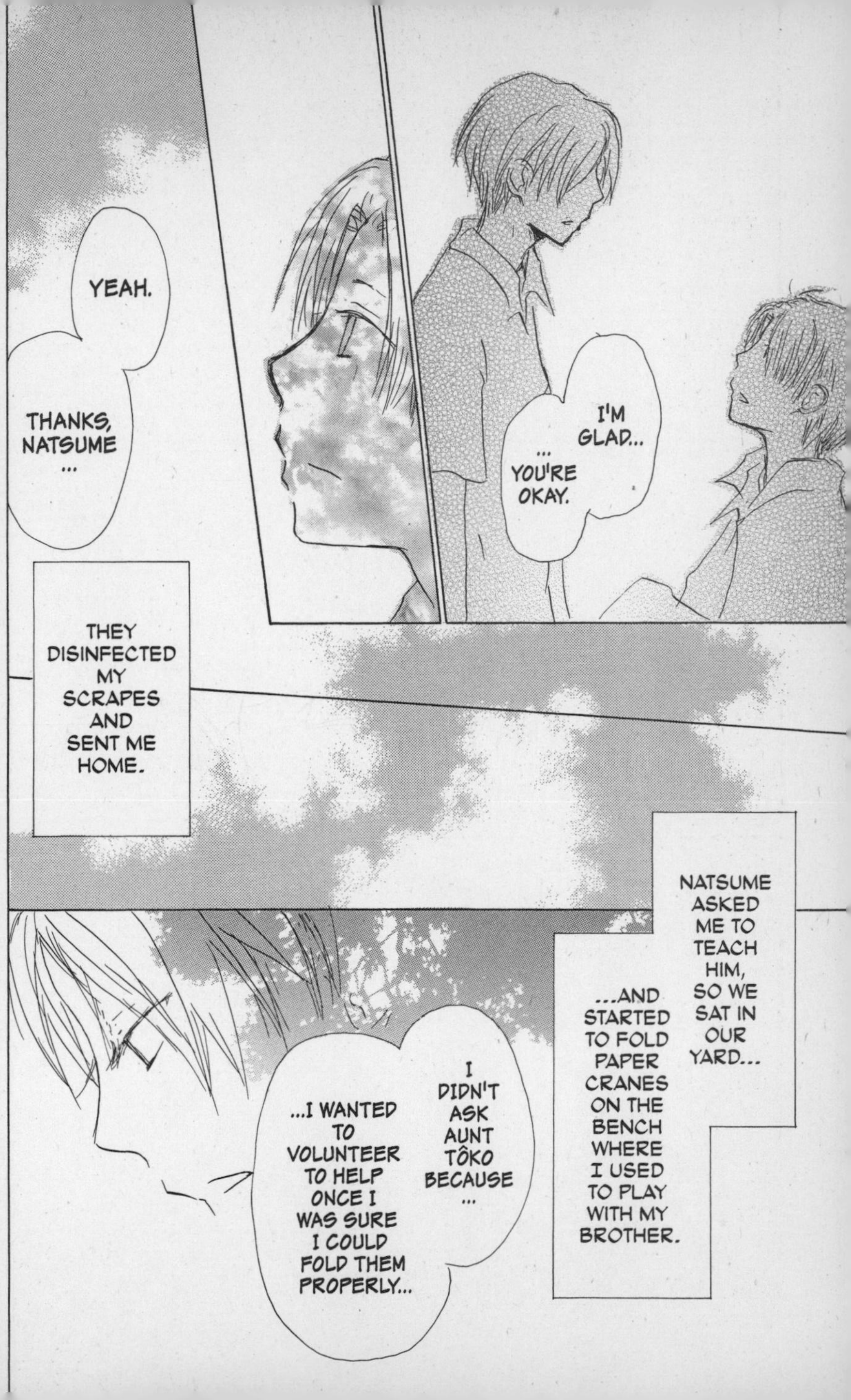
I'M GLAD... ... YOU'RE OKAY.
YEAH.
THANKS, NATSUME ...
THEY DISINFECTED MY SCRAPES AND SENT ME HOME.
NATSUME ASKED ME TO TEACH HIM, SO WE SAT IN OUR YARD...
...AND STARTED TO FOLD PAPER CRANES ON THE BENCH WHERE I USED TO PLAY WITH MY BROTHER.
I DIDN'T ASK AUNT TÔKO BECAUSE ...
...I WANTED TO VOLUNTEER TO HELP ONCE I WAS SURE I COULD FOLD THEM PROPERLY...

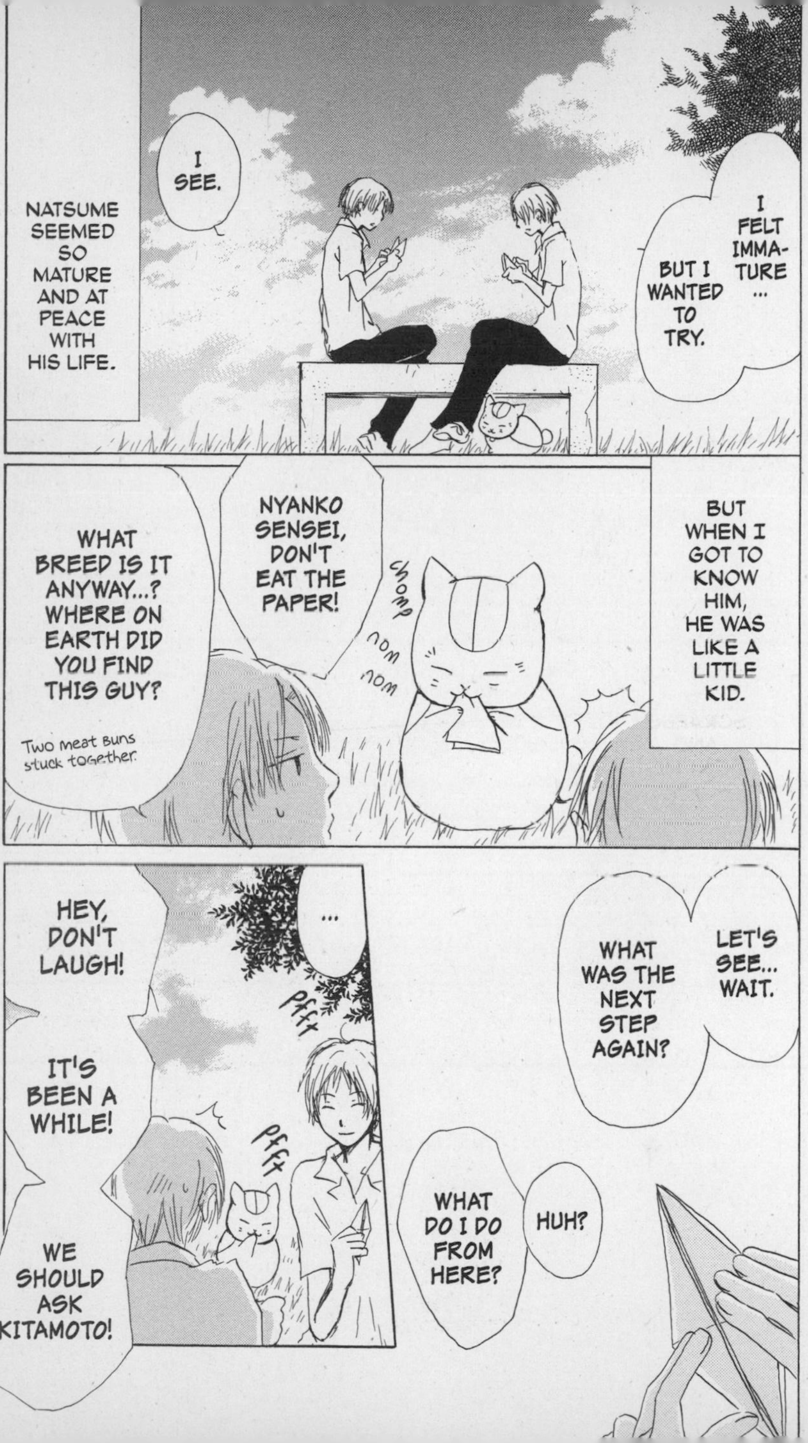
I FELT IMMA-TURE...
BUT I WANTED TO TRY.
I SEE.
NATSUME SEEMED SO MATURE AND AT PEACE WITH HIS LIFE.
BUT WHEN I GOT TO KNOW HIM, HE WAS LIKE A LITTLE KID.
NYANKO SENSEI, DON'T EAT THE PAPER!
chomp
nom nom
WHAT BREED IS IT ANYWAY...? WHERE ON EARTH DID YOU FIND THIS GUY?
Two meat buns stuck together.
LET'S SEE... WAIT.
WHAT WAS THE NEXT STEP AGAIN?
HUH?
WHAT DO I DO FROM HERE?
...
Pffft
HEY, DON'T LAUGH!
Pffft
IT'S BEEN A WHILE!
WE SHOULD ASK KITAMOTO!

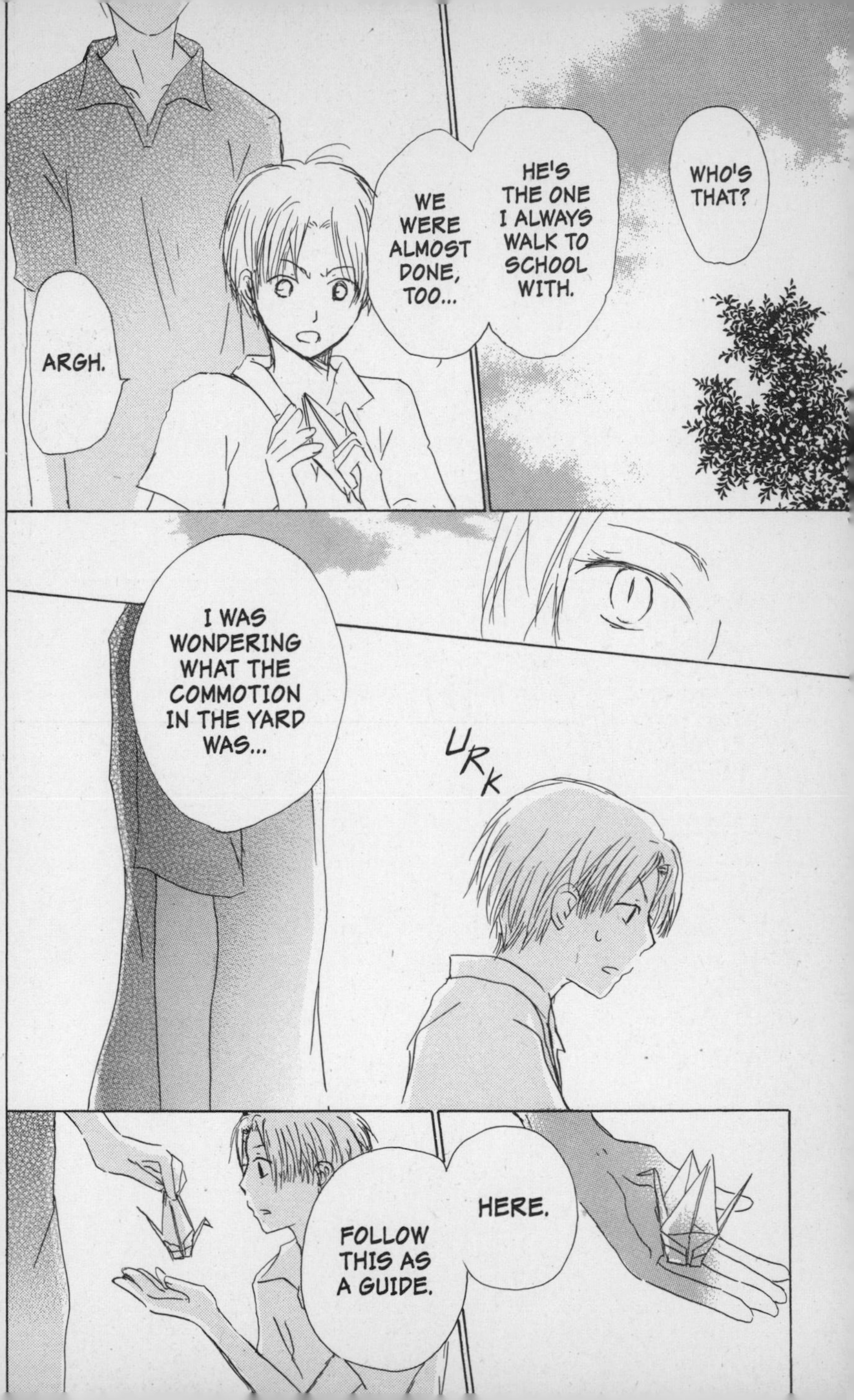
WHO'S THAT?
HE'S THE ONE I ALWAYS WALK TO SCHOOL WITH.
WE WERE ALMOST DONE, TOO...
ARGH.
I WAS WONDERING WHAT THE COMMOTION IN THE YARD WAS...
URK
HERE.
FOLLOW THIS AS A GUIDE.

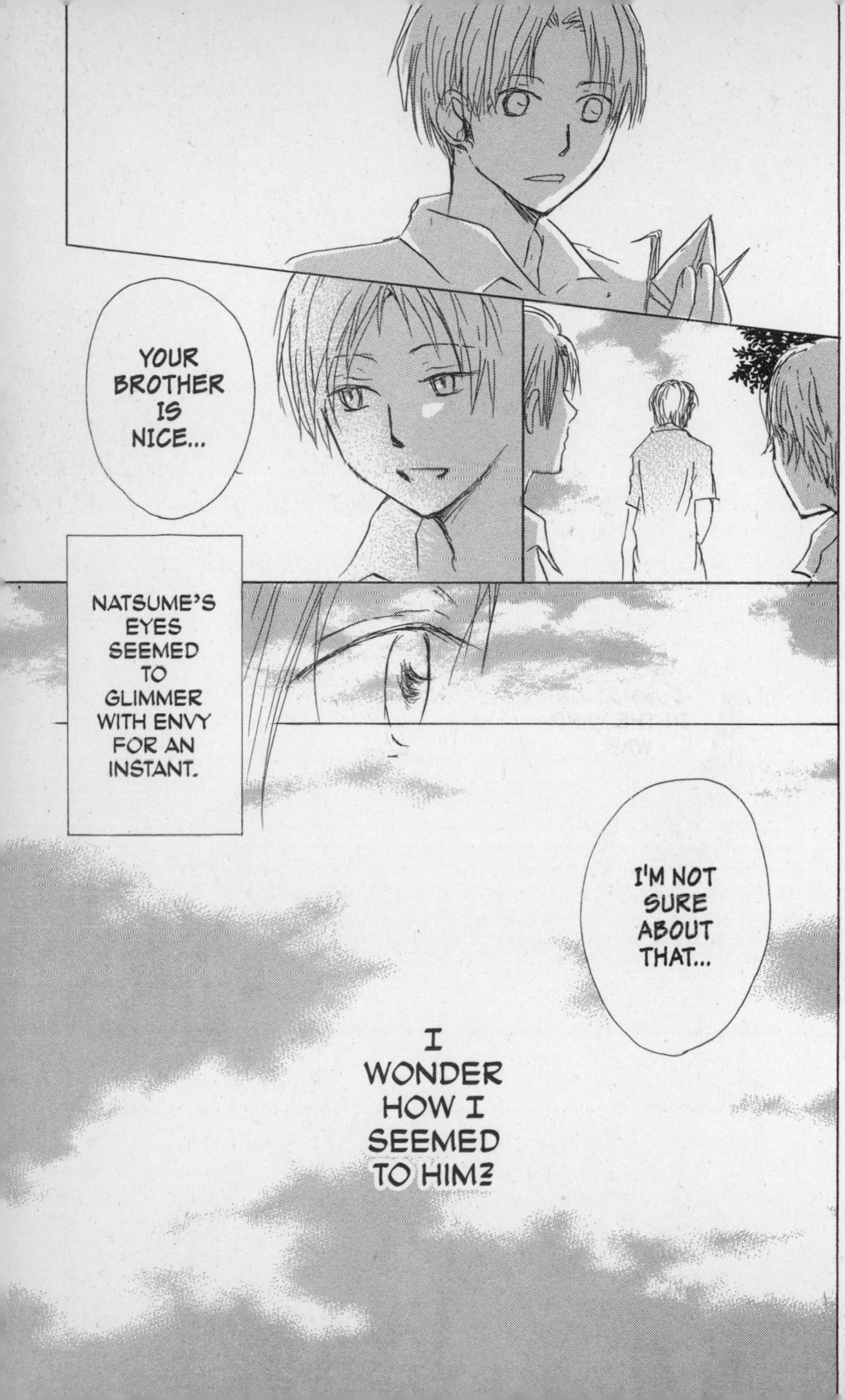
YOUR BROTHER IS NICE...
NATSUME'S EYES SEEMED TO GLIMMER WITH ENVY FOR AN INSTANT.
I'M NOT SURE ABOUT THAT...
I WONDER HOW I SEEMED TO HIM?

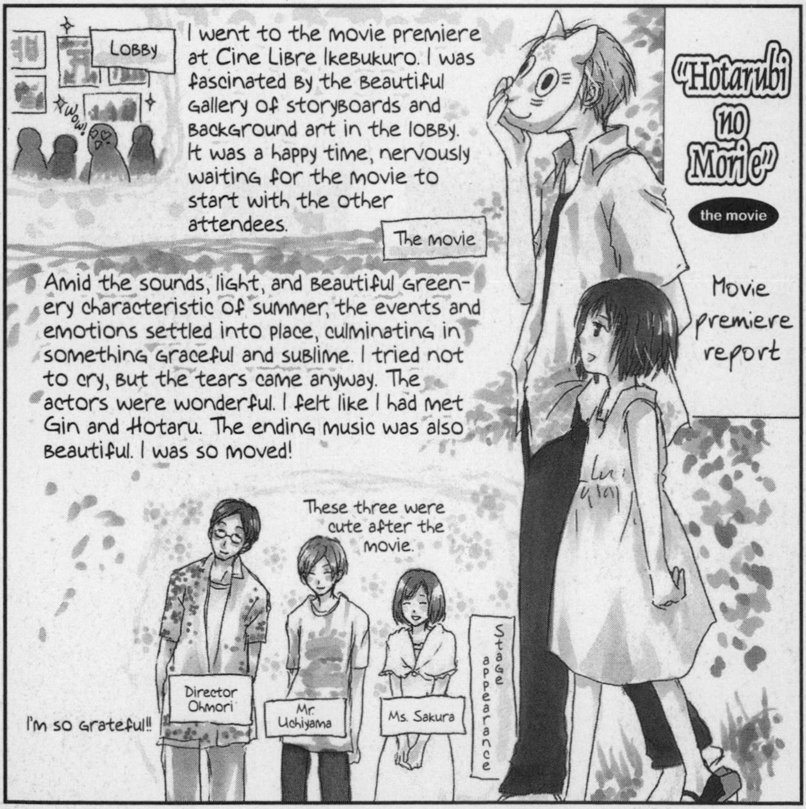
"Hotarubi no Mori e"
the movie
Movie premiere report
Lobby
Wow!
I went to the movie premiere at Cine Libre Ikebukuro. I was fascinated by the beautiful gallery of storyboards and background art in the lobby. It was a happy time, nervously waiting for the movie to start with the other attendees.
The movie
Amid the sounds, light, and beautiful greenery characteristic of summer, the events and emotions settled into place, culminating in something graceful and sublime. I tried not to cry, but the tears came anyway. The actors were wonderful. I felt like I had met Gin and Hotaru. The ending music was also beautiful. I was so moved!
These three were cute after the movie.
Stage appearance
Ms. Sakura
Mr. Uchiyama
Director Ohmori
I'm so grateful!!

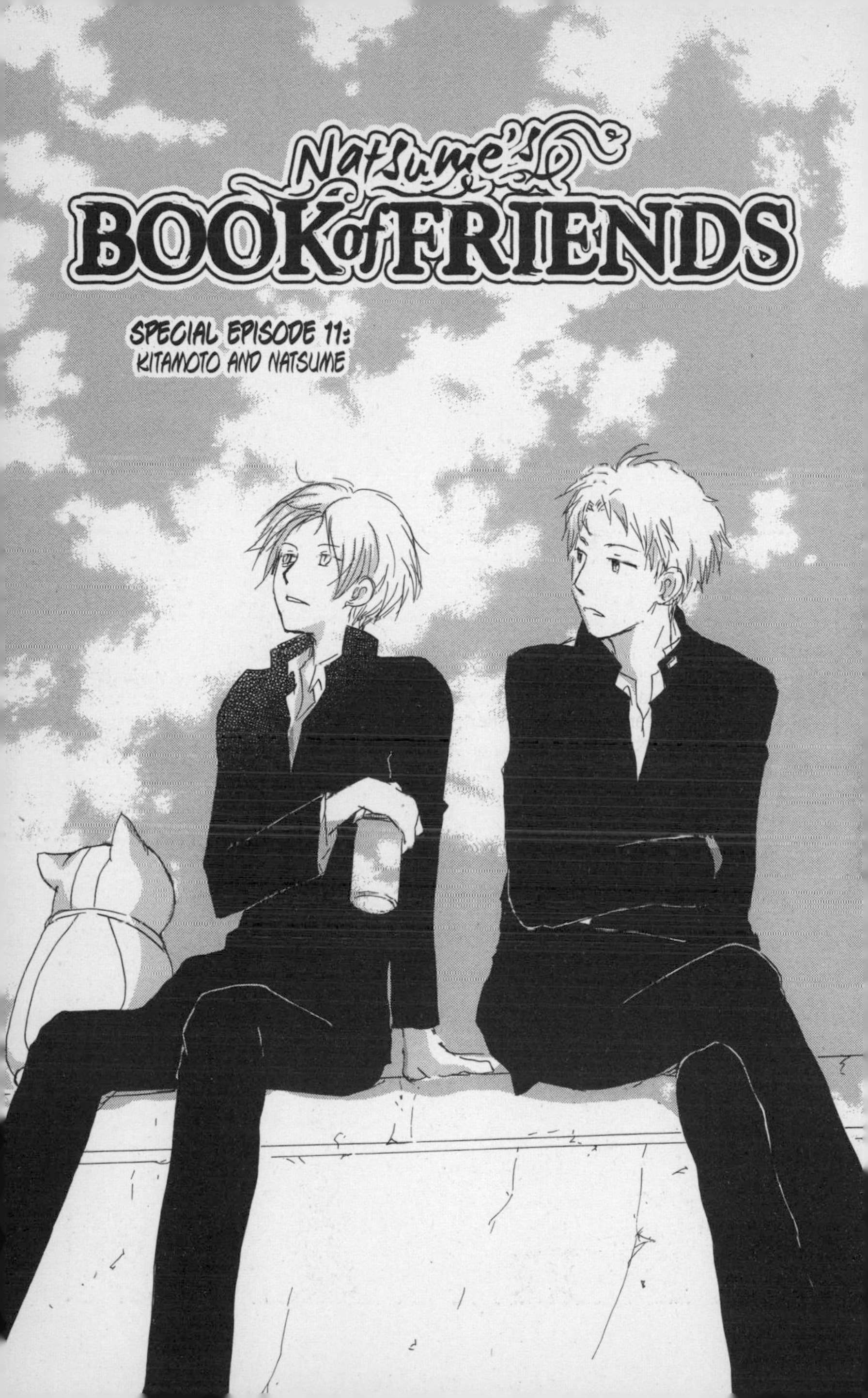
Natsume's
BOOK of FRIENDS
SPECIAL EPISODE 11:
KITAMOTO AND NATSUME

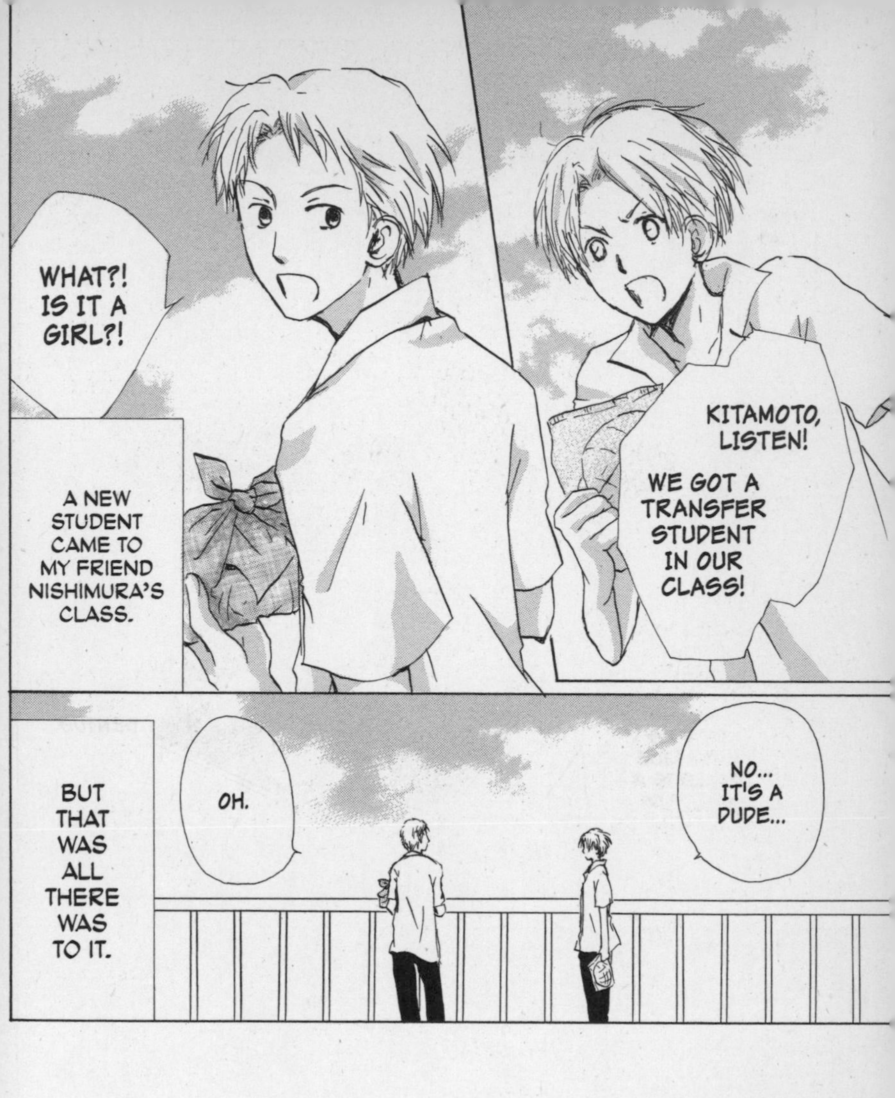
KITAMOTO, LISTEN!
WE GOT A TRANSFER STUDENT IN OUR CLASS!
WHAT?! IS IT A GIRL?!
A NEW STUDENT CAME TO MY FRIEND NISHIMURA'S CLASS.
NO... IT'S A DUDE...
OH.
BUT THAT WAS ALL THERE WAS TO IT.

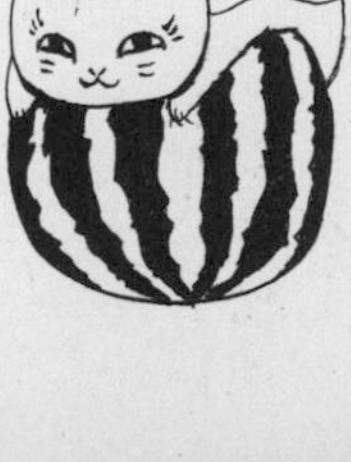

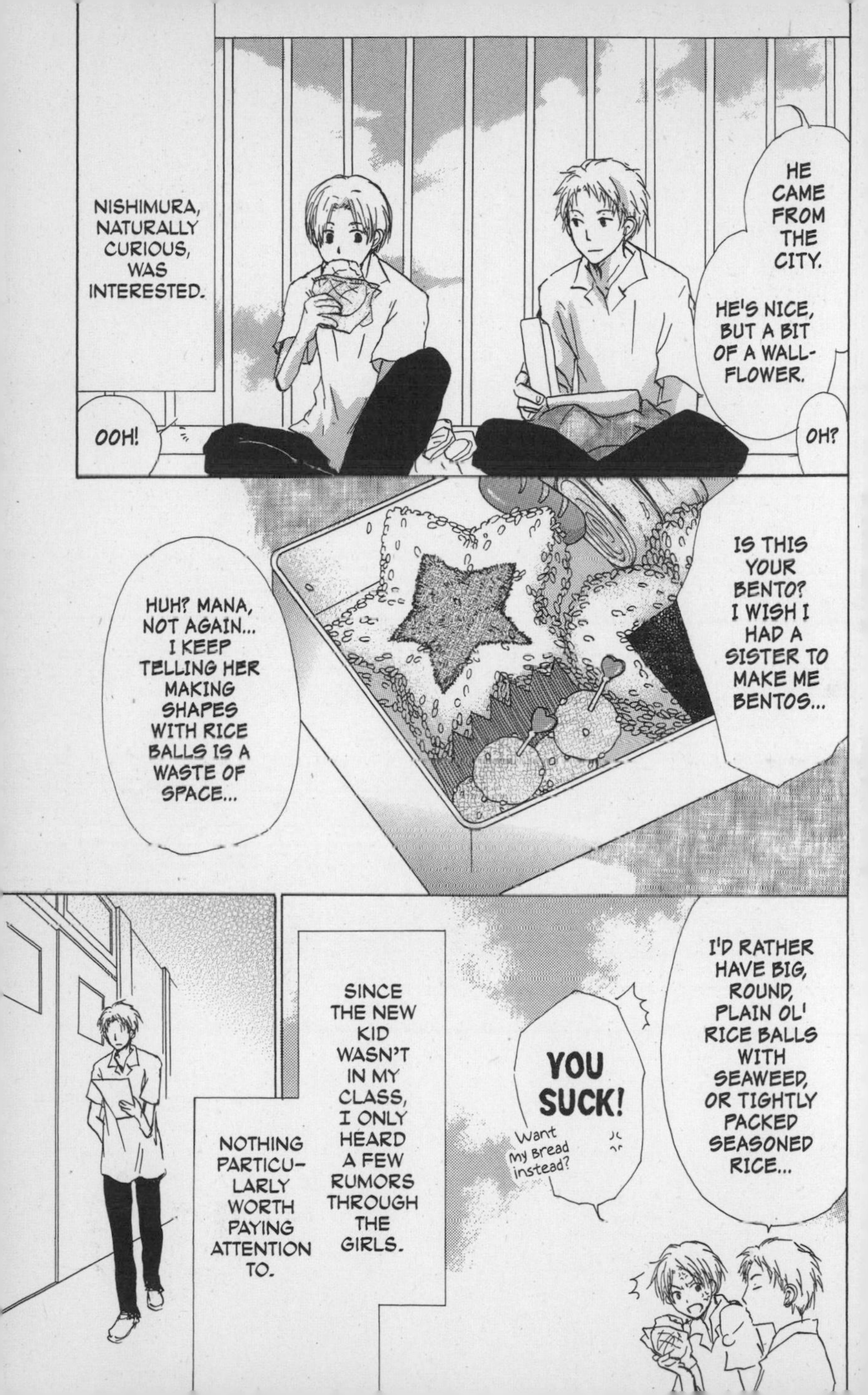
HE CAME FROM THE CITY.
HE'S NICE, BUT A BIT OF A WALL-FLOWER.
OH?
NISHIMURA, NATURALLY CURIOUS, WAS INTERESTED.
OOH!
IS THIS YOUR BENTO? I WISH I HAD A SISTER TO MAKE ME BENTOS...
HUH? MANA, NOT AGAIN... I KEEP TELLING HER MAKING SHAPES WITH RICE BALLS IS A WASTE OF SPACE...
I'D RATHER HAVE BIG, ROUND, PLAIN OL' RICE BALLS WITH SEAWEED, OR TIGHTLY PACKED SEASONED RICE...
YOU SUCK!
Want my Bread instead?
SINCE THE NEW KID WASN'T IN MY CLASS, I ONLY HEARD A FEW RUMORS THROUGH THE GIRLS.
NOTHING PARTICU-LARLY WORTH PAYING ATTENTION TO.

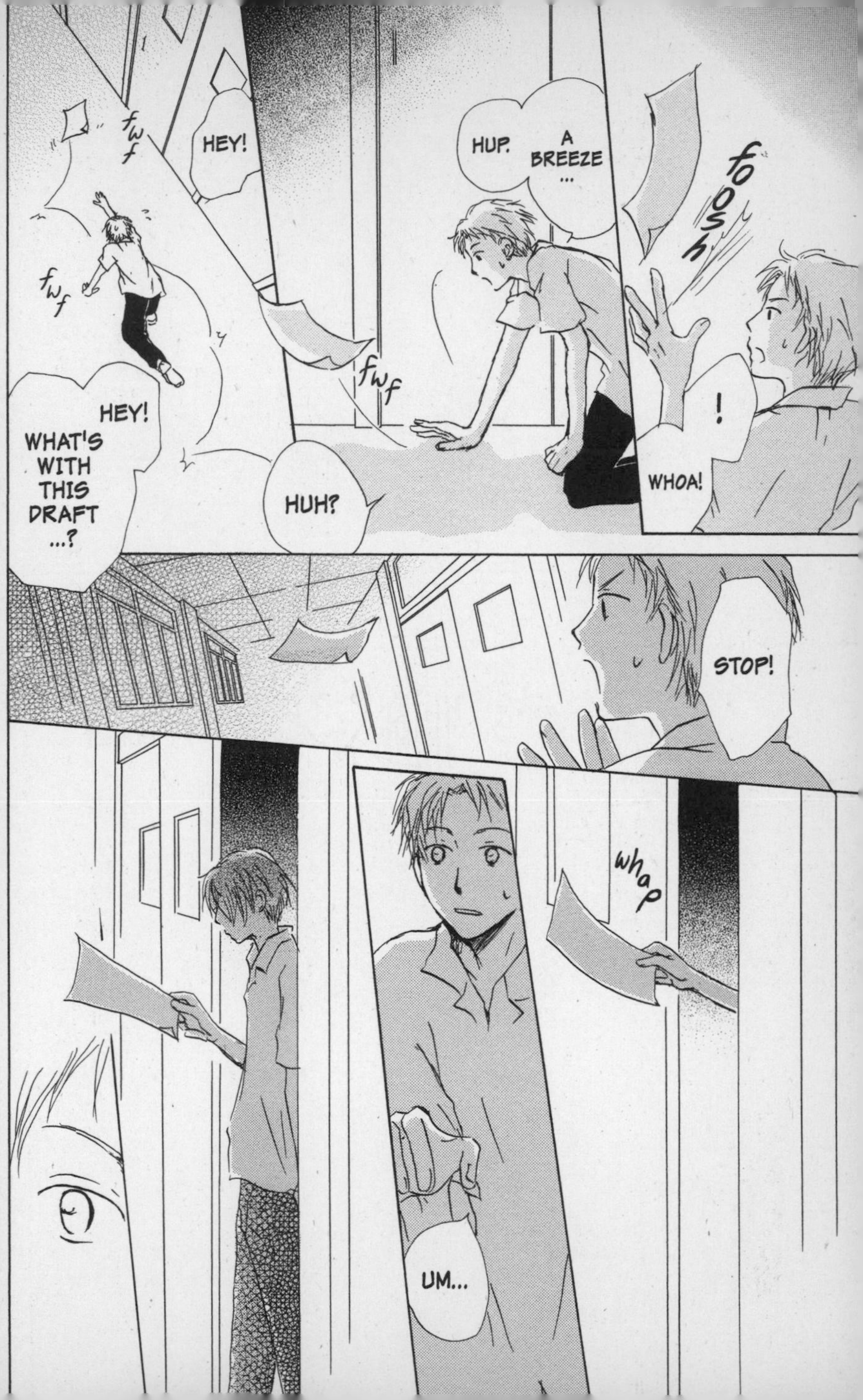
foosh
!
WHOA!
HUP.
A BREEZE ...
fwf
HUH?
HEY!
fwf
fwf
HEY! WHAT'S WITH THIS DRAFT ...?
STOP!
whap
UM...

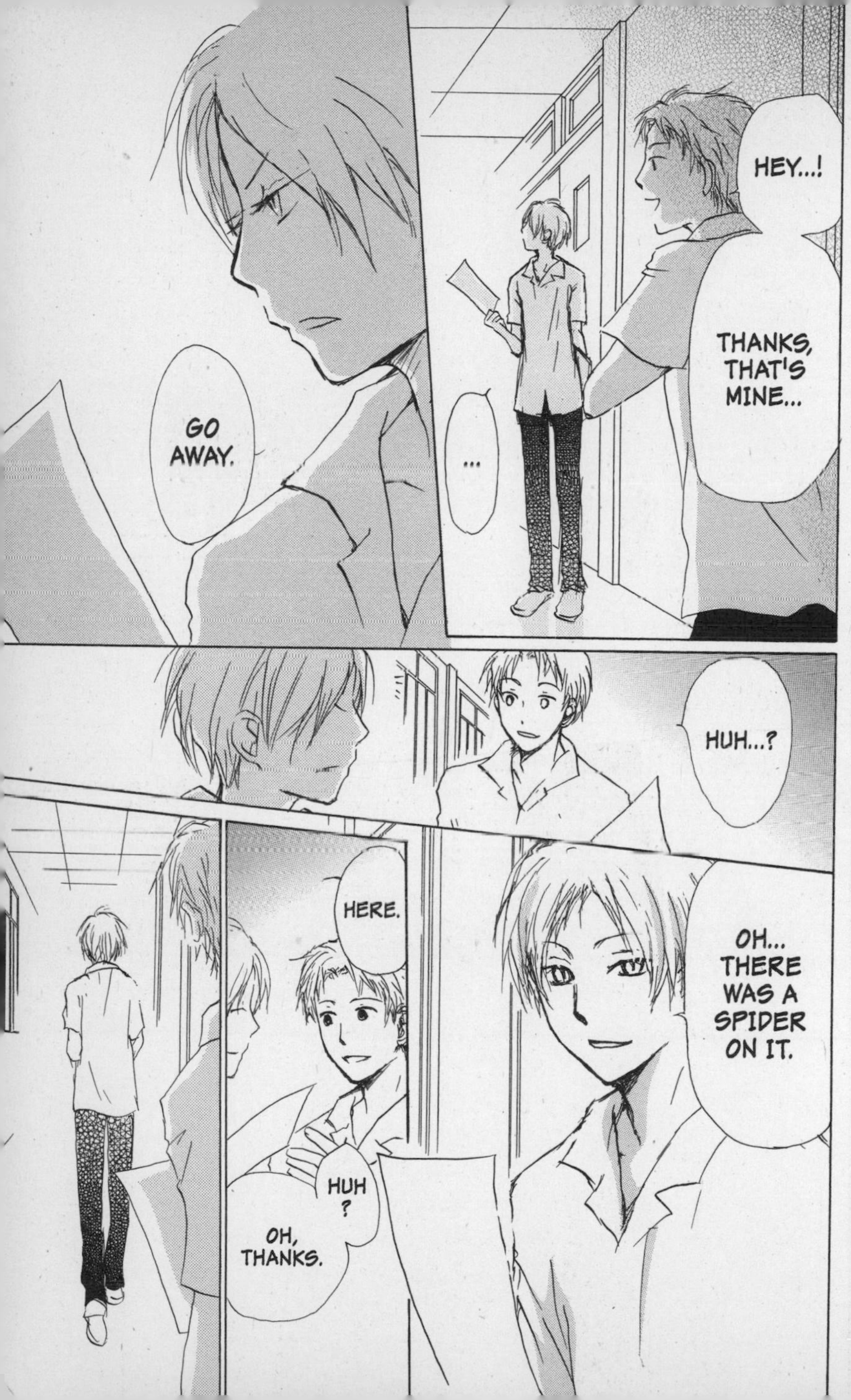
HEY...!
THANKS, THAT'S MINE...
...
GO AWAY.
HUH...?
OH... THERE WAS A SPIDER ON IT.
HERE.
HUH ?
OH, THANKS.

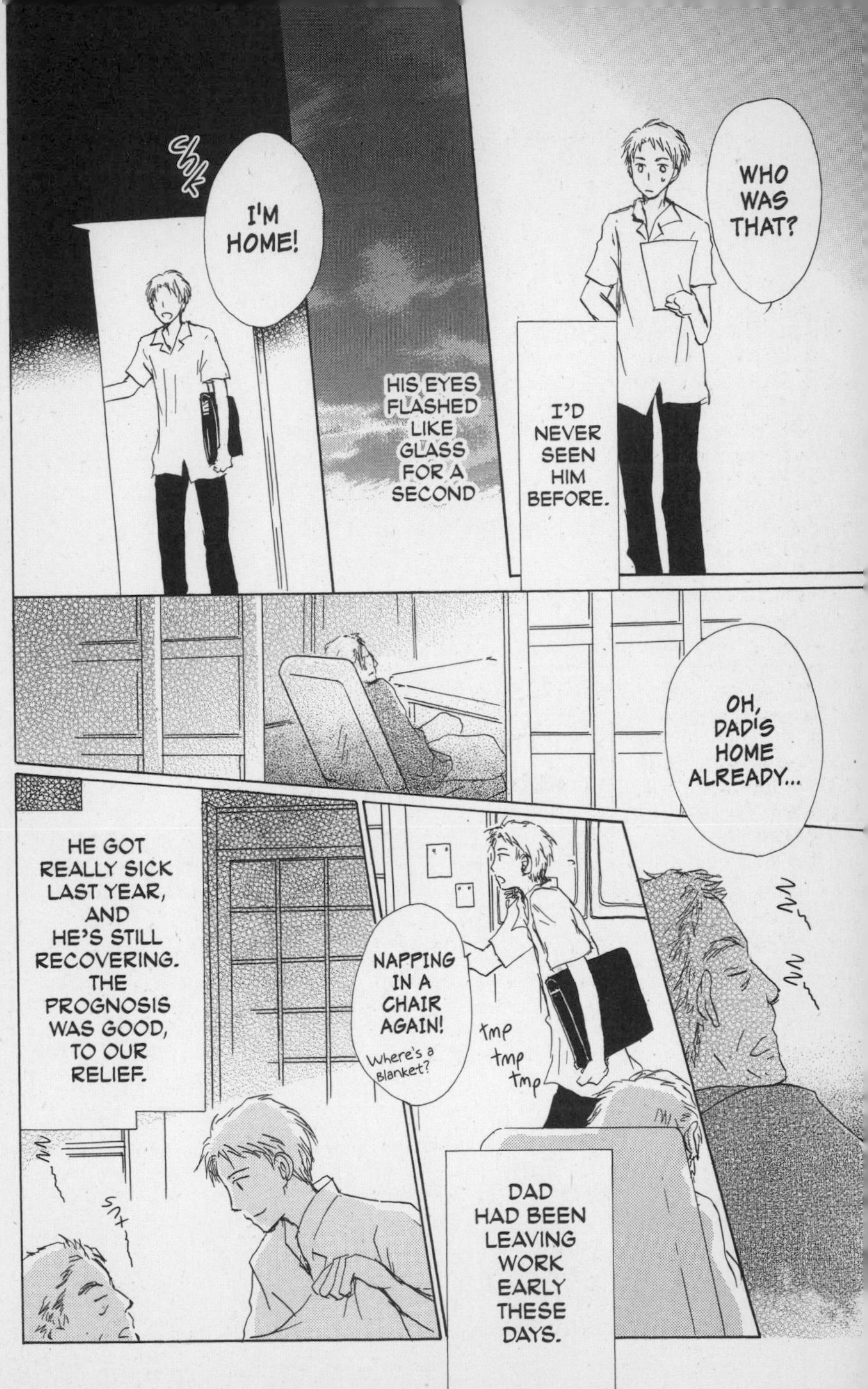
WHO WAS THAT?
I'D NEVER SEEN HIM BEFORE.
I'M HOME!
chk
HIS EYES FLASHED LIKE GLASS FOR A SECOND
OH, DAD'S HOME ALREADY...
DAD HAD BEEN LEAVING WORK EARLY THESE DAYS.
NAPPING IN A CHAIR AGAIN!
Where's a Blanket?
tmp tmp tmp
HE GOT REALLY SICK LAST YEAR, AND HE'S STILL RECOVERING. THE PROGNOSIS WAS GOOD, TO OUR RELIEF.
snx

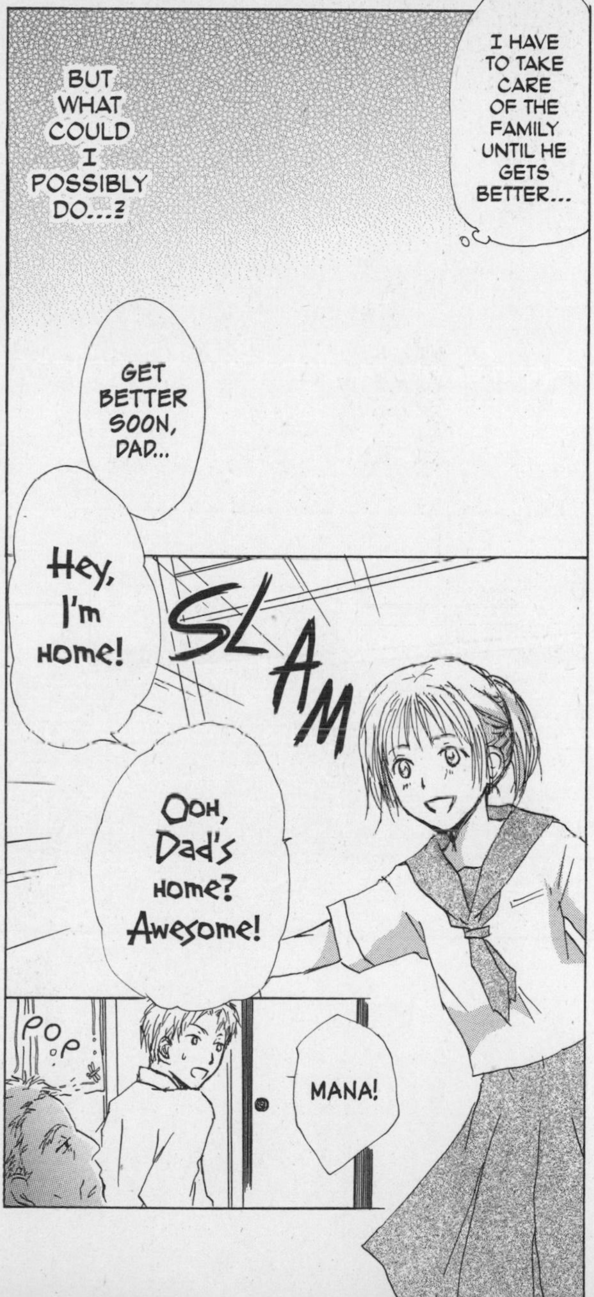
I HAVE TO TAKE CARE OF THE FAMILY UNTIL HE GETS BETTER...
BUT WHAT COULD I POSSIBLY DO...?
GET BETTER SOON, DAD...
SLAM
Hey, I'm home!
Ooh, Dad's home? Awesome!
MANA!
POP

05

❋ Tanuma

When the name and the face fit perfectly as I start working on a character, it usually develops from there as I expect. But Tanuma didn't easily become fast friends with Natsume as I planned. He seems endlessly nervous. He's actually quite calm, but when Natsume's around, he becomes nervous trying to become better friends with him, making Natsume also nervous in the process. He's difficult to figure out. But it's a new experience, so he's fun to draw.

❋ Urihime and Sasago

I really like these two, but they don't like Natsume very much, so Natori puts them away when he meets with Natsume. I haven't had much opportunity to draw them in depth. I'll get to it one day.

End of $\frac{1}{4}$ columns.

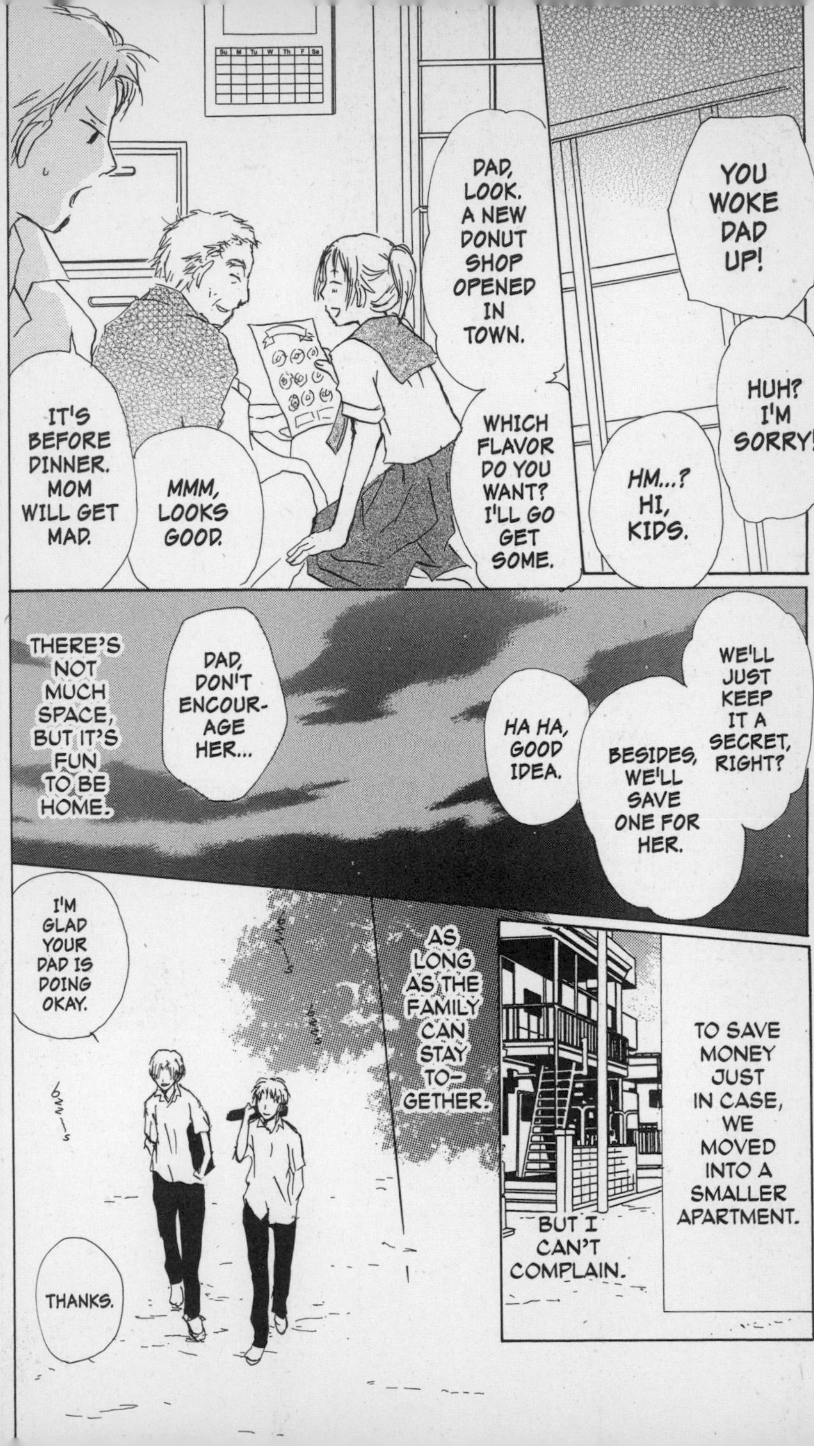
YOU WOKE DAD UP!
DAD, LOOK. A NEW DONUT SHOP OPENED IN TOWN.
HUH? I'M SORRY!
HM...? HI, KIDS.
WHICH FLAVOR DO YOU WANT? I'LL GO GET SOME.
MMM, LOOKS GOOD.
IT'S BEFORE DINNER. MOM WILL GET MAD.
WE'LL JUST KEEP IT A SECRET, RIGHT?
BESIDES, WE'LL SAVE ONE FOR HER.
HA HA, GOOD IDEA.
DAD, DON'T ENCOURAGE HER...
THERE'S NOT MUCH SPACE, BUT IT'S FUN TO BE HOME.
TO SAVE MONEY JUST IN CASE, WE MOVED INTO A SMALLER APARTMENT.
BUT I CAN'T COMPLAIN.
AS LONG AS THE FAMILY CAN STAY TO-GETHER.
I'M GLAD YOUR DAD IS DOING OKAY.
THANKS.

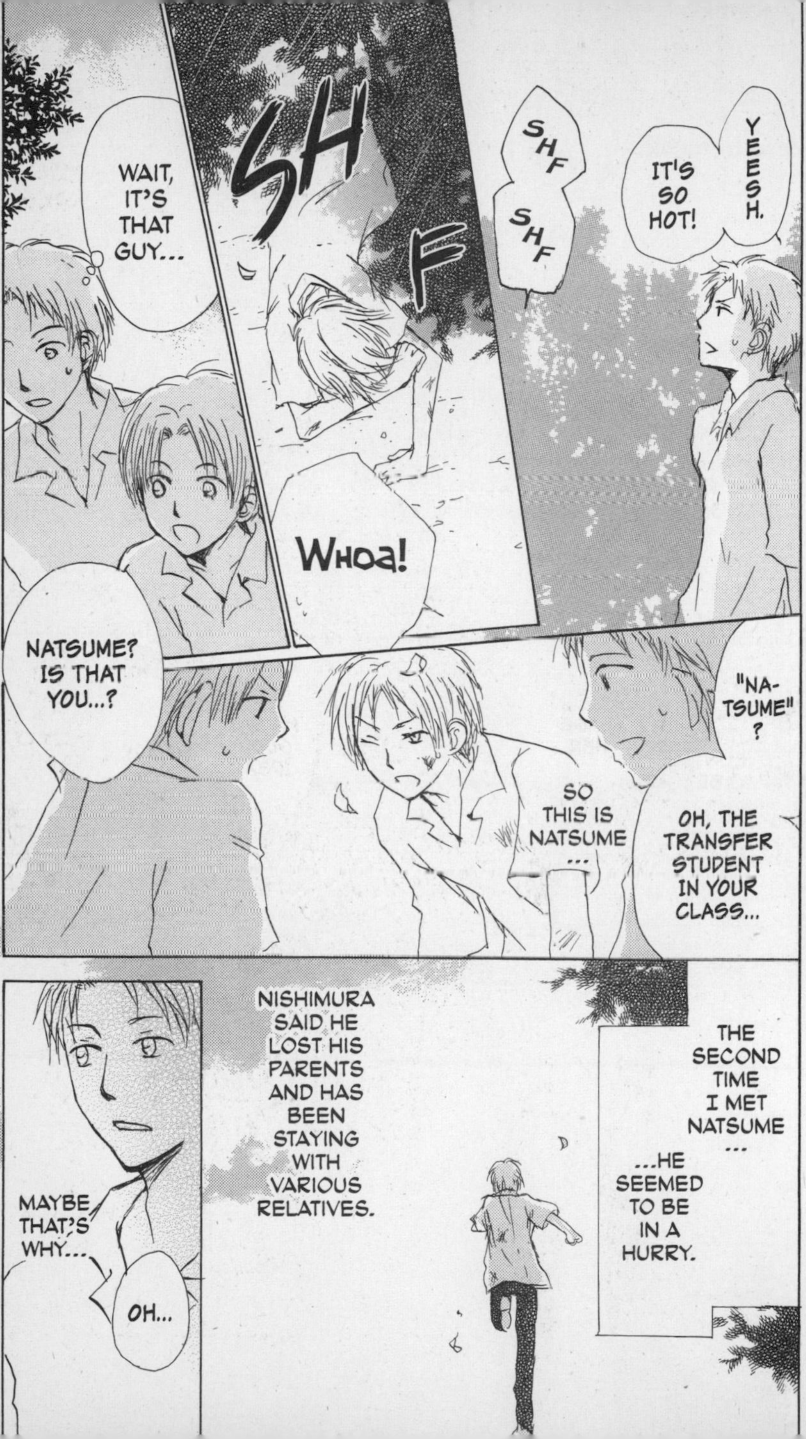
YEESH.
IT'S SO HOT!
SHF SHF
SHF
Whoa!
WAIT, IT'S THAT GUY...
NATSUME? IS THAT YOU...?
"NA-TSUME"?
OH, THE TRANSFER STUDENT IN YOUR CLASS...
SO THIS IS NATSUME...
THE SECOND TIME I MET NATSUME...
...HE SEEMED TO BE IN A HURRY.
NISHIMURA SAID HE LOST HIS PARENTS AND HAS BEEN STAYING WITH VARIOUS RELATIVES.
MAYBE THAT'S WHY...
OH...

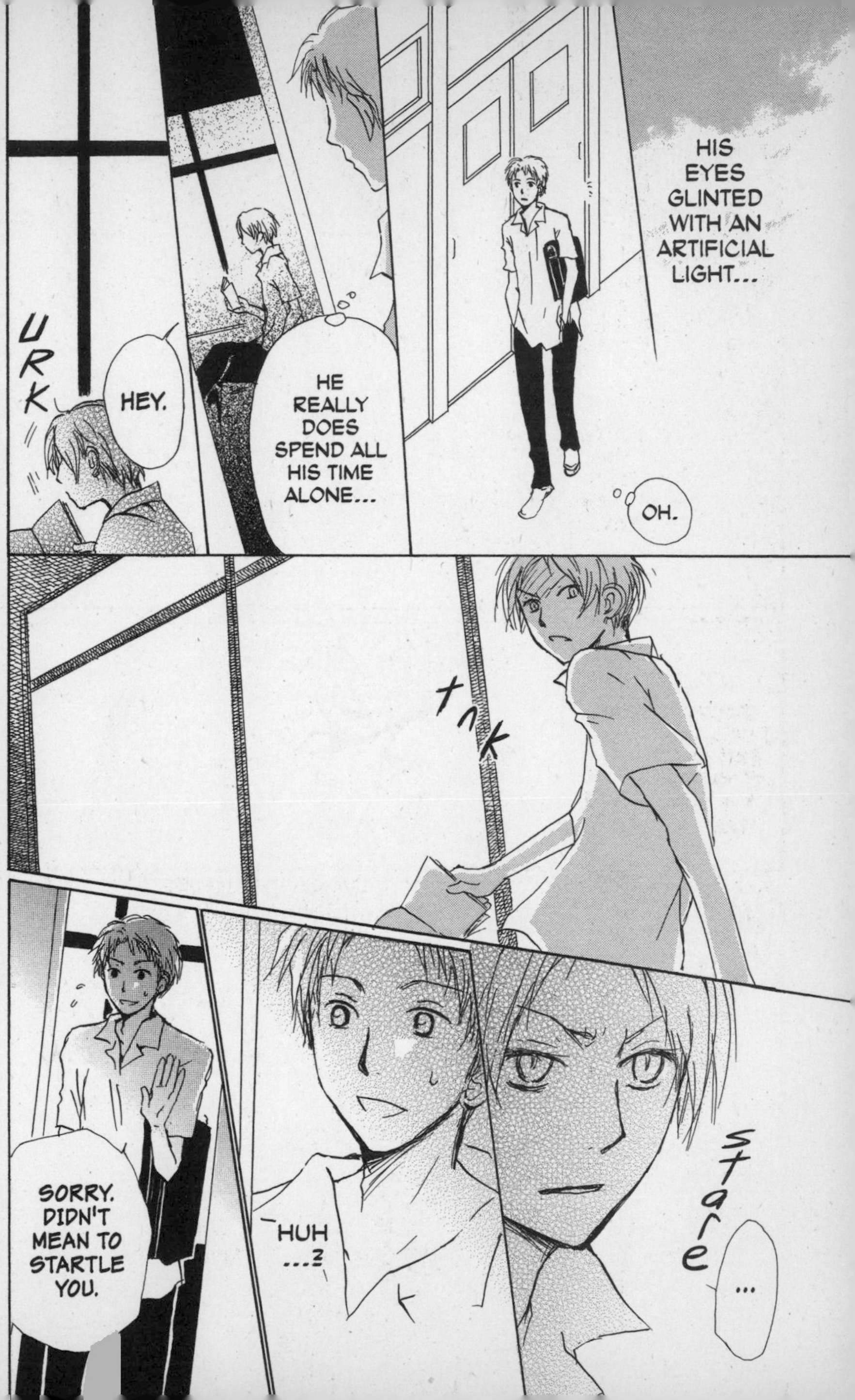
HIS EYES GLINTED WITH AN ARTIFICIAL LIGHT...
OH.
HE REALLY DOES SPEND ALL HIS TIME ALONE...
HEY.
URK
tnk
stare
...
HUH ...?
SORRY. DIDN'T MEAN TO STARTLE YOU.

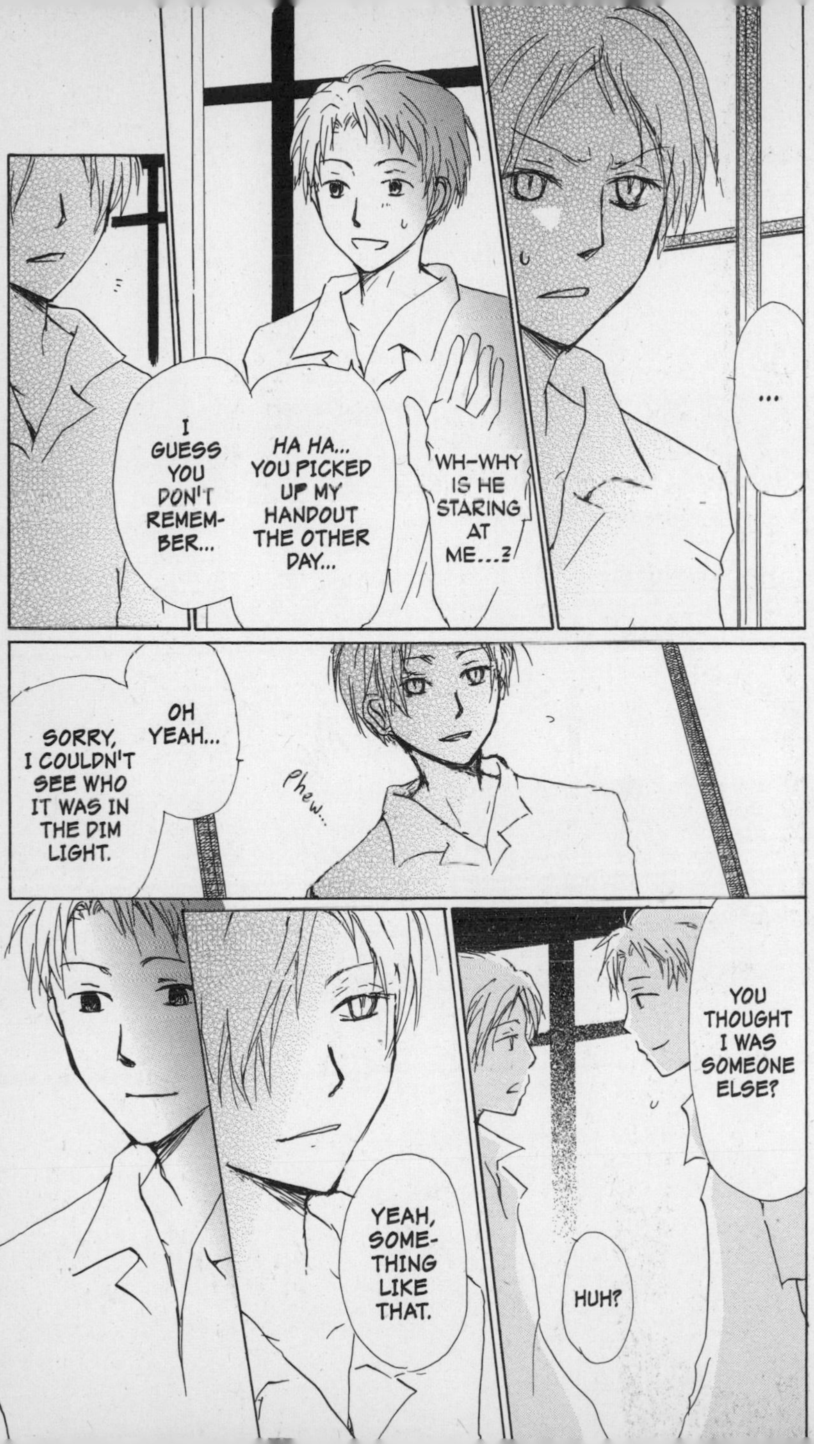
...
WH-WHY IS HE STARING AT ME...?
HA HA... YOU PICKED UP MY HANDOUT THE OTHER DAY...
I GUESS YOU DON'T REMEMBER...
OH YEAH...
SORRY, I COULDN'T SEE WHO IT WAS IN THE DIM LIGHT.
Phew...
YOU THOUGHT I WAS SOMEONE ELSE?
HUH?
YEAH, SOMETHING LIKE THAT.

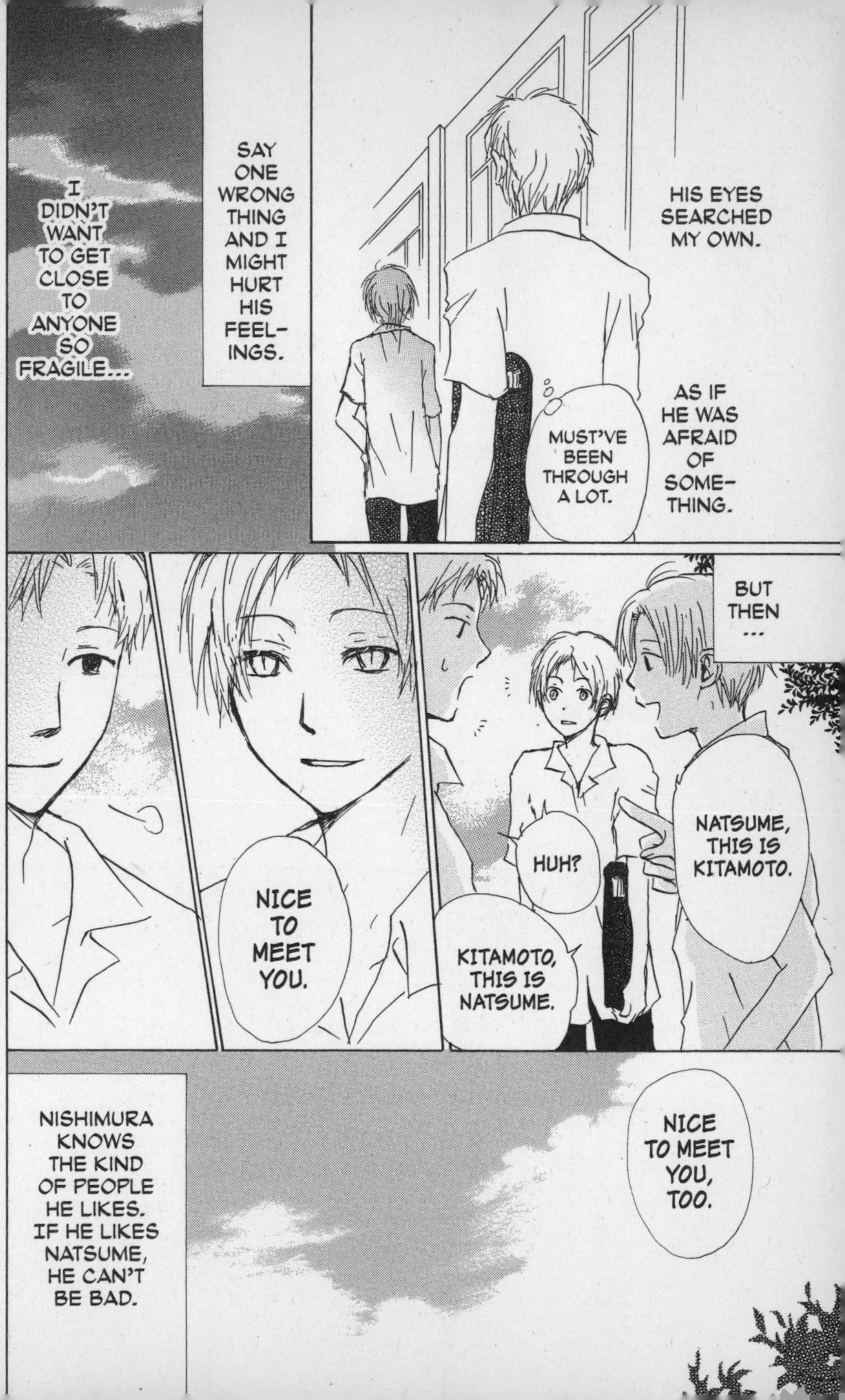

HIS EYES SEARCHED MY OWN.
AS IF HE WAS AFRAID OF SOME-THING.
MUST'VE BEEN THROUGH A LOT.
SAY ONE WRONG THING AND I MIGHT HURT HIS FEEL-INGS.
I DIDN'T WANT TO GET CLOSE TO ANYONE SO FRAGILE...
BUT THEN ...
NATSUME, THIS IS KITAMOTO.
HUH?
KITAMOTO, THIS IS NATSUME.
NICE TO MEET YOU.
NICE TO MEET YOU, TOO.
NISHIMURA KNOWS THE KIND OF PEOPLE HE LIKES. IF HE LIKES NATSUME, HE CAN'T BE BAD.

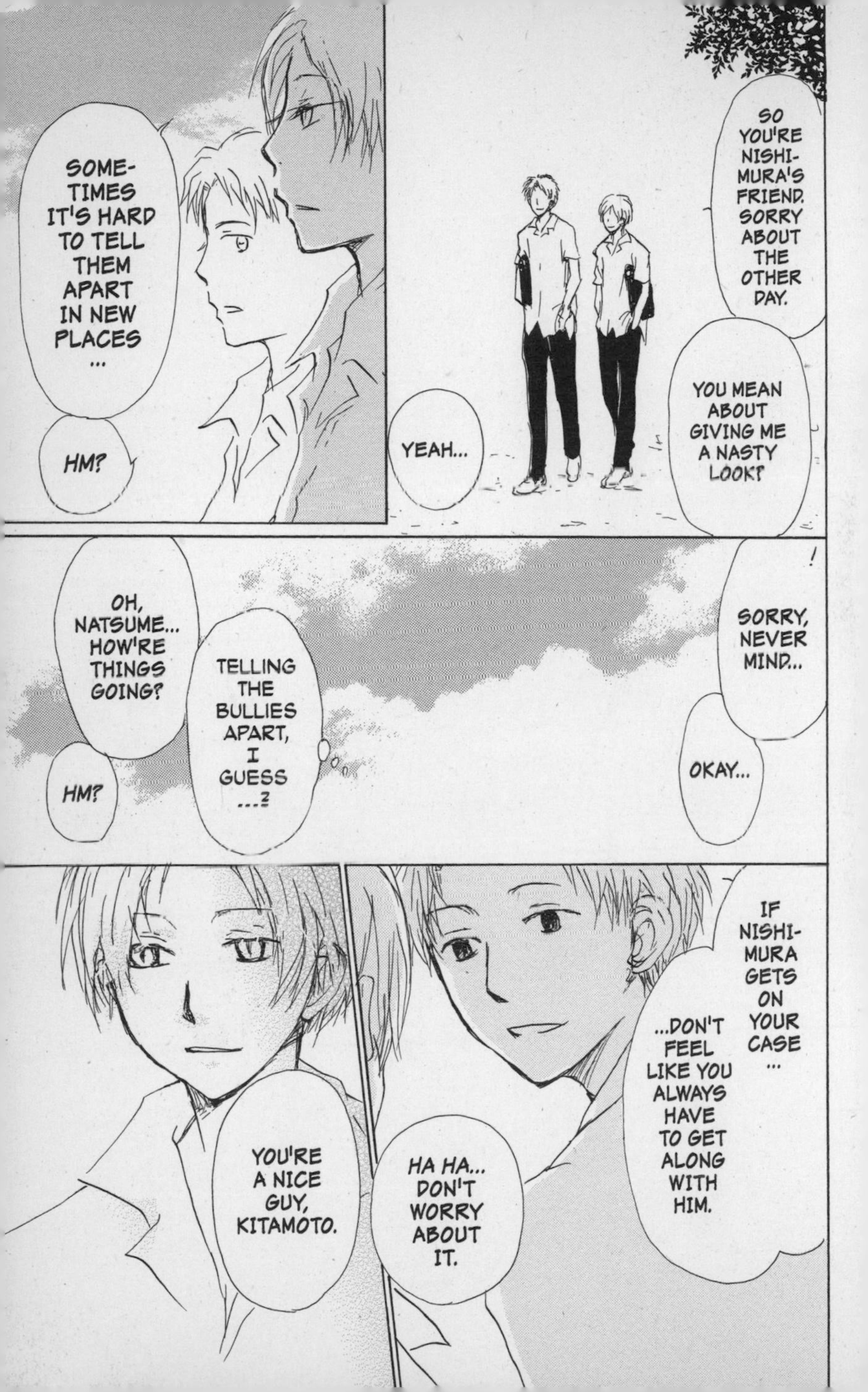
SO YOU'RE NISHIMURA'S FRIEND. SORRY ABOUT THE OTHER DAY.
YOU MEAN ABOUT GIVING ME A NASTY LOOK?
YEAH...
SOMETIMES IT'S HARD TO TELL THEM APART IN NEW PLACES ...
HM?
!
SORRY, NEVER MIND...
OKAY...
TELLING THE BULLIES APART, I GUESS ...?
OH, NATSUME... HOW'RE THINGS GOING?
HM?
IF NISHIMURA GETS ON YOUR CASE ...
...DON'T FEEL LIKE YOU ALWAYS HAVE TO GET ALONG WITH HIM.
HA HA... DON'T WORRY ABOUT IT.
YOU'RE A NICE GUY, KITAMOTO.

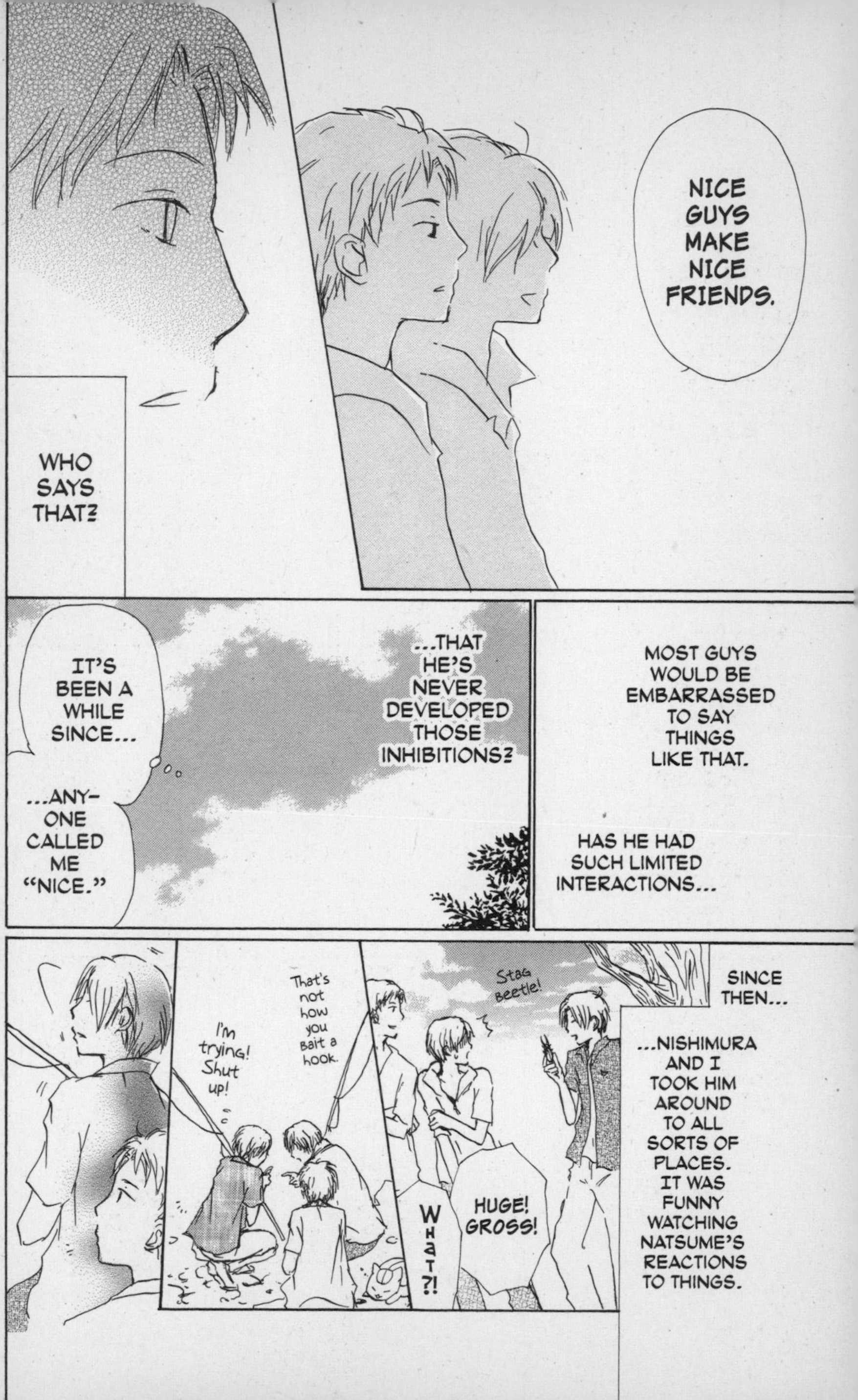
NICE GUYS MAKE NICE FRIENDS.
WHO SAYS THAT?
MOST GUYS WOULD BE EMBARRASSED TO SAY THINGS LIKE THAT.
HAS HE HAD SUCH LIMITED INTERACTIONS...
...THAT HE'S NEVER DEVELOPED THOSE INHIBITIONS?
IT'S BEEN A WHILE SINCE...
...ANY-ONE CALLED ME "NICE."
SINCE THEN...
...NISHIMURA AND I TOOK HIM AROUND TO ALL SORTS OF PLACES. IT WAS FUNNY WATCHING NATSUME'S REACTIONS TO THINGS.
Stag Beetle!
HUGE! GROSS!
WHAT?!
That's not how you bait a hook.
I'm trying! Shut up!

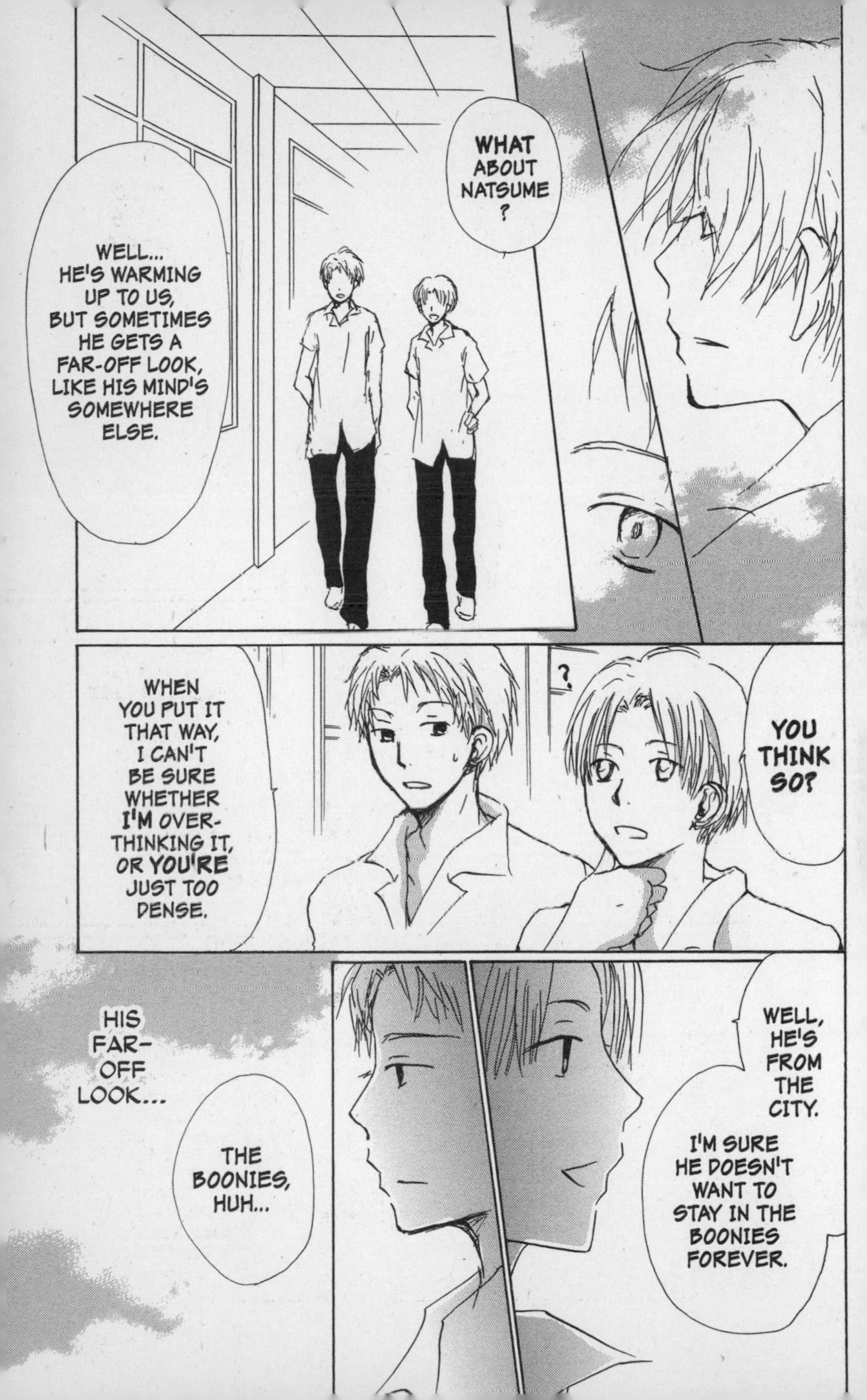
WHAT ABOUT NATSUME ?
WELL... HE'S WARMING UP TO US, BUT SOMETIMES HE GETS A FAR-OFF LOOK, LIKE HIS MIND'S SOMEWHERE ELSE.
YOU THINK SO?
?
WHEN YOU PUT IT THAT WAY, I CAN'T BE SURE WHETHER I'M OVER-THINKING IT, OR YOU'RE JUST TOO DENSE.
WELL, HE'S FROM THE CITY.
I'M SURE HE DOESN'T WANT TO STAY IN THE BOONIES FOREVER.
THE BOONIES, HUH...
HIS FAR-OFF LOOK...

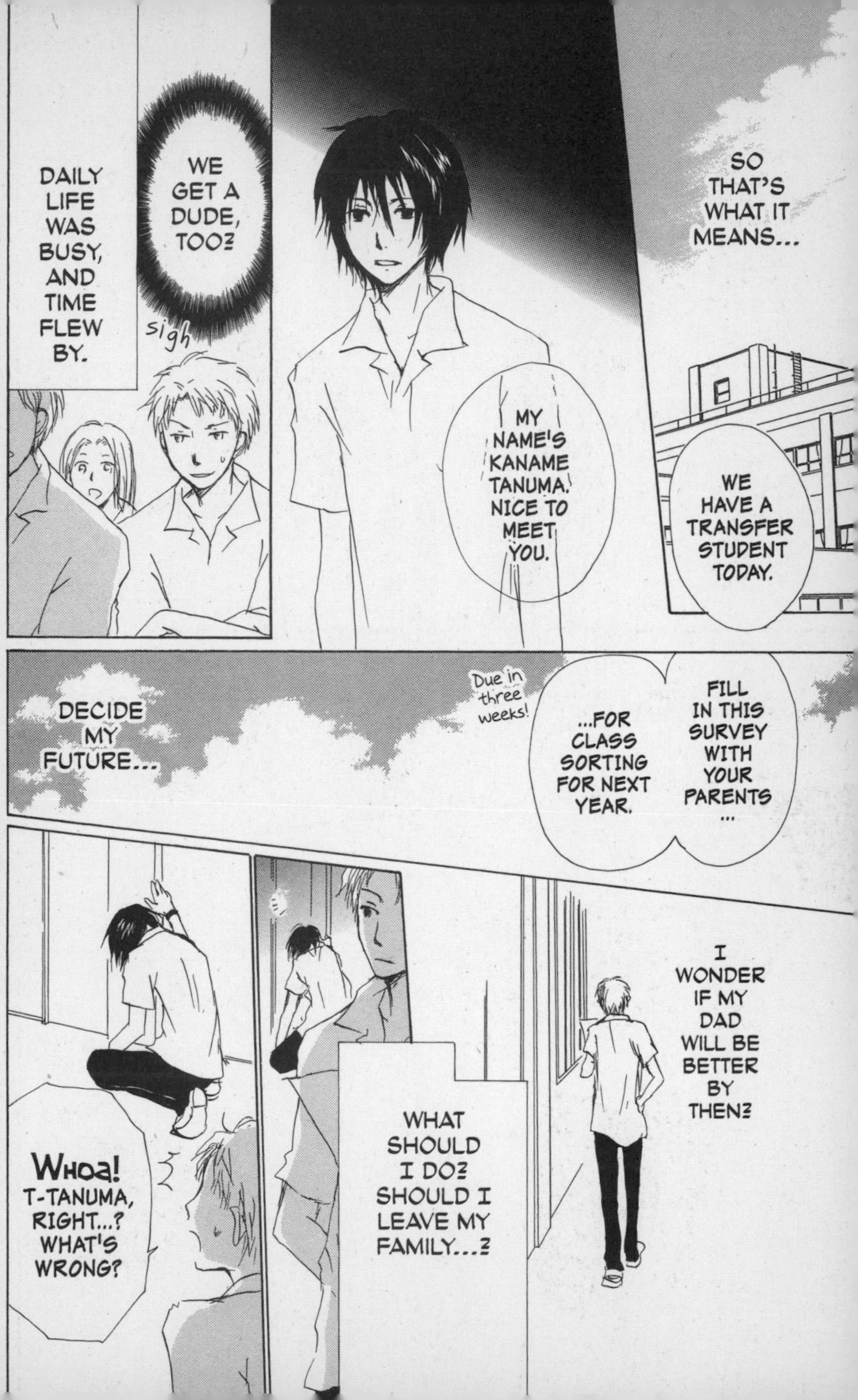
SO THAT'S WHAT IT MEANS...
WE HAVE A TRANSFER STUDENT TODAY.
MY NAME'S KANAME TANUMA. NICE TO MEET YOU.
WE GET A DUDE, TOO?
DAILY LIFE WAS BUSY, AND TIME FLEW BY.
sigh
FILL IN THIS SURVEY WITH YOUR PARENTS ...
...FOR CLASS SORTING FOR NEXT YEAR.
Due in three weeks!
DECIDE MY FUTURE...
I WONDER IF MY DAD WILL BE BETTER BY THEN?
WHAT SHOULD I DO? SHOULD I LEAVE MY FAMILY...?
WHOA! T-TANUMA, RIGHT...? WHAT'S WRONG?

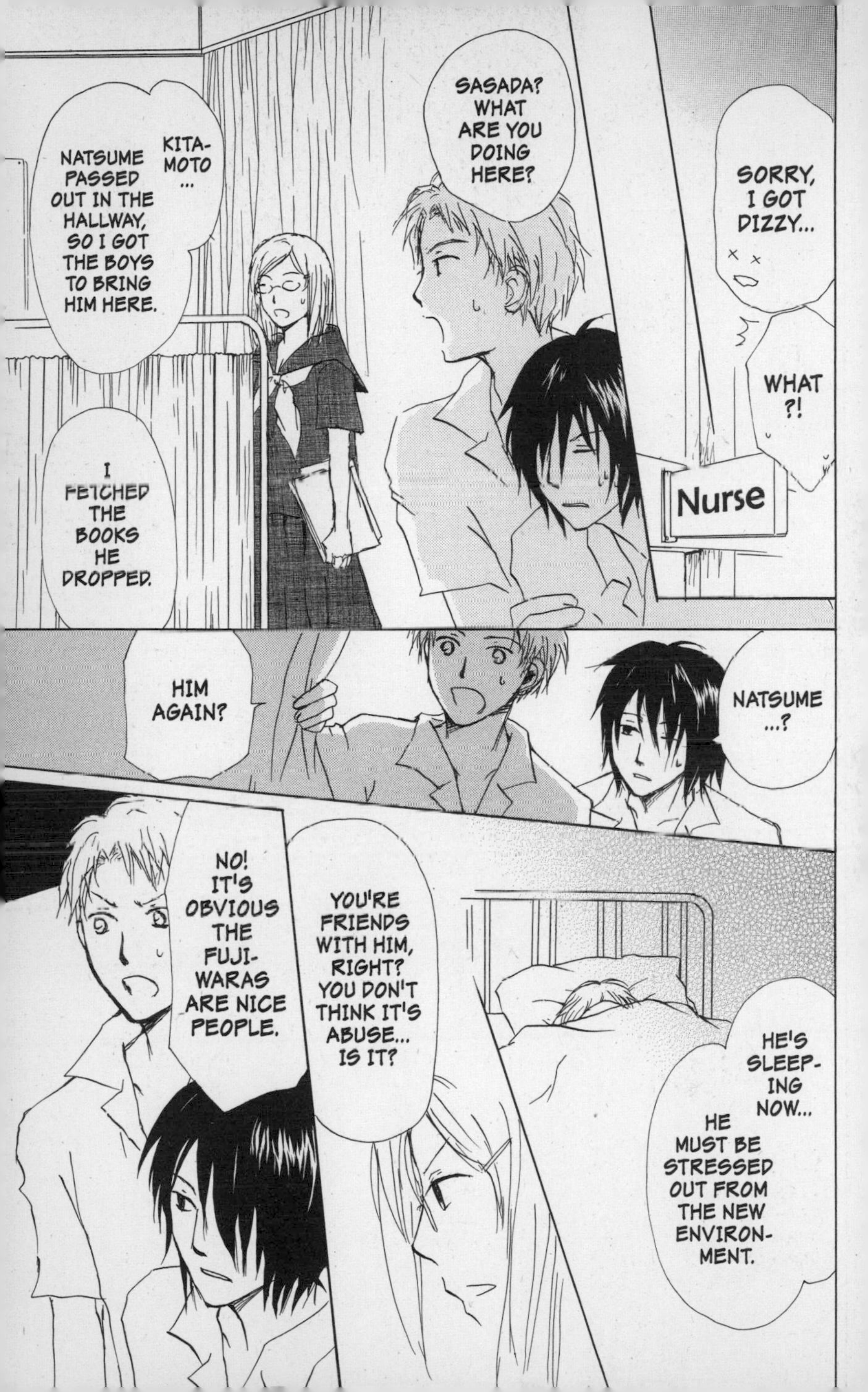
SORRY, I GOT DIZZY...
WHAT?!
Nurse
SASADA? WHAT ARE YOU DOING HERE?
KITA-MOTO...
NATSUME PASSED OUT IN THE HALLWAY, SO I GOT THE BOYS TO BRING HIM HERE.
I FETCHED THE BOOKS HE DROPPED.
NATSUME...?
HIM AGAIN?
HE'S SLEEP-ING NOW...
HE MUST BE STRESSED OUT FROM THE NEW ENVIRON-MENT.
YOU'RE FRIENDS WITH HIM, RIGHT? YOU DON'T THINK IT'S ABUSE... IS IT?
NO! IT'S OBVIOUS THE FUJI-WARAS ARE NICE PEOPLE.

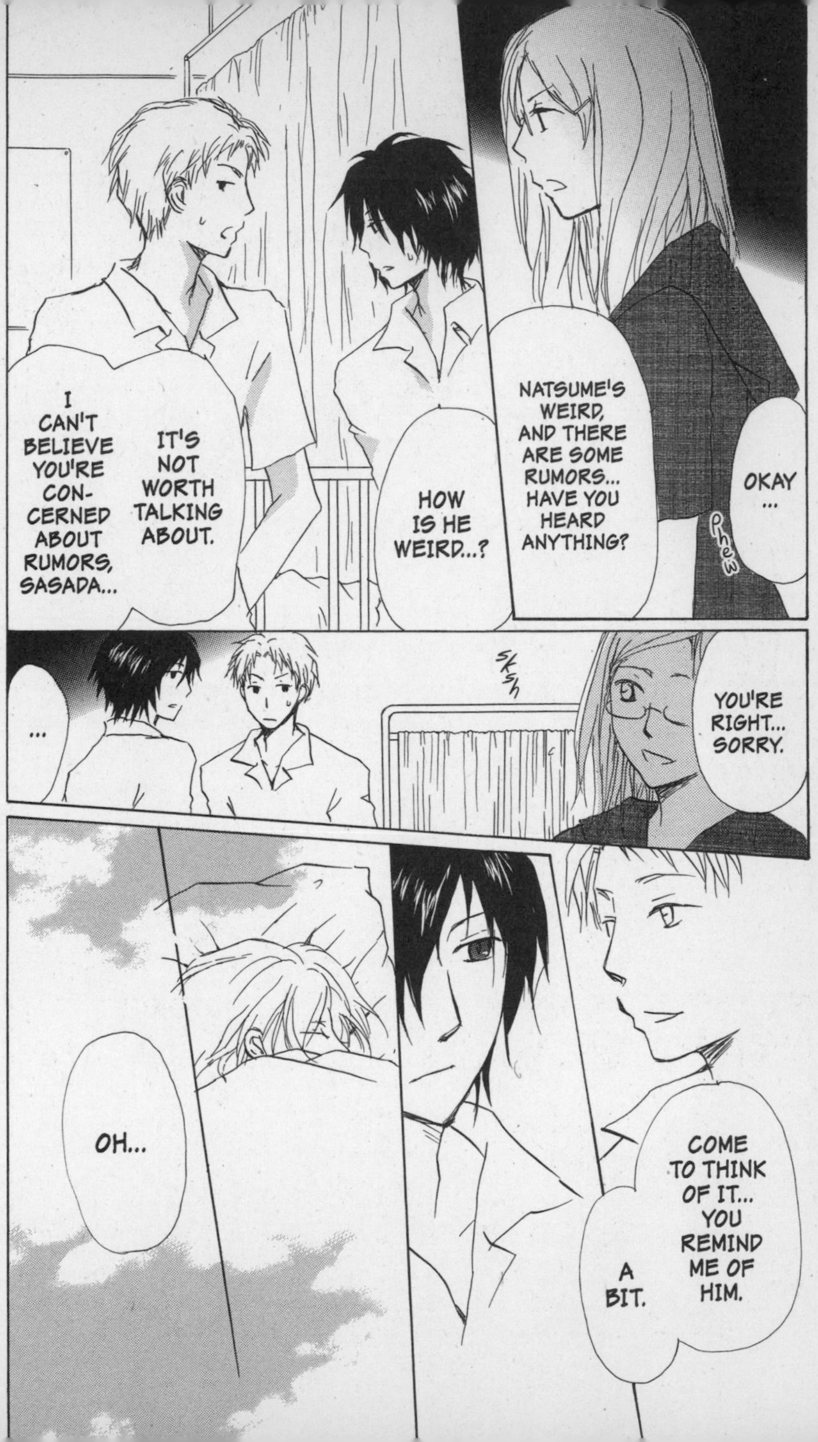
OKAY ...
Phew
NATSUME'S WEIRD, AND THERE ARE SOME RUMORS... HAVE YOU HEARD ANYTHING?
HOW IS HE WEIRD...?
IT'S NOT WORTH TALKING ABOUT.
I CAN'T BELIEVE YOU'RE CON-CERNED ABOUT RUMORS, SASADA...
YOU'RE RIGHT... SORRY.
SKSH
...
COME TO THINK OF IT... YOU REMIND ME OF HIM.
A BIT.
OH...

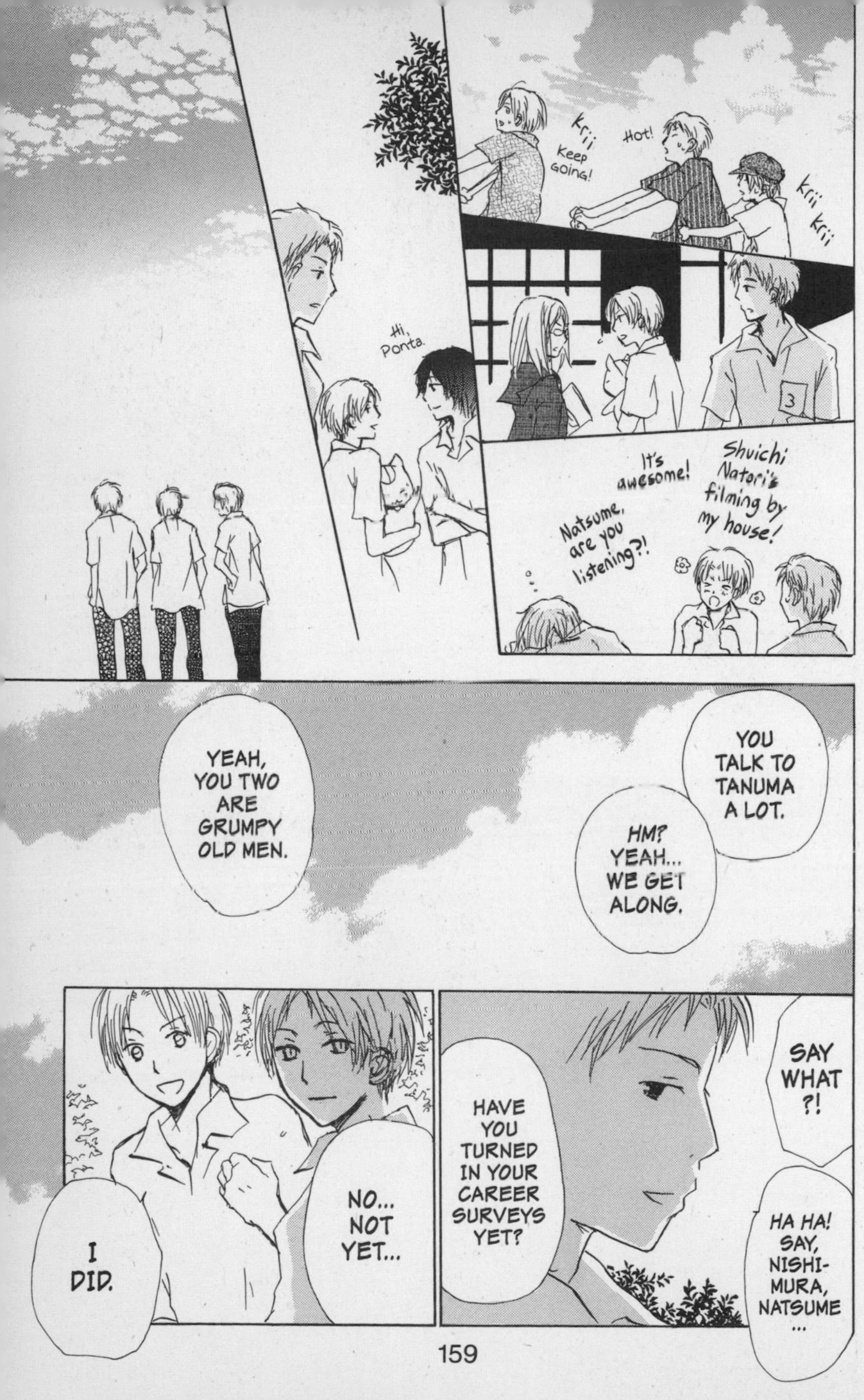
krii krii
Hot!
Keep going!
krii
Shuichi Natori's filming by my house!
It's awesome!
Natsume, are you listening?!
Hi, Ponta.
YOU TALK TO TANUMA A LOT.
HM? YEAH... WE GET ALONG.
YEAH, YOU TWO ARE GRUMPY OLD MEN.
SAY WHAT?!
HA HA! SAY, NISHIMURA, NATSUME...
HAVE YOU TURNED IN YOUR CAREER SURVEYS YET?
NO... NOT YET...
I DID.

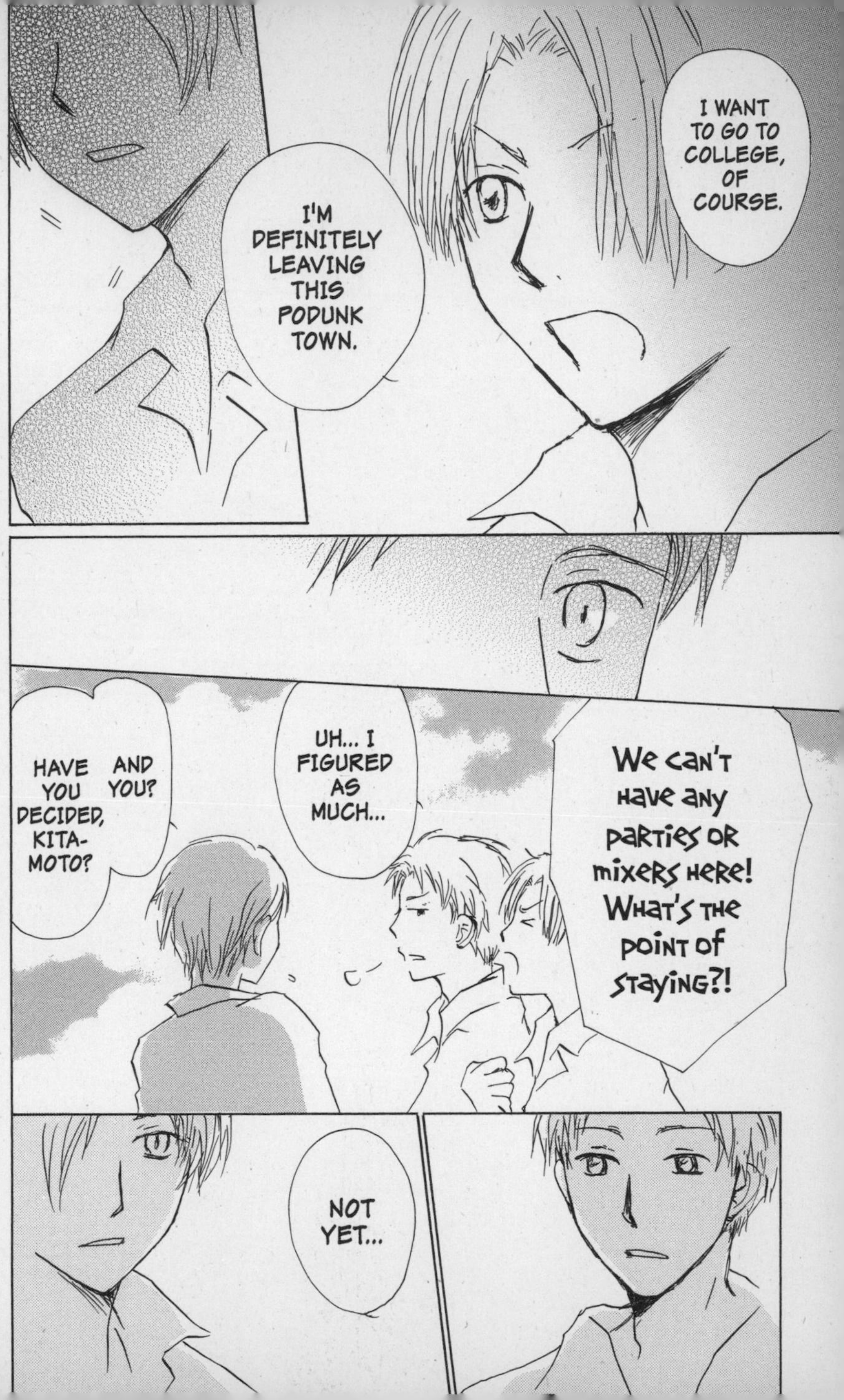
I WANT TO GO TO COLLEGE, OF COURSE.
I'M DEFINITELY LEAVING THIS PODUNK TOWN.
We can't have any parties or mixers here! What's the point of staying?!
UH... I FIGURED AS MUCH...
AND YOU?
HAVE YOU DECIDED, KITA-MOTO?
NOT YET...

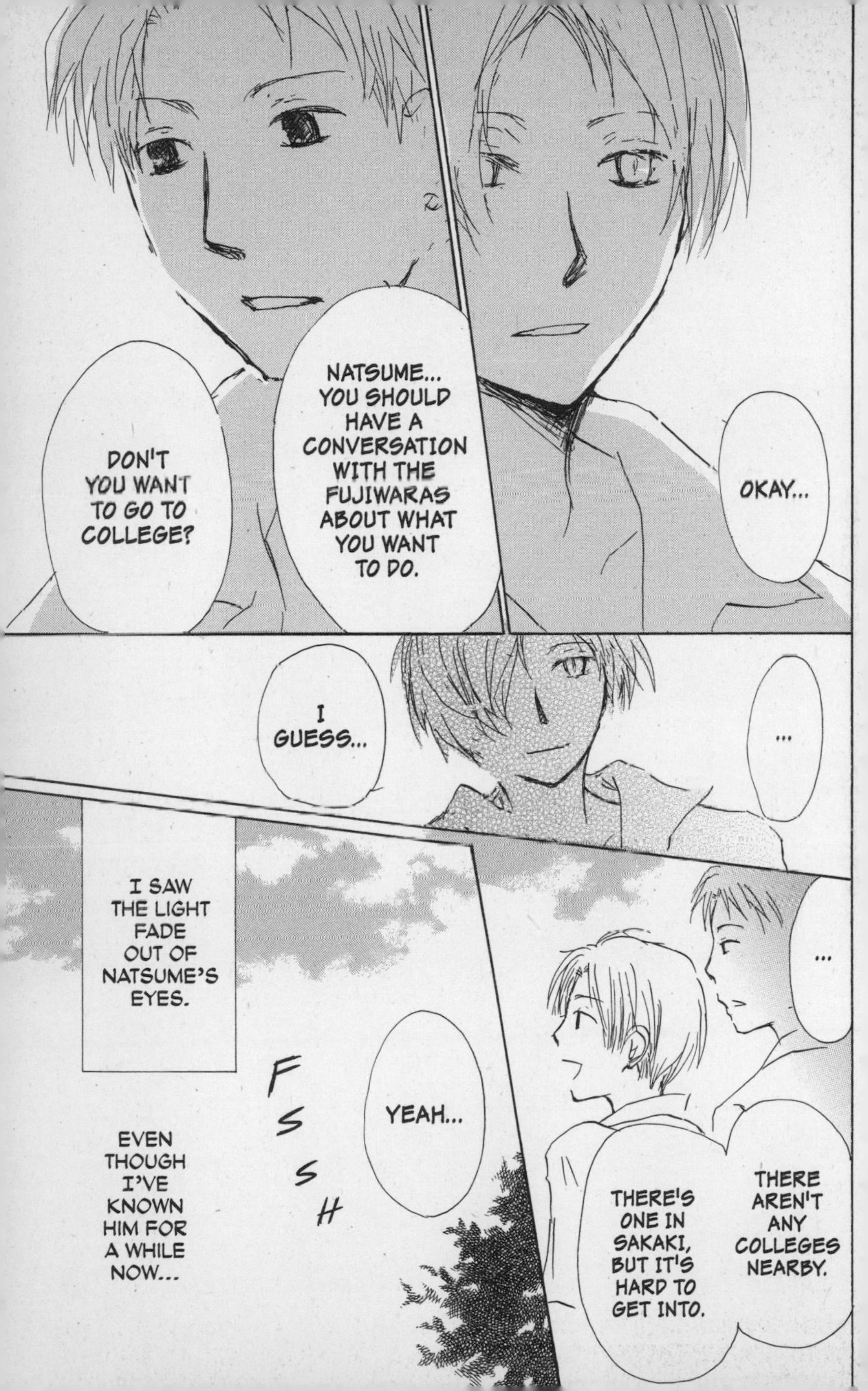
OKAY...
NATSUME... YOU SHOULD HAVE A CONVERSATION WITH THE FUJIWARAS ABOUT WHAT YOU WANT TO DO.
DON'T YOU WANT TO GO TO COLLEGE?
...
I GUESS...
...
THERE AREN'T ANY COLLEGES NEARBY.
THERE'S ONE IN SAKAKI, BUT IT'S HARD TO GET INTO.
YEAH...
FSSH
I SAW THE LIGHT FADE OUT OF NATSUME'S EYES.
EVEN THOUGH I'VE KNOWN HIM FOR A WHILE NOW...

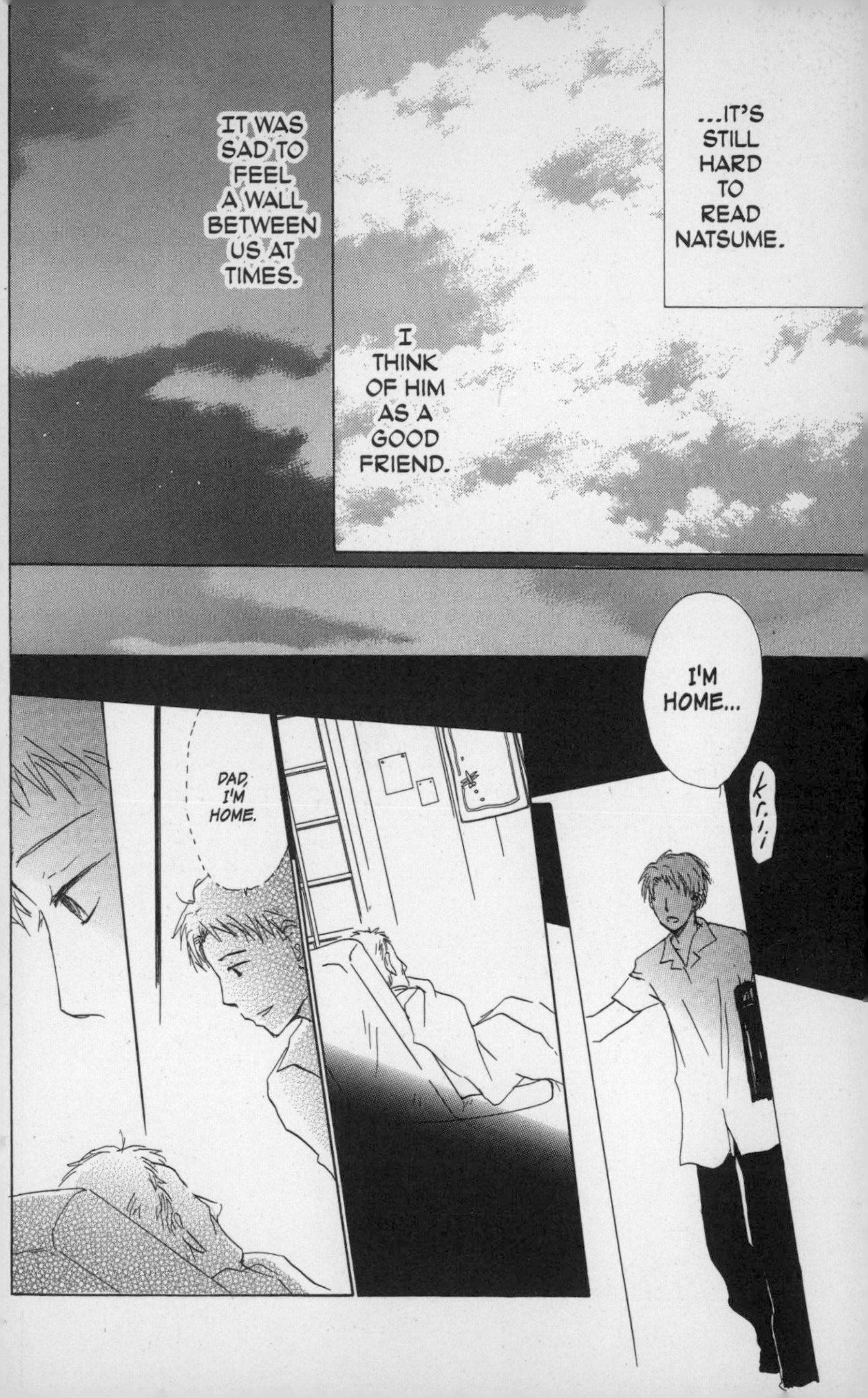
...IT'S STILL HARD TO READ NATSUME.
I THINK OF HIM AS A GOOD FRIEND.
IT WAS SAD TO FEEL A WALL BETWEEN US AT TIMES.
I'M HOME...
kri
DAD, I'M HOME.

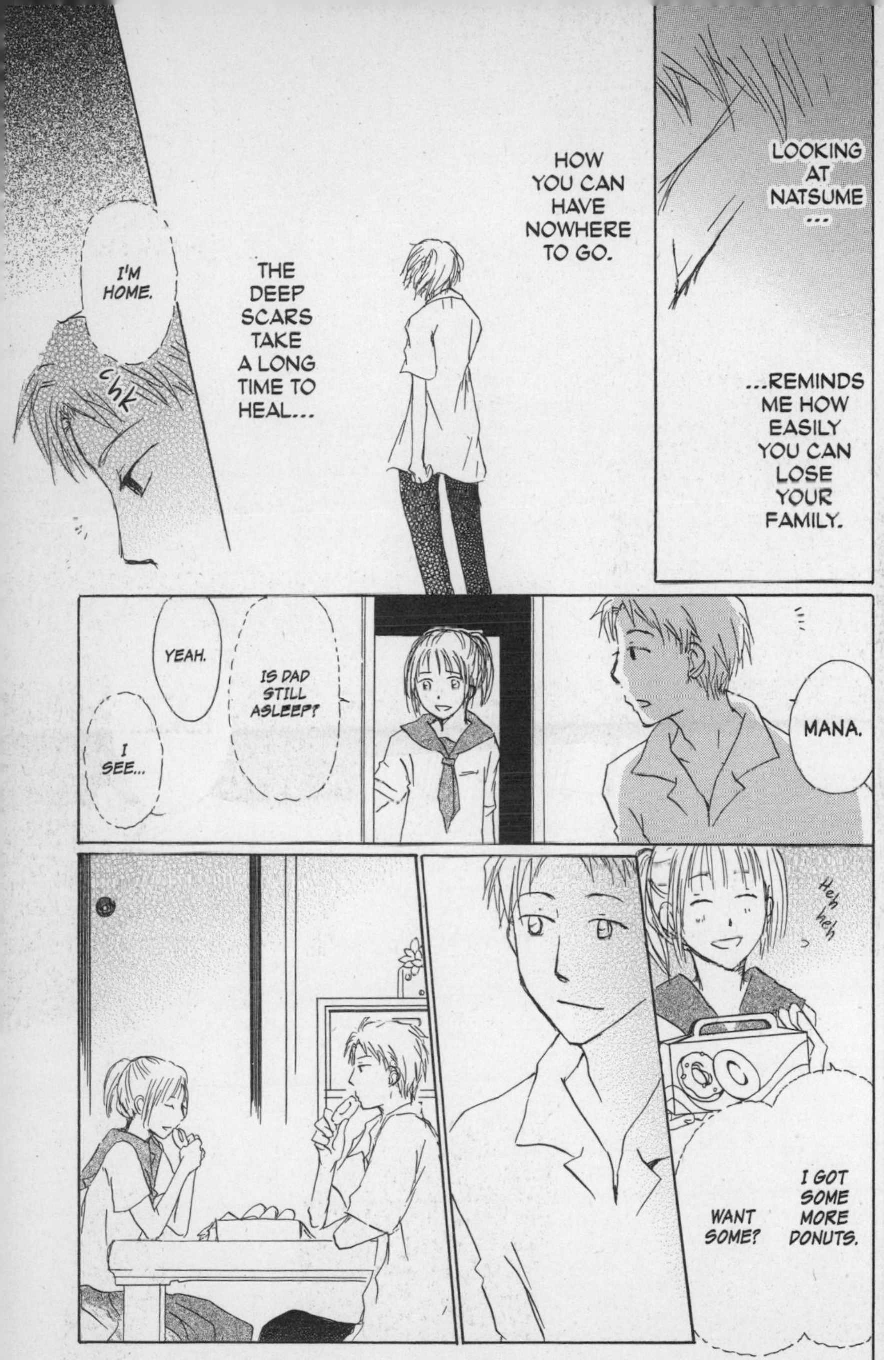
LOOKING AT NATSUME...
...REMINDS ME HOW EASILY YOU CAN LOSE YOUR FAMILY.
HOW YOU CAN HAVE NOWHERE TO GO.
THE DEEP SCARS TAKE A LONG TIME TO HEAL...
I'M HOME.
CHK
MANA.
IS DAD STILL ASLEEP?
YEAH.
I SEE...
Heh heh
I GOT SOME MORE DONUTS.
WANT SOME?

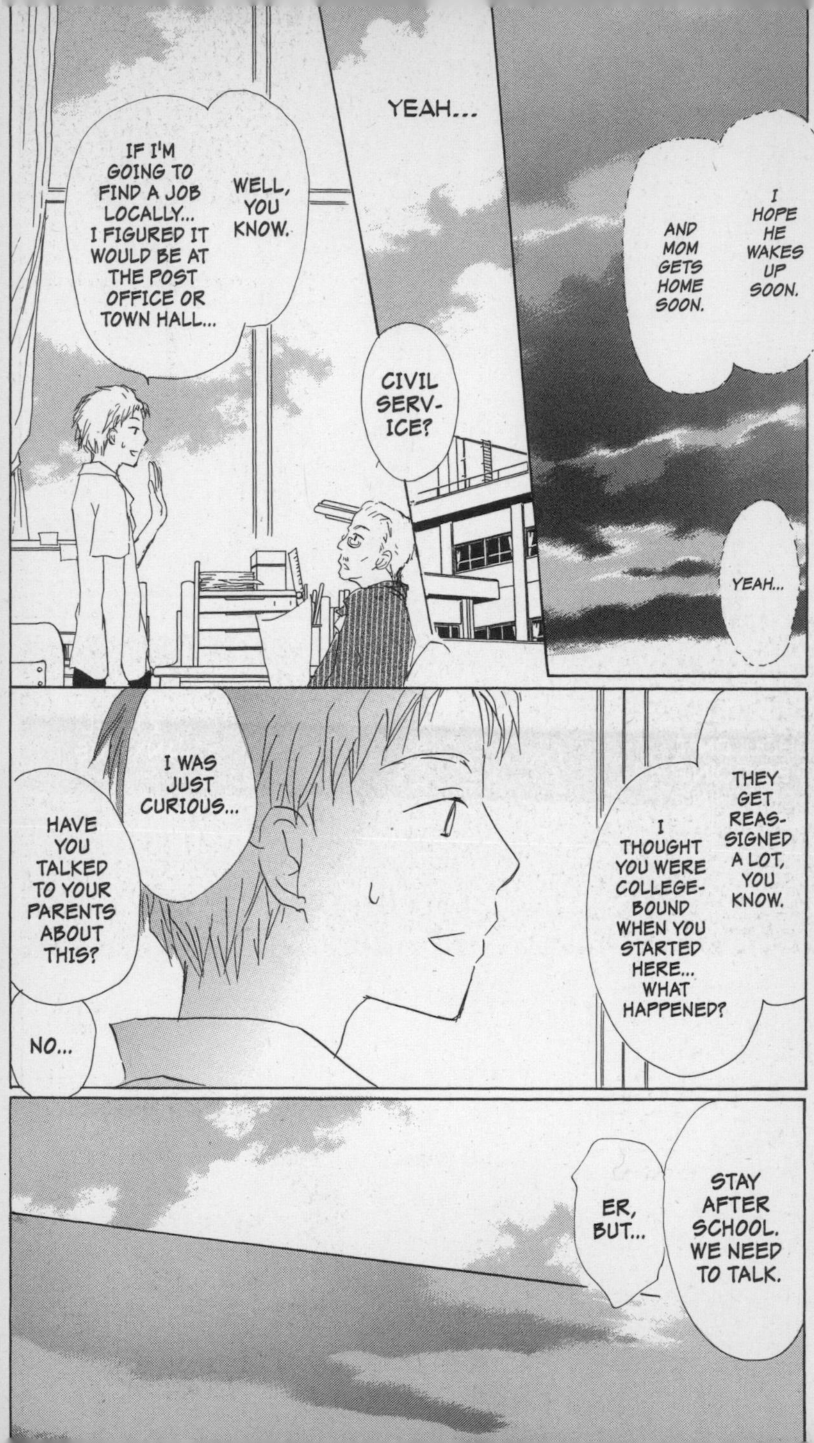
I HOPE HE WAKES UP SOON.
AND MOM GETS HOME SOON.
YEAH...
YEAH...
WELL, YOU KNOW.
IF I'M GOING TO FIND A JOB LOCALLY... I FIGURED IT WOULD BE AT THE POST OFFICE OR TOWN HALL...
CIVIL SERV-ICE?
THEY GET REAS-SIGNED A LOT, YOU KNOW.
I THOUGHT YOU WERE COLLEGE-BOUND WHEN YOU STARTED HERE... WHAT HAPPENED?
I WAS JUST CURIOUS...
HAVE YOU TALKED TO YOUR PARENTS ABOUT THIS?
NO...
STAY AFTER SCHOOL. WE NEED TO TALK.
ER, BUT...

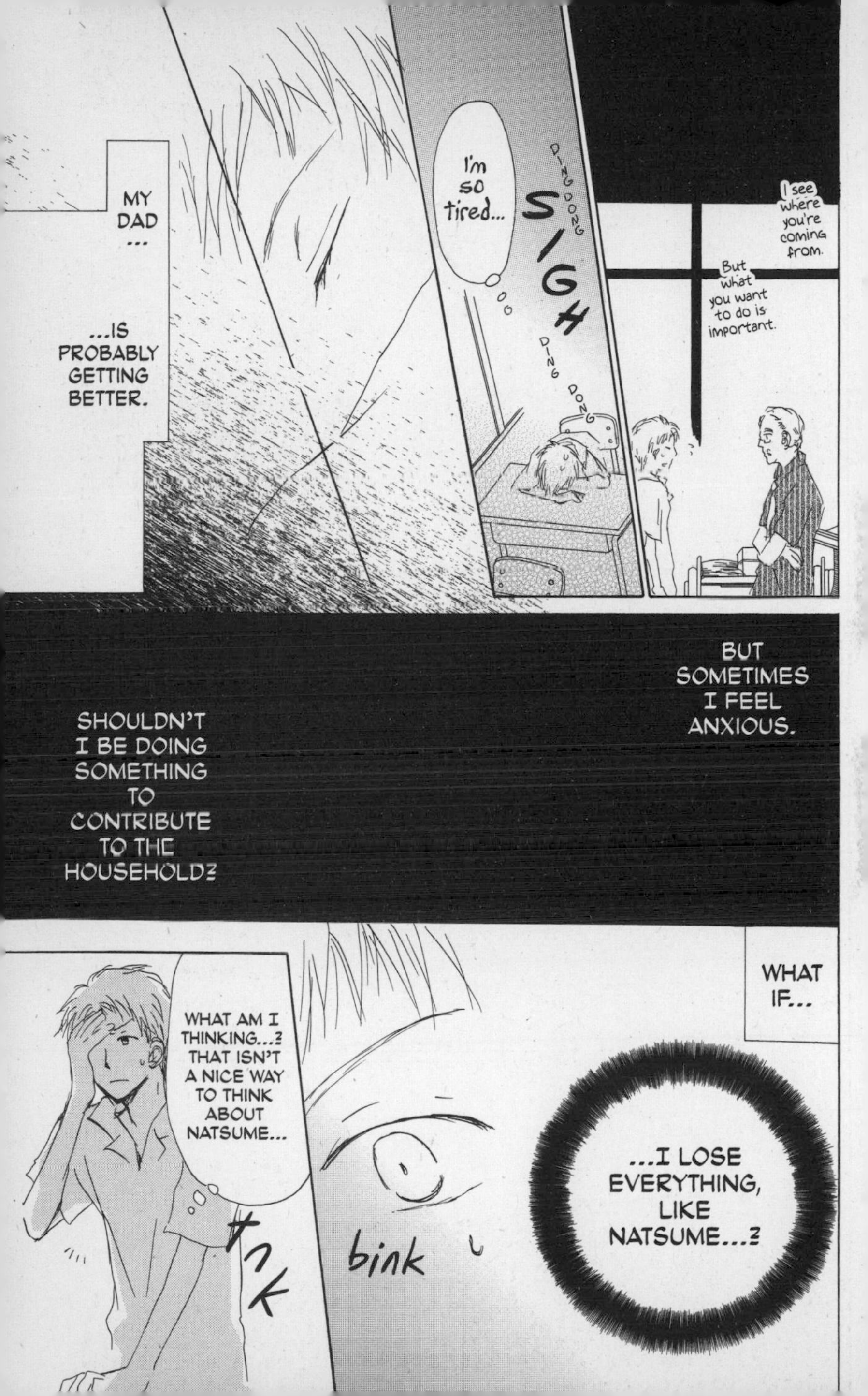
I see where you're coming from.
But what you want to do is important.
DING DONG
SIGH
DING DONG
I'm so tired...
MY DAD...
...IS PROBABLY GETTING BETTER.
BUT SOMETIMES I FEEL ANXIOUS.
SHOULDN'T I BE DOING SOMETHING TO CONTRIBUTE TO THE HOUSEHOLD?
WHAT IF...
...I LOSE EVERYTHING, LIKE NATSUME...?
bink
WHAT AM I THINKING...? THAT ISN'T A NICE WAY TO THINK ABOUT NATSUME...

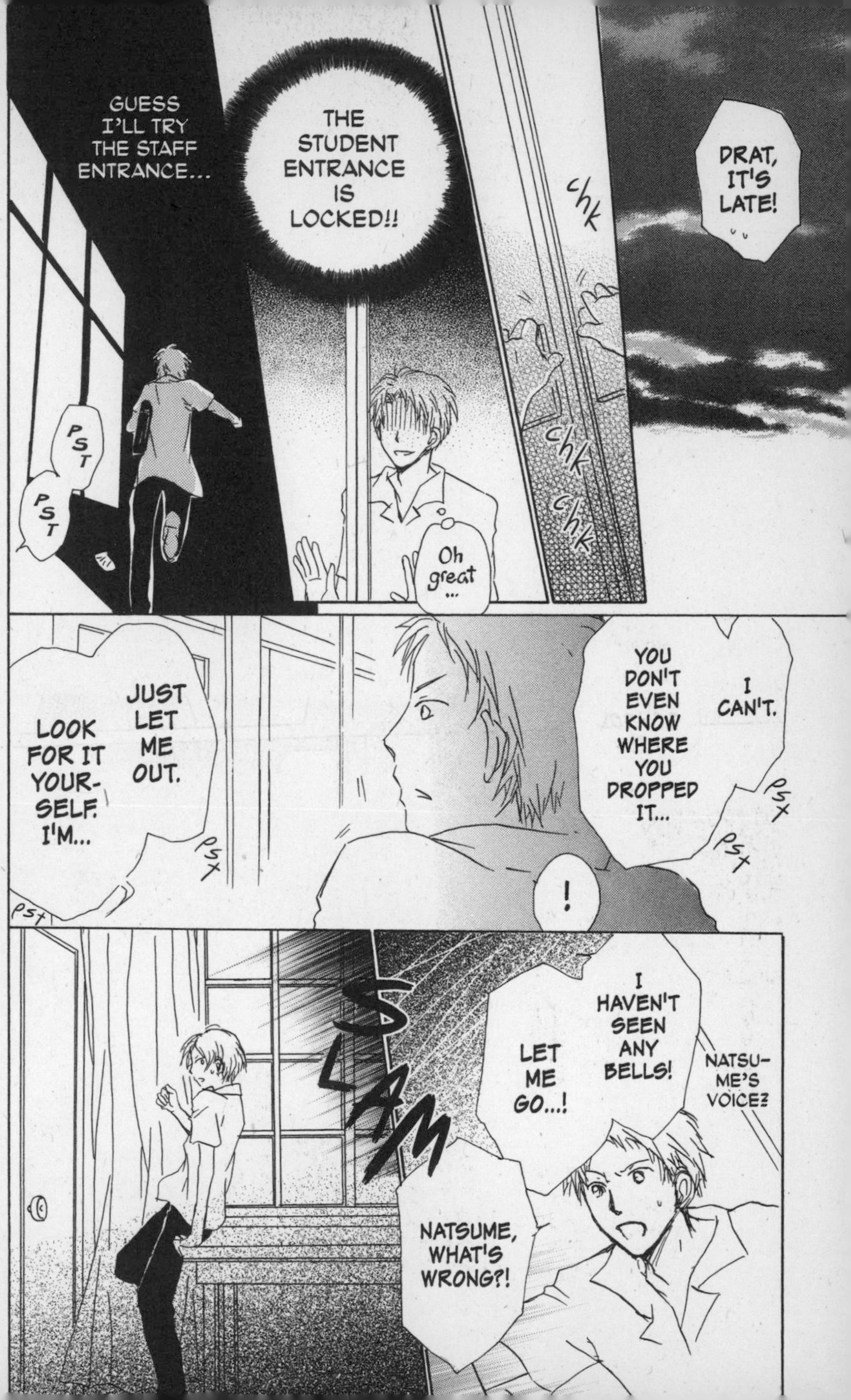
DRAT, IT'S LATE!
chk
chk chk chk
THE STUDENT ENTRANCE IS LOCKED!!
Oh great...
GUESS I'LL TRY THE STAFF ENTRANCE...
PST PST
I CAN'T.
PST PST
YOU DON'T EVEN KNOW WHERE YOU DROPPED IT...
!
JUST LET ME OUT.
LOOK FOR IT YOURSELF. I'M...
PST
PST
NATSU-ME'S VOICE?
I HAVEN'T SEEN ANY BELLS!
LET ME GO...!
SLAM
NATSUME, WHAT'S WRONG?!

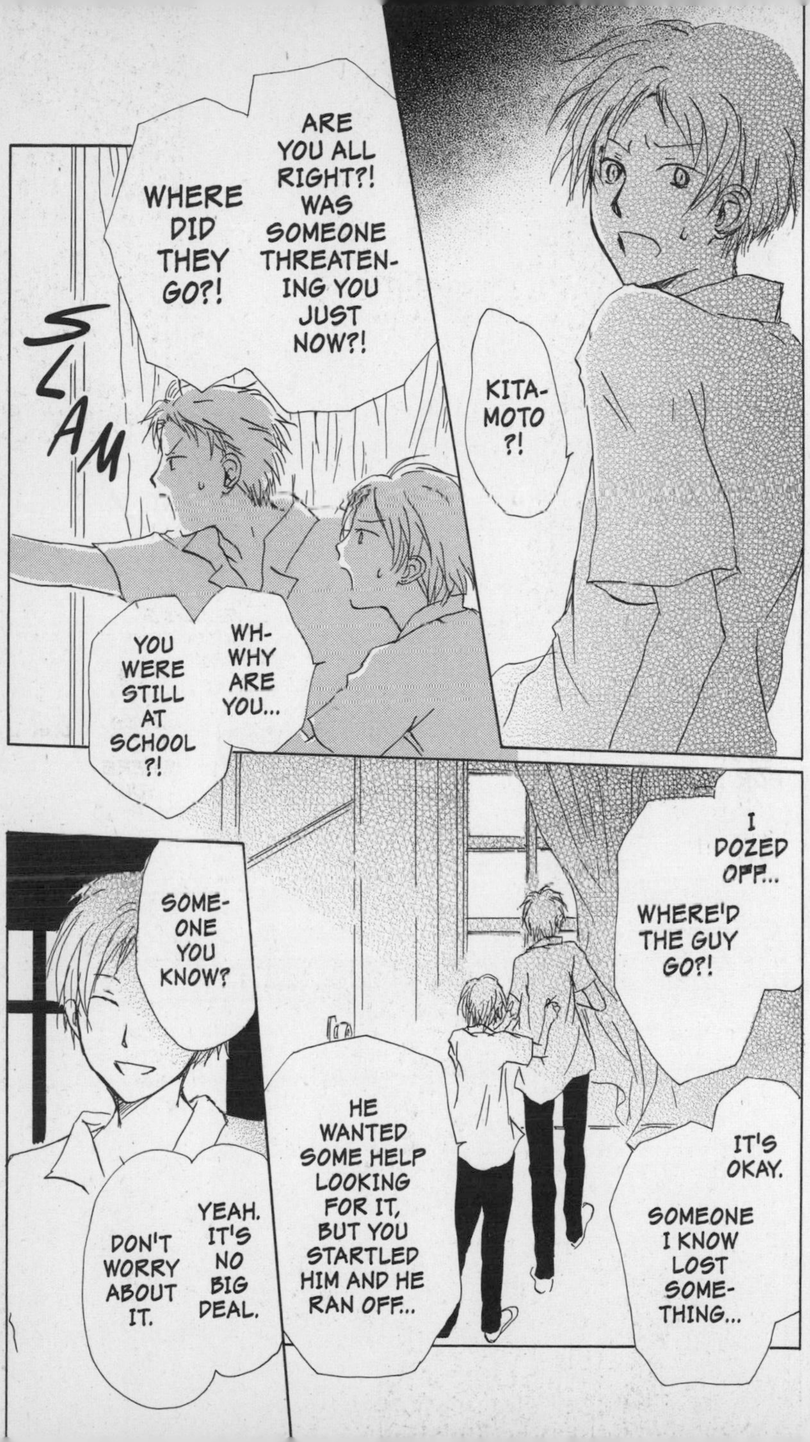
KITA-MOTO?!
ARE YOU ALL RIGHT?! WAS SOMEONE THREATEN-ING YOU JUST NOW?!
WHERE DID THEY GO?!
SLAM
WH- WHY ARE YOU...
YOU WERE STILL AT SCHOOL?!
I DOZED OFF... WHERE'D THE GUY GO?!
IT'S OKAY.
SOMEONE I KNOW LOST SOME-THING...
HE WANTED SOME HELP LOOKING FOR IT, BUT YOU STARTLED HIM AND HE RAN OFF...
SOME-ONE YOU KNOW?
YEAH. IT'S NO BIG DEAL.
DON'T WORRY ABOUT IT.

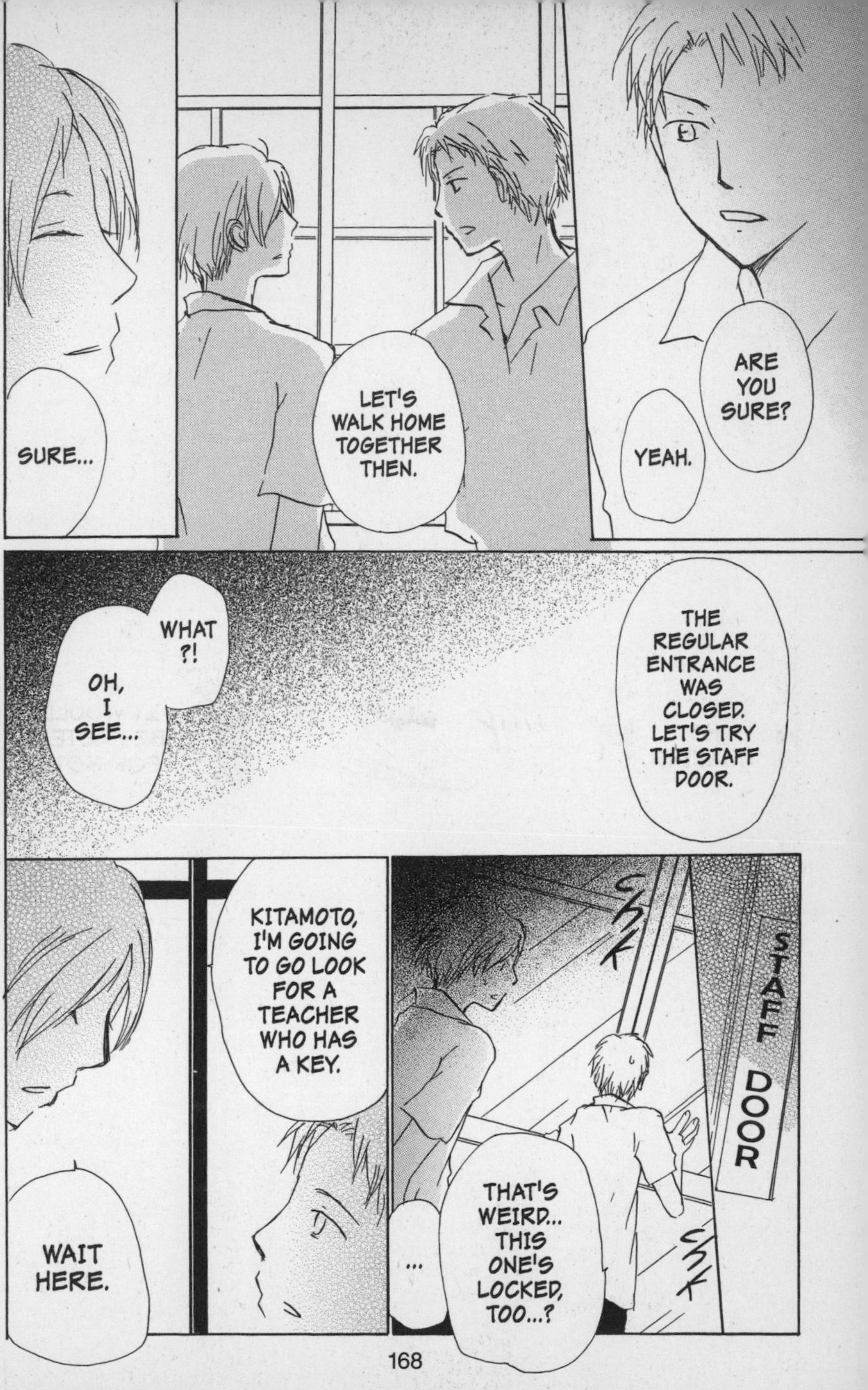
ARE YOU SURE?
YEAH.
LET'S WALK HOME TOGETHER THEN.
SURE...
THE REGULAR ENTRANCE WAS CLOSED. LET'S TRY THE STAFF DOOR.
WHAT ?!
OH, I SEE...
CHK
STAFF DOOR
CHK
THAT'S WEIRD... THIS ONE'S LOCKED, TOO...?
...
KITAMOTO, I'M GOING TO GO LOOK FOR A TEACHER WHO HAS A KEY.
WAIT HERE.

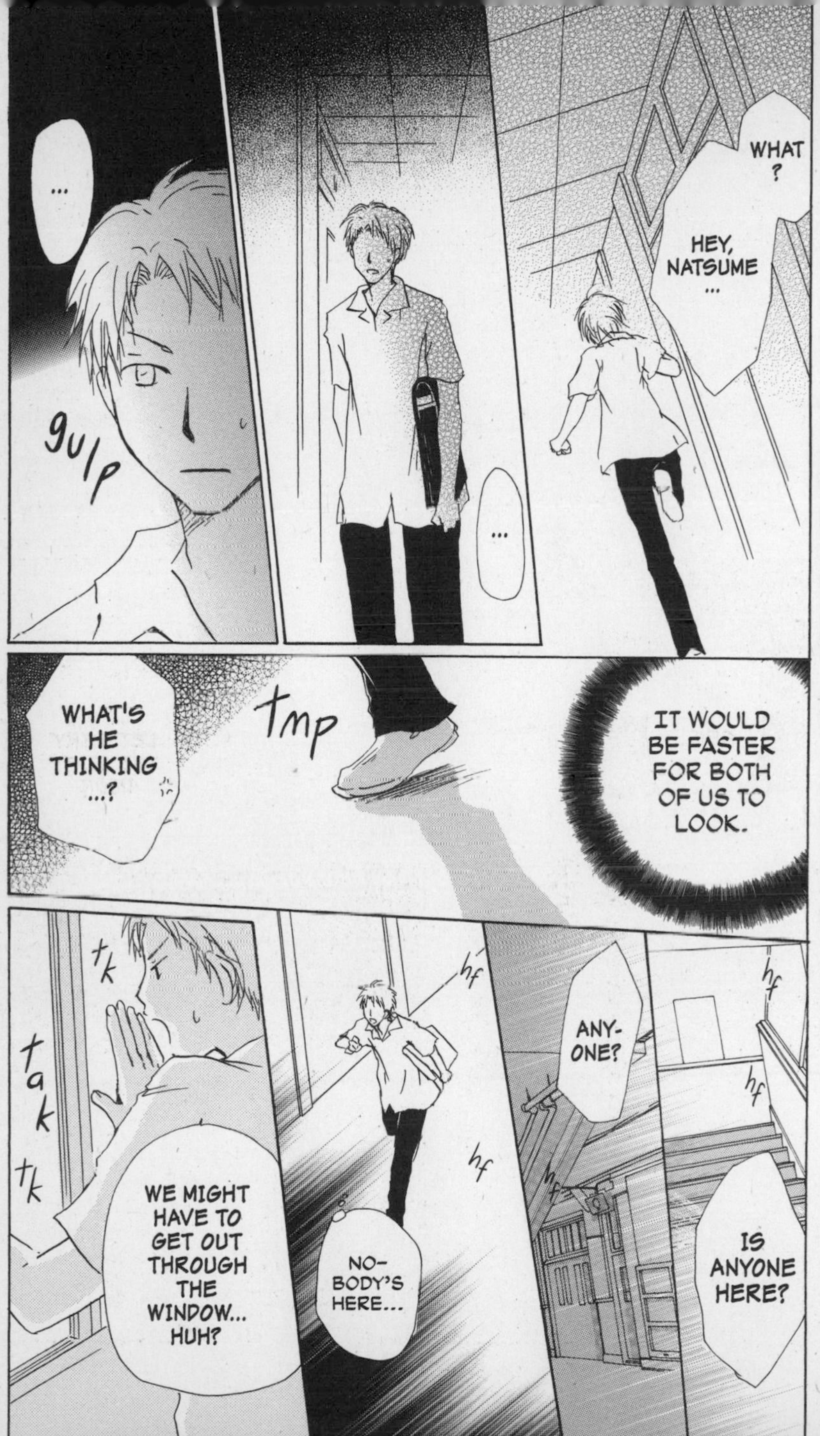
WHAT ?
HEY, NATSUME ...
...
...
gulp
IT WOULD BE FASTER FOR BOTH OF US TO LOOK.
tmp
WHAT'S HE THINKING ...?
hf
hf
IS ANYONE HERE?
ANY-ONE?
hf
hf
NO-BODY'S HERE...
tk
tak
tk
WE MIGHT HAVE TO GET OUT THROUGH THE WINDOW... HUH?

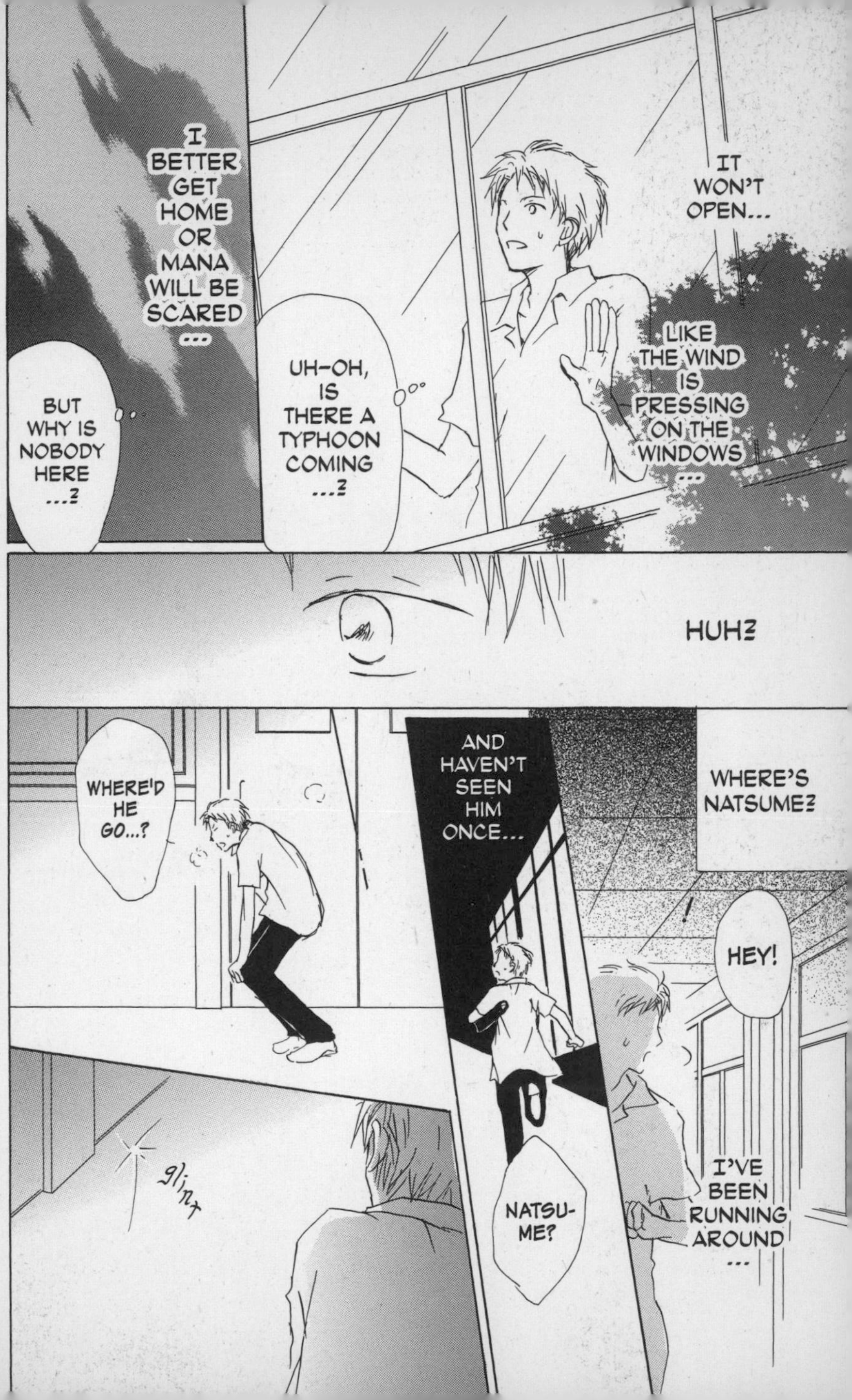
IT WON'T OPEN...
LIKE THE WIND IS PRESSING ON THE WINDOWS...
UH-OH, IS THERE A TYPHOON COMING...?
I BETTER GET HOME OR MANA WILL BE SCARED...
BUT WHY IS NOBODY HERE...?
HUH?
WHERE'S NATSUME?
HEY!
I'VE BEEN RUNNING AROUND...
AND HAVEN'T SEEN HIM ONCE...
NATSU-ME?
WHERE'D HE GO...?
glint

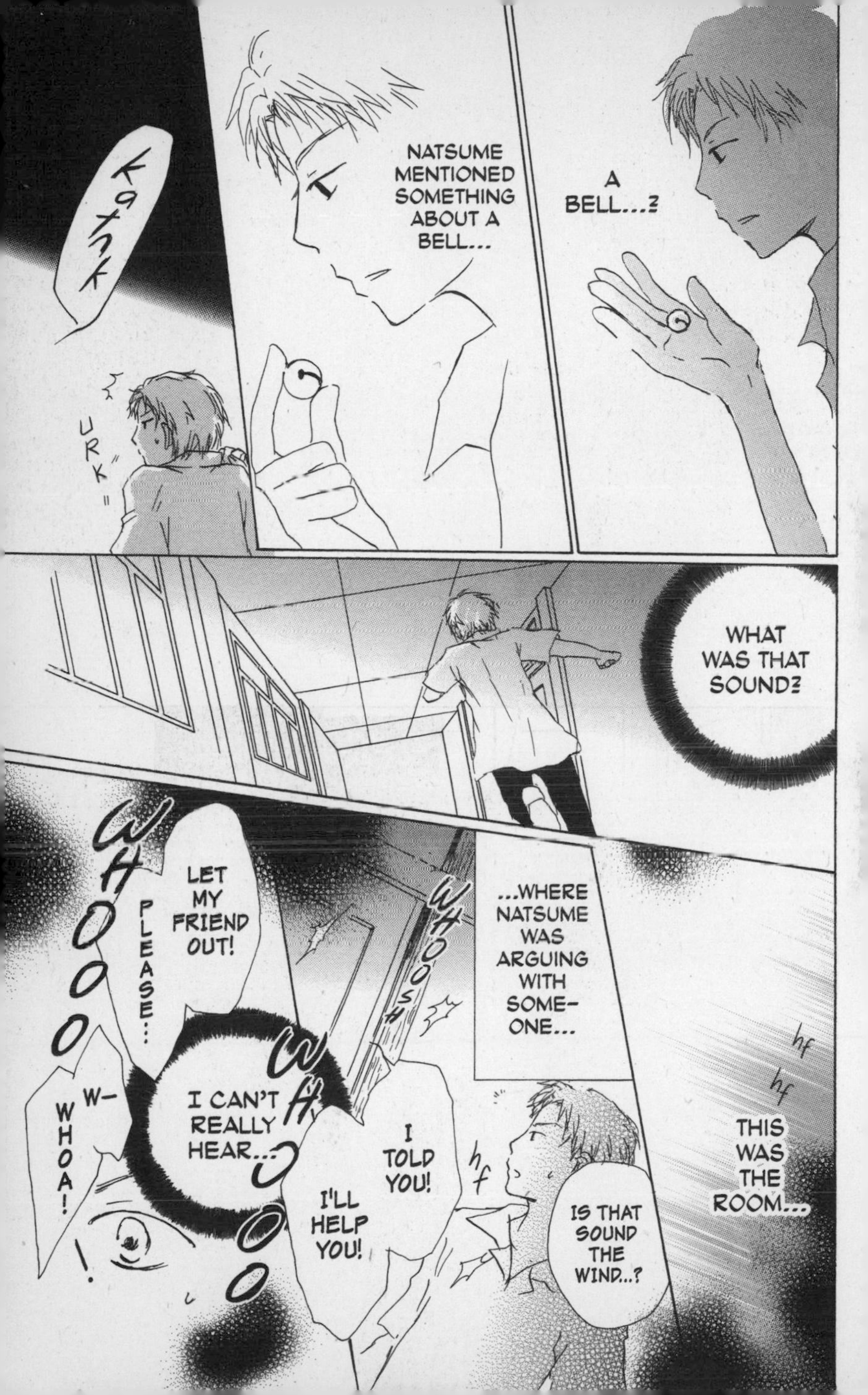
A BELL...?
NATSUME MENTIONED SOMETHING ABOUT A BELL...
katnk
URK
WHAT WAS THAT SOUND?
THIS WAS THE ROOM...
hf hf
...WHERE NATSUME WAS ARGUING WITH SOME-ONE...
IS THAT SOUND THE WIND...?
hf
WHOOSH
I TOLD YOU!
I'LL HELP YOU!
WHOOOO
I CAN'T REALLY HEAR...
LET MY FRIEND OUT!
PLEASE...
W- WHOA!
WHOOOOO

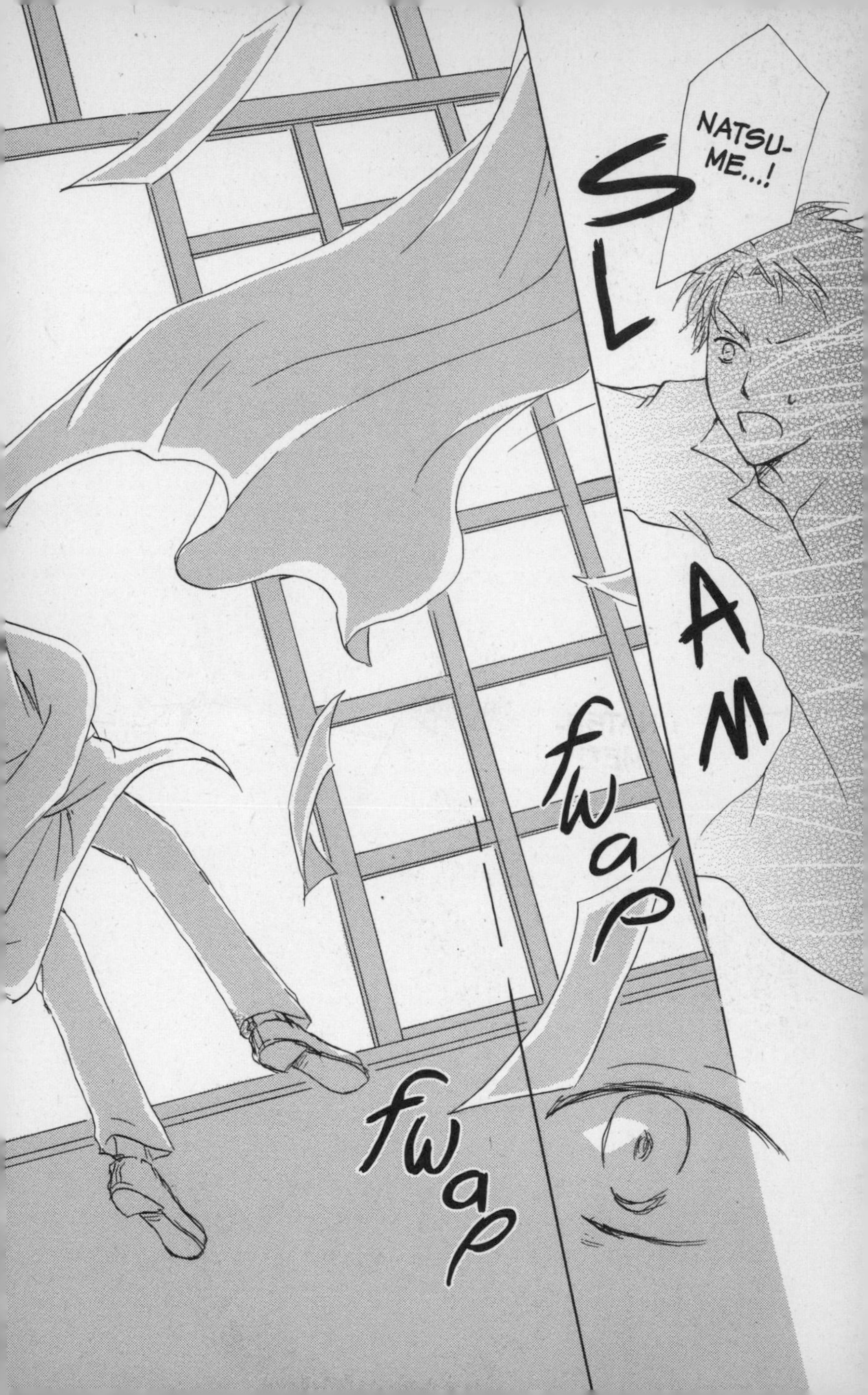
NATSU-
ME...!
SLAM
fwap
fwap

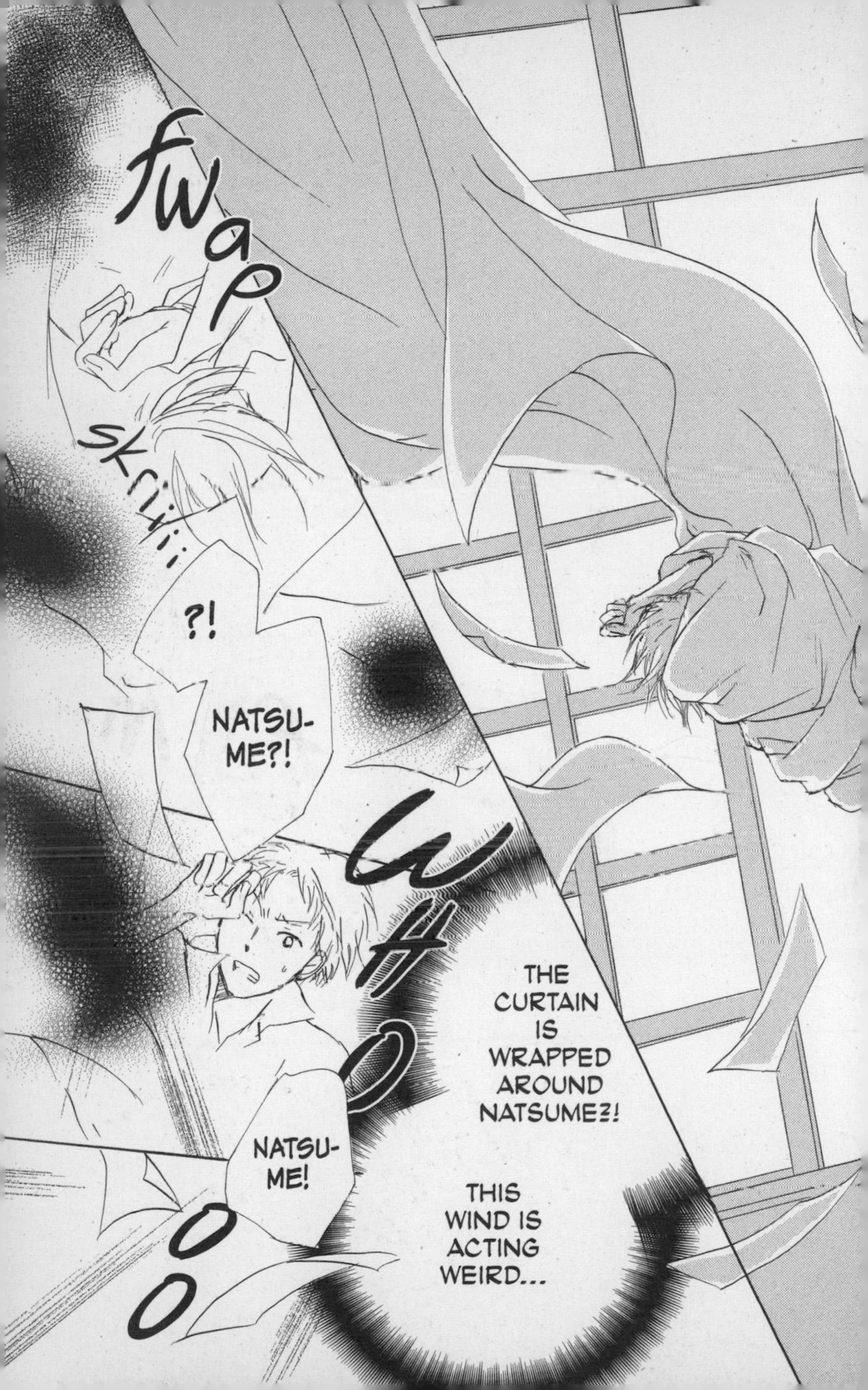
FWAP
SKRIIIII
?!
NATSU-
ME?!
THE
CURTAIN
IS
WRAPPED
AROUND
NATSUME?!
WHOOOO
NATSU-
ME!
THIS
WIND IS
ACTING
WEIRD...

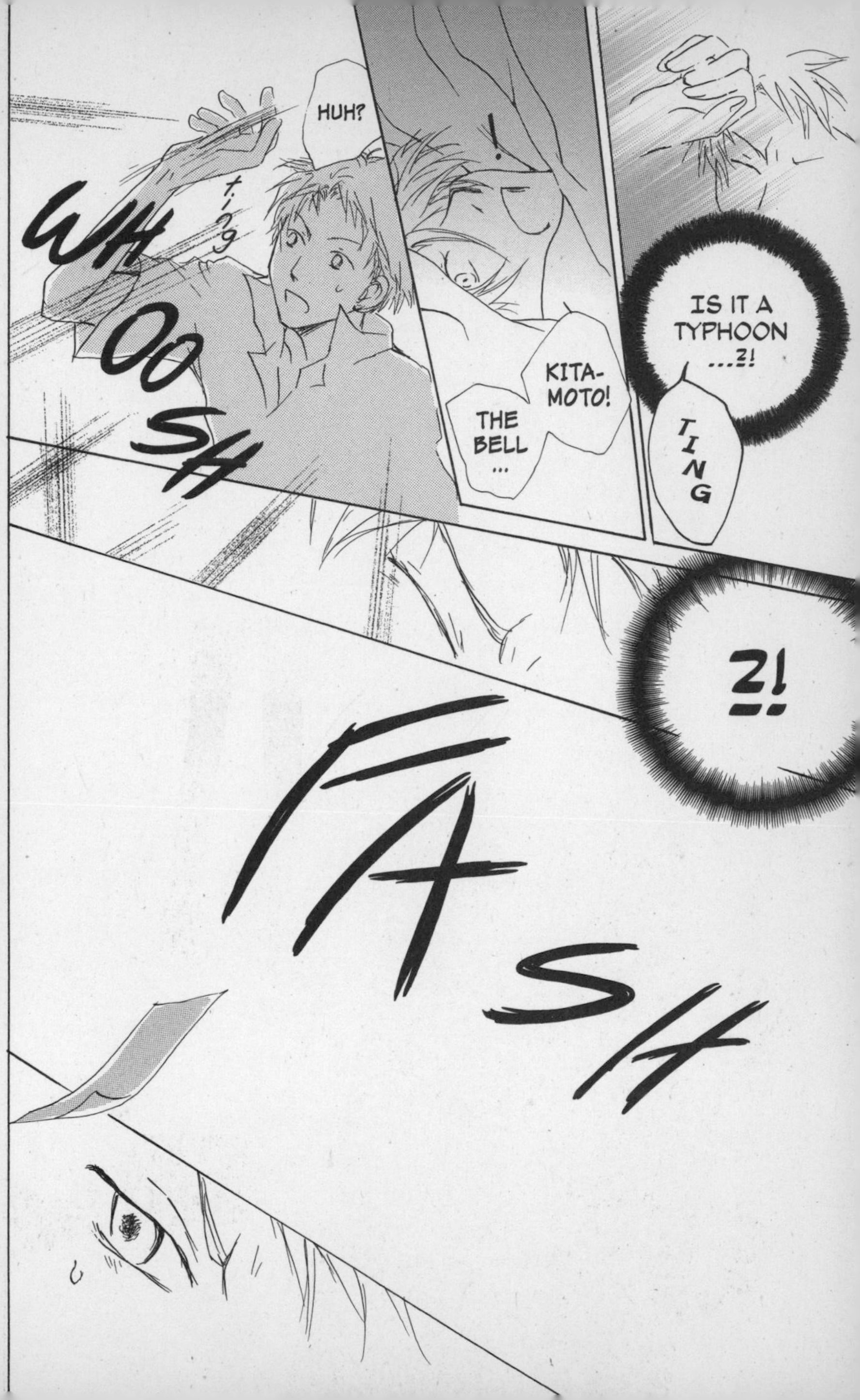
IS IT A TYPHOON ...?!
TING
!
KITA-MOTO!
THE BELL ...
HUH?
ting
WHOOSH
?!
FASH

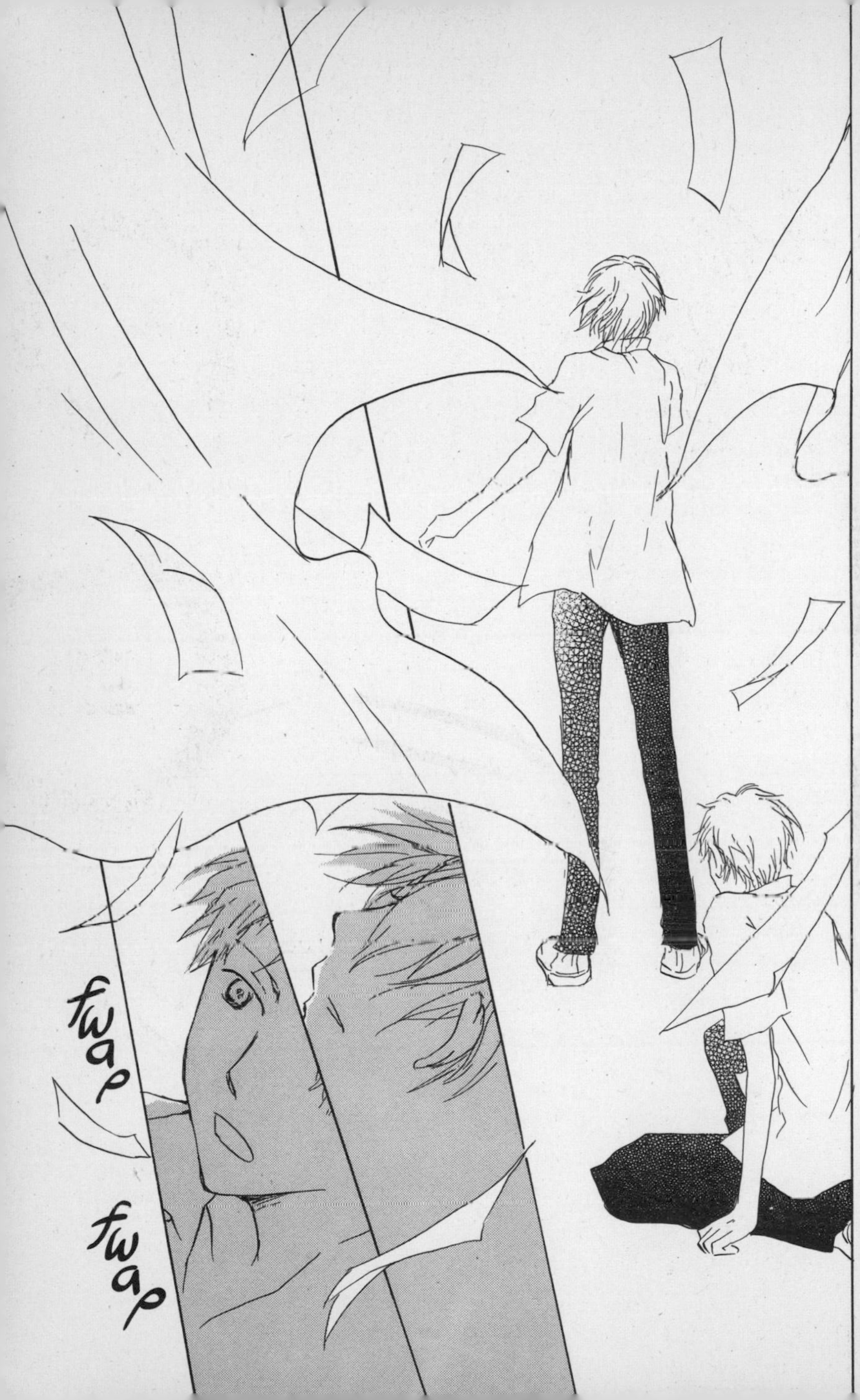
fwap
fwap

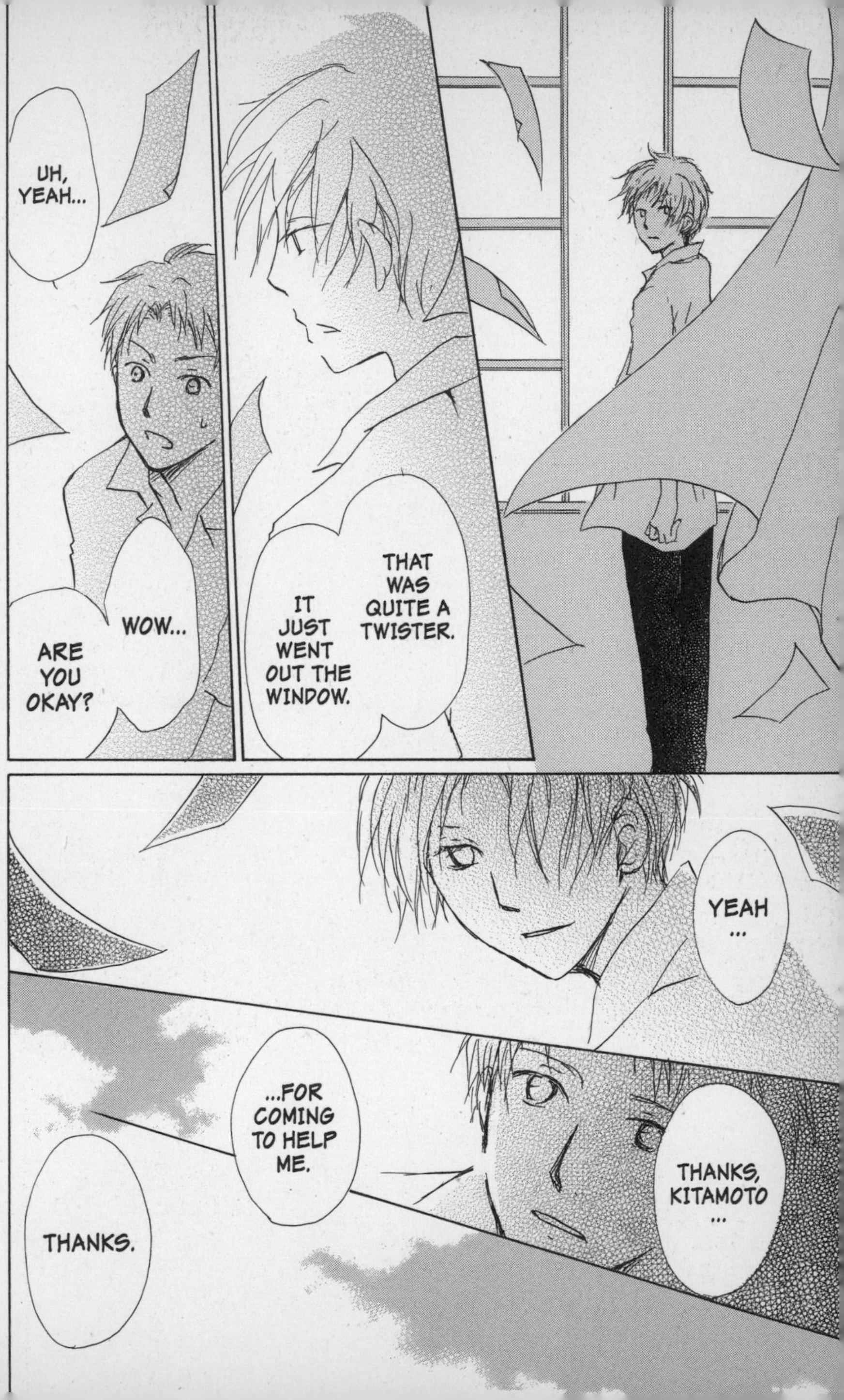
THAT WAS QUITE A TWISTER.
IT JUST WENT OUT THE WINDOW.
UH, YEAH...
WOW...
ARE YOU OKAY?
YEAH ...
THANKS, KITAMOTO ...
...FOR COMING TO HELP ME.
THANKS.

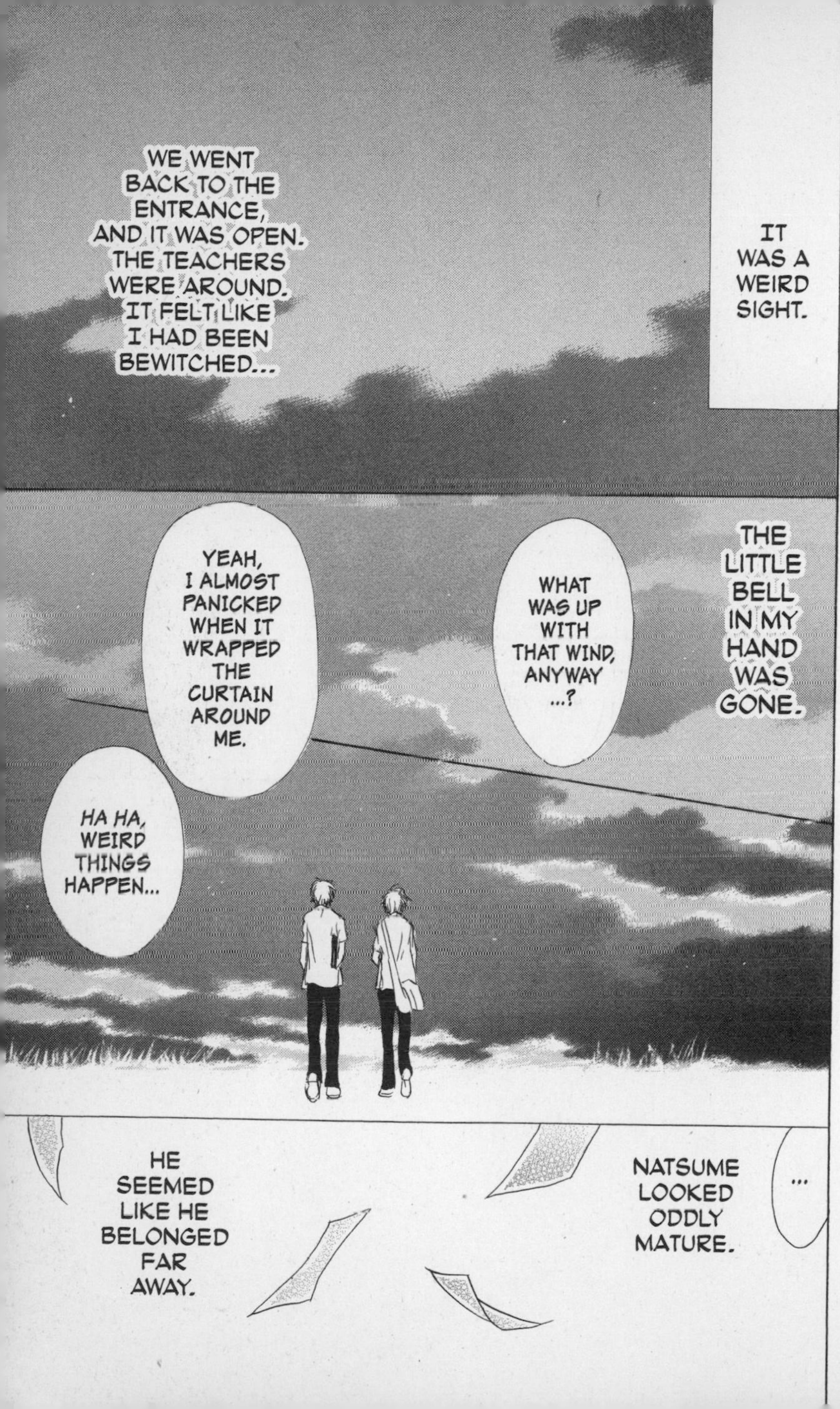
IT WAS A WEIRD SIGHT.
WE WENT BACK TO THE ENTRANCE, AND IT WAS OPEN. THE TEACHERS WERE AROUND. IT FELT LIKE I HAD BEEN BEWITCHED...
THE LITTLE BELL IN MY HAND WAS GONE.
WHAT WAS UP WITH THAT WIND, ANYWAY ...?
YEAH, I ALMOST PANICKED WHEN IT WRAPPED THE CURTAIN AROUND ME.
HA HA, WEIRD THINGS HAPPEN...
...
NATSUME LOOKED ODDLY MATURE.
HE SEEMED LIKE HE BELONGED FAR AWAY.

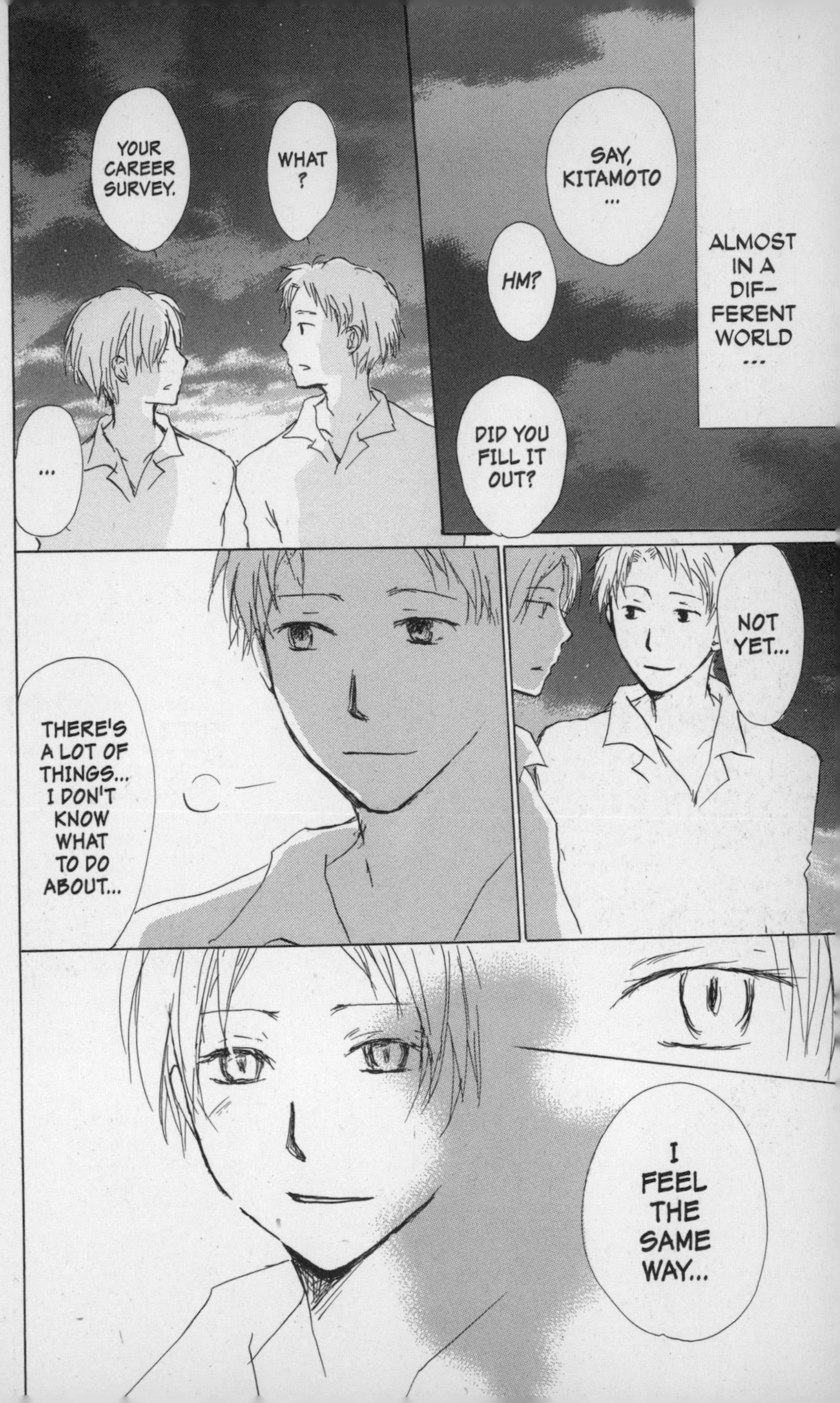
ALMOST IN A DIF-FERENT WORLD...
SAY, KITAMOTO...
HM?
DID YOU FILL IT OUT?
WHAT?
YOUR CAREER SURVEY.
...
NOT YET...
THERE'S A LOT OF THINGS... I DON'T KNOW WHAT TO DO ABOUT...
I FEEL THE SAME WAY...

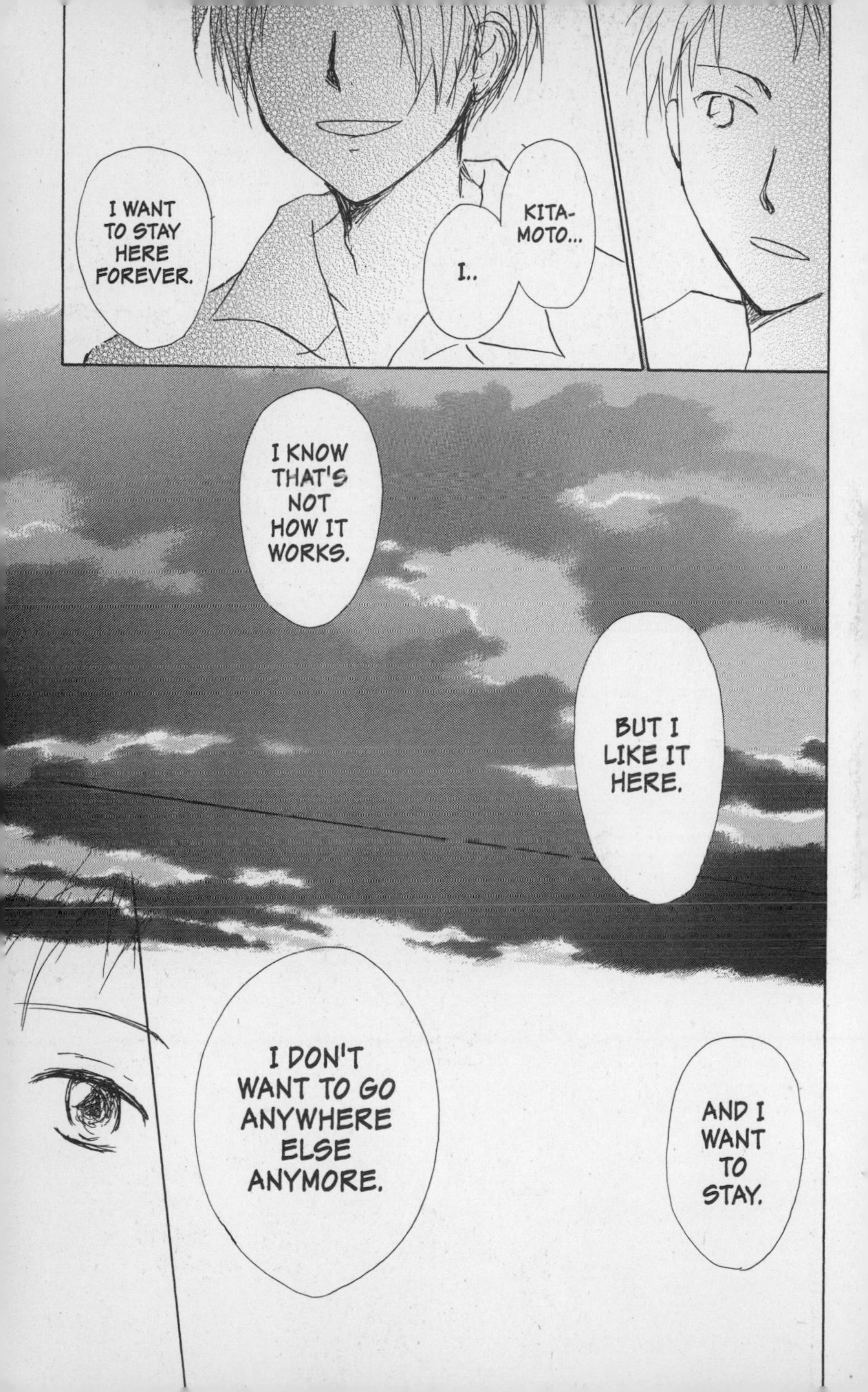
KITA-MOTO...
I..
I WANT TO STAY HERE FOREVER.
I KNOW THAT'S NOT HOW IT WORKS.
BUT I LIKE IT HERE.
AND I WANT TO STAY.
I DON'T WANT TO GO ANYWHERE ELSE ANYMORE.

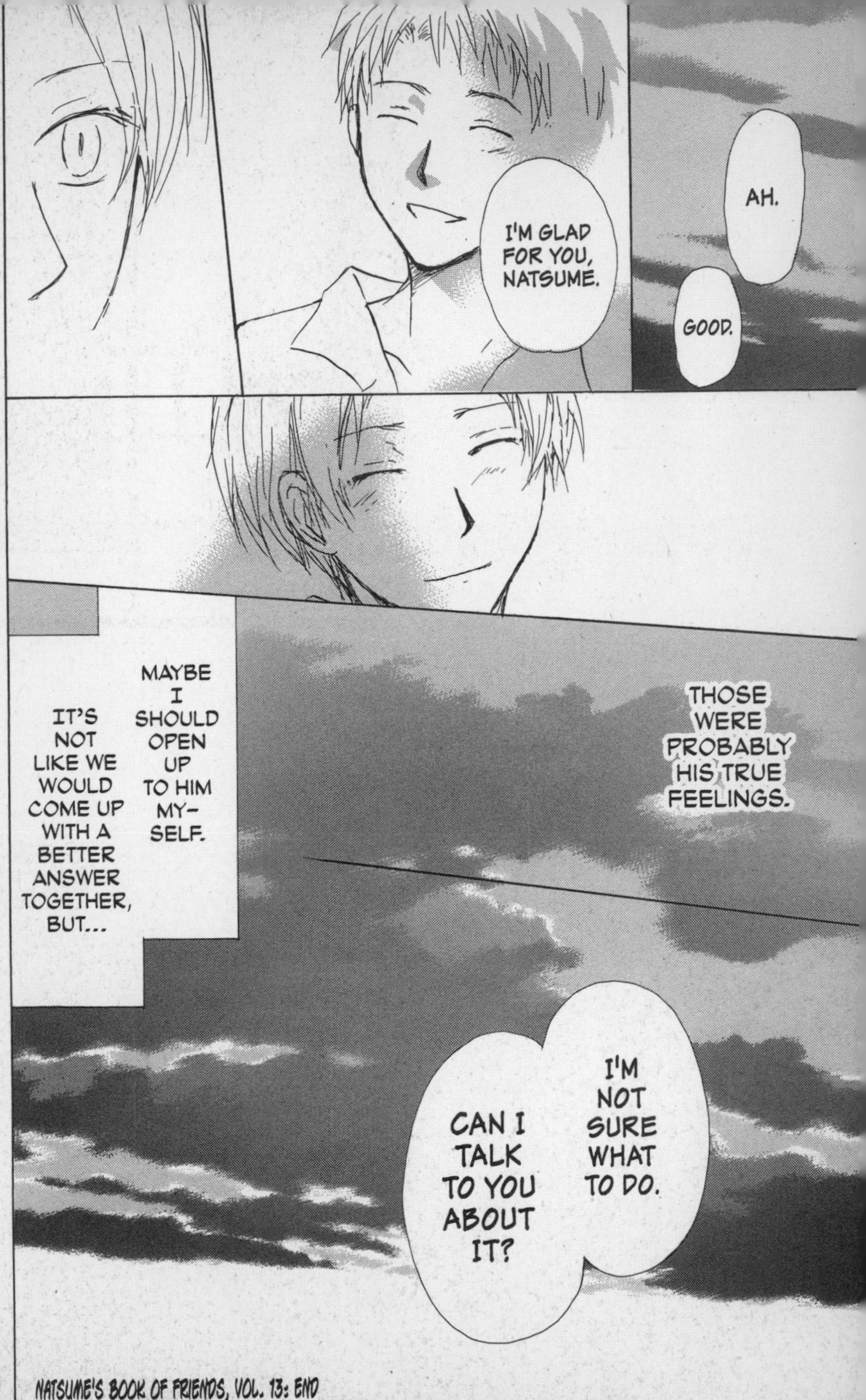
AH.
GOOD.
I'M GLAD FOR YOU, NATSUME.
THOSE WERE PROBABLY HIS TRUE FEELINGS.
IT'S NOT LIKE WE WOULD COME UP WITH A BETTER ANSWER TOGETHER, BUT...
MAYBE I SHOULD OPEN UP TO HIM MYSELF.
I'M NOT SURE WHAT TO DO.
CAN I TALK TO YOU ABOUT IT?

NATSUME'S BOOK OF FRIENDS, VOL. 13: END

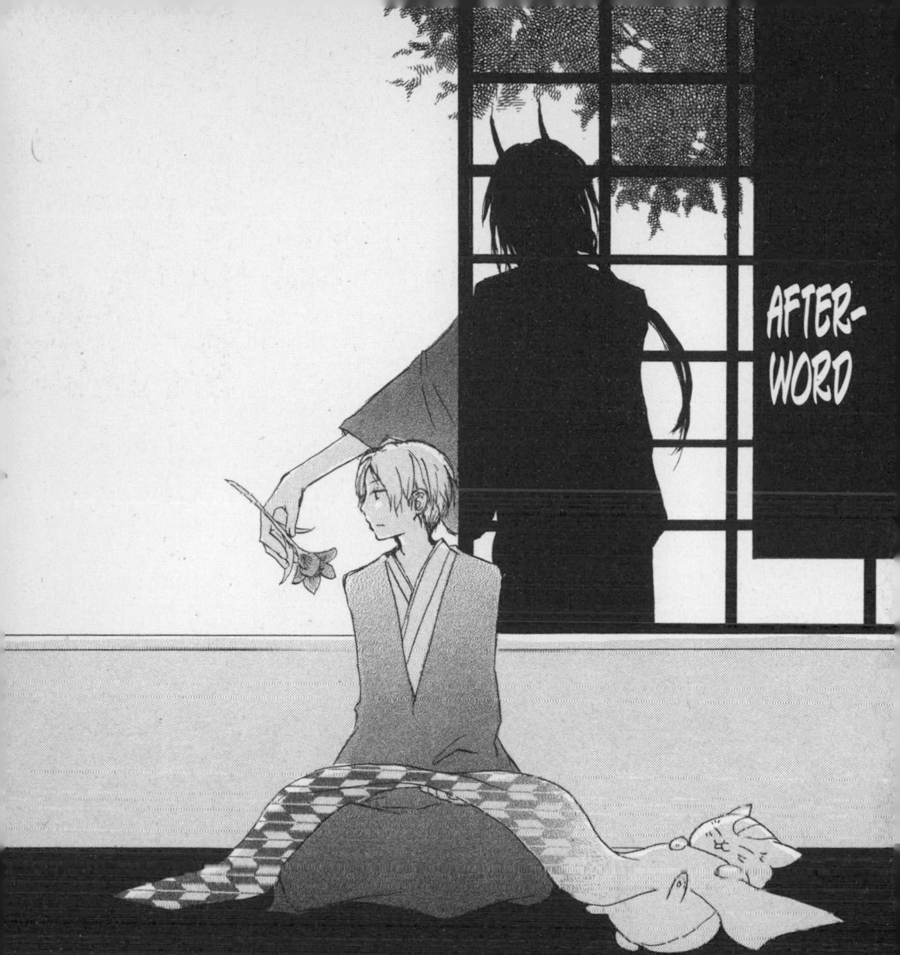
AFTER-
WORD

Now that he has more friends and people who understand him, Natsume is better able to make a stand for what he believes in. But he has to face that there's a dark side to both humans and yokai that he can't fully deny or embrace. Also, there's something in his life that doesn't disappear the way yokai do, and it's slowly starting to scare him.

Please read the rest of this afterword only after reading the entire volume, to avoid spoilers.

CHAPTERS 52-54
Behind the Chains

Natsume is now able to face a variety of things. But I also feel that the distance between him and Natori grows each time they encounter one another. They see the same things and hope for the same outcome, but because their paths are a little different, it's hard for them to take action when they're together. It's a strange feeling. I'm sure Natori wants to remain Natsume's ally, and Natsume wants the same with Natori.

I'm happy I got to draw more about Matoba, too. Whereas Natori tries to do what's right and is afraid of making a mistake, I think Matoba is the kind of person who doesn't fear making mistakes.

SPECIAL EPISODES 11 & 12
Nishimura and Natsume, Kitamoto and Natsume

I'm so happy I got to write these stories of Nishimura and Kitamoto meeting Natsume for the first time. I've wanted to draw them for a while. I've felt a bit of empty nest syndrome as Natsume grows and softens in expression these days, so it was pretty emotional to draw him back again when he was still tense about himself. Nishimura seems straightforward, but is quick-tempered and has a peculiar obstinate streak; Kitamoto is occasionally impatient because he's burdened by a sense of responsibility. They're different from Natsume, but I hope I'll get another chance to draw how they grow and do their best in their lives. It was also refreshing to do some episodes without yokai (besides Nyanko Sensei).

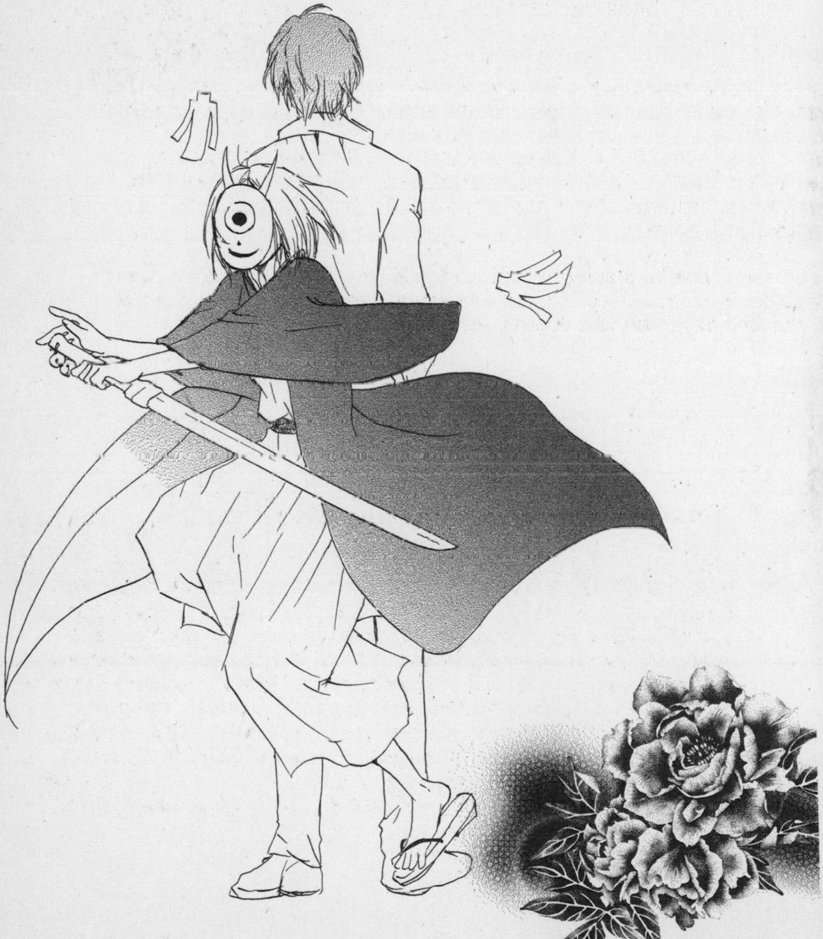

I'm so blessed that they're producing a fourth season of the anime. I would like to thank the director, the animation staff, voice actors, and everyone who helped with the first and second seasons, and worked together to develop the third and fourth seasons. And thank you to all the viewers, the readers of the manga, and the editors.

For me, Natsume has become a precious title that brought me to work with so many people. I would like to apply myself, episode by episode, to keep making manga people can enjoy.

Thanks to:

Tamao Ohki
Chika
Mika
Mr. Fujita
My sister
Mr. Sato
Hoen Kikaku, Ltd.
          Thank you.

AFTERWORD: END

Natsume's
BOOK of FRIENDS
13 VOLUME END NOTES

PAGE 7, PANEL 3: *Cram school*
After-school supplementary classes to help with the rigorous Japanese entrance exams.

PAGE 14, PANEL 3: *Yokan*
A traditional Japanese dessert made from sweet bean paste jellied with agar (a seaweed that acts like gelatin). Often served chilled in the summer.

PAGE 87, PANEL 2: *Tanuki*
An actual Japanese animal also known as a "raccoon dog." They have a reputation for being quite plump.

PAGE 112, PANEL 2: *Melon bread*
A sweet pastry common in Japanese bakeries, it is a round fluffy bun with a thin cookie crust. The name comes from the crust's crosshatch pattern which resembles melon skin.

PAGE 128, PANEL 2: *1,000 cranes*
Cranes symbolize longevity in Japan, and legend says folding a thousand origami cranes grants a wish. It is often done to wish for somebody's speedy recovery.

PAGE 170, PANEL 1: *Typhoon*
Cyclones that form in the northwest Pacific Ocean are called "typhoons" (as opposed to hurricanes, which form in the Atlantic Ocean).

Yuki Midorikawa
is the creator of *Natsume's Book of Friends*, which was nominated for the Manga Taisho (Cartoon Grand Prize). Her other titles published in Japan include *Hotarubi no Mori e* (Into the Forest of Fireflies), *Hiiro no Isu* (The Scarlet Chair) and *Akaku Saku Koe* (The Voice That Blooms Red).

NATSUME'S BOOK OF FRIENDS

Vol. 13
Shojo Beat Edition

STORY AND ART BY Yuki Midorikawa

Translation & Adaptation Lillian Olsen
Touch-up Art & Lettering Sabrina Heep
Design Fawn Lau
Editor Pancha Diaz

Natsume Yujincho by Yuki Midorikawa
© Yuki Midorikawa 2012
All rights reserved.
First published in Japan in 2012 by HAKUSENSHA, Inc., Tokyo.
English language translation rights arranged with HAKUSENSHA, Inc., Tokyo.

The rights of the author(s) of the work(s) in this publication to be so identified
have been asserted in accordance with the Copyright, Designs and Patents Act 1988.
A CIP catalogue record for this book is available from the British Library.

The stories, characters and incidents mentioned in this publication are entirely fictional.

Printed in Canada

Published by VIZ Media, LLC
P.O. Box 77010
San Francisco, CA 94107

10 9 8 7 6 5 4 3 2 1
First printing, December 2012

PARENTAL ADVISORY
NATSUME'S BOOK OF FRIENDS is rated T for
Teen and is recommended for ages 13 and
up. This volume contains fantasy violence.
ratings.viz.com

www.viz.com

www.shojobeat.com

Enter_the_world_of_

LOVELESS

story_+_art_by_YUN_KOUGA

2-in-1 EDITIONS

Each 2-in-1 edition includes 6 color pages and 50 pages of never-before-seen BONUS comics, artist commentary and interviews!

only $14.99!
($16.99 CAN / £9.99 UK)

Available at your local book store, comic book shop or library, or online at:

store.viz.com

www.viz.com

SURPRISE!

You may be reading the wrong way!

It's true: In keeping with the original Japanese comic format, this book reads from right to left—so action, sound effects, and word balloons are completely reversed. This preserves the orientation of the original artwork—plus, it's fun! Check out the diagram shown here to get the hang of things, and then turn to the other side of the book to get started!

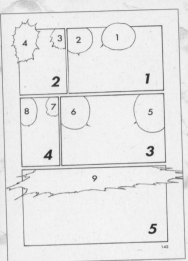

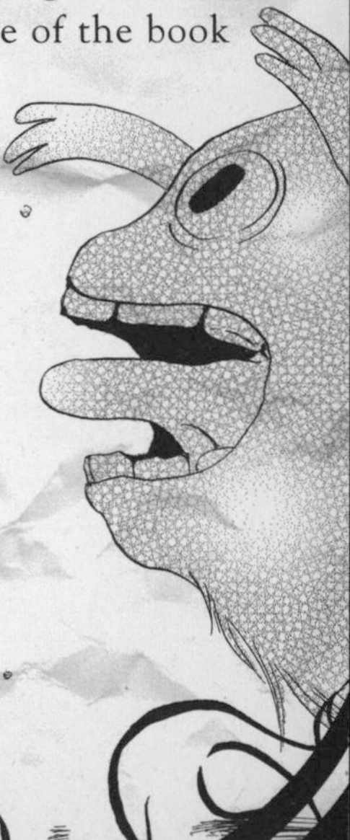

142